Castoriadis's Ontology

John D. Caputo, *series editor*

PERSPECTIVES IN
CONTINENTAL
PHILOSOPHY

SUZI ADAMS

Castoriadis's Ontology
Being and Creation

FORDHAM UNIVERSITY PRESS
New York ∎ 2011

Fordham University Press has no responsibility for the persistence or accuracy of URLs for external or third-party Internet websites referred to in this publication and does not guarantee that any content on such websites is, or will remain, accurate or appropriate.

Fordham University Press also publishes its books in a variety of electronic formats. Some content that appears in print may not be available in electronic books.

Library of Congress Cataloging-in-Publication Data

Adams, Suzi.
    Castoriadis's ontology : being and creation / Suzi Adams.—1st ed.
        p.   cm.— (Perspectives in Continental philosophy)
    Includes bibliographical references (p.   ) and index.
    ISBN 978-0-8232-3458-5 (cloth : alk. paper)
    ISBN 978-0-8232-3459-2 (pbk. : alk. paper)
    ISBN 978-0-8232-3460-8 (epub)
    1. Castoriadis, Cornelius, 1922–1997.   2. Ontology.   I. Title.
B2430.C3584A64   2011
194—dc22

                                                           2011009662

Printed in the United States of America
13 12 11   5 4 3 2 1
First edition

Contents

Abbreviations

AC	"Autonomie et Complexité," unpublished archival document
CL	*Crossroads in the Labyrinth*
CQFG	*Ce qui fait la Grèce*, vols. I and II
DD	"Done and to be Done"
DH	*Domaines de l'homme*
EA	*De l'écologie à l'autonomie*
ETSS	"Epilegomena to a Theory of the Soul which has been presented as a Science"
GI	"General Introduction" to *Socialisme ou Barbarie*
GMPI	"The Greek and the Modern Political Imaginary"
IIS	*The Imaginary Institution of Society*
ISCS	"Imaginaire sociale et changement scientifique"
ISR	"Institution of Society and Religion"
MSPI	"Modern Science and Philosophical Interrogation"
OIHS	"The Ontological Import of the History of Science"
PA	"*Physis* and Autonomy"
PSS	"Pour-soi et subjectivité"
SST	"The State of the Subject Today"
STCC	"Social Transformation and Cultural Creation"
SU	"The Sayable and the Unsayable: Homage to Merleau-Ponty"
SV	*Sujet et verité*

TE   "Technique"
TC   "Time and Creation"
VEJP   "Value, Equality, Justice, Politics: From Marx to Aristotle,
          From Aristotle to Us"

Acknowledgments

This book would not have been possible without the support of a great number of people along the way, to whom I would like to express my gratitude. My greatest thanks go to Johann Arnason for his immense intellectual generosity and acuity, his interest and encouragement. I would like to particularly thank him for his valuable feedback on many of the revised chapter drafts, and also for his intellectual and practical wisdom in responding to the 3,957 questions that floated his way during the redrafting process. I would also like to extend my deepest thanks to Charlie Ambrose for supporting my work over the past several years. He generously read and commented on each chapter of the book and provided me with insightful feedback as well as lively discussions on various aspects of Castoriadis's oeuvre. I have had the opportunity to draw on unpublished archival material for this study, and the privilege of various research sojourns in the Castoriadis Archives (Paris). I am particularly grateful to Zoé Castoriadis, Myrto Gondicas, and Cybèle Castoriadis for their intellectual support and generosity in facilitating my research in the archives, as well as for the warmth of their hospitality. I would also like to thank the Castoriadis Association for its kind permission to use archival material in this book. I worked on this book in several institutional contexts. I would like to thank my friends and colleagues at La Trobe University (Melbourne), the Universiteit voor Humanistiek (Utrecht), Monash University (Melbourne), and Flinders University (Adelaide) for supporting my endeavors. I would especially like to thank Anthony Elliott and my colleagues in the

Sociology Department at Flinders University for affording me much needed time and space in the decisive final stages of redrafting and editing the manuscript.

This book has been enriched through the feedback and advice of key people. I would like to thank the two anonymous referees who reviewed the original manuscript for Fordham University Press for their detailed comments and criticisms that led me to clarify and refine key aspects of the work. I also thank Fabio Ciaramelli, Vincent Descombes, and Dick Howard for their generous engagement with the argument I was developing in an earlier drafts of the manuscript; Peter Beilharz and George Vassilacopoulos were crucial for the development of my argument in the final stages; Harry Kunneman and Frederic Vandenberghe in Utrecht for their many kindnesses during my research sojourn; Beryl Langer, who has provided wise intellectual counsel and friendship since my Honors year; Stathis Gourgouris for his feedback and encouragement; and Craig Calhoun for his enduring and generous support of all my endeavors. I would like to thank Helen Tartar at Fordham University Press for supporting this project; without her, it would not have seen the light of day. I would also like to thank Eric Newman and his editing team for their many improvements to the manuscript, and Tom Lay for his assistance throughout the publishing process. I am grateful, too, to Thomas Welzenbacher for his kind permission to use the glass painting *Ray Man* on the cover and to Carolyn Corkindale for her help with the index.

I am fortunate to have friends with whom I can discuss all things Castoriadis and who inspire me to think more deeply: Thanks to Angelos Mouzakitis, Mats Rosengren, Jeremy Smith, Karl Smith and Ingerid Straume. I am also grateful to the organizers and participants of the Castoriadis conferences in Paris (2006), Melbourne (2008), Sydney (2009) and Stockholm (2010) for their engaged discussion and conviviality. My friends and family have come to accept if not completely understand the idiosyncrasies of my writing rhythms; they have made me soup in winter, and made sure I enjoyed the fresh air in summer. Many thanks to Anne and John Adams, Al and John Lamont, Lou Coventry, George and Ro Marriott, Jenny Williams, Toni Bentley, Lisa White, Ken Strachan, Emile White, Dan and Jonathon Katz, the lovely Langers, Anne Hahn, Mary Reilly, Eric Coventry, Marty Grace, Nik Taylor, Gillian Keightly and Cassandra Star.

Castoriadis's Ontology

General Introduction

Castoriadis in Context

Ontological creation was long held to be an extrahuman affair and occupied a central place in philosophical and theological discussions alike. In Western philosophical traditions, the civilizational constellations surrounding Athens and Jerusalem have provided dual cultural sources for its historical elaboration. It was the arrival of modernity, however, that first ushered in the social-historical horizons from which the ontological implications of human creation could be more fully grasped.[1] What were the historical preconditions of this turn of events? Hans Blumenberg (2001 [1957]) emphasizes the protracted breakdown of the idea of *mimesis* as the "imitation of nature," especially in relation to *"techne"* as the historical precondition for the consideration of human creation as ontological. Interwoven with these innovations, although less discussed by Blumenberg, was the gradual institution of a subject-centered metaphysics—classically formulated by Descartes—and attendant versions of humanism. In a related vein, Ricoeur highlights the shift toward the modern conception of the imagination as *productive*, instead of the premodern view of the imagination as *reproductive*.[2] He poses the question: "Are we not ready to recognise in the power of imagination, no longer the faculty of deriving 'images' from our sensory experience, but the capacity for letting new worlds shape our understanding of ourselves?" (1981: 181).[3] Castoriadis's ontology of creation is to be understood against this background. Although his elaboration of social-historical being is arguably drawn along philosophical-anthropological lines, its

1

elucidation is made possible by the horizons of modernity through which the ontological significance of human creation can be thought at all.[4] In the first instance, Castoriadis's philosophical elucidation of the being of creation takes a radical view of the novelty and ontological importance of *human* creation, which he articulated in terms of absolute creation *ex nihilo*. Although the idea of "*creatio ex nihilo*" draws on a theologically rich tradition, Castoriadis's ontology is directed against all forms of theological thinking. In his hands, creation *ex nihilo* is meant to characterize the specificity of human not divine creation. Indeed, the very notion of "divine" creation was antithetical to his project, as it implies "creation" from a basis external to anthropos. Castoriadis's intellectual sources are found instead in ancient Greek images of anthropic being as self-creating, as well as in Romantic conceptions of the productive (or creative) imagination.

Castoriadis's philosophy of creation is intimately linked to his project of autonomy. As will become apparent, the connection between autonomy and creation is maintained not only with his first ontological turn in the early 1970s, in which he focused on the being of human creation, but also with his second ontological turn in the early 1980s, in which he reconsidered the creativity of nature in its various regions and modes. In his most systematic work, *The Imaginary Institution of Society* (1987 [1975]),[5] Castoriadis embarks on an elaboration of the ontological preconditions of autonomy, but it metamorphoses along the way into an ontology of the social-historical.[6] Integral to Castoriadis's ontological turn of the 1970s is his link to the imaginary element of the human condition, and, in turn, the elaboration of the creative imagination as the basis of meaning. The imaginary element, as we shall see, points to a fundamental hermeneutical dimension in Castoriadis's thought that was at odds with his more explicit, ontological program. This is especially evident in his approach to the phenomenological problematic of the world horizon, on the one hand, and social imaginary significations, on the other.[7]

Castoriadis's philosophy can be situated within French phenomenological strands that take a hermeneutical or an ontological turn. The former highlights the importance of Ricoeur, the latter Merleau-Ponty. To claim a hermeneutical aspect to Castoriadis's thought is something he himself repudiated: That his philosophy reveals an implicit hermeneutics, however, is a central contention of the present study.[8] Merleau-Ponty must be considered a central intellectual source for the development of Castoriadis's thought and merits particular reference. Although the influential connection between Merleau-Ponty and Lefort has been well documented, Merleau-Ponty's bearing on Castoriadis's philosophical trajectory has been less discussed.[9] In this vein, however, Howard (1988) has noted the importance of Merleau-Ponty not just for Lefort, but also for Castoriadis and *Socialisme ou barbarie* in general.[10] The early Castoriadis (and the *Socialisme ou barbarie* collective more broadly) worked within French phenomenological Marxism, and it continued as an important intellectual source for Castoriadis's philosophical orientation.[11] In the French context, Merleau-Ponty was significant for phenomenological Marxism and *Adventures of the Dialectic* was an influential text. Merleau-Ponty was also one of the first to introduce a Weberian element into his analysis; Weber was of course also crucial to Lefort's and Castoriadis's analyses of capitalism and bureaucracy.[12] Castoriadis's thought underwent several alterations following *Socialisme ou barbarie*. Four are particularly important in the present context. First, Castoriadis's critique of Marx is, among other things, an attempt to redefine the relationship between theory and history in order to open a space for the open-ended creativity of history, with a central focus on meaning.[13] Second is his sustained encounter with psychoanalysis, which began in the late 1960s, although he first started to practice as a psychoanalyst in 1973. Third is the ontological turn of the 1975 section of the *IIS* where he looked to elucidate a *regional* ontology of the social-historical as a way of fleshing out the being of *nomos*. Finally, there was his reconfiguration of the *nomos* and *physis* problematic, which incorporated a second ontological shift to a *transregional* ontology of creative *physis* in the 1980s. Castoriadis's earlier focus on the excavation of a regional ontology of *nomos* (as human modes of being, in particular, the social-historical) presumed that ontological creation of form was limited to human modes of being; concomitantly his image of being was one of irregular stratification. An understanding of being as incorporating a variety of regions points to the heterogeneity of being and to the heterogeneous *logics* of being. In his later work, albeit implicitly and unsystematically, Castoriadis began to elucidate a second image of being that, while still intrinsically heterogeneous, was characterized by *self-creation* in *all* of its regions, not just human regions. Hence, his image of the social-historical and the psyche as the only regions of being to be characterized by self-creation gave way to a deeper sense of the "transregionality" of being as creation. This overarching "logic" of creation that pervaded all regions of being, which was ultimately seen as transregional, came to be articulated as creative *physis* as *à-être*, although, in order to make the new emphasis on the omnipresence of self-creation compatible with the older one on the heterogeneity of being, Castoriadis needed to provide extra clarification of the differences between modes of self-creation, for example, those between living beings and societies.[14]

As with Lefort, Castoriadis's "political ontology"—to use Howard's term—has clear sources in Merleau-Ponty's writings. More than that, however, his shift to ontology proper (that is, with the publication of the *IIS* in 1975) emerged from a sustained encounter with Merleau-Ponty's own ontological reconfiguration of phenomenology. Unlike Merleau-Ponty, however, Castoriadis came to ontology through a reconsideration of human, that is, social-historical creation; it was only later that a re-thinking of the ontological creativity of nature became visible in his philo-sophical reflections. Castoriadis wrote two important meditations on Merleau-Ponty's thought. Significantly, each of Castoriadis's encounters with Merleau-Ponty occurred on the eve of—and in close connection with—major ontological breakthroughs in his own thought. The first essay reflecting Castoriadis's encounter with Merleau-Ponty was "The Sayable and the Unsayable: Homage to Merleau-Ponty" (1971).[15] Castor-iadis wrote it on the cusp of his first shift to ontology and the elucidation of the being of the social-historical in the *IIS*. Themes encountered in this paper prefigured what were to become central problematics—society, history, imagination, meaning, creation, and institution—for his overall philosophical trajectory. These problematics constitute the main focus in the first section of the present study.[16] Castoriadis's second meditation on Merleau-Ponty's thought—"Merleau-Ponty and the Weight of the Onto-logical Tradition"—was written after completion of the *IIS*.[17] This essay emphasized the centrality of the imagination and radical creation as an-thropic modes of being, which in Castoriadis's view, went unrecognized by traditional philosophy as its overall tendency was to reduce an under-standing of "being" to "determinacy" that obscured the creative mode of the social-historical.[18] For Castoriadis, ultimately Merleau-Ponty re-mained held back by the inherited ontological tradition; this meant that openings toward the radical creativity of the imaginary in Merleau-Ponty's philosophy were left unrealized. In the same paper, however, we find Castoriadis's earliest indication of a shift toward rethinking the cre-ativity of nature—termed a "*hyper physis*" in that paper—and the conse-quent move toward a general ontology of creative emergence as *à-être* (understood as an "always-becoming-being").[19] Consideration of the being of creation as it plays out in nature, that is, beyond the anthropic limits of the social-historical (and the psyche) originally imposed by Cas-toriadis in the *IIS*, comprises the focus of the second half of this study.

Like Merleau-Ponty, Castoriadis's philosophy cannot be properly un-derstood without reference to Heidegger.[20] In contrast to the second-gen-eration phenomenologists, however, Castoriadis's critical dialogue with

Heidegger is more implicit and ancillary to his central philosophical concerns. That being said, and Castoriadis's own protestations to the contrary notwithstanding, Castoriadis's rethinking of the connections between "being," "time," and "creation" draws in a general way on Heidegger's early thought.[21] In particular, he formulated his own most seminal and consistent insights, especially concerning the ontological importance of the imagination, as well as the central importance of the temporality of being, through a radicalization of Heidegger's thought. Castoriadis's engagement with Heidegger tends to focus more on Heidegger's pre-*Kehre* period, especially on the *Kant and the Problem of Metaphysics* as the mooted sequel to *Being and Time*.[22] Heidegger's argument that Kant's *Critique of Pure Reason* provides us with not only an epistemology but an ontology, and his discussion of the transcendental imagination as Kant's key but neglected element, also affords Castoriadis with a starting point for rethinking the temporality of the social-historical.[23] Conversely, although Castoriadis, too, radicalizes our understanding of the temporal mode of being, he does not take it in the direction of a phenomenology or fundamental ontology. Instead, he elucidates an ontology of the *social-historical* as an ontology of human creation and as the region of being that has been occluded by the inherited philosophical tradition. Although Castoriadis and Heidegger both criticize a whole tradition of occidental philosophy, Castoriadis does not accuse it so much of a *forgetting of Being*, but of a reduction of being to *determinacy*.

Castoriadis's reworking of phenomenology can be situated as part of a broader move toward "post-transcendental phenomenology." This is a trend also apparent in Lefort and Merleau-Ponty's writings, as well as in Levinas and Patočka's. Post-transcendental phenomenology—a term first coined by Johann P. Arnason—forms part of a broader cultural turn in the social and human sciences that has been evident in the latter decades of the twentieth century.[24] It constitutes a heterogeneous field, and emphasizes the ways in which phenomenology has transformed itself from a subjective and intersubjective philosophy to one that interrogates trans-subjective (and transobjective) horizons. It thus continues the critique of the philosophy of consciousness that led to Husserl's elaboration of the lifeworld in his later work, and broadens its ongoing reconstruction. In moving beyond a subject-oriented (or intersubjective) analysis, post-transcendental phenomenology highlights the importance of (socio-)cultural analysis, and of culture as the articulation of the human encounter with the broader world horizon. In this vein, the problematic of the world becomes central, and is regarded as a transsubjective (and transobjective) horizon. So considered, the cultural dimension of analysis, especially as it pertains to the emergence of meaning formations, is the most important.[25] In this sense, a focus on the transsubjective, or cultural context, goes beyond a focus on the subject or intersubjective, since cultural constellations of meaning provide the infrastructure within which the embodied subject-self can navigate and participate in intersubjective relations.[26] The transsubjective level of analysis corresponds more or less, in Castoriadian terms, to the " anonymous collective" of the "social-historical," or, to draw on another tradition, and from a slightly different angle, the "objective Spirit." Post-transcendental phenomenology seeks to elucidate concrete cultural interpretations of the world horizon—as well as their philosophical preconditions—from interdisciplinary perspectives of sociology, politics, philosophy, history, and anthropology.[27]

In response to the twentieth-century phenomenological and hermeneutic challenge of "the meaning of meaning,"[28] the problematic of culture as the inescapable symbolic context of social-historical being was rethought from diverse angles.[29] Culture was conceived variously as the realm of freedom—or creativity—in contrast to civilization, or anthropologically as a constitutive symbolic order, or, finally and most pertinently for our current purposes, as the ongoing confrontation between anthropos and world. In this respect, Castoriadis's (and Merleau-Ponty's) approach to the problematic of anthropos and world is unusual in that they rethink the natural as well as the sociocultural world and their interrelations. Finally, post-transcendental currents of phenomenology tend to incorporate a hermeneutical dimension and openness to the cultural—or transsubjective—level of investigation. Part of this has seen the partial shift from a focus on "faculties of the subject" to "cultural configurations," such as the move from "the imagination" to "the imaginary" (or "cultural imagination" as per Ricoeur (1976), or "the social imaginary" as per Castoriadis),[30] from "reason" to forms of "rationality" (Arnason 1994), and most recently toward an interest in "cultural memory" (Assmann 1992).

The problematic of culture has also been central to recent social theoretical concerns and Castoriadis's emphasis on the *creative imagination* adds a distinctive twist to such interpretations. The French phenomenological tradition—the French philosophical tradition, more broadly—has historically pursued conversation with social theoretical currents, where "social theory" is understood to incorporate not only sociological but also political, philosophical, and anthropological aspects. The case of Durkheim is particularly instructive. Long hailed by sociologists for his early work, it was his later work (often coauthored with Marcel Mauss), especially *The Elementary Forms of Religious Life* (1995 [1912]), in which he made his well-known "anthropological turn" that was important for

French debates.[31] More recently, Durkheim's later thought has become an important source for the cultural turn in sociology (Alexander and Smith 2005). Castoriadis, too, drew in central ways on Durkheim's thought and, as with Anderson's *Imagined Communities* (1982), it can be situated within post-Durkheimian currents. If Durkheim's interest in the anthropological aspects of society were important for Castoriadis, so, too, was Weber's more historical approach, and the connection between history and meaning. Indeed, one of his earliest essays discussed Weber and the social sciences (1944).[32] The tensions that emerge from his anthropological elucidation of the social-historical and the anthropological versus the historical figurations of the creative imagination are never quite exorcised but remain fruitful to his overall trajectory.[33] Weber's thought, too, has recently undergone a renaissance with more interest being shown in the cultural aspects of his thought. An important thinker here is Johann P. Arnason, who fused Weber's early theory of culture as the "relations between man and world" (1982) and Merleau-Ponty's understanding of *mise en forme du monde*, which Arnason further refined through a reconstruction of Castoriadis's notion of social imaginary significations.[34]

Ever since Husserl's articulation of the lifeworld, the world horizon has taken on increasing importance for succeeding generations of phenomenologists; in this regard, Merleau-Ponty and Patočka's respective reconfigurations and radicalization of Husserlian and Heideggerian themes are the most striking. The post-transcendental phenomenological context points to the signification of *the world* as our ultimate horizon in need of perpetual interpretation. The double sense of Merleau-Ponty's *mise en forme du monde*—as *world articulation* or *world forming*—is pertinent: The world becomes the horizon where the "true transcendental" (Merleau-Ponty) of nature and culture entwine. An emphasis on (inter)-cultural articulations of the broader world horizon implies a hermeneutical dimension to our ontological condition in the world. To paraphrase Merleau-Ponty: Because we are in the world, we are condemned not only to meaning, but also to interpretation. The human encounter with the world, then, results in its cultural articulation. This perspective regards the human condition not only as self-interpreting (Taylor) but *also* world-interpreting (this aspect has been most explicitly elaborated by Arnason): Such an approach thus offers a critique of sociocentric images of culture common to the humanist imaginary.

As mentioned, the horizons of modernity form the backdrop to reflections on the ontological import of human creation, and, more broadly, extrahuman modes of creation. As such, a cultural hermeneutics of modernity is needed, both in general, and, more pertinently for our current purposes, to situate Castoriadis's philosophy more concretely. "Ways of worldmaking," to draw on a well-known motif from Nelson Goodman, are historically diverse.[35] In modernity, the world is no longer a taken-for-granted horizon but is inherently problematic and problematizable. Following Arnason, modernity is regarded as a "field of tensions" (1988), in which the (partially structured) conflict of interpretations play out. In this way, interpretative frameworks are required to make sense of rival approaches to the various configurations of meaning constellations that structure this field of tensions (Arnason 1988, 1989a, 1991, 1994).[36] Rather than seeing Romanticism as a conservative reaction to the modernity of the Enlightenment, or the Enlightenment as the sole bearer of the project and promise of modernity, Romanticism and the Enlightenment are better regarded as general cultural currents that structure modernity's field of tensions and offer rival images of the world and worldhood. "Enlightenment" and "Romanticism," then, are neither reduced to historical periods, nor to intellectual movements, but are envisaged as cultural currents indicative of particular configurations of meaning constellations and transsubjective contexts. In this vein, the Enlightenment is broadly understood as emphasizing rationality and explanation, while the imaginary and the ongoing quest to reactivate contexts of meaning are seen as characteristic of Romanticism.[37]

Within this context, philosophy as a civilizational form makes a significant contribution to the shape and direction of broader cultural currents. Kant's critical philosophy constitutes a watershed moment in Western thought, and is pivotal for the elaboration of a hermeneutic of modernity: Not only does it articulate the most sophisticated version of Enlightenment thought, it opens onto incipient Romantic contexts, too. One of the first to recognize this was Herman August Korff, who, in a decisive essay "Das Wesen der Romantik" (1929), identifies not only the imagination as the chief characteristic of Romanticism, but also Kant's thought as a bridge between Enlightenment and Romantic currents. These can be considered along two axes: First, there is the identification and problematization of the role and scope of the imagination in the first *Critique*; and, second, there are the implications of its mutations from the first to the second editions.[38] Kant is a central figure for Castoriadis's thought, both in terms of the philosophy of the three *Critiques* and the dialogue and tension between Enlightenment and Romantic thematic.[39] Like Kant, Castoriadis builds bridges between Enlightenment and Romantic worldviews. In the first instance, Castoriadis makes the occluded theme of the imagination central to his philosophy—especially to his theory of meaning—and elucidates its implications both at the psychical and social-historical levels.[40] Kant's recognition of—and recoil from—the role of the imagination as the basis of reason in the two different editions of the first *Critique* is a key site of interrogation for Castoriadis. He takes up the ontological role of the imagination as the ground of reason, which was neglected by Kant, and links it to his theory of the creative imagination within his broader theory of meaning.[41] From his earliest phase, Castoriadis took up the Weberian theme that meaning is the elementary medium of social life. Castoriadis's point, however, is that the role of meaning in social life cannot be understood unless the imagination is brought in. In this way, there is a dual Romantic motif: the imagination and meaning. For Castoriadis the reappraisal of the creative imagination was the way to restore contexts of meaning (and by linking it directly to meaning, to radicalize theories of meaning), especially as the reactivation of a milieu of meaningful contexts that had been emptied by broad Enlightenment trends constitutes a significant part of the Romantic critique of the Enlightenment.[42] At the level of an elaboration of modernity, the Enlightenment as an intellectual source is most obvious in Castoriadis's emphasis on autonomy and self-reflection;[43] at the philosophical level it is evident not only in his unwillingness to reject rationality, but also in his refusal to envelop human modes of being within a cosmic whole.[44] The project of autonomy in its dual aspects of a strong and explicit politics (*la politique*) and philosophy (*la philosophie*) remains fundamental throughout Castoriadis's philosophical trajectory.[45] Of most relevance to the present study is Castoriadis's notion of philosophical autonomy, which imagines the world both as an interpretative creation of human *nomos*, and as an inescapable context to be encountered.

To properly consider both Kant and Castoriadis as respectively connecting Romantic and Enlightenment cultural currents, the inclusion not just of Kant's two editions of the first *Critique*, but also the third *Critique*—where aesthetics and nature are central foci, and, as such, Romantic problematics are first introduced—is needed. In considering the aesthetic aspect, there is good reason to see in Kant's idea of the creative genius an important source for Castoriadis's idea of the creativity of the social-historical in general. Although Castoriadis moves the idea of creation to the institutional level (the creation of Athenian democracy or the creation of monotheism, for example), there is nonetheless a tendency to see in aesthetic creations (and aesthetic creations of the "genius artist") the perfection of the human capacity to create new forms, and create them *ex nihilo*.[46] Second, Kant's third *Critique* was a vital text for the early Romantics: It emphasizes not only the autonomy of the aesthetic sphere and the paradigm of the genius as creator, but also incipient articulations of the creativity of nature. In this way, Kant, too, can be incorporated within the intermittent modern tradition of *natura naturans/natura naturata* (although he himself does not use the term), which was reinvigorated in early modernity by Spinoza and deepened further by Schelling.[47] In the *Critique of Judgment*, Kant recognizes the inadequacy of the scientific framework of the first *Critique* to grasp the living being; hence the teleology of nature in the third *Critique*. Although Kant did not—and could not within the constraints of his critical philosophy—grant the protocreativity of nature the ontological status that Castoriadis does. Castoriadis's later shift toward creative *physis* can be seen as a critical reactivation of *naturphilosophical* themes.[48] A critical *naturphilosophical* agenda can be interpreted in Whiteheadian terms, in that it imagines alternative visions to the various interlacements of science and nature via a rethinking of ontological premises, and thus links up with philosophical aspects of the project of autonomy. Castoriadis's later conception of *physis* radicalizes the classic Aristotelian formulation of internal qualitative movement and change (*alloiosis*) to creative emergence, interpreted through a critical reconsideration of the Romantic idea of nature and the intermittent tradition of *natura naturans/natura naturata*. A fusion of key Aristotelian and Kantian motifs is thus to be regarded as a central aspect of Castoriadis's philosophy.[49]

There is growing interest in Castoriadis's work within a variety of national and regional contexts, but it tends to be directed less toward a systematic discussion of his philosophical—that is, ontological—elucidations (and the phenomenological milieu from which it emerges), and more toward his social-political and psychoanalytic writings.[50] This is partially due to the nature of Castoriadis's elucidations themselves, where no clear division between the philosophical and the political exist.[51] When the philosophical aspects of Castoriadis's work do come into focus, they are mainly taken up within political-philosophical contexts. There are exceptions to this: Arnason develops the philosophical hermeneutic implications of Castoriadis's ontology toward a culturological phenomenology; Ciaramelli pursues the ontological and psychoanalytic implications of Castoriadis's thought alongside his interest in Levinas; Descombes addresses philosophical themes in Castoriadis that build bridges with the analytic tradition; and Waldenfels has written on the philosophical-phenomenological aspects of Castoriadis's project, in tandem with a focus on Merleau-Ponty and a development of the ethical notion of *Aufmerksamkeit*. A growing interest in the philosophy of Castoriadis is discernable in a new generation of researchers: Most recently, Klooger's (2009) monograph offers illuminating insights on the links between autonomy, society, and the psyche; Smith (2010) critically compares Castoriadis's and Taylor's approaches to self and subjectivity; and Mouzakitis (2008) investigates notions of time and historicity in Castoriadis, Heidegger, and Gadamer. Although there is increasing (and enduring) interest in Castoriadis in the French (and broader francophone) context, recent book publications have tended toward the introductory and include, for example, Poirier's book on the radical imaginary (2004), Caumières (2007) text on autonomy, and Prat's booklet on the key dimensions of Castoriadis thought (2007).[52] There has not yet been a sustained engagement with Castoriadis's most central work, *The Imaginary Institution of Society*, especially with its 1975 section. Neither has much systematic research been undertaken with respect to Castoriadis's post-*IIS* philosophical path, in general, and to his reconsideration of the philosophical idea of nature in particular; this is, no doubt, due, at least in part, to its more unsystematic character. The present study addresses these gaps.

The announcement of Castoriadis's initial ontological turn in *The Imaginary Institution of Society* and his later, reconfigured ontology during the 1980s forms the primary focus of this study. Accordingly, it examines the internal shifts in Castoriadis's philosophical trajectory beginning with the publication of his *magnum opus* in 1975, *The Imaginary Institution of Society*, up to and including his reply to his critics in "Done and to be Done" (1989). It also seeks to contextualize Castoriadis's thought within the history of philosophy. In so doing, it draws on three overarching and overlapping interpretive contexts: First, it revives ancient Greek sources, in particular, the problematic of *nomos* and *physis*, which, it is argued, were pivotal to Castoriadis's overall ontological reflections on human institution and nature. Second, it draws on an emergent line of philosophical enquiry—post-transcendental phenomenology—to engage with Castoriadis's thought (I return to this later). Finally, it takes a hermeneutic of modernity—represented here philosophically by Kant and the *Frühromantiker*—as a central context in reconstructing Castoriadis's ontological reflections within broader currents of philosophical thought. Writing a monograph can entail the hazard of losing critical distance. To minimize this, I draw on hermeneutical methods of critique, tracing subterranean and unfinished lines of arguments, tensions and latent tendencies internal to Castoriadis's oeuvre. This leads me to take issue with Castoriadis's own professed understanding of his philosophical project. In addition, by situating Castoriadis within the history of philosophy and current debates in social theory, phenomenology and beyond, the book opens onto broader contexts of comparison and discussion; this is especially important as Castoriadis himself tended to minimize the extent to which he drew on specific intellectual currents of thought. The book draws on a hermeneutic approach that is consequently critically interpretative rather than strictly exegetical. Its affinities lie more with Ricoeur than Gadamer: The written text and engagement with the contexts of meanings that are "charged with latent philosophy" form the basis of interpretation.[53] Simultaneously, the autonomy of the text as the site of interpretation is privileged over the author's erstwhile intentions. Thus, although offering close textual analysis of key Castoriadis texts, as a reconstructive hermeneutics, the present work is reducible to neither an exegesis of, nor a commentary on, those works. Instead it provides a critical engagement with Castoriadis's ontological project as a whole that goes beyond his explicit intentions, and opens onto areas of discussion to which, at first glance, they may not appear to readily lend themselves.

Castoriadis announced his shift to ontology in *The Imaginary Institution of Society* (1989 [1975]). The *IIS* is a heterogeneous book consisting of two sections. The first section comprises three papers elaborating Castoriadis's critique of Marx—known as "Marxism and the Revolutionary Project"—which were first published in *Socialisme ou barbarie* in 1964–65. During this time Castoriadis rediscovered the ancient Greeks as a key intellectual source, which facilitated his move away from an articulation of "socialism" to the "project of autonomy." The second part of the *IIS* was written 1970–1974 and indicates his original turn to ontology. Overall, the second part of the *IIS* can be seen as four, loosely woven responses to perennial philosophical questions concerning the human condition: ontological, epistemological, anthropological, and hermeneutical. In the 1975 section of the *IIS*, Castoriadis proposes in a relatively systematic form a regional ontology of the social-historical—the realm of *nomos*—and its preconditions as a self-creating mode of being. At this juncture, he interprets *physis* (as natural norm) primarily in its opposition to *nomos*. From the late 1970s—and gaining momentum in the early-to-mid 1980s—a second ontological shift starts to emerge. During this time, Castoriadis begins to rediscover the creative aspect to *physis* that he had previously minimized, and extends the mode of self-creation to all regions of being. His radicalization of *physis* signals the shift from an ontology of regional social-historical *nomos*, to transregional *physis*, whereby all regions of being—indeed, being *qua* being—are interpreted as self-creating. Thus, Castoriadis's mature philosophy incorporates two overlapping ontological configurations. Castoriadis's reconfiguration of the *nomos/physis* problematic—indicated by his shift toward an ontology of transregional *physis*—is neither fully systematic nor fully realized. The task of the present book is to hermeneutically reconstruct the ontological transformations of Castoriadis's philosophical path. It does so primarily by way of a close reading of a selection of his texts—both published and unpublished—in the period 1975–1989. The year 1975 marks Castoriadis's publication of the *IIS* and his turn to a regional ontology of the social-historical. The year 1989 has been selected as the upper limit for the present study on the basis that it is the year in which Castoriadis wrote "Done and to be Done" as a mature statement of his thought and response to his critics.[54]

The book is organized around two thematic sections: *Nomos* and *Physis*. In the first section—*Nomos*—a close reading of the four chapters of the 1975 section of the *IIS* that comprise Castoriadis's initial turn to ontology is undertaken as a regional ontology of the social-historical. After sketching the importance of *nomos* for Castoriadis's philosophy, the first chapter takes up ontological themes and discusses the self-creative and temporal aspects of the hitherto occluded mode of the social-historical. In this vein, Castoriadis's discussion of Plato's *Timaeus* provides a crucial discussion to Castoriadis's overall philosophical aim to elucidate an ontology of (human) creation as an qualitative, temporal mode of being, reminding us of the predilection of "inherited thought" to reduce the creativity of time to frameworks of determinacy, and revealing subterranean openings onto his later, transregional ontology. The second chapter argues that in discussing the proto-institutions of *legein* and *teukhein*, a Kantian element emerges. In addressing this epistemological aspect, Castoriadis begins to build a critique of elementary reason. The third chapter takes up the first pole of the creative imagination: the radical imagination as psychic flux and as an anthropological feature of subjectivity. The link between imagination and meaning first begins to emerge here, although ultimately "psychical meaning" can only be considered properly as a "proto-meaning." The fourth chapter considers the other pole of the creative imagination: the radical imaginary (which emerges at the social-historical level). It discusses Castoriadis's theory of meaning as a contribution to philosophical hermeneutics and grapples with the phenomenological problematic of the world horizon as it appears (and disappears) in Castoriadis's thought. Chapter 4 not only closes the first section of this book, it also acts as a bridge between the two book sections (Part I: *Nomos* and Part II: *Physis*) and is, along with the Introduction to Part II, "*Physis* and the Romanticist Imaginary of Nature," and Chapter 5, which elaborates Castoriadis shift to creative *physis*, probably the most structurally important chapters of this study.

Castoriadis's later elucidations of the being of creation go beyond his original formulations in *The Imaginary Institution of Society*. In retrospect, the *IIS* was less about providing answers and more about opening a series of new questions: These form the focus of the second part of this study. To contextualize Castoriadis's usage of creative *physis*, it is situated within the Romanticist imaginary of nature, which includes the fragmentary tradition of *natura naturans/natura naturata* and *Naturphilosophie*. Chapter 5 provides an overview of Castoriadis's shift toward transregional radical *physis* and the creativity of nature through examination of an archival document and hermeneutical reconstruction of a key, if little discussed essay by Castoriadis, "*Physis* and Autonomy" (PA). It argues for the significance of Castoriadis's conjoint reimmersion in ancient Greek sources, his encounter with autopoietic debates, as well as the enduring importance of Aristotle as his chief interlocutor. Chapter 6 takes up Castoriadis's deepening reassessment of objective knowledge. It discusses his critique of the Kantian approach to knowledge through his requirement, in continuation and radicalization of phenomenological themes, to problematize not only the subject but also the object of knowledge. At the same time, the chapter highlights Castoriadis's continued emphasis on the overlap of the ontological dimension with the epistemological: Knowledge of nature also entails a philosophy of nature. Chapters 7 and 8 address Castoriadis's two later regional ontologies and their place within his overall transregional ontology of *physis*: a philosophy of the living being and a philosophical cosmology, respectively. In the former, it is argued that the two central themes of Castoriadis's thought—self-creation and autonomy—reemerge at the level of the living being. This is discussed in relation to the relocation of the *physis* and *nomos* problematic, and the possibility of "biological autonomy," with respect to Castoriadis's ongoing engagement with Francisco Varela. The final chapter considers Castoriadis's philosophical cosmology and takes up the problematic of a qualitative theory of time and creation in the physical world. Castoriadis critiques the reduction of time to a spatial dimension in physics and argues that an overarching interpretation of time as radical *physis* is needed to make sense of subjective (as the social-historical) and objective approaches to time. Plato's *chora* makes a reappearance, and its "chaotic" elements with respect to an elucidation of the world are reconsidered. The conclusion returns to the being of creation via the interplay of *nomos* and *physis*. The idea of *nomos*—which Castoriadis conceives broadly as *human institution*—is interpreted as encompassing the two central motifs of his thought: radical autonomy and creation *ex nihilo*. However, in that it situates the idea of *nomos between* autonomy and creation, *nomos* as human self-institution is understood as *creative interpretation* and relativizes Castoriadis's overly strong notions of creation and autonomy (especially in its stark polarization to heteronomy). As a result, it emphasizes the hermeneutical undercurrents to Castoriadis's thought; the circle of *physis* and *nomos* is envisaged not only as the "circle of creation" (in Castoriadis's words), but also as a hermeneutical circle of creative interpretation and the cultural (and intercultural) articulation of the world as a shared horizon.

Nomos

For the being of the *nomos*, no ontological place exists.

—VEJP 326

Nomos is our creative imaginary institution by means of which we make ourselves qua human beings. It is the term *nomos* that gives full meaning to the term and project of autonomy.

—PA 332

Introduction to Part I

The Importance of Nomos

The significance of the ancient Greek institution of the *physis* and *nomos* was a lasting problematic for Castoriadis.[1] As distinguished from the normative order of *physis*, *nomos* indicated the order of self-institution and human convention for Castoriadis, and, as such, it encompassed the two central motifs of his thought: Autonomy and human creation.[2] As the epigraph states, he considers it as "our imaginary creative institution" (PA). Nevertheless, as he observed in an earlier, 1974 essay "no ontological place," it had not been elaborated for the being of *nomos* (VEJP: 326). Rectifying this situation was the result, in retrospect at least, of his ontological turn in *The Imaginary Institution of Society* (1989[1975]) and his elucidation of the social-historical as a regional ontology of *nomos*. The order of *nomos*, as a distinctly *human,* that is, *self-creating* order, was originally directed against all versions of *physis* as an order in which preexisting, extrasocial "natural norms" were embedded.[3]

The separate etymological and social-historical trajectories of *nomos* and *physis* emerge first in archaic Greek thought. As such, their respective elaborations are not straightforward; much is obscure and contested.[4] Nonetheless, a couple of points are worth noting: It seems clear that Homer utilized an early form of *physis*—*phua*—that indicated variously generation and growth, although it was limited to the vegetative domain (Kaulbach 1984), as well as prefiguring the *polis* and human forms of autonomy (*CQFG*). However, it was Heraclitus who first extended an anthropological dimension to *physis*, that is, as an order with direct relevance to the human condition. The idea of *physis* received its classic articulation in Aristotle, and as Gadamer (1998) maintains, it is only by way of Aristotle that one can hermeneutically access the shifting pre-Socratic imaginary of *physis* at all. According to Cornford (1957), *nomos* was prefigured in archaic thought in the impersonal power of *moira*. The order of *nomos* appears also in Hesiod, where the gods gave not only humans but also animals their appropriate *nomoi*: Humans were separated from animals by the bestowal of *dike*. Although the invention of *physis*, in particular, has long been regarded as the watershed moment that marks the shift from mythic to rational, that is, philosophical thought in ancient Greece, Castoriadis (*CQFG*) agrees with Gadamer (1998) in noting that only after *physis* comes into opposition with *nomos* is real philosophical momentum and creativity achieved.[5] One of the many reasons for which Castoriadis critiqued Heidegger can be traced to Heidegger's interest in and reliance on a *physis* that was pre-*nomos*, and hence an acceptance of a certain kind of a *top-down* unveiling (or "disclosure") rather than a *bottom-up* institution (or "creation").[6] Castoriadis takes an alternative approach. Although the importance of *physis* to pre-Socratic thought is acknowledged, in his ancient Greek seminars, Castoriadis traces the archaic antecedents to *nomos*, not *physis*, as the key motif by which to grasp the importance of the Greek breakthrough and trajectory.[7] He argues that *nomos*, as a particular kind of human order that created itself *ex nihilo*, was implicit in Greek thought as an imaginary signification—instituted in Greek social doing—even before its later opposition to *physis*.

In his seminars on Ancient Greece, Castoriadis counted the *physis/nomos* problematic as the most important of three Greek philosophical creations (*CQFG*). In emphasizing the uniqueness of the ancient Greek trajectory—in comparison to other axial civilizations—and its breakthrough to autonomy, Castoriadis identifies three vital philosophical oppositions particular to the Greeks: *aletheia* (truth/opinion), *einai/phainesthei* (being/appearance), and the *nomos/physis* problematic.[8] Emerging in the fifth century BCE, the invention of the *nomos/physis* opposition was both later and more enigmatic than the earlier two (*CQFG*). The elaboration of the *nomos/physis* distinction did not signal the invention of absolutely new terms, but rather the transformations and creative interpretation of particular historical meaning-constellations. In this vein, the *nomos/physis* opposition of the Sophist debates concerned the naturalness or conventionality of language; this is a key point to which Castoriadis continually returned. Conversely, Plato relocated the *nomos* and *physis* problematic. In Plato, the problematic of human convention and innovations previously associated with *nomos* is relegated to the realm of appearances as subject to incessant change and opinion, whereas the place of *physis* is taken by the immutable Forms that determine the nature of things in the sensible realm. For Plato, however, the idea of self-movement is transposed from *physis* to the world-soul.[9] Aristotle, in response to the Sophists and Plato, sought to reintegrate *nomos* and *physis* and to bring them into the domain of human affairs. For him, anthropos is by nature a political animal. Aristotle reintegrated movement back into *physis* but could not ultimately uphold *nomos* over *physis* in the human domain: His was the thought of classical teleology.

Reflecting on *nomos* also alerts us to the period of Greek history to which Castoriadis had the greatest affinity and drew upon the most heavily: The so-called Greek Enlightenment. It includes, for Castoriadis, not only the more theoretical thinkers Protagoras and Democritus, but also the writers of tragedy (Sophocles), as well as the historians Herodotus and Thucydides. Aristotle, too, is included for Castoriadis, at least in terms of his thought if not his chronology. The fifth century BCE witnessed the innovation and blossoming of politics and cultural thought that was anchored, for Castoriadis, in the creation of the democratic *polis*. Thus broadly speaking, the ancient—as opposed to the archaic or Hellenistic—Greek world provided central motifs and impetus to Castoriadis's thought, at least during the period in which he was occupied with the *IIS*.[10] Although Castoriadis sees in Democritus a certain greatness in his thinking about *nomos*—and in Plato its ultimate occultation—it is Aristotle who, throughout his trajectory, remains his greatest interlocutor.[11] Aristotle offers abiding inspiration for Castoriadis, and he finds the openings Aristotle makes toward the idea of *nomos* of particular fecundity and interest, even if he judges Aristotle as ultimately unable to surmount the ontology of *physis* as a natural norm (PA). Not only Aristotle but also Castoriadis are heirs to the Platonic heritage, with which they each in their various ways continually grappled. As I shall show during the course of this book, although Castoriadis is critical of Plato's withdrawal from democratic ideals and of his projection of *nomos* into the heavens, the final status of Plato's philosophical thought for Castoriadis remains somewhat ambiguous.

Castoriadis's most sustained engagement with the dichotomy between *nomos* and *physis* is to be found in the early essay "Value, Equality, Justice, Politics: From Marx to Aristotle and from Aristotle to Ourselves" (1984 [1975]), but it was a problematic that continued to absorb him throughout his life.[12] VEJP is contemporaneous with the *IIS* (both were published in 1975), and so it is particularly pertinent for our discussion. In the *IIS*, Castoriadis seeks to elucidate the mode of being of *nomos*, for which, as our epigraph notes, "no ontological place exists" (VEJP, 326). As I shall show, in the course of his long journey through *nomos*, Castoriadis argued that "society" and "history" had been thought about using frameworks informed by investigations of other regions of being (by which he means particularly those of the natural-mathematical sciences). Thus the real "object" of their study—the social-historical as self-instituting and self-creating—remained invisible to their gaze. Consequently, Castoriadis set out early on to argue that the philosophical idea of *physis*—understood as a natural norm—had no place in theorizing the social-historical: The social-historical was to be elucidated via *nomos*.[13] The enigma of the *nomos/physis* opposition seems an inescapable problematic: "To posit *nomos* is itself to be driven back ineluctably to a positing of *physis*, of a fact of being which indubitably exists as a mode of being" (VEJP, 284). Although in VEJP Castoriadis did not focus explicitly on the non-anthropic dimensions of *physis*, in recognizing its indeterminacy, it suggests a prefiguring of the space in which *physis* could be later radicalized. Later in VEJP, Castoriadis—in discussing the status of knowledge—refers to this enigma in passing once more, but this time in the context of the indeterminacy of *physis*. Here Castoriadis links the indeterminacy of *physis* to a physical existence of indeterminacy "in itself" (that is, not pertaining to *nous*) and to an ontological foundation that limits human knowledge. From this discussion, Castoriadis concludes that the "indeterminate" and the "possible" do "objectively" exist (VEJP p. 323 ff), in which both the incipient beginnings of a context to theorize radical *physis* and the interpenetration of *physis* and *nomos*, at least in regard to matters epistemological, begin to appear.[14]

The ancient Greek achievement has been variously characterized by classical commentators. Vernant credits it with "the discovery of the political" (2000), Raaflaub (2004) with the discovery of "political freedom," while Meier goes so far to elaborate it as a "political revolution" (2000). Castoriadis is in general agreement with these thinkers, but focuses on a slightly different aspect. Instead of casting the discovery of the "political" as the greatest achievement of the ancient Greeks, for Castoriadis their most important achievement was the institution of "politics" (*la politique*). For him, "politics" is to be understood in the strong and explicit sense of public discussion, contestation, recognition, or the problematization of society's self-institution that was inaugurated by the Athenian form of direct democracy. "Politics" for Castoriadis is quite different from "the political" (*le politique*), which is understood as the social arrangement of power that each polity institutes (and must institute) in its own way. *Nomos*, as a philosophical concept, has a special affinity to the philosophical aspects and elucidation of autonomy.[15] In this sense it points to the invention of "philosophy" proper—in contrast to the merely "philo-sophical"—as the difference between questioning and problematizing the world in a strong sense or the mere interpretation of it.[16] Echoing Castori-adis's distinction between *la politique* and *le politique*, the distinction be-tween "philosophy" and "the philosophical" might also suggest the invention of *la philosophie* (philosophy) in the strong sense, in contrast to *le philosophique* (the philosophical).[17] Here the links between philosophy (*la philosophie*) to politics (*la politique*) seem readily apparent. The emer-gence of "*nomos*" in ancient debates signals the birth of philosophy as one of the twin aspects of the invention of the project of autonomy in ancient Athens, the other being politics. It signifies for Castoriadis not only the beginning of Greek philosophy, properly speaking, in the strong sense, but also of philosophy, in general. In DD he writes:

> The historical creation of philosophy is rupture of this closure [of instituted society]: explicit putting into question of these S.I.S. [so-cial imaginary significations], of the representations and words of the tribe. Whence its consubstantiality with democracy. The two are possible only in and through an onset of rupture in social heteron-omy and the creation of a new type of being: reflective and delibera-tive subjectivity. The creation of reflection—of thought—goes hand in hand with the creation of a new type of discourse, philosophical discourse, which embodies unlimited interrogation and itself mod-ifies itself throughout its history (DD p. 370).

However, even though Castoriadis links the invention of *la philosophie* to the project of autonomy, he is far more ambivalent about *le philosophi-que* as *world interpreting*, even though, at an earlier juncture, he seemed to indicate otherwise: "Man is an unconsciously philosophical animal, who has posited the questions of philosophy in actual fact long before philosophy existed as explicit reflection; and he is a poetic animal, who has provided answers to these questions in the imaginary" *(IIS* p. 147). Later, though, his view seemed to have changed and the overall tension is similar to that between the social-historical as an anthropological category and the project of autonomy as historically specific. For Castoriadis, world-interpreting philosophies misconstrue themselves and do not em-phasize the world as humanly created (and as such problematizable); that is, they do not envisage the world as belonging to *nomos*. They tend to lapse into heteronomous ways of lending meaning to the world, especially in monotheistic contexts. Thus, *le philosophique* as a world-interpreting mode misses the point for Castoriadis: Philosophy as *nomos* presupposes the form of the world as a self-creation that can be subsequently altered and put into question. The world becomes *always already* problematiza-ble. Here it turns out to be more complicated than Castoriadis was wont to acknowledge: The creation of a world of meaning (as instituting soci-ety) still needs to interpret the already existing instituted world of imagi-nary significations, and a new (or even novel) interpretative configuration by its very existence could conceivably be seen to problematize—even if obliquely—the antecedent world. Thus, this is, I suggest, to find ourselves in the thick of the problematic of interpretative creation and the world horizon, or, the problematic of *cultural articulations of the world*.[18] For present purposes, however, it suffices to note that, for Castoriadis, philos-ophy in its strong form (*la philosophie*) has close links to *nomos* and em-phasizes the conventionality of the sociopolitical world as a specifically human creation and innovation.

For Castoriadis, the failure of inherited philosophy to recognize the social-historical and its world-creating modality is a central problematic. For him, *nomos* as the human order of the self-creation of social-political forms (or worlds) points us directly to that mode of being which can cre-ate and alter itself: *the social-historical*. Indeed, recognition of *nomos* can be said to relativize the totality of the social-historical's occlusion in the inherited tradition: With the recognition of *nomos*, openings onto the so-cial-historical, no matter how oblique or inarticulate, are always already made. At the end of *CQFG*, Castoriadis traces the multiple significations of *nomos* to archaic thought, where he suggests that the idea of a humanly created order was implicit to the Greek imaginary.[19] The main point for Castoriadis is that it is only with the Greeks that this distinction is in-vented/recognized; it is occluded in all other, especially monotheistic, constellations. The invention and recognition of *nomos* in its opposition to *physis* enables Castoriadis to articulate the social-historical mode of being as a mode of being *nomô* and insert it within a historical-philosophi-cal constellation—intermittent to be sure—that challenges the grip of the inherited tradition.

During the composition of the second part of the *IIS*—that is, from the early to the mid 1970s—a focus on *nomos* (in particular, on the social-historical as its most privileged form) and its philosophical elucidation was neither at the foreground of Castoriadis's thought nor was it a sus-tained guiding thread to his larger concerns. As such, it requires herme-neutical reconstruction. What he emphasized during this period was instead a settling of accounts with Marx, and the new departure points these toward the social-historical.[20] In the following four chapters, we ac-company Castoriadis on his long journey through *nomos* and his elucida-tion of its ontological place.

Toward an Ontology of the Social-Historical

If the 1964–65 section of the *IIS* announced Castoriadis's farewell to Marx, the second section (written 1970–74) heralds his shift from phenomenology to ontology.[1] It declares itself with the programmatic chapter on the social-historical as an occluded ontological region that has remained unrecognized by traditional philosophy. Castoriadis's original purpose in the second part of *The Imaginary Institution of Society* was to elucidate the ontological preconditions of "autonomy." Along the way, however, it became an elaboration of *self-creation* as the mode of being of the *social-historical*. His contention, forcefully made, is that Western philosophy has reduced the richness and plurivocity of *being* to an assumption of determinacy, and, as a consequence, is unable to come to grips with the notion of ontological creation without reducing it to "identity" and the "reproduction of the same." Castoriadis proposes to critique the Western philosophical tradition—and its interpretation of being—through an elucidation of the social-historical as the very mode of being that eludes deterministic thought.[2] In so doing, two dimensions of social-historical creation become central: First, its radical temporality as the "time of otherness"; and, second, its fundamental connection to the creative imagination.[3] For Castoriadis, ontological creation highlights the importance of history as the region of change, self-alteration, and the emergence of the radically new. The intimate nexus of time and being appear as history. Heidegger's rethinking of being and time notwithstanding, Castoriadis argues that traditional philosophy lacks the resources to think time *qua* time, especially in its connection to being *qua* being.[4]

We receive the clearest indication of Castoriadis's philosophical focus in the opening sentence of the second section of the *IIS*: "Our aim in this chapter is to elucidate the question of society and that of history, questions that can be understood only when they are taken as one and the same: the question of the social-historical" (p. 167).[5] Let us unpack this sentence. First to the term "elucidation": "Elucidation" is seldom used in philosophical parlance. Jaspers (1932) employed a similar idiom in his *Existenzerhellung* (*Erhellung* has been translated as *elucidation* in the English literature), where he sees the task of philosophy to *elucidate* existence, in the first instance, rather than to acquire *understanding*. Castoriadis's usage of "elucidation" is not unrelated in that he can be broadly interpreted as radicalizing existential currents.

The achievement of phenomenology—in its various incarnations—was its emphasis on meaning as fundamental to the human condition.[6] Castoriadis inherited this legacy, and concern for "meaning" remained crucial to the development of his thought. "Elucidation" itself incorporates notions of "making clear" or illumination, and is, in the broadest sense, to be understood as "making sense of" or the "putting into meaning of" our historical world and our world-as-history. In looking back, "elucidation" as a philosophical task already appears in the 1965 section of the *IIS*, where, in contrast to the totalizing project of theorizing as reason/rationality, Castoriadis's practice of elucidation draws on the intellectual sources of phenomenology and phenomenological Marxism. This is especially strong in the 1964–65 section of the *IIS* but carries into his ontological phase. An interesting example can be found in the very final paragraphs of the 1964–65 section of the *IIS* (p. 164), for example. Castoriadis posits an "articulated unity" between elucidation and action in a radicalization of Marx's eleventh thesis, where Marx no longer presents a stark choice between "interpretation" or "revolutionary action" but argues that the real purpose is to "interpret the world *in order* to change it" (p. 164). Elucidation then for Castoriadis is a kind of philosophical *praxis*, and philosophical action is a part of "social doing" and a vital aspect of the project of autonomy. In this sense, elucidation is inherently a form of *la philosophie*, as opposed to *le philosophique*.[7] Crucially, as the above quotation indicates, elucidation is interrogative: It problematizes—in this case the questions of being and the social-historical—in line with philosophy in the strong sense of *la philosophie*. However, in a rare instance, and as the 1965 passage on Marx's eleventh thesis reveals, Castoriadis also implicitly accepted an *interpretative* element of elucidation.[8] I say "rare," as, in general, Castoriadis was hostile to the hermeneutic tradition of philosophy. For him "interpretation" sought to give a "faithful rendering" (MSPI) of the truth of the text, which he saw as neither creative nor interrogative. At best, hermeneutics can be situated within *le philosophique*; it could not ever aspire to *la philosophie*. And yet, in this one place in the *IIS*, Castoriadis's understanding of *interpretation*—as elucidation—of the world is interrogative, creative and transformative.[9] Thus, for Castoriadis, elucidation of the social-historical signals a shift—or perhaps expansion—of the project of autonomy to incorporate a philosophical interrogation that begins with the elaboration of the social-historical as the mode of being whose very existence makes questioning, and hence autonomy, possible: the mode of being *nomô* , for which, as he observed in a contemporaneous text, "no ontological place exists."[10]

Castoriadis tends to frame his elucidation of the social-historical as if he were standing "outside" it from some kind of Archimedean point (perhaps in part explicable in light of his self-identification as a revolutionary);[11] he does not take into account the currents of interpretative patterns that provide his overarching horizon. He is, of course, clearly situated within them, especially, as the present book suggests, within phenomenological currents upon which he draws and remains dependent, even when he repudiates them. At the same time, from the very outset, Castoriadis pits his elucidation against a generalized tradition of inherited thought, whose contribution in his view, as the opening paragraph of this chapter on the social-historical makes clear, is at best "limiting and negative" (p. 167).

Within traditional philosophical approaches, in what way can society and history be said *to be*? The problem for Castoriadis is that they are unable to identify the "true object of the question" for itself (p. 167). Castoriadis points to the governing idea of determinacy for inherited thought and the univocal meaning of being as "being determined."[12] For Castoriadis, determinacy—or the determinist imaginary—is crucial to Western thought. In turn, it is also its chief obstacle to grasping a mode of being that is essentially creative and temporal. It is only by steadfast occultation of the modes of being of the social-historical and the creative imagination that the inherited logic-ontology could maintain the idea of the determinacy of being. For Castoriadis, the social-historical makes manifest a realm or region of being that escapes the onto-logics of traditional thought. The mistake of these approaches, according to Castoriadis, has been to misrecognize the mode of being of the social-historical, by splitting it into separate questions of the "social" and the "historical."

The former was determined from an "elsewhere," that is, from an extrasocial source, and the latter subordinated to the posited *raison d'être* of the former. Inherited thought is thereby unable to grasp the temporal mode of anthropic being (and all the consequences ensuing from this claim), without exploding their interpretative frameworks. Their methodologies—the logics of their ontologies—assumed that being was the atemporal, stable, enduring essence—*ousia*—of a "thing." However, when the "social" would emerge into focus, problems were encountered, which were, in turn, a consequence of the failure to realize that the social—as belonging to *nomos* rather than *physis* and to *doxa* rather than *aletheia*—posits its own *eide* of, by and for itself. The order of *physis,* although perhaps sufficient to explain natural modes of being, could not do justice to anthropic being. In Castoriadis's view, therefore, the inherited tradition had failed to take into account the distinction between *nomos* and *physis* and to adequately theorize the ensuing implications.

One of the problems with determinacy is that it is conceived as occurring through an external source. As such, inherited thought could not grasp a mode of being that was not only creative but also *self-creative* (such as the social-historical). Yet at the time of the *IIS*, it does seem that Castoriadis juxtaposes the creative mode of the social-historical against the onto-logics of determinacy of inherited thought. Two things are significant to note here. First, although the idea of the social-historical as self-creating is evident at the time of the *IIS*, it took on a sharper focus in Castoriadis's thought during the 1980s, after a deeper immersion in ancient Greek sources; at this later point, the autocreation of the social-historical was explicitly contrasted to external and divine creation by a (monotheistic) God. Indeed, from the early 1980s, in his seminars on ancient Greece (*CQFG*), Castoriadis drew on a Hesiodian image of self-creating anthropos emerging from the abyss. Second, the idea that creation was to be understood as *creation of new determinations*, and hence, as not repudiating the idea of determinism but only its wholesale usage, was a theme that emerged later.[13] This later reframing of the problematic may be in part contextualized within Castoriadis's polyregional ontology of the living being, which he developed as part of his shift to radical *physis* in the 1980s. I shall return to this at length in the second half of the book.

The inherited tradition's preoccupation with the external determinations of society and the "nonbeing" of history also blinded it to "doing" as a mode of being (p. 168) in the broadest sense of "making be" (*faire être*) as the self-deployment of history and its attendant ontological implications. When the idea of action was considered by the philosophical tradition, it was reduced to one of two moments, both of which remained governed by an external source: the ethical moment by good/evil and the "technical" moment by derivatives of good/evil (efficient and inefficient). The mode of being of "doing" as social action emerges from, and radicalizes, the anthropological turn in Marxian thought, which included a critique of Marx's notion of labor (Arnason 1988a, Joas and Honneth 1980). Yet "the being of doing," and some versions of philosophical anthropology, also point to the ambiguity between philosophical anthropology and ontology. In some influential versions, humans and nature (and nature imbued by an order of meaning) are often portrayed in terms of radical discontinuity. It is most famously seen in Husserl's (1941) "Phenomenology and Anthropology," which can be read as a critique of Heidegger's *Being and Time* and *Kant and the Problem of Metaphysics*. A similar ambiguity resonates, too, for Castoriadis and his journey through the *IIS*: Does he elucidate an anthropology? Or a regional ontology of the social-historical?[14] Perhaps there are inevitably elements of both in modern constellations where anthropos is taken as the ontological basic datum, and ontologically divorced from divine and natural orders of meaning. This ambiguity and tension is exemplified in the reception of Castoriadis and the *IIS*, especially in the German context: Honneth and Joas, who jointly authored the above mentioned text on the German tradition of philosophical anthropology (1980), in later works take up the idea of social action in Castoriadis's thought, but from different aspects. Fusing insights from theories of action and Castoriadis, with Mead and the pragmatist tradition, Joas (1992) developed the idea of the "being of doing" into an anthropology of creative action. Honneth (1986) (and Habermas), on the other hand, criticizes Castoriadis for, in his view, resorting to saving the idea of revolutionary action through ontological recourse.[15]

With the opening sentence of the 1975 section of the *IIS*, Castoriadis delineates the boundaries of his philosophical investigations. In contrast to Heidegger's univocal interpretation of being—and, more generally, the inherited tradition's reduction—Castoriadis takes up the Aristotelian (and later, Husserlian) insight of multiple modes and categories of being. Castoriadis opts to begin with a regional ontology of the social-historical in explicit opposition to the individualistic—as well as naturalistic—assumptions that have vitiated the philosophical anthropological approaches (including Heidegger's *Dasein*).[16] In elucidating society and history as the social-historical—or rather in elucidating the being proper to the social-historical (p. 167)—Castoriadis directs and limits his focus to anthropic modes of being. In the *IIS*, natural modes of being do not really figure in their own right, but feature as a counter image to anthropos. As such, in delineating the region of the social-historical as the mode of being that escapes determinacy, Castoriadis leaves the question of nature—or regions of being beyond the anthropic—unaddressed.

At the time of the *IIS*—and this is borne out in the earlier paper MSPI—Castoriadis argued that, despite the internal crises that they might experience, the natural sciences—and the knowledge they produce—have a more or less fundamental grip upon the respective regions of being that they investigate.[17] As such, "nature"—broadly if amorphously understood by Castoriadis as the "first natural stratum"—can be grasped within traditional onto-logics. The methodologies used in other branches of knowledge are not appropriate when imported to elucidate the social-historical: It cannot be grasped via frameworks of determinacy, and, as such, eludes them. There are glimpses here of shifts to come: In MSPI, Castoriadis speaks of being as "irregularly stratified," for example, but the implicit sense is that natural modes of being are more or less governed by ensemblistic-identitarian logic, or, minimally, that they are characterized by a fundamentally different modality to the social-historical. There are preliminary indications in Castoriadis's framing of the living being in the *IIS* that open onto the idea of being as *à-être*, but these remain in the background.[18] However, the other side of *physis*—creative *physis* as a transregional fundament of being as *à-être*—has already existed as a subterranean theme in his thought. The implication that will be teased out further in the present study is that, unlike Heidegger in rethinking the *Seinsfrage*, the meaning of Being is not singular, but plural, more in the vein of Aristotle (even in the more or less "determined" regions of nature). Castoriadis rejects Heidegger's ontological difference: As he stated already in the earlier SU in regard to Merleau-Ponty, Being can only be manifested as beings. But with the advent of the transregional ontology of radical *physis* in the 1980s, Castoriadis's rejection of Heidegger's ontological difference is reformulated, as we shall see.

In raising the question of the being of the social-historical, Castoriadis reactivates the *Seinsfrage*. His philosophical debt to the early Heidegger is clearly identifiable, though unacknowledged.[19] In *Being and Time*, Heidegger renewed the question of being, and saw the vital connection between the meaning of being and temporality. The result was the (incomplete) fundamental ontology of *Dasein*. Like Heidegger, Castoriadis reopens the question of being primarily as a reconsideration of human modes of being, and their elemental link to time and being, as in some way privileged.[20] In the first instance, Castoriadis sought to ground human autonomy ontologically, which mutated into an ontology of the social-historical and a reopening of the question of being. In this sense, he is closer to Heidegger than he would care to acknowledge: Not only does he charge the entire philosophical tradition—evident at least since Plato—with having made a fundamental error, but he is also convinced that clarification of human modes of being can impart something important and hitherto perplexing about being.[21] A rethinking of the concept of time is crucial to this clarification. Again reminiscent of Heidegger, Castoriadis claims a profound covering over of fundamental aspects of being. His path was different, however. In his view, it was neither the forgetting of Being, nor a negative philosophy that was the mistake of the ontological tradition, but its reduction to a univocal determinacy (Descombes 1991a).[22] In this context, however, it is also relevant to note immediate and important preliminary differences, chief among them being Castoriadis's complete rejection of a transcendent realm as well as of a radical ontological distinction between *Sein* and *Seiende*. For Castoriadis, a transcendent explanation of the world, however else it might be understood, would first be interpreted as the ontological creation of a particular social-historical constellation within a tradition that denies the creativity of the social-historical.[23] Second, his resolute pursuit of a thisworldly path echoes his Ionic sources—as opposed to the Eleatic or Southern Italian current, which emphasized transmigration—and their pessimism about the after world: In opposition to Kant, there is nothing to hope for.

Castoriadis's project, although politically to the other extreme of Heidegger's, nonetheless remains philosophically entwined in developing, albeit implicitly, a phenomenologically and hermeneutically sensitive ontology of anthropic regions of being. Central to both is a philosophical elucidation of time and the imagination; as such, as mentioned earlier, Castoriadis builds on the general Heideggerian themes developed not only in *Being and Time* but also in the *Kantbuch*. Castoriadis rejects the preoccupation of inherited thought with essence/*ousia*, as did Heidegger, but Castoriadis takes it in a different direction. Rather than identifying *ousia* with presence—something for which Castoriadis later critiques Heidegger, on the basis that Heidegger did not fully understood the *nun* of Aristotle in relation to the measuring of time (TC)—Castoriadis identifies a preoccupation with essence as an obsession with equating being with determinacy in two elemental ways. The first way is exemplified by Kant, whose maxim of Being as Determinacy is understood to be a basic assumption of the philosophical tradition. Plato epitomizes the second way, where the self-creation of the social world is subsumed under an ultimately theological account of the production of difference.[24] In asserting the temporal mode of being, the fundamental link of time and creation, and their centrality to an elucidation of social-historical being, Castoriadis, on the other hand, envisages the social-historical as a self-determining, self-creative mode of being, that stands in stark contrast to a conventional conception of extrasocial determination. Castoriadis's elucidation then of the social-historical is neither existential nor phenomenological in a traditional sense, although he could be read in some respects as radicalizing Heidegger's privileging of *Dasein*'s authentic existence into the reactivation of the project of autonomy and its ongoing "doing" as "making-be." Instead, he sets out to prescribe ontological weight to the respective modes of being of the creative imagination and the social-historical by drawing on interwoven Aristotelian and Husserlian approaches to the idea of polyregional being. As Castoriadis writes in MSPI: "Every phenomenon is an interphenomenon. The borderline between them become hazy and the idea of region reasserts the enigma of the central place it must be accorded in the categorical schema of knowledge" (MSPI 167). As we are beginning to clarify, he approaches the same problematic from a different perspective in the *IIS*:

> For we see that [the social-historical] does not fall under traditional categories—except in a nominal and empty manner—but instead it makes us recognize the narrow limits of their validity, and permits us to glimpse a new and different logic and, above all, radically to alter the meaning of being. (p. 169)[25]

The Problematic of "Society" and "History"

Traditional thought has separated the question of the social-historical into two separate object-domains, "society" and "history" (p. 170). In explaining how inherited philosophy went astray, Castoriadis follows suit and considers each object-domain separately. He asks: How are we to explain temporal alteration in the social realm? His response is that "history" is "temporal alteration" par excellence; the social occurs—can only occur—as historical, that is, as temporal alteration and deployment. Thus Castoriadis's identification of the "social-historical" as a single region unites two terms that have been generally considered distinct in their relation to being: "society" and "history." These two questions have been considered from a variety of angles, but for Castoriadis the problem of society must also be approached *philosophically*. For him, the inescapable conclusion, even after a cursory examination of history, is that each society is deployed—deploys itself—as temporal alteration. That is, each society *has* a—and *is* its—history. There is no "once and for all determination" of "the social" as it is lived across space and time. Rather, what strikes Castoriadis is the myriad of differences instituted by each society and how these differences are irreducible to the identical-as-the-same, that is, to a singular definition or meaning of "society." In this way, Castoriadis emphasizes the discontinuity rather than continuity of social-historical formations. How are these differences to be explained under the rubric of the same? Or within the framework of identitarian logic? Castoriadis believes it futile. This notwithstanding, he proceeds to elaborate what he sees as the most important traditional responses to these questions. Overall, however, he sees the question of society and history as the question of the origin of *otherness*, whereas traditional thought sees the question of society and history as answerable in terms of *identity*.

At first glance, the terms "society" and "history" seem to refer to opposite kinds of object-domains altogether: Society is essentially a question of its particular identity, whereas history is the domain of change. Three things quickly become evident. First, Castoriadis posits history as the mode of temporal alteration of society—that is, as an inherent aspect of society—and asks how and why it occurs. Second, he delves into the meaning of such alteration (*qua* alteration). Finally, he raises the possibility of historical novelty and its meaning. Castoriadis proceeds to unify these apparently disparate issues and object-domains by identifying the crux of the matter: In traditional thought, the great number of different societies and their (subordinated) histories are reduced to an equation of identity and unity. He proposes to take the empirical fact of their concrete differences and their untold plurality as a philosophical question of consequence: "Why does the identical appear as different?" (p. 170). Castoriadis's task is to provide an analysis that goes beyond an "impoverished philosophy of history," while elevating the question of history to a question of *society* as a *philosophical* question.[26] Nonetheless, differences in his approach to these respective aspects are evident: For Castoriadis the question of "society" can be framed around a single point—that of *ecceity*; "history" requires a plurality of questions to adequately address its thematic.

Castoriadis identifies "the physicalist" and "the logicalist" as an identifiable typology within Western thought that responds to the question of the social (p. 170). At this point, Castoriadis reveals a greater engagement with the social-theoretical rather than the philosophical field, which is not unusual within French philosophical currents. His emphasis on anthropological, especially the functionalist and structuralist approaches of that time, rather than the more strictly sociological accounts of society, is particularly noticeable and Castoriadis would seem to be to responding to two interpretative contexts in this respect. First, as Merleau-Ponty in

"From Durkheim to Mauss to Lévi-Strauss" (1964 [1960]) has argued, the French current took an anthropological turn in thinking through the social world. Second, and overlapping with the first, the 1960s and 1970s were dominated by structuralist debates in the French context. Although Castoriadis had some early sympathy for Saussure (see MSPI and *IIS*), his argument is antistructuralist, as Joas and Knöbl (2009) have noted. The problem of history would seem to be the most pressing for Castoriadis to elucidate, yet both physicalist and logicist approaches demonstrate a reductionist view of history. In developing his typology and responding to the questions of "society" and "history," Castoriadis, too, is guilty of neglecting an appropriate discussion of theories of history (apart from reference to Marx and Hegel).[27] This is even more curious when recollecting the discussions of the idea of history in the French twentieth-century context in general, but especially in the narrower context of *Socialisme ou barbarie* and French phenomenology, in which currents he was situated.[28] There is also a dearth of concrete histories considered in developing his account. Although in the 1980s, mainly during his seminar courses at the EHESS, he did develop a concrete historical approach to ancient Greece, it is, as Vidal-Naquet (2004) has noted, an idiosyncratic interpretation.[29] It is moreover explicitly a political account: As Castoriadis tells us, to elucidate an incipient ontology of the social-historical and to situate it in the Greek tradition is ultimately to advance the project of autonomy through transformation of our contemporary world.

The problem with physicalism for Castoriadis is that it reduces society and history to nature; that is, it subsumes society to the laws of nature as determined and atemporal. His critique operates on two levels: First, it is aimed at functionalism, in particular anthropological functionalism—such as practiced by Malinowski (1944)—where society is reduced to biological needs. He does not engage with later developments within functionalism, for example, Parson's (although Castoriadis's critique would also apply at the level of Parson's organismic model of society). Castoriadis's second target within the physicalist typology is Hegelian-Marxism—as a synthesis of logicist and functionalist approaches—and especially Marx of the *German Ideology*, where "species being" is interpreted as a variant of the Aristotelian organism and of the idea of *physis* "that reproduces itself without ever changing" (p. 170). These may be reduced to unchanging "biological" needs that are then mobilized and utilized to explain social organization and social needs. Such explanatory frameworks cannot account for the diversity of nonfunctional and transfunctional components, activities, and institutions of any given society, nor do they address the question of the many differences between societies. Instead, they posit a transhistorical social "identity." They disregard the fact that neither "needs" nor their "objects" are reducible to biology; they are instead socially instituted, that is, social-historically instituted, interpreted and created. Functionalist approaches reduce the social to natural, that is, functionalist imperatives, and ignore two things: First, the question of meaning and interpretative frameworks that give rise to the myriad interpretations of "the world," "needs," or "the social"; second, that "the surplus of meaning" exceeds functional imperatives. In this way, Castoriadis contends that, while there are some quasi-functional elements to society, they coexist alongside constellations of meaning.

Logicism forms the second dimension of Castoriadis's typology (p. 171), with French structuralism, especially Lévi-Strauss, constituting the main focus of his critique. On Castoriadis's account, structuralism reduces the social to a questionable set of finite and discrete elements that can only be combined in a (finite) variety of ways, through the positing of binary oppositions in a series of logical operations. As in his critique of cybernetics (MSPI), Castoriadis charges structuralism with the failure to perceive the socially instituted nature of the "sets" in questions: A "natural set" does not exist. In the same vein, Castoriadis highlights the paucity with which structuralism accounts for the existence of meaning.[30] What the structuralists fail to see is that meaning, like language, is a social convention, not a natural datum: It pertains to *nomos* (p. 172). At this juncture, Castoriadis does no more than briefly allude to Hegelian-Marxism as epitomizing the opposite end of the logicist spectrum, having critiqued it extensively in the first part of the *IIS* (1964–65). It is worth noting that there is an implicit, third image of society in this *IIS* chapter: the individualistic. This approach decomposes the social-historical into the individual. When the attempt is made to regenerate the social-historical from the individual, it transforms itself into either a physicalist approach—for Castoriadis, this would apply to the "needs" of Marx, which could include new versions of the old Marxist project (for example, G.A. Cohen, 1978)—or into the logicism of rational choice theory where the ability of individuals to apply rational rules of conduct is emphasized and thus ultimately dissolved into elements of the other two approaches.

For Castoriadis, the problem with the physicalist and logicist approaches to society is that they proceed from determinations and logics that reduce "society" to what is known from other modes of being and regions of knowledge, specifically those from the "natural sciences." On these accounts, history is added almost as an afterthought. Castoriadis asserts that, when considering history, physicalism is transformed into causalism, which erases the question of history entirely. At this point,

Castoriadis provides us with an implicit definition of creation in the guise of a definition of history: "For the question of history is the question of the emergence of radical otherness or of the absolutely new" (p. 172). He contrasts this to causalism, as the repetition of the same, whereas the production of difference is the negation of otherness, a formulation again used later in his explicit delineation of creation from production, otherness from difference. Logicism becomes finalism.[31] Finalist approaches rely on identitary operations of *potentiality,* posited as a "primordial principle" (p. 173).[32] Hegel's dialectic articulated its most classical form, but it also draws on the potentiality/actuality distinction formulated by Aristotle. In these schemas, time dissipates into atemporality, or what Castoriadis later called "the imperfect tense of ontological infinity," (PA) where history is erased from the question and becomes a receptacle of coexistence. In critique of this position, Castoriadis introduces his definition of time (which will later become explicit as creation). Time is constitutive of history: "True time, [is] the time of radical otherness, an otherness that can neither be deduced nor produced" (p. 173).

Unlike a *univocal* interpretation of being, a *pluralistic* elucidation of being assumes different logic-ontologies for different regions, and for the identity of their objects. The discovery of new regions requires critical reflection on the logic-ontologies created for already known regions of what is and their respective interpretations of modes and meanings of being. This is especially the case for the modes of being of the social imaginary and the social-historical. Interwoven with the mode of being of the social-historical is the mode of being of the creative imagination. Castoriadis established an affinity between the social-historical and the imagination, although it is spelled out more in the 1965 part of the *IIS.* However, as Castoriadis wrote later in the *IIS* preface (noted earlier), a properly philosophical elucidation of the imagination is absent. Nonetheless, the task of introducing it was there from the beginning, together with the elucidation of the social-historical and critique of traditional approaches. The actual phrase Castoriadis uses here is: "In particular, the regions considered here—the radical imaginary and the social-historical—imply a profound questioning of the received significations of being as determinacy and of logic as determination" (p. 174). Thus, in addition to a typology of traditional responses, it might also be considered that Castoriadis might, from a different perspective, be considered to be problematizing the *determinist imaginary.*

In what appears to relativize his earlier argument, Castoriadis now seems to assert that the inherited logic-ontology does indeed have a deep hold on social life (p. 175). Its presence is an inescapable necessity of the elementary proto-institutions of *legein* and *teukhein*, although the existence of the social-historical lays to rest the claim of the full determinacy of being.[33] The validity to which the inherited logic can aspire is modest, yet its reach, even into the social-historical and its institution, is profound (p. 175). Thus in the very region of being that the logics of determination cannot fathom—the social-historical—there is nonetheless a continuity between "the natural world" and the "social world" in terms of the hold this logic has on both. However, the grasp of identity logic on the social is of a different kind in that it cannot "explain" the social-historical in the way that it does natural regions. Thus, despite Castoriadis's assertion that the starting place for thinking about society and history was in their radical singularity, there appears to be some quasi-philosophical anthropological features to the social-historical after all.[34] One such aspect is the necessary social-historical institution of its form of identity logic that itself emerges in some kind of continuity from the first natural stratum and its exigencies; yet, Castoriadis does not address this issue fully.

The point of Castoriadis's objections to traditional interpretations of being as determinacy and logic as determination, particularly as they pertain to the social-historical and the social imaginary, is that, in the fleeting documented moments when these modes of being were "discovered," they were subsequently subsumed to the demands of the given framework that resulted in their ongoing reocculation. This can be illustrated by the case of the creative imagination.

Glimpses of the creative imagination can be occasionally found in the history of philosophy, but each thinker who has tried to grapple with it has, in turn, recoiled from its ontological implications. Castoriadis proceeds to map what he sees as the key moments in the philosophical history of the imagination. First, Aristotle's positing of *phantasia* in *De Anima III (3)* as reproductive, and as situated between sensation and intellect (p. 174), was foundational for the course of the imagination in philosophy. Yet the place in which Aristotle glimpses its radical character remains on the whole undiscussed.[35] Kant encounters the imagination thrice (in the two editions of the first *Critique* and then again in the third *Critique*), while Freud perpetually encounters the imagination without explicitly saying so. As Castoriadis tells us: Freud "talks throughout his work about what is in fact imagination, and accomplishes the feat of never mentioning the term" (1994, p. 318). Ten years earlier, in the 1964–65 section of the *IIS*, a footnote points to the importance of Kant, and especially Fichte, for thematizing the imagination.[36] Curiously absent from the list is Heidegger and his discovery of the temporalization of the imagination and its relation to being in the *Kantbuch*,[37] as well as more generally the submerged tradition of the imagination in phenomenology and hermeneutics, with the most obvious cases in the French tradition being Sartre (1936), Merleau-Ponty (1968, 1974b), Bachelard (1942), and Ricoeur (1976, 1978).[38]

In occulting the being of the radical imagination and the social-historical, the inherited logic-ontology could maintain the determinacy of being; the core of this logic is identitary-ensemblistic and its rule over the proto-institutions of *legein* and *teukhein*. Castoriadis begins therewith to clarify the fundamentals of identitary logic. Although its pretensions are always much grander and totalitarian, inherited onto-logics do not have validity over anything, other than the first natural stratum (as ensidizable nature). In the previously discussed examples of physicalism and logicism (as causalism and finalism), Castoriadis wants to demonstrate the inadequacy of borrowing methodologies and frameworks that might be valid for one domain and to assume a general validity for all regions of being. He explains that identitary logic, as the logic of determination—though it can be particularized in various ways (logicism, causalism)—can only posit itself as a relation between elements of a set (here Castoriadis introduces elements of a philosophy of mathematics to the discussion) and is present "from the start of the institution of *legein* and *teukhein*" (p. 176). Mathematics is a social-historical creation and yet Castoriadis seems to grapple with an ambiguity here by positing it as "naturally" fundamental to *legein* and *teukhein*. As I shall suggest throughout the course of the book, the strange case of mathematics remains a constant source of fascination and inspiration for Castoriadis, but its onto-epistemological status remains ultimately unresolved.[39]

The inherited logic of determination—and its linked ontology—upholds a conception of being as determined/determinacy: Something can only be grasped as being if it can be understood as fully determined (p. 176). Let us note in passing that to speak of being, Castoriadis has needed to rapidly introduce an epistemological element to his ontological elucidation that points to the ultimate impossibility of separating ontology from epistemology.[40] Thus, in concluding this first section of the social-historical chapter, which Castoriadis entitled "Possible Types of Traditional Responses," he finds himself confronted with Kantian concerns. In writing on being, Castoriadis quickly acknowledges the need to question (in order to critique) the logical foundations of ontology: What are the ways in which being can be *thought* at all? On a hermeneutical note, it is significant that, in speaking of the "typology" of the approaches to "society" and "history," Castoriadis claims they are the "only" answers available within this framework (p. 176). Yet, this is internally inconsistent with his own ontological argument in that no onto-logic or imaginary—not even the determinist imaginary—can circumscribe or predict the number of creative responses to a given context. In so doing, Castoriadis himself appeals to an *inherited historical tradition*—that is, to a specific interpretative pattern—that could have been interpreted and/or created otherwise.

What, then, is society? Castoriadis proceeds to examine the common ground of different approaches to this question. He ultimately concludes that "society" provides us with a way of coexistence beyond the reach of traditional identitary thought, since the inherited tradition cannot accommodate the idea of a mode of being as temporal creation. Again, he relates them to physicalism/causalism or logicism/finalism, with the added inclusion of individualist schema.[41] If conceived as a system, society would be closed on itself. In that case, society would be ultimately reducible to distinct elements, which would stand in clear relation to each other and could be univocally defined. No matter whether the system is conceived as causal or logical, ensemblist-identitarian logic is always used. Another common approach is to conceive of the ultimate element of society as the individual. The best-known example is Locke's social contract, but the individual is also the final element in Aristotle, Marx, and Freud: The truly *social* dimension of society is not considered.[42] Neither is the problem resolved with Durkheim's collective consciousness (p. 179) or Jung's collective unconscious. Nothing in society is given once and for all; social relations, spheres and forms give rise to new ones, and thus our elucidation of it can only be fragmented and partial.[43]

In recognizing the social-historical, the very question of being *qua* being is posed. For Castoriadis, the discovery of the social-historical destroys Heidegger's ontological difference: Being cannot be thought of in separation from beings, for "each region of beings unveils another sense of being" (p. 183). Being is neither a determinable ensemble nor a set of well-defined elements. At this juncture Castoriadis introduces the idea of being as magma: "a mode of organization belonging to a non-ensemblist diversity" (p. 182). He does not elaborate at length, referring us in a footnote to the final chapter of the *IIS* for further discussion. However, I note the shift from the first part of the *IIS*—pre-magma—where he referred to the social world as a "system of significations" (p. 146). He does not explain further whence he was inspired to use the idea of magma. Its affinities are mainly—but not exclusively—geological, as molten rock material under the earth's crust. It is a metaphor rather than a category; indeed, as

I shall show, the importance—even necessity—of metaphor for speaking of being as magma is well founded.

If society has been conceived as a mode of coexistence, history has been understood as temporal succession. Yet, because inherited thought has necessarily approached this via ensemblistic-identitarian thinking, the nature of radical historical temporality has eluded it. Viewed through the lens of identitarian succession, which is ultimately but an aspect of coexistence, varieties of difference are reduced to exemplars of the same. Time becomes nothing other than a relation of order subsumed to the imperatives of an external other. Castoriadis now makes explicit that to which he had earlier gestured: History's temporality resides in the emergence of *radical otherness*. History brings the new into being (p. 185). Time, as a theme in need of urgent discussion, is hence introduced via the idea of history as "succession" in a nontraditional interpretation of "radical alteration," that is, creation.

Time, Creation and Subterranean *Physis*

Castoriadis pursues a twofold aim in his discussion of time. First, he wants to show that traditional philosophy has instituted a tradition of time as identitary: Time is as an "image of non-time" (p. 188). Second, he argues that time *qua* time needs to be interpreted as the emergence of ontological novelty as *creation of otherness*. For Castoriadis, this is most apparent in the region of the social-historical. In not recognizing the true modality of time, the inherited tradition generally confused the relation between time and space: Time was treated as a dimension of space. The presupposition and consequence of this situation for Castoriadis is an onto-logics of determinacy that is reinforced by the actual *de-temporalization* of time. This particular way of conceiving being underlies the Western tradition: A new interpretation of being would be needed for time and being to be elaborated more appropriately. Although not made explicit, Castoriadis seeks to recover and radicalize a submerged and fragmented philosophical current that interprets "being as temporal." As we shall see, he draws on an archaic Greek image of being as neither fully chaotic nor fully ordered, but as the interplay of both. There is, also, a duality in the argument that Castoriadis takes up in the present context. On one hand, Castoriadis pursues a general ontology of time, while, on the other, he undertakes a more limited discussion of social-historical time. The delineation between the two aspects is not always distinct: In the former case, subterranean glimpses of radical *physis* begin to emerge.

Castoriadis opens his discussion on the philosophical institution of time by drawing on the concept of *the world*: "Every society exists by instituting the world as its world, or its world as the world, and by instituting itself as part of the world" (p. 186). Here, as elsewhere, the problematic of the world remains relatively underdeveloped in his thought, yet, like radical *physis*, its submerged presence continues to intrude on his more explicit discourse. At this point, we confine ourselves to noting that in light of the two lines of argument mentioned above, and in relation to his introduction of the world concept, Castoriadis's discussion of time sits somewhat uneasily between cosmogony and cosmology. Castoriadis asserts that time is a necessary institution of the social-historical—it must always be instituted as part of its world—but he does not elaborate further as to why this is the case. Time is enigmatic: It seems obvious at the level of everyday life, yet, in echo of Augustine, its mystery confounds all who would grapple with it. Castoriadis is nevertheless certain that time is distinct from space and is neither reducible to nor separable from the content of a spatial receptacle, as inherited thought would have it. Already we see in his allusion to Plato's *chora* that he is setting up his discussion of time in preparation for the problematic of the *Timaeus* and the twofold aspect of time that primarily concerns him: First, that time is not reducible to a dimension of space; second, as a qualitative modality, time is not separable from its content. From another angle, he reframes the Kantian question of the multiplicity of the manifold: Being exists in a spatial and temporal dimension yet is separable from these very same dimensions in which it exists (p. 187).

The philosophical tradition has unceasingly grappled with time's elusive character. Castoriadis turns to Plato's *Timaeus* to confront the intractable questions of time in inherited thought.[44] Castoriadis uses the *Timaeus* to make his case that frameworks of determinacy go hand in hand with the nontemporal, which for Castoriadis is conceived as a spatial dimension. He establishes that the *Timaeus*—here symbolic of the Western tradition as a whole—treats time as identitary. Castoriadis's strategy in "The Philosophical Institution of Time" (the fourth section of the *IIS* chapter on the social-historical) is one of *Destruktion* via immanent critique. His goal is to indicate "the *impossibility* for inherited thought truly to think of time, a time essentially different from space" through textual reconstruction of key passages in the *Timaeus* (p. 187). Although it is unsurprising that Castoriadis takes Plato as the "Founding Father" of identitary time, it is somewhat more surprising that his discussion of "The Philosophical Institution of Time" is entirely represented by the *Timaeus*. Another option could have been to engage more fully with Aristotle either to marshal resources for his critique of Plato, or, indeed, to glean insights for a more positive philosophical program, as he was later to do in the final chapter of the *IIS*. Unusually for Castoriadis, Aristotle is the more shadowy figure in the discussion at hand. Normally his preferred classical interlocutor, Aristotle's presence in this discussion confines itself, in the main, to a few footnotes.

Although Castoriadis designates the *Timaeus* as the first philosophical text in which the questions of time are raised, discussions of time hearken back to Zeno's aporia and the idea of creation evident in Heraclitus. The pre-Socratics, however, did not pursue a program of "being as determinacy," and perhaps for this reason, they are absent.[45] However, the *Timaeus* is emblematic for Castoriadis in ways that other canonical texts of philosophy are not. It focuses not just on time, but also draws together the idea of time as a spatial relation and the separability of the content of time/space from its receptacle. It also highlights the inability of inherited thought to think creation with the specificity that Castoriadis gives it. Plato's Demiurge epitomizes not only the idea of production as a pseudo-creation, but, moreover, a pseudo-*theological* creation, that is, creation from an extrasocial (extracosmic), personalized-divine source. At the time of writing the chapter on the social-historical in 1970–71, Castoriadis had recently been immersed in a reading of the *Timaeus*: A footnote in the *IIS* draws our attention to a finished manuscript of the *Timaeus* which he "hope[d] to publish soon" and in which he would discuss matters of time and creation in greater detail. He signals that the discussion of time and the *Timaeus* in the *IIS* is but a summary of that longer manuscript.[46]

Castoriadis's analysis of the *Timaeus* in the *IIS* falls into two parts: First, the consideration of the transcendent and sensible realms and, second, their respective modes of being as the *aei on* and *aei gignomenon*. In the transcendent domain, the Demiurge is presented with neither time nor space but with the *aei on* as *always being*. The problem for Castoriadis is that *aei on* assumes a radical atemporality which rules out the possibility of qualitative *movement* and *change* and hence of time as well. The *always being* of the transcendent forms can only be understood as determinacy, whose characteristic features are atemporality and identity. Having rather summarily dealt with the question of time by establishing its nonexistence, Castoriadis moves to consider the sensible realm. Does time fare any better there? The sensible realm is characterized by *aei gignomenon* as *always becoming*, but given that there is not yet any "time," there cannot be any "becoming" that does not "become" in or with time. However, *genesis* in the sensible realm—"with becoming in the world"—is indeed subject to partial determinations, where "the becoming *aei*,[47] and of being *aei*—of the determined, *peras*—must rely on the *eidos* of genesis as 'absolute and pure becoming-ness'" (p. 188). Again, however, as there is not yet time in which the form could "become," it must constantly have contradictory determinations, which Castoriadis interprets as having no determination whatsoever. In the sensible world, though, actual *genesis* could account for some sense of time as it contains within itself a sense of movement and mobility, should *genesis* be related to the time of the world. To "become" in the world is to be subject to partial determinations, "and it is among these partial determinations that the time of the world is to be counted" (p. 188). This proves to be less than straightforward as *genesis* again points to a sense of time as cyclical repetition that indicates an essential returning or repetition of *the same* rather than the *creation of otherness*. These cycles are not so much *in time*, rather time features as a "local property."

In inherited thought, then, as inaugurated with Plato, an image of time is institutionalized as that which allows or "realizes" the return or repetition of the same. There may be diverging conceptions of time—either as causal determination or cyclical repetition of becoming—but Castoriadis argues that, at bottom, they are governed by a single understanding of time. The philosophical tradition does not deny the existence or importance of time, but, in Castoriadis's eyes, it can neither recognize nor accommodate the existence of an overarching or genuine time as creation. Inherited thought has thus instaurated an essential indistinction between temporal and spatial dimensions: "Time *is* space to the extent that nothing allows us to distinguish the mode of co-belonging of its parts or moments from the mode of co-belonging of the parts or points of space" (p. 189). Subsequently, and in echo of Plato's new beginning in the *Timaeus*, Castoriadis asks abruptly, "For what is space?" Indeed, we find that Castoriadis has reached that part of the *Timaeus* where Plato stops in his tracks and begins anew.[48] Castoriadis notes, but does not elaborate further, that this occurs "after the world has been made" (p 189). After considering time in the transcendent and sensible realms, Plato, somewhat surprisingly introduced a third and enigmatic kind—the *chora* as a spatial receptacle.[49] Through the voice of Timaeus, Plato says: "But if we call it an invisible *eidos*, formless, all-receiving, and, in a most perplexing way, partaking of the intelligible and most difficult to catch, we will not be speaking falsely" (51a–b). It is called a "third kind" of being, but in the sense of a "kind of kind beyond kind" (Sallis 1999, p. 113). The *chôra*, which manifests a residue of pre-Socratic *physis*, and Hesiodian *chaos*, shares features of Kant's transcendental imagination, in that it ultimately neither participates wholly in the intelligible nor the sensible. It is "a sort of invisible and formless *eidos* . . . Hence a formless form and invisible aspect . . . sensible insensible, unthinkable thought," (p. 189) that is separable yet inseparable from what is found "there." In his essay on *Khôra*, Derrida writes: "They always consist in giving form to [*khôra*], by determining it, which, however, can offer itself or promise itself only by escaping from all determination" (1993, p. 26). Sallis and Derrida have pointed to the "intrinsic untranslatability" of the *chora*, even questioning whether it has a "meaning" in any conventional sense, as its introduction was also simultaneously an interruption of meaning (Sallis 1993, p. 115). Surprisingly, however, Castoriadis does not discuss the difficulties in translating the term "*chora*." He refers neither to its chaotic aspects, nor to the ambiguities between "space" and "place," nor to the ambiguities of meaning as "receptacle" and "reception," nor to the sense of its errancy as both "wandering" and "leading to error" (p. 93), nor to its sense as a matrix (p. 109), nor to its feminine aspect as that which "supports, aids, succors" as the "nurse of all generation," which Kristeva was pursuing (1984). Perhaps most surprisingly of all, Castoriadis does not pursue the implications of encountering the *chora* "as if in a dream"—as he did conversely for his evocation of the magma—for his elucidation of being. He accepts the *chora* simply as a "spatial receptacle," in which exists everything that is-becomes. Had he taken more account of the generative aspect, the receptacle would not just have been "in which" all generative content occurs but also *from which*. At this point of his trajectory, however, Castoriadis was concerned to demonstrate the constancy of time as identitary in inherited thought; his later awareness of the creative aspects of the chaotic aspects of being did not yet figure. This, coupled with his resistance to the idea of the "creation of forms" taking place within a context of weak determinacy, that is, that there could be an interpretative element to creation, might explain why he overlooked aspects of the *chora* that potentially opened onto creative aspects of the world. Instead he contented himself with equating the *chora* with the identitary dimension of being.[50] Before proceeding further, let us recall that for Castoriadis the question of time as the "making different" is characterized in inherited thought through two aspects: First, via its subordination to the spatial dimension, and, second, by the relation between receptacle and content as separable.

Castoriadis opens a (triple) parenthesis (p. 189). He observes that the separability-inseparability of the receptacle reemerges in contemporary physics with the dimension of space-time which "'depends[s]' on the quantity of the energy-matter that it 'contains.'" (I will return to this in Chapter 8.) Castoriadis moves briefly to consider Kant's interpretation of space (and time) in the first *Critique* as a pure form of intuition. Kant's conception is more radical than Plato's. Not only does Kant separate space from its *particular* content, he separates it from *all* content whatsoever. In Kant, space and time figure as the "pure possibility of the self-difference of identity, or the pure production of difference out of nothing" (p. 189). Somewhat in passing, Castoriadis notes that Kant, following Aristotle, and followed by Hegel, represents time/non-time as a line upon which it can be measured and abstracted. In this vein, a footnote a few pages later (p. 196) refers us to Aristotle and "motion."[51] As I explore at a later point, in rediscovering the other, eminently creative side to *physis*, Castoriadis simultaneously rediscovers the radical potential of Aristotelian understandings of qualitative movement within *physis* as deteleologized *alloiosis* change, alteration, and also creation of form.[52] Although Aristotle was Plato's pupil, he was more influenced by the Ionian rather than the Eleatic tradition, as well as drawing on pre-Socratic motifs. Aristotle's reintroduction of *physis* into philosophy was a critique of Plato, yet Castoriadis did not turn to him directly as a way of interrogating Plato. Perhaps part of the problem with Aristotle could be that, at the time of the *IIS*, Castoriadis's focus on *nomos* as the antithesis of *physis* meant that, because he rejected it as a "natural norm" for anthropos, the order of *physis* was relevant for natural regions of being only.[53]

Castoriadis was yet to fully see the possibilities of the creative side to *physis*, in general, but also, and more specifically, in regard to human regions of being. In relation to the discussion of time in the *IIS*, Castoriadis does not interrogate Augustine, Aristotle, Bergson, or Heidegger (to list but the most obvious); Kant is briefly discussed, but only in the succeeding section on "Time and Creation." In the early 1970s, however, Castoriadis had not explored this creative side to *physis*. The footnote in question (mentioned above) draws out the connection between Aristotle's notion of time and movement in book IV of *Physics*, as "the number of motion in respect of 'before' and 'after' and motion as 'the movable *qua* movable'" (p. 396). The movable "or that which changes," is not understood in terms of creation, rather in terms of teleologically understood determinacy, as it moves toward a predestined end or finality. In pointing to Aristotle and Hegel and their respective conceptions of time, Castoriadis is alluding to an alternative philosophical current of thinking, the concept of time that simultaneously problematizes the "vulgar time" of Heidegger's *Being and Time*. Castoriadis does not elaborate further here on that tradition or on Heidegger's conception of time, although he will return to them as part of his cosmological reflections in the 1980s.[54] Interesting at this juncture, however, is the existence of another footnote (p. 189)—

actually a footnote on a footnote on a footnote—which refers us to the "rigorous" early text by Derrida, "Ousia et Grammē," in which Derrida critiques Heidegger's interpretation of time in *Being and Time* as the idea of presence.[55] To the best of my knowledge, it is the only reference Castoriadis makes to Derrida. In this context, however, it is just as interesting to note that despite this reference to Derrida's essay on Heidegger's interpretation on time, Castoriadis excludes Heidegger's understanding of time in his discussion, and, indeed, only refers in passing to broader phenomenological articulations of time.[56]

The point of Castoriadis's brief excursus on Plato's *chora* and beyond is to demonstrate the inadequacy of received interpretations of time as space and a receptacle, for:

> to the extent which what emerges is not in what exists, not even "logically" or as an already constituted "potentiality" to the extent that it is not the actualisation of predetermined possibility (the distinction between power and act is only the most subtle and most profound manner of suppressing time), hence, to the extent that time is not simply and not only in-determination but the springing forth of determinations or, better yet, of other *eide*-images-figures-forms. *Time is the self-alteration of what is, which is only to the extent that it is à-être.* For this reason, any separation between time and what is reveals itself to be reflexive, analytical, secondary—identitary. And it is as this time, the time of otherness and alteration (*alteration-alterité*) that we have to think of history. (p. 190, emphasis added)

This quotation is decisive for the present reconstruction of Castoriadis's philosophical trajectory and his shift to a general ontology of creative *physis*. Here he points to an important difference between time and space: Unlike space, time cannot be thought as separable from its concrete content. It is not separable from the emergence of new *eide* with and through and as time, not just social-historical time, but the time of being more generally. The dual argument—pursued along general and regional lines—is apparent.[57] The above passage also introduces his neologism *à-être*—*an incessant always becoming-being, but never so closed unto itself that it could not create new forms*—for the first time. *À-être* is a term first coined in the "General Introduction" of *Socialisme ou Barbarie* 10/11 series in 1974; Castoriadis wrote the GI in 1973.[58] Although somewhat speculative, it would seem to me that its introduction in the *IIS* is indeed Castoriadis's first coining of it. This second half of the *IIS* was written in

1970–74; the chapter on the social-historical—currently under discussion—is its opening chapter and would have presumably been written at the beginning of this period. In addition, the closing pages of the social-historical chapter contain significant overlap with sections of MSPI—a discussion of Saussure, linguistics, synchrony and diachrony, as well as brief mentions of the fields of cosmology and biology—which was first written in 1970, and first published in 1973. The idea of being as *à-être* breaks with traditional philosophical conceptions. In its magmatic mode, being is interpreted as heterogeneously stratified and incessantly autocreative. In the *IIS*, Castoriadis focuses on a regional ontology of anthropic being as radically self-creative. He contrasts this with the non-anthropic regions of being, which could more or less be grasped by frameworks of identitary thought. Even so, for the first time in the *IIS*, the nascent discourse of radical *physis*—of transregional autocreative being—can be glimpsed.

With the introduction of *à-être,* the argument in the *IIS* proceeds to develop on two, entwining levels. First, there is the explicit focus on the being of the social-historical as a new region of being. The discovery of the social-historical presumes a diversity of regions and modes of being, but there is also the strong, albeit implicit, sense that the social-historical is a mode of being *sui generis.* Second, a more inchoate current exists alongside the first. The second strand incorporates a broader sense of being in its polyregionality, or transregionality: an ontology of creation, of radical *physis* as *à-être.* The latter current remains subterranean at the time of the *IIS* and throughout the 1970s, but emerges as the more significant in Castoriadis's thought during the 1980s. The extent of the transregional ontological implications of *à-être* were neither realized nor even properly considered at this point because Castoriadis was concerned primarily with elucidating anthropic modes of being, especially in their regional otherness from natural modes of being which he considered amenable to ensemblistic-identitarian thought. However, as will be discussed in Chapter 4 of this study, by the end of the *IIS,* Castoriadis expands the reach of magmas to include natural modes of being as well. In the 1980s, Castoriadis increasingly comes to recognize in *à-être* the other side of *physis* as ontologically creative; he begins to build a positive, transregional ontology that is nurtured by insights from inherited philosophical fragments. Indeed, much of what Castoriadis discusses in this section on the philosophical institution of time (and the succeeding section on "Time and Creation") lays the foundation for his later shift to an ontology of radical *physis* (to which point I shall return in Chapter 8). Castoriadis's argument is that time is essential to theorizing being, an insight he shared with Heidegger. However, Castoriadis radicalizes this by connecting time to radical autocreation, and to the ontological importance of the creative imagination as the core of anthropic being.

Castoriadis closes the parenthesis and returns to Plato's discussion of the *chora* (p. 190). As indicated above, there is a sense of temporality to the *chora*, although it remains muted, but Castoriadis does not pursue it. He begins instead a discussion of place (*topos*) and space (*chora*) but tends not to distinguish clearly between them. He views them in mathematical rather than phenomenological terms. Castoriadis quotes Plato's musing that all being must be *somewhere, in some place*. For him this means that if the Forms as "always being" were to exist in a supracelestial place, they would still be in a relation of *coexistence* for them to exist together in one place. The *chora/topos* is implied as soon as there is a "plurality": It is "the first possibility of the Plural" (p. 191), and allows for the *identity of difference* (as opposed to the *otherness of alterity*) in a unity of a spacing. Without the *chora/topos*, where would the "different" exist? Even the order of "succession" is but a modality of the coexisting: "Pure succession has never been thought, and could never be, except as a modality of the *co*existence of the terms of a series" (p. 191). Time would seem to be necessary here, but it is only required to allow the same to differ from itself: "The 'same' thing is never exactly the same, even when it has suffered no 'alteration,' for the very reason that it is *in* another time. But in what way is this other time *other*?" (p. 191). Castoriadis is alluding here to his important distinction, to which he will later return, between the repetition of the same as "difference" and alteration as the creation of "otherness." In the inherited tradition, time cannot really exist (take place), "precisely because we must look for a place for time, an ontologically determined place in the determinacy of what is, hence that time is but a mode of place" (p. 191). Although time is still seen according to its spatial dimension, temporality makes possible plurality as "different determinations that do not annihilate identity."[59] Time in the *Timaeus* was of a second-degree order; it confused (spatial) difference with (temporal) otherness, and was aligned to determinacy (p. 193). However, there is no "pure time" as time is not separable from its content. Time is the emergence of other forms in and as the (social-) historical. Yet even so, Castoriadis tells us,

> More precisely: the "pure" schema of time is the schema of the essential alteration of a figure, the schema that presentifies the breaking up and the suppression of one figure through the emergence of a(nother) figure. As such, it is independent of any particular figure, but not of any figure whatsoever. Time as the "dimensions" of the radical imaginary . . . is the otherness-alteration of figures. (p. 193)

Despite his erstwhile intentions, the interpretative element ("alteration of a figure") as essential to creation ("otherness-alteration") creeps into his thought, although it remains in tension to his explicit argument for absolute creation as the emergence of new forms altogether.

Space is briefly discussed by Castoriadis (pp. 193–95). Its status was not as straightforward as it was for Plato, and inherited thought more generally, would have it. However, Castoriadis judges—somewhat inconclusively—that it is left unresolved. He accepts that "pure space" is a precondition of thought but wants to distinguish it—as externally determining as a dimension of "difference" and the "repetition of the same"—from time as the autocreation of "otherness." Unlike an "empty space," an "empty" time is inconceivable. Castoriadis radicalizes Kant's categories of time and the role of the imagination—via an implicit reading of Heidegger's *Kantbuch*—but he leaves Kant's category of space barely changed, as he agrees that it is a logical, *a priori* condition of identitary thought. Somewhat cryptically he also tells us that, "[t]o be sure, time—in the sense we give the term here, time as otherness-alteration—does imply space, since it is the emergence of other *figures* and since figures, that is the Plural as it is ordered or minimally *formed*, presuppose spacing" (p. 195). However, he lingers no further to elucidate this intriguing problematic but moves straight into a more positive elaboration of time as creation.

Yet what if we were to take the implications of these hastily brushed aside marginalia more seriously? By "starting from the immense questioning to which the Philosopher's work opens us, and by knowingly transgressing its limits" the beginnings of a positive elaboration of time as creation could be reconstructed from the latent possibilities of the *chora* that were left unexplored by Castoriadis.[60] What if a phenomenological rather than mathematical context were our starting point? How might "creation" as not only referring to the emergence of absolutely new forms, but also including the self-alteration of existing forms as "otherness alteration," then appear to us? How should the figuring of space implied by time as otherness-alteration be thought? Instead of ignoring it—or reducing it to abstract space—perhaps *place* as a phenomenological modality of meaning implies a concrete context from which imaginary forms emerge. How might we think of the *chora* as the "primordial spacing" when we take into account its chaotic, that is, creative aspects? Would the relativization of the identitarian modality of the *chora* have implications for Castoriadis's relegation of the question of the One and the Many to the identitarian domain? Recall that for Castoriadis the problematic of the One and the Many—unlike other significant philosophical questions elaborated by the ancient Greeks such as *physis/nomos*, being/appearance, truth/opinion—was not part of his philosophical reflection. It could be argued, however, that the problematic of the One and the Many is presumed by the others. Nevertheless, Castoriadis's preoccupation with creation as the creation of otherness (as well as his acceptance of the Aristotelian *dyad* as the first number) precluded this.[61] Would the reactivation of the problematic of the One and the Many in turn help elucidate the *chora*'s separability-inseparability in relation to its content (but not its complete separability, as with Kant)?[62] How might the introduction of the "enigmatic *chora*" immediately after the production of the world, which required Plato to take a backward step and start afresh, be rethought in relation to the world horizon, phenomenologically speaking? Given the preeminence of imaginary institutions as primary social-historically created forms, what would happen if we rethought the *chora* as part of the becoming-being of meaning, as a modality of the world "inseparable-separable" from its many social-historical articulations and concretizations? Part of Castoriadis's difficulty here lies in the recurring ambiguity of "the world" in his thought: Does he interpret the creation of Plato's kosmos as the natural world? The social world? The world *qua* world?

Having established a radically different interpretation of time than was found in the inherited tradition, Castoriadis moves to link it to the idea of creation. He does this by distinguishing between identitary and non-identitary modes of beings as ensemblist and magmatic respectively. Although time as the creation of other forms does imply a spatial element, in his view they are radically different: The temporal dimension of being creates otherness, the spatial dimension produces difference. "Difference" and "Otherness" have conventionally been interpreted as broadly synonymous, yet Castoriadis's distinction between them is crucial to his philosophical approach: The emergence of *temporal otherness* with the measuring of *spatial difference* shatters the inherited onto-logics of determinacy, for the emergence of otherness cannot be predicated, predicted, or deduced from its precedents. In this sense, an ellipse is *different* from a circle, but democracy is *other* than monarchy. The invention, form, and determinations of democracy cannot be determined on the basis of a pre-existing monarchy: "[I]t comes from *nothing* and out of *nowhere*" (p. 195).[63] In traditional thought, however, ontological genesis has been interpreted as imperfect or less-than being; only complete determinacy, as in Kant, could be considered *to be*. In this way, the being of creation has no ground, no origin, no *Ursprung* by which it could be determined; it is rather an *Ur-sprung* into forms of otherness.[64]

Can traditional thought really come to terms with creation? Castoriadis remains doubtful. In particular, Castoriadis critiques monotheistic and Platonic versions as pseudo-creations. In his view it signifies nothing more than a production of an imitation of something that was already there, determined by the "elsewhere" and atemporality of the Creator-Legislator God (p. 196).[65] Returning to Plato, Castoriadis points out that in some places Plato upholds a sense of creation as "the cause of the passage from non-being to being," that which "leads a former non-being to a subsequent beingness (*ousia*)?" (p. 197), where he opens onto *poiesis* and *techne*, art and artisans.[66] Castoriadis takes a different tack: He follows Aristotle in seeing the *eidos* as the essence of the form. As such it draws on *poiesis* but also *techne*, such that artisans as well as artists are seen as creators, as human creations of *eide*: "The statue is brought into being as a statue and as this particular statue only if its *eidos* is invented, imagined, posited out of nothing" (p. 197). Castoriadis transposes divine acts of cosmic creation *ex nihilo* to the human realm, bringing the idea of creation down from the heavens and into the concrete world, something that would only be possible in modern philosophical contexts (Blumenberg 2001). In fact, he privileges human creation of a new *eidos* as more ontologically significant than the cosmological creation of a new galaxy, as the following quotation shows:

> The wheel revolving around an axis is an absolute ontological creation. It is a greater creation; it weighs, ontologically, more than a new galaxy that would arise tomorrow evening out of nothing between the Milky Way and the Andromeda. For there are already millions of galaxies—but the person who invented the wheel, or a written sign, was imitating and repeating nothing at all. (p. 197)

However, there is an underlying tension here between the creative doing of artisan activity and the creative doing of the artist. The artisan does not incessantly create new forms, but also produces exemplars of the same, whereas the artist creates new forms in order for art to be art. Foremost in the present context, the tension is seen between Castoriadis's divergent strands of social-historical radical imaginary as manifest in "doing" and "signification," exemplified in the difference between artisans and artists. Although Castoriadis maintains, even privileges at this point the activity of "doing," the latter mode of being comes to be more important for his work. Art in the sense of Kant's third *Critique,* as the positing of a new *eidos,* becomes increasingly emphasized in his thought. Gradually, a philosophical elucidation of the being of "doing"—especially as it pertains to the realm of everyday life—becomes marginalized. Although the being of doing—for example, as expressed in noncommodified, popular forms of art—is seen as potentially creative, its philosophical implications, especially in relation to interpretative creation, are hinted at but not taken very much further.[67] Its mode of being raises questions about Castoriadis's increasing emphasis on the ever-new positing of new forms as emblematic of creation, and his rejection of a more interpretative and contextual form of creation, which could do more justice to the creative dimensions of artisan activity and folk art. A greater sensibility for interpretative forms of creation would also give greater due to the context in which new forms of art are posited. For example, while an Athenian tragedy is *other* than—not merely *different* from—a Shakespearean play, they are both still part of an identifiable current of Western literature. Nevertheless, the ontological weight of human creativity as made possible by the ontological weight of the imagination is neglected in Western philosophy. Creation, in Castoriadis's sense, ruptures frameworks of being as determinacy—the *eide* as immutable and unalterable—and, as such, they cannot account for it. Kant, for Castoriadis, may be seen as a partial exception: In the third *Critique* he rediscovers the creativity of the "productive imagination," and its role in the work of art, but it carries with it no ontological significance. Plato's Demiurge, as artisan and creator, is really "producing" (in Castoriadis's sense) the world after a given image, governed by a preexisting paradigm.

The final discussion of the twofold philosophical institution of time and its relation to creation returns to the issue of otherness and determination, except now it is posited from a different angle: that of an essential indetermination to being. Being must be considered not homogenous but as heterogeneous. Castoriadis is not arguing, though, for an image of being as completely indeterminate, which would be an image of total formlessness, total chaos such that no (new) forms could be formed. Instead he draws on the ancient Greek image of the world as an overlap of kosmos and chaos: neither totally ordered nor totally unordered. He does not use this terminology here, developing it more explicitly in his later trajectory, but its presence was already discernable in the 1964–65 part of the *IIS*.[68] To accept some kind of indetermination to being challenges central metaphysical concepts of causation and categories as "closed, certain and sufficient" (p. 200), as well as questioning their *apriori* deduction, which is itself a logical requirement. In contesting the "closed, certain and sufficient" concept of being, further intrusions of the more general ontology of being as *à-être*, that is, as heterogeneous, multilayered, overlapping and—importantly—never ultimately systemized or closed on itself, are discernable. Here in the *IIS*—similarly with Heidegger at the time of *Being and Time*—Castoriadis primarily confines the development of the elucidation of this traditionally elusively temporal mode of being to anthropos. It is via consideration of "history," "society," and the "imagination/imaginary" that new insights into the multiple meanings of being are gained. To preserve an exclusively identitary sense of being, traditional philosophy has needed to negate the "being-ness" of these three interrelated anthropic modalities. Nonetheless, Castoriadis's ultimate drawing on a more general sense of being displays at least an implicit openness, even at this relatively early stage, to the idea that more than merely anthropic modes of being might be characterized by the capacity to create ontological form. If this be the case, moreover, then other regions of being may be said to be characterized by a certain indeterminacy and heterogeneity—and self-creativity, too.

From Plato onward, inherited philosophy has instituted a tradition of thinking about time as identitary and being according to atemporal essence/substance. Castoriadis is seeking to challenge this reading of being. In so doing, he picks up fragmentary countermoments and submerged traditions in reinterpreting being by a reexamination of the underlying constituents of time, creation, and the imaginary element. Inherited philosophy has instituted being and time as identitary (p. 200). Castoriadis tells us that this is a consequence of reducing the diversity of social-historically instituted interpretations of time into but one of its dimensions—that of *legein* and ensemblist-identitary logic. Identitary time is necessary for identitary determination. It becomes in this context "the homogeneous and neutral medium of 'successive coexistence,' which is coexistence itself for the Gaze (*Theoria*) that examines the latter spread out before it." Identitary time takes place in the 'identitary present' which is moreover but the innumerable (and numbered) repetition of identitary presents, always identical as such and different only by their 'place'" (p. 201). The identitary present, and here Castoriadis draws on Aristotle, as represented by the "*nun*" as the "absolute present," is different on one level, but its substratum involves the "same." Something is found "in time"—an identity, determination, *peras* of a being—but in essence it excludes time.[69] True time is not identitary: It is "bursting, emerging, creating. The *present*, the *nun* is here explosion, split, rupture—the rupture of what is as such. This present exists as originating, as immanent transcendence, as source, as the surging forth of ontological genesis" (p. 201). Although "true time" is not reducible to time as it is manifest in the social-historical, nonetheless, "social-historical time—time that is the social-historical itself—allows us to apprehend the most pregnant, the most striking form of this time" (p. 201) as instituting society irrupts between society as instituted, in echoes of *natura naturans/natura naturata*, as perpetual and permanent self-alteration.

Social-Historical Aspects of Time

Castoriadis proceeds to consider social-historical aspects of time. He argues that the radical imaginary of instituting society manifests itself as two overlapping moments, as "doing," and as "signification" that posit something that is *not yet*.

> If [history] includes the dimension that idealist philosophers called freedom . . . this is because this *doing* posits and provides for itself something other than what simply is, and because in it dwell significations that are neither the reflection of what is perceived, nor the mere extension and sublimation of animal tendencies, nor the strictly rational development of what is given. (p. 146)

Castoriadis's emphasis on the being of "doing" is more evident and its implications more clearly spelled out in the first half of the *IIS*. Although Castoriadis begins to pursue a "theory of action" in earnest in this 1975 section of the *IIS,* it ultimately remained more marginal to his overall elucidation than the being "signification." This will become clearer as we continue our journey through the *IIS*.

Castoriadis turns to consider the relation of the social historical to natural time. Although he agrees that there is something akin to a "natural" time, he argues that we can never move beyond the social institution of the world and its particular institution of time to "experience" socially purified data (p. 202). He concedes, however, that the elaboration of the world "X" that occurs at the interface of social-historical and natural modes of being must mean that it lends itself to elaboration, and moreover, carries within it a "certain organization" (p. 202). The organizability of the "X" becomes important, too, in a later context, where Castoriadis questions Kant's *"glücklicher Zufall"* as elaborated in the third *Critique* in his rethinking of objective knowledge.[70] Castoriadis introduces the idea of *Anlehnung* (*étayage*) to grasp the relation between the social-historical and the first natural stratum (I return to this more fully in the following chapter), which for him is an attempt to come to grips with the modality of the social-historical in its elaboration of partial aspects of the first natural stratum in a selective and nondetermined way. The local irreversibility of time will be instituted in a singular fashion by each society and invested each time with a different meaning. The instituting signification comprises the being proper to the social-historical; traditional responses to the idea of social nature of time do not bring us further, in Castoriadis's view. The transcendental tradition—from Kant to Husserl—cannot conceive a plurality of subjects if they confine themselves to nonempirical criteria, and hence cannot make sense of the social institution of time; again Castoriadis encounters the individualist—monadological or egological—frameworks that cannot support notions of the social *qua* social-historical.

For Castoriadis, social-historical being is a rupture of being *qua à-être* and is, as such, a creation of *otherness* (p. 204). Notice that the presence of subterranean *physis* as *à-être* again intrudes even when the discussion is strictly confined to the social-historical aspects. However, it also points to the tension in Castoriadis thought in terms of being *qua* being as *à-être*, and its confinement at this point to anthropic modes of being, without considering the natural world for itself. At this juncture of his thought, all modes of natural being are considered to be adequately grasped by onto-logics of determinacy, yet at the same time Castoriadis acknowledges that the emergence of the social-historical in its exceptionality is inscribed in a pre-social/natural temporality (p. 204). In the second half of the book, we begin to see that Castoriadis moves to emphasize the rupture of living being from being *qua à-être* as part of a wider polyregional—or dimensional—ontology of the *for-itself* (*pour soi*), which redraws anthropic and natural regions of being along lines of greater continuity. Castoriadis begins to merge what hitherto he had kept analytically separate: the social-historical and the radical imaginary, where the social-historical is characterized as radical imaginary and an incessant self-figuration.

Although there is the enigma of natural temporality and natural identity, it does not determine the quality of socially instituted temporality. The social-historical is its own implicit temporality as a manner of "making time" (p. 206); it brings its own temporality into being as a specific and concrete social-historical temporality that is not reducible to the explicit institution of social-historical time. Castoriadis illuminates this with two examples. The first example is a comparison of modern capitalism with ancient Greece. The social manifests itself and institutes itself as a concrete and actual temporality. Castoriadis has been arguing that history is the self-alteration of this specific mode of coexistence. Yet curiously, although the crux of Castoriadis's argument is that it is impossible to think time without its concrete content, for nigh on the entire chapter he has been doing just that. Even his two concrete illustrations of social-historical time—modern capitalism and ancient Athens—remain brief and cursory. Nonetheless, for Castoriadis, whatever else capitalism may be, it is the social-historical institution of time as a homogenous identitary time immersed in the magmatic significations of an infinite time as unlimited growth and progress, as well as its actual temporality, which makes it be what it is: An unprecedented quickening of time as incessant rupture and revolution.[71] From another angle it also appears as the freezing of time, as an "immobility in perpetual change" (p. 207) and a suppression of otherness. He might well have added the institution of perpetual novelty, but curiously does not.

The second example looks to the contrast between ancient Athens and Sparta as seen by Thucydides. Here the distinction between innovation and swiftness on the part of the Athenians and hesitancy and stagnation on the part of the Spartans (p. 208) represents their respective modes of doing—which itself is interpreted through its significations of past and the future as they relate to the institution of reality as what is signified to be ultimately meaningful or of value—is evident.

The social institution of time consists in two overlapping dimensions: The identitary and the imaginary as the time of marking and the time of signification respectively, with each existing in a "relation of reciprocal inherence" (pp. 209–10). Identitary time leans on the first natural stratum and indicates time as calendar time. The identitary dimension indicates time as markings; social imaginary time indicates the time of signification. Notice, too, that Castoriadis devotes a section to the time of "doing" as part of the being of "doing," something that, after the focus on the proto-institutions of *legein* and *teukhein*, he generally leaves aside. The tension in STCC, as discussed above in relation to *eide*, artisans and artists, can be directly attributable to the different directions and emphases in which Castoriadis ultimately developed what were at this point two overlapping but irreducible aspects to the radical imaginary. As we have seen, the time of doing is raised as inseparable from imaginary time. Here Castoriadis makes a connection, which he did not develop further, between *kronos* and *kairos* by invoking the Hippocratic writings: "Time is that in which here is *kairos* (propitious instant and critical interval, the opportunity to take a decision) and *kairos* is that in which there is not much time" (p. 212). The time of "doing" is thus instituted to contain singularities not determinable in advance: moments requiring creative action, as irregular and heterogeneous, and is thus intrinsically closer to a true temporality and hence being than social representation. (Interestingly, Castoriadis uses the term "representation" here rather than "signification.") Imaginary time on the other hand for Castoriadis tends to cover the idea of temporality as otherness-alteration, be it cyclical or linear representations of time such that it occults to itself the very nature of its temporality. Castoriadis does not use the terminology of "autonomy" and "heteronomy" here, but the implications are clear. Nevertheless Castoriadis seems to qualify this by suggesting that it is a necessity for the institution to institute itself outside of time (p. 214) in order to maintain its identity. Again the *natura naturans/natura naturata* of instituting and instituting society reemerges. Castoriadis now draws the explicit link of heteronomy and autonomy, exhibiting a Marxian residue by recourse to the idea of alienation (p. 214). Yet history is inherently creative and ruptures can and do occur through revolutionary social doing. It is possible for society to recognize in its institution its own self-creativity: The institution of *la politique* and *la philosophie* in the ancient Athenian democratic *polis* testifies to this. Thus society and history when separately thought do not capture the mode of being of the object in question (p. 215). Only when thought of as the social-historical, as both doing and signification, can time as radical otherness be grasped in its perpetual self-alteration and creation of other forms.

After going to great lengths to emphasize and even recover the temporal nature of being as the social-historical, Castoriadis moves somewhat surprisingly to a discussion of synchronic and diachronic approaches in the closing pages of the chapter (p. 216 ff). He finds insights in Saussure to critique the radical atemporality of structuralism, but also, more positively, to find support for thinking the creative mode of being of the social-historical in a radicalization of the linguistic turn. Given the similarity of the content, and its reach into cosmological and biological domains, it may be speculated that this section of the *IIS* is contemporaneous with the relevant sections of MSPI, in which the thematic is the same. Written in 1970 for a 1971 interdisciplinary symposium, MSPI was first published in 1972 and in its present, expanded form in November 1973 in *Encyclopaedia Universalis*. Therein, Castoriadis surveys the state of play in the natural and human sciences. A conclusion to be drawn from his analysis is his conviction that each discipline has a particular if partial grasp upon the world, upon a particular stratum of being, and has partial overlap with neighboring—and sometimes distant—disciplines. Each contributes to the elucidation of being *qua* being. Yet MSPI is less about a world in fragments than about the social-historical as a separate region of being in need of its own elucidation. At this point, philosophy is seen as an elucidation of the *human* ontological condition (not of natural being) and more particularly, of the hitherto occluded mode of being of the *social-historical*.[72]

In the section on linguistics (MSPI p. 194 ff), Castoriadis points to the intimate nexus between language, meaning, and philosophy. However, his discussion of Saussure occurs in the section on "society and history" (MSPI pp. 203 ff), where the discussion is identical in substance to the one here in the closing pages of the *IIS* chapter on the social-historical. The early Saussure recognized the important overlap of synchronic and diachronic approaches, unlike the later structuralists, in particular Lévi-Strauss, but also Foucault, where they were understood in absolute opposition, with the synchronic approach given privilege: History becomes the "mere juxtaposition of different structures" (*IIS.* p. 216).[73] Castoriadis emphasizes instead the overlap of structure and becoming, pointing to the domains of cosmology and biology as those in which the overlapping element is particularly evident.[74] In affirming the impossibility of distinguishing synchrony from diachrony, Castoriadis takes what seems to be a different tack from the rest of the chapter, which accentuates the radically temporal dimension of the social-historical. In turning to Saussure, he looks to language as a way into a discussion of signification in a radicalization of the linguistic turn. The being of language, like the being of doing, contains the inherent possibility of generating the new. Language is code and *langue* to the extent that it refers to significations: "The possibility of the emergence of other significations is immanent in language and permanent as long as language is living" (p. 218). As such Castoriadis critiques structuralism's conception of language as a reduction to the "ensemble of its relations," for synchronic language must always be open to diachronic change. The final point about language—that it assures every society's access to its own past (p. 219)—opens onto the thematic of his early essay (1944) on Weber. Castoriadis argued that Weber was the first to see that history was the bearer of social meaning, and begins to link the two aspects of the social-historical: Imaginary signification and meaningful doing.[75]

The *IIS* chapter on the social-historical is in many ways a transitional chapter in Castoriadis's philosophical journey. It thematizes two overlapping—yet diverging—currents of instituting society that sometimes confront each other in tension: The time of creation as doing, and the time of creation as signification. Hitherto, it had seemed as if the mode of being of "doing" was the privileged mode of human existence *qua* social-historical; "doing" as a mode of being is seen as closest to the true temporality of being as creation. Earlier in the chapter, I suggested, too, that social significations as social representations seemed mainly to act to occult the nature of the social-historical as intrinsic creative doing; from the opposite perspective, "doing" was the privileged mode of being concerning the project of autonomy; it was "doing" that activated or created significance. Only in the closing pages of the chapter does Castoriadis explicitly address the mode of being of signification as temporal creation. Also evident is that the notion of radical self-alteration, which Castoriadis often uses here, can more readily support the idea of interpretative creation than "creation of otherness out of nothing." In the former example, something is altered from *something* to something else, while in the latter case it is seen as being from *nothing* to something. And it is in this light interesting that although creation *ex nihilo* is implicit to his argument, in his discussion of social-historical creation, the term is not yet used. As well, the sole focus on anthropic modes of being results in unnoticed tensions at the interface of the social and the natural; these continue into the next *IIS* chapter. This in part explains the submerged but ever-intruding presence of a more general notion of being as radical *physis*. I will continue to map these threads in the course of our journey through the *IIS*. Although the importance of the mode of being of "doing" persists into the next chapter on the proto-institutions of *legein* and *teukhein*—and an epistemological element begins to appear—the mode of being of "signification" gradually becomes the more important to the ultimate configuration of the *IIS*.

2

Proto-Institutions and
Epistemological Encounters

Since Kant and the transcendental turn, the status of ontology—in the sense of philosophical claims about being—has been questioned.[1] In the previous chapter, Castoriadis boldly approached the subject of being in an elucidation of the social-historical, but he quickly encounters heightened epistemological issues and a corresponding Kantian problematic: Onto-logical foundations are inseparable from logical foundations. Similar to Kant, Castoriadis discovers the imperative of interrogating the frame-works and categories of thought through which the idea of being can even begin to be thought, although Castoriadis's arguments are epistemologi-cally and ontologically substantive. In this sense, the Kantian theme is one derived from the Heideggerian context of the *Kantbuch*. Like Heidegger, Castoriadis finds that ontology and epistemology cannot be definitively divided. Heidegger saw the necessity of interpreting Kant's productive imagination as temporal, but Castoriadis further radicalized Heidegger's interpretation from the egological Kantian imagination into the radical imaginary of the social-historical.[2] Yet, as with Heidegger and Kant of the first *Critique*, Castoriadis, too, constructs an inescapable abyss between human and nonhuman nature (the makeshift bridge of *Anlehnung* not-withstanding).[3] At the time of the *IIS*, Castoriadis remains in dialogue with the *Critique of Pure Reason*.[4] Although he attempts to bridge the gap between the social and the natural with the introduction of the idea of *Anlehnung*, ultimately it is not until he rediscovers the significance of Kant's third *Critique*, as part of his shift toward creative *physis*, that he can more fully come to grips with the problematic that it entails. The connection between the previous *IIS* chapter on the social-historical and the present chapter on the proto-institutions of *legein* and *teukhein* is that, for Castoriadis, Western logic prevents us from thinking the full sense of creation (p. 181). In this vein, the chapter on *legein* and *teukhein* continues the argument introduced in the chapter on the social-historical, in that the core of the inherited logic is ensemblistic-identitarian.[5]

In this chapter, Castoriadis's articulation of a *critique of elementary reason* is in the foreground. His critique of elementary reason is intended as a preparatory step for his overall critique of *totalizing* reason. It centers on an elucidation of the primordial institutions of what he terms *legein* and *teukhein*, which are elementary forms of thinking and doing. A feature of Castoriadis's critique of reason is seen in the analysis of the social-historical—that is, institutional—underpinning of ensemblistic-identitarian logic. Castoriadis, as with post-Husserlian phenomenological thought more generally, criticizes the idea of a transcendental subject of knowledge, and instead theorizes reason by way of institutions and the social-historical.[6] For Castoriadis, reason and its operations are in central interplay with the imagination; indeed, for him, the imagination is at the basis of reason. Concomitantly, this can be extended to say that culture is the "other" of reason.[7] Here the important novelty of Castoriadis's approach to the imagination begins to emerge, in that he links the creative imagination not only to works of human creation but also to *meaning*.[8] Castoriadis, however, goes beyond Kant's use of the imagination. Kant took up the role of the creative (that is, productive) imagination in the first edition of the *Critique of Pure Reason*, but modified it in the second edition.[9] He subsequently rediscovered it in the third *Critique*, but could not lend it ontological weight. Castoriadis did not shy away from theorizing the ontological role of the imagination: He had already signaled this in his previous chapter on the social-historical. For Castoriadis, the imagination pointed the way to liberty, not chaos, as the inherited tradition was wont to think. In thematizing the role of the imagination, Castoriadis encounters the problematic of language, whereby he reflects on the structuralist—originally Saussurean—perspective that a critique of reason proceeds by way of a discussion of language, especially in its significatory dimension. Thought itself is only feasible through language, which in and of itself points to a social *institution* rather than a transcendental subjective *constitution*.

There are two points to note about Castoriadis's critique of reason. First, despite his critique of totalizing reason, Castoriadis's own critique incorporates a totalizing aspiration in that he intends it to span the whole of the philosophical tradition (both precritical and postcritical). This is especially evident in his account of the philosophical "obsession" with mathematics from Plato to Husserl (p. 222).[10] In this chapter on *legein* and *teukhein* he extends the critique beyond Husserl to focus on the importance of Cantor. Castoriadis's critique of reason develops a particular critique of mathematical reason, hence, in the first instance, this comprises a critique of logic, not of substantive reason. Second, Castoriadis links up—more or less significantly—with a whole spectrum of approaches to reason that specifically problematize Kant's own critique. Nietzsche comes to mind, as does the earlier Frankfurt School: There are some parallels with Adorno's critique of identitarian logic from the *Negative Dialectics*.[11] As the *IIS* is written in the early 1970s, structuralism (in particular Lévi-Strauss) emerges as the target of his critical discussion.[12] Here, too, a Kantian connection is apparent: Lévi-Strauss of *La pensée sauvage* (1962) can be read as providing an analysis of reason, but without the transcendental subject. Indeed, in the now famous 1963 "roundtable" with Ricoeur (among others) in *Esprit*, Lévi-Strauss admitted as much.[13] For Lévi-Strauss, internal structures are inborn and unconscious; meaning, in this sense, is a mere epiphenomenon that consciousness experiences under the impact of these quasi-transcendental structures. Castoriadis, on the other hand, does not relate transcendental structures to the unconscious mind, but rather to institutions and the social-historical.

In the present chapter, Castoriadis extends his analysis of *legein* and *teukhein,* and its deepening examination of the epistemological issues at hand, to modes of knowing in the natural sciences and mathematics by introducing the psychoanalytical concept of *Anlehnung*.[14] Using the idea of *Anlehnung*, Castoriadis tries to articulate the relation between the social-historical and the natural world (as the first natural stratum) as one of partial dependency, yet nonetheless as a relation mediated by creation (not determinacy).[15] This also lays the basis for Castoriadis's deepening critique of knowledge. *Legein* and *teukhein,* as elementary categories and primordial institutions of the social-historical, delineate the ways in which being can be articulated. As social-historically instituted, they point to the social-historical mode of being as the emergence of otherness, as well as to the limits of reason in thinking being. Yet because they are anchored in nature, they problematize these same two contexts. Castoriadis does not always fully confront these frictions, especially at the time of the *IIS*. Our access to the world is achieved neither through unmediated reason nor through the purely (natural) senses.[16] It is not naturally determined, rather we think/experience/construct/act through categories. For Castoriadis these categories are not "natural," nor are they constituted by the transcendental ego/subject; they are instead socially created and instituted. In this way, the rules of *legein* and *teukhein* regulate how being is approached and imprint general frameworks on our encounters with being, thus functioning as quasi-Kantian categories. Castoriadis incorporates a dual approach to these modes of being—epistemological and substantively ontological. In short, the way in which the *how* of thought is instituted will condition the *what* of thought. In more concrete terms, being—understood as determinacy—can only be thought via a corresponding and consubstantial logic and vice versa. Nevertheless there are problems with this articulation, not the least of which are the natural underpinnings that *legein* gives to reason as a social-historical institution, as well as, in the same vein, the difficulties that Castoriadis encounters with articulating the problematic of a "partial determinacy" between the first natural stratum, and *legein* and *teukhein*.

From his opening sentence in the *legein* and *teukhein* chapter of the *IIS*, Castoriadis indicates his intent to tackle the tradition of "necessary and sufficient reason" (p. 221). It signals an engagement with a Leibnizian interpretation of reason (that is, pre-Kantian) that has become the sole representative of the historical variants of *reason*. Castoriadis informs us anew (following on from his observation in the preceding *IIS* chapter) that the reasons for this are deeply embedded within the institution of the social-historical itself. This is ambiguous and could seem to indicate quasi-ontological or anthropological reasons rather than concretely historical reasons and precursors, or a deeply layered sedimentation of the concrete unfolding of the institution. Castoriadis charges the inherited logic-ontology with the autonomization of one dimension of "thinking as Reason" that reaches the pinnacle of its achievement in mathematics.[17] He deepens his argument that for every ontology there is a corresponding logic, and the logic that informs the unbroken ontological tradition of Western thought since its Greek inception is consubstantial to the central tenet of this logic, which posits *being as being-determined*.[18] The trajectory of the inherited tradition, concludes Castoriadis, is anchored in the very requirements and totalizing ambitions of this logic (p. 221).

Castoriadis provides us with an immanent critique of the logic of Reason by turning to its internal foundations. Unlike his discussion of the institution of time (in the previous chapter), however, where he focused on a single philosopher (Plato), his present strategy sees him seeking insights from a mathematician, in this case, Cantor. Here a more thoroughgoing explanation of the connection between identitarian and ensemblistic modes of reasoning begins to appear. Castoriadis considers the question of the foundation of mathematics to be most developed in the area of set theory, which simultaneously elucidates the immanent necessities of this dimension of social life. Castoriadis finds Cantor's "naive" theory of sets to be the most useful for his purposes: "A set is a collection into a whole of definite and distinct objects of our intuition or of our thought. These objects are called the elements of the set" (p. 223). Because Cantor's definition *presupposes* "signs posited as distinct and definite elements" (p. 226), it presumes the elementary mathematical activity of *legein* as being able to "distinguish-choose-posit-assemble-count-speak" in a universal manner (p. 223), itself presupposing the schema of union and separation (p. 224). Castoriadis is working toward an immanent destruction of the possibility of sets: Union and separation presuppose an element that must be already posited as "pure self-identity" and determinacy, which further assumes the *presupposition of its own positing*. Castoriadis in essence critiques its circular logic and undefinable axioms. Conversely, Castoriadis does not consider these very same elements to hinder the circle of creation. However, if mathematics has a natural anchor in *legein*, and is, too, a social-historical necessity, whence these axioms? There is an implicit creative moment even in *legein,* as elementary mathematics, that continues to problematize the ontological status of mathematical reason. Although sets cannot really exist in full, it is intrinsic to their logic that they posit themselves as if they did. For Castoriadis, the main problem with the idea of a set is that it must be able to—in advance—enumerate the totality of its elements, which is a direct critique and reframing of Kant: "To say that a thing is is to say that it is determined as to all its possible predicates" (p. 226).

At this point in his thought, of the two aspects of social-historical being—the being of doing and the being of signification—the being of "doing" is still foremost for Castoriadis. The being of signification is less developed and Castoriadis continues to oscillate between an elucidation of "signification" and "representation." Both are contrasted to mathematical *legein*, but are nonetheless reliant on its operation and support: "The existence of society—as collective and anonymous social doing/representing would be impossible without the institution of *legein* and the application of the inherent identitary-ensemblist logic" (p. 227). Ensembles must be socially instituted. An organization, if it is organized, must be meaningfully organized, but Castoriadis demarcates these aspects of meaning from the social-historical significations invested in an ensemble and only fleetingly addresses them.[19] For him, signification is absent from ensemblistic-identitarian operations in that they are reducible to elementary mathematical enumerations.

For Castoriadis, the being of the social-historical cannot be reduced to sets (or to its biological substratum)—it is rather a magma and a "magma of magmas." Yet the social-historical seems to exist in an uneasy relationship with the essential component of *legein* as ensemblist-identitarian logic of determinacy, whereas the being of doing or "representation" is only possible when anchored in *legein*. Castoriadis tends to gloss over the question of the being of ensemblistic-identitarian logic, especially in the social-historical. In the same way, neither is the new logic required by magmatic being elucidated properly: To say that an "elucidation," inevitably fragmentary, is needed, does not in itself take us very far. What is needed is a hermeneutic-phenomenological corrective that takes account of our corporeal being in the world, the creativity of interpretation, and the importance of metaphor and symbols as an indirect and oblique route to knowledge.[20]

Anlehnung: At the Intersection of the Social and the Natural

Castoriadis's conception of *Anlehnung* holds a significant, albeit undeveloped, place in his thought (pp. 229ff). He employs the idea of *leaning on* in the first instance as a makeshift term to explain the relation between the social-historical and its natural preconditions as being irreducible to a deterministic explanation. The "first natural stratum," as Castoriadis terms it, can neither be "disregarded" nor forced at will: The social-historical must take account of it, but in a selective, partial, and nondetermined way. *Anlehnung* provides the natural context of creation, as well as emphasizing that the connections and interrelations between different regions and modes of being are mediated by relations of creation, not determinism. This notwithstanding, *Anlehnung* remains in many ways a *Verlegenheitsbegriff*; it is related to Castoriadis's central concerns, but not an accurate expression of them. It would, however, be wrong to dismiss it out of hand; the idea of *Anlehnung* is more complex than a first glance might reveal. As presented in the *IIS*, the idea of *Anlehnung* has four aspects. First an anthropological dimension is indicated; second, a quasi-sociological, where the grafting of institutions onto nature occurs; third, an epistemological in that the application of ensidic logic relies on already ensemblized/ensemblizable primary layers of being; and finally, an ontological, where complex layers of being and their interrelations are brought into play. In the *IIS*, the epistemic dimension of *Anlehnung* is emphasized, as it allows for the elaboration of the first natural stratum as a form of objective knowledge.

Castoriadis first draws on the concept of *Anlehnung*—originally a Freudian term—not in the *IIS* chapter under discussion, but in the subsequent chapter (p. 289). Nevertheless, the problematic behind the concept is visibly present in this earlier chapter on *legein* and *teukhein*. More often, he refers to the idea of *Anlehnung* as "*s'étayer sur*" or "*étayage*" (*leaning on*).[21] Principally a psychoanalytic term, Castoriadis primarily intends it to elucidate the relationship of the social-historical *leaning on* nature, and it represents an attempt to extrapolate a psychoanalytical concept into the social domain. From the outset, the idea of *Anlehnung* was strengthened by Castoriadis's own leaning on Fichte's idea of *Anstoss* ("shock" or "check"), which indicates the facility of the being for-itself for affect, that is, to be affected by the shock created by the collision between the for-itself and the world. The notion of *Anlehnung* (*s'etayage*) can also be approached as Castoriadis's attempt to look for a way around the Kantian dilemma that all experience/knowledge is codetermined by the mind. In Castoriadis's account, the "fact" that the mind's processes nonetheless find some correlation and grip with the phenomenal world cannot be explained by Kant as other than a "*glücklicher Zufall.*"[22] The idea of *Anlehnung* acts as a bridge between nature and the social-historical. *Legein* and *teukhein* are not merely existent in the anthropic realm; they occur in living nature, too, as a prefiguration or a preformation of the elementary operations of reason within nature. In this way, *legein* and *teukhein* in the social-historical may be understood as an institutional radicalization of trends that are already operative within nature. Here preliminary correctives to the radical dualism of the first two Kantian critiques begin to emerge: Castoriadis does this intentionally, by building bridges between nature and the social-historical.[23] This becomes more explicit within his later ontology of *physis*, but it is prefigured here in the *IIS*. In a sense, *Anlehnung* becomes undifferentiated and introduces a zone of indeterminacy between society and nature.

Castoriadis extends his analysis of *legein* and *teukhein* and links epistemological issues to modes of (objective) knowledge in the natural sciences and mathematics (although not in a focused way in the *IIS*) via the concept of *Anlehnung*. In a variant of transcendental realism, Castoriadis accepts that there is an external world, whence the social-historical emerges.[24] He argues furthermore that anthropic modes of being are not simply reducible to the social-historical but also incorporate psychical and "natural" dimensions. However, of these three, the "natural" is the least important in Castoriadis's thought at this point; from another angle, it is also the most difficult to satisfactorily reconcile with the rest of his thought during the 1970s. Those aspects of human forms of life considered in their "naturalness" or "animality" are considered of little import in that they tell us nothing that is not "merely trivial." Castoriadis may ultimately be justified in this belief, but, at this point, it remains merely his assertion. By dismissing the first natural stratum and its relation to the social-historical, it disguises the tension to which the relationship of *Anlehnung,* that is, the relation between the social-historical and the first natural stratum, particularly in the example of the living being, gives rise in the first place. This can be explained by way of Castoriadis's focus and project in the *IIS*: In delineating or distinguishing the social-historical and its mode of being as one of ontological creation and therefore not graspable by traditional logic-ontologies, Castoriadis posits the (mode of being of the) social-historical as a magma of imaginary significations, that is constellations of meaning. It is not characterized by determinacy/is not determined; rather it is underpinned by an ontological principle of unceasing creation. However, tensions arise because, in focusing on the being of the social-historical, Castoriadis neglects to theorize other regions of beings and the relation of the social-historical to them. These make themselves most apparent in the relation between the social-historical and the first natural stratum, which the makeshift notion of *Anlehnung* is meant to breach.

Tension is visible, for example, between "internal" and "external" forms of leaning on the first natural stratum by the social-historical. Although Castoriadis admits that "internal" and "external" is a "gross abuse of language," this in and of itself does not provide a resolution. The difficulty occurs in the way the first natural stratum is instituted for the social-historical. In the "internal" version, "male" and "female" are naturally given biological categories which social imaginary significations then bring into being as "being male" or "being female": a cultural meaning is grafted onto a biological given. Yet in the "external" leaning on nature Castoriadis insists, in a continuation of his critique of cybernetic approaches to biology from MSPI, that there is no "information" to be found in nature. To be more precise, the living being, or in this case, the social-historical, organizes/creates what for it is information by partial and selective leaning on the first natural stratum. This tension persists even after his shift toward radical *physis* in the mid-1980s, although his later argument, especially concerning the living being, can be seen as a radicalization of his critique of cybernetics, and as such, links more strongly to the "external" aspects of *Anlehnung* rather than the "internal." Indeed, the "internal" aspects of leaning on by the social-historical are generally not further elaborated after this point, and the "internal" aspects of lean-ing on by the living being are not broached at all. In fact, the interiority of the living being—or access to it—is later problematized for objective knowledge.[25] There is added friction here between the "external" and "in-ternal" in regard to the strictly epistemological aspects. Dreyfus (2004) in his discussion of Taylor's "anti-epistemology" points to the importance of the "embedded" knowing of the phenomenological tradition as well as its critique of the external/internal divide. Castoriadis, at least in the context of the problematic of *leaning on*, does not address such issues, although it is possible that forms of "embedded" knowing could be made congruent with his more fragmentary elucidation of *teukhein*. This is to say, there appears to be a stratum of being that is able to be organized by the first natural stratum, the theorization of which allows Castoriadis to preserve the idea of "objective knowledge." For there is something existing in the first natural stratum which "always lends itself interminably to an analysis that constitutes in it distinct and definite elements, elements that can al-ways be grouped into specifiable sets, always possessing sufficient proper-ties and of the excluded middle, and classifiable in terms of hierarchies, permitting the juxtaposition or unambiguous interconnection of hierar-chies" (p. 228), a "formidable example" of which is embodied in "the person of the living being." Castoriadis's final observations in this section on the living being seem to suggest not just that it is amenable to our identitary-ensemblist organizations but that being contains in itself a stra-tum which is already in some way organized, that is, in which "sets" are preformed. This may be because at this point the only stratum of being that is interpreted as indeterminate is that of the social-historical. Be that as it may, the capacity to ensemblize is not limited to the social-historical; it is also to be found in nature, and as an already ensemblized nature. However, if living beings already perform identitary-ensemblistic opera-tions, how much then can these be said to be an "ontological creation" of the social-historical (as *legein*)? Can "sets" be said then to be an "ontologi-cal" decision in the sense that Castoriadis meant it, if living beings—and anthropos in its dimension as a living being—make/create/construct the same ontological world?

In this early stage of his ontological turn, Castoriadis characterizes liv-ing beings as "identitary automata." He takes a generally Aristotelian view of the organism in that he considers them as self-moving, but they are seen to simply *organize* (in the sense of elaborate) the world rather than create their own *Eigenwelt* (as he was later to propose a decade or so later), their "transforming filter" notwithstanding (p. 232). A prefiguration of creative *physis* is evident here: Living beings organize objective elements of the world as information/events (even the living being has a being of doing) for themselves by partial selection, rather than finding a given order in nature (Castoriadis does not yet speak of the relation of the living being to the first natural stratum as a process of leaning on). However, living beings are not seen as self-creating but self-organizing, nor do they seem to be characterized by an interior world: Castoriadis's elucidation of them remains firmly rooted in their constitution by *legein*. Even when they lend "weight" or "value" to objective elements, they do this by way of a "series of mechanisms" rather than an enacting of (proto)meaning.

At this point, Castoriadis introduces a preliminary interpretation of the inseparability of the *organizing* subject from the *organizable* object, which he will later develop in the 1980s. In so doing, he moves from Kant's first *Critique* to the third, and his beginning ventures into his problematization of Kant's "*glücklicher Zufall*." Yet he struggles with a sense of partial determinacy, for, if the first natural stratum is organizable, it must also in some sense be partially formed. In other words, the first natural stratum cannot be complete chaos; if it were complete indeterminacy, it would be formless. Castoriadis tends to stumble at this aspect of the required elucidation. Part of the difficulty is that for him the "kosmos" that is interwoven in the chaos is an order of *meaning* (p. 46), and since he has radically separated significatory *meaning* from ensemblistic-identitarian *organization*, he does not have the resources to adequately address it. Thus, the first natural stratum does not just consist in ensemblizing living beings, and ensemblizable aspects of living beings and inorganic nature, but is somehow already ensemblized in itself.

Anthropic being is sundered for Castoriadis. He adopts a strict demarcation between anthropic being in its animal aspects as a living being (p. 233) and in its significatory aspects as the social-historical.[26] At this juncture the dissimilarity lies therein that the living being is thinkable as an ensemble that establishes itself in and through other ensembles; the living being does not create ontological form, as does the social-historical. With the advent of radical *physis* in Castoriadis's thought, and the stronger emphasis on ontological creativity of the living being, the demarcation between anthropos and the organism is maintained, but is drawn along different lines. The distinguishing point becomes the capacity for *autonomy* and the difference between autonomy and self-constitution.[27] If the metaphor "automaton" is apt for the living being, it loses all import in reference to the social-historical (p. 234). The social-historical institutes a world of *meaning*, which for Castoriadis points to the existence of "entities" for the social-historical that are in no way drawn from an organization of the first natural stratum. On his account, these are primarily "supernatural" creations, such as the gods, myths and so forth (with the very important exception of "democracy"). In the same way, the question of "nonbeing" is still a signification suffused with meaning, rather than the absence of a presence. Another point of contrast with the living being is that "noise," per se, does not exist for the social-historical. Rather, in echo of Merleau-Ponty's point that the human condition is to be "condemned to meaning," Castoriadis argues for the absolute requirement of signification in the social-historical, itself the defining marker between the social and the animal (p. 235). The relationship then between the social-historical and the first natural stratum is characterized as one of partial dependency, but, through the advent of signification, the leaning on by the social-historical "ontologically alters" the first natural stratum, whereby the "signification" of the social-historical is privileged over the "ensemblist organization" of the (human) living being, which for all intents and purposes ceases to have any relevance in the face of signification.[28]

At this point, Castoriadis makes a decisive move by proceeding toward an implicit emphasis of the being of signification over the being of doing: "The institution of society is the institution of a *world of significations*—which is obviously a creation as such, and a specific one in each case" (p. 235, emphasis added). Here we see that it is the creation of a world of significations that separates social-historical being from anthropic-animal being; from here, an elucidation of the being of doing becomes increasingly less prominent in his philosophical elucidation. To think of the social-historical world's self-creation as a world of signification is already to suggest—or anticipate—a critique of reason, especially modern forms of reason in that the institution of infinite pursuit of pseudo-rational mastery over nature, evinced by the cultural project of capitalism and modern science, also has cosmological implications in that it challenges the idea that the world comprises a fully rational organization amenable to scientific manipulation and control. The world is not transparent to reason; that is to say, it is not an identitary-ensemblist organization. Thus to posit that the social creation of a world of significations exists to cover over the occasional gap in the world's rational organization is misplaced and indicative of the modern entrenchment of the institution of reason. From another angle, the social-historically created world of significations serves to problematize Lévi-Strauss's reduction of mythical thought to classificatory thought.[29] What appears to modern rationality as "lacunae" in the first natural stratum, "actually appear as lacunae of this sort only on the basis of the institution of unlimited interrogation within the horizon of identitary logic. The given is logically or rationally incomplete only when completeness has been posited as logical or rational completeness" (p. 237).

Here, I suggest, Castoriadis's critique of mathematical reason is linked rather more closely to an implicit critique of the excesses of modern forms of the rationalist imaginary than his comments at the beginning of the chapter would indicate.[30]

The first natural stratum cannot be ignored by the social historical—it provides stimuli and supports, and a place must be found for it within the/each world of significations. However its stimuli are never directly "taken up" as it were, but are mediated and ontologically transformed by the magma of instituted significations. In this way its mode of organization is no longer that of the ensemblist mode of the first natural stratum, but rather is inserted into a matrix of significations. At this stage of his philosophical trajectory, Castoriadis operates within a quasi-dualistic framework, similar to Kant's first *Critique*, his attempt at bridge building through *Anlehnung* notwithstanding. There is a gap between human and other modes of being. Human modes of being, in the case of the psyche and the social-historical, are ontologically creative; they are supported by a quality of indeterminacy. Other regions of being are implicitly (and sometimes explicitly with the case of the living-being) understood as determined. At this point, Castoriadis is not challenging the determinist imaginary *in toto*; it would seem to have a significant grasp on natural domains of being. The analysis of *legein* and *teukhein* shows being cannot be simply "known" in a direct fashion; knowledge of being (or, better, our encounter with being) is mediated through a categorical schema of *legein* and *teukhein*. *Legein* incorporates a form of elementary reason as identitary, ensemblizing reason, which extends even into the realm of nature (as living being). *Legein* has a dual status in anthropic modes of being: First, the constitution of the "world" *qua* living being, and, second, the institution of a social-historical world of signification via social *legein* that still necessarily incorporates an identitary-ensemblistic dimension. In this way, we organize, create, separate, transform, and invest what we know with signification—in order to know it—rather than it being the case that our knowledge reflects the merely given order of nature. Not only does it plumb the depths of the living being, but *legein* also has a relation with the natural world *tout court*, for, if we can *ensemblize* the given natural world, this implies that it in turn is *ensemblizable*. Castoriadis's notion of the world as ensemblizable is discussed at an earlier stage in his trajectory, in the 1971 "The Sayable and the Unsayable," his homage to Merleau-Ponty.[31] In SU, his discussion is more directly focused on language, and his subsequent shift to a discussion of *legein* within the auspices of language in the *IIS* shows the radicalization of meaning from the confines of language proper to a focus on signification. There in SU, as here in the

IIS, he begins to critique Kant's "happy accident" (SU p. 125) and, thinking in Merleau-Ponty's wake, finds no final separation between subject and object. Even though Castoriadis focuses on the being of the social-historical, and not on humans "as a herd of bipeds," nonetheless, he cannot and does not dismiss this level of anthropic being. There is a seeming and unexplained gulf between the two, and the fact of "signification" does not seem to adequately bridge it.

Nonetheless Castoriadis does want to argue that, in a sense, signification as the mode of being of the social-historical bridges the gap. In the world of the living being, irrelevant information appears as "noise." For the social-historical, however, there is "no irrelevant information; the irrelevant exists only as a limiting case of the relevant" (p. 235). This brings Castoriadis to the crux of the social-historical and its leaning on the natural world—the world of the social-historical is always endowed with signification—therefore always weighty with meaning. Even at the limits, it is only through the possibility of signification that "noise" can be distinguished as without meaning and as irrelevant. From the point of view of an identitary automaton—"a completely formalized calculus" as in the case of the living being and anthropic animality—for something to be is to say that its form is determined (as an instance of a given *eidos*); the form further governs its entry into a predetermined "syntax of operations." However, in the case of the social-historical, to say that something *is* means that it signifies/that it is tied to a signification: "the institution of society is the institution of a world of significations," and, as such, ontological creation is a way that the positing of "is" by the living being is not.

The Proto-Institutions of *Legein* and *Teukhein*

Legein and *teukhein*, as primordial institutions of the social-historical, delineate our ways of articulating/making being. Through their elementary categorical frameworks, they point us to the social-historical's mode of being as one of creative institution, as well as to the limits of reason in thinking being. Our access to the world does not occur via unmediated reason nor the purely (natural) senses; it is not naturally determined, rather we think/experience/construct/do through categories. For Castoriadis these categories are not "natural," nor are they individually constituted; they are created and instituted by, through and as, the social-historical. *Legein* and *teukhein* regulate and imprint general frameworks on our encounters with being; they function as quasi-Kantian categories. Hence Castoriadis incorporates a dual approach to the meanings of being—epistemological and substantive. "Being" within the determinist imaginary can only be thought via a corresponding and consubstantial logic and vice versa.

As discussed, the social-historical emerges from—and as—nature, but also ruptures natural being, and being *qua* being. How does the social-historical achieve this simultaneous transcending and prolonging of nature? Castoriadis argues that it does so through signification. Here we continue to see the being of *signification,* as the social-historical *qua* social-historical, gradually becoming more privileged over the mode of being of *doing.* Castoriadis approaches the being of signification—and *legein* —through language. Or, from another perspective, his emphasis on meaning emerges from an engagement with and radicalization of phenomenology and the linguistic turn of the structuralists. Indeed, Castoriadis writes in the concrete context of the structuralist debates of the 1960s and his work is often a polemic directed against Lévi-Strauss and his notion of a "super reason." Here a strong Merleau-Pontian element is apparent in Castoriadis: Meaning presupposes language but is not collapsible into language.[32] For Castoriadis, there can be no linguistic meaning without reference to a translinguistic context, which, moreover, provides support for the emergence of new significations (p. 238). Castoriadis explains that language is bifurcated into a more general division of meaning: *Langue* and *code.* As *langue,* language is the repository of significations, but significations are not exhaustible by language as *langue* transcends the structural aspects of language. Language as *code* on the other hand refers to *legein* in the broadest sense as the ensemblizing dimension of not just an external (natural) world, but more broadly organizing itself in an identitary or univocal manner as an internal aspect of language itself. *Legein* as code takes in language, but also incorporates operations beyond language. Language is always of necessity a code: It exists only by instituting itself in, by, and as an identitary dimension as well as instituting a system of ensembles; that is, in its abstract material aspect, as a formal system, formalizable into distinct elements of grammar and phonetics (p. 239). In this vein, Castoriadis suggests that *legein* as code is comparable to the ensembles of formalizable mathematics. In its signifying aspect, language as *code* is also present, especially in terms of designation, properties, and linguistic terms (such as sentences, words): "It is evident that the ensemblization of the world (implied in counting out a herd of goats just as much as in sending a man to the moon) is consubstantial to the institution of language as a code of significations and that the former operates in and through the latter" (p. 239). Not only present in rational "concepts," the identitarian-ensemblist dimension paradoxically penetrates into the indefinite, indeterminate magma of significations themselves, in that it must be graspable in at least one of its aspects as definite and distinct. It can never be a closed system unto itself, as significations can always refer to something beyond themselves, and as such a magma of significations is always in some sense *open*. A signification is an indirect pointer to something else: "We can describe it only as an indefinite skein of interminable referrals to something other than (than what would appear to be stated directly)" (p. 243).[33] Castoriadis continues to elaborate the magma metaphor through an almost poetic evocation of social-historical being (but it implicitly incorporates the extended interpretation of transregional being as *à-être*) that reveals its geological context as well as the importance of metaphor as an indirect route to knowledge. However, the paradox of the poetic openness of significations as magma is inescapably entwined with ensemblistic-identitarian logic: "In this magma, there are flows that are denser, nodal points, clearer of darker areas, bits of rock caught in the whole. But the magma never ceases to move, to swell and to subside, to liquefy what was solid ant to solidify what was almost inexistent" (p. 244).

Legein's primary operation, on the other hand, is designation. The seemingly simple declaration "this is called . . ." already incorporates "the entire bundle of operators that we normally think of as separate and separable" (p. 244).[34] A *Kategorienlehre*—commencing with the category of identity—begins to be discernable in a way that draws on the ontological approach of Aristotle and the epistemological perspective of Kant. The sign (in a non-Saussurean sense) is a concrete but distinct instance, and formal *eidos* is a type of sign in a *sui generis* relation between the two (p. 244). The graphic abstract material form of the *eidos* is identical with all other instances of the *eidos* in the relation of a universal figure, in which, in a further process of ensemblization and objectification, the object can appear as a separable-separate member of a class (but not confused with the class per se). Finally, it is grasped as identical and self-identical in the substantial sense of *Selbstheit*; thus, "in positing a sign, the social imaginary, for the first time in the unfolding of the universe, brings identity into existence, an identity that does not, and cannot, exist anywhere else" (p. 245).

Underlying the self-identity of *legein* as category is the signitive relation—the social-historical aspect *par excellence*. In its magmatic diversity, the signitive relation defies ensemblistic operations in an interplay of two *eide* as the particular and the universal (again drawing on his earlier interpretation of Merleau-Ponty in SU, pp. 130–31) as an institution of the *quid pro quo*: "the relation between the sign and the object as absolutely specific, unanalysable and unconstructable, which posits and takes both terms together as co-belonging, although between them there is no real or logical relation of any sort" (p. 245). As a "re-presentation" (p. 246)— and in an echo of the sophist arguments of the conventionality of language—it is an institution *nomô*; that is, it is conventional. Underlying *legein* as designation and identity is the object and subject, which further presupposes the signitive relation held together by phantasma as the radical imagination. Here, the all-pervading importance of the imagination starts to appear for the first time in the *IIS*—and with it the reiteration of the link between Castoriadis and Heidegger of the *Kantbuch*. That being said, its presence is more latent in this chapter on *legein* and *teukhein*. Castoriadis tells us:

> But what is also put into play by the signitive relation is a concrete material-sensuous figure (usually audible or visible) which is a sign only inasmuch as it exists as sensuous without matter for the members of the society in question, beyond the concrete existence of any particular individual. Sensuous without matter: this is precisely Aristotle's definition of the phantasma, the phantasy, the "image." (p. 246)

In the above passage, Castoriadis merges together Aristotle's approach to the imagination as the *making be* what is not present, with Kant's insight in the first *Critique*, from which he later retreated, of the imagination at the very basis and root of reason. As such, the imagination can be interpreted as "the other of reason." Although often in shadows or occluded, the creative imagination completes the operations (and substance) of reason. Castoriadis takes the problematic of the imagination a step further than Kant, however, and posits it rather as the social-imaginary, which he defines as follows: "Imaginary: an unmotivated creation that exists only in and through the positing of images. Social: inconceivable as the work or the product of an individual or a host of individuals" (p. 247).

Legein as the overlap of designation and the signitive relation is a fundamental institution of the social-historical and provides a partial response to the dilemma of the border zones and lines of (dis)continuity between the social-historical and nature. Although particular signitive relations encounter the natural world and must respond to its context, "an abyss separates this from the institution of a system of signs" (p. 248). The signitive relation is impossible to construct and is irreducible to identitary logic operations. In a critique of informational and cybernetic approaches, Castoriadis argues that a sign does not designate a (logical) object, but evokes a magma of open-ended meanings in something that stands in for something else. Indeed the signitive relation creates/institutes the relation between the sign and the object: "Designation (re-presentation, *Vertretung*), *quid pro quo*, is original institution" (p. 247). Castoriadis points to the intrinsic overlap of *legein* and *teukhein* and again points to the social-imaginary in its twofold aspect of doing/representing and the necessity of the instrumental "doing" and "representing" of *teukhein* and *legein*. The institution of ensemblist-identitarian *legein* and *teukhein* is "still itself a doing and a representing—a 'making be' as presentation, a figuring and a figure; the institution of *legein* and of *teukhein* as such is still a *legein-teukhein*" (p. 249). Thus the signitive relation is distinctively human and synthesizes and radicalizes tendencies already existing in nature.

The signitive relation is irreducible to psychologism (pp. 250–52); it can only be thought as a social institution, not as an egological constitution of associations. It is not present in the psychic flux of representations. Although the psychic flux is at the base of language, it cannot account for it; we have the ability to conceive of representations in the mind as examples of many others. The designatory relation refers to something in the world.[35] The signitive relation is instituted: Castoriadis provides us with a definition of institution as neither real nor arbitrary, in an implicit allusion to Husserl, who, in Castoriadis's view, did not develop his notion of *Stiftung* far enough: "Particular realizations of the object-sign relation by each individual can exist only because signitive co-belonging and rules themselves exist as social, as instituted—that is to say, as non 'real,' as without any particular place or outside of any place ('real' or 'logical')" (p. 251).[36]

Criticizing logical and psychological approaches, Castoriadis critiques Kant's inability to account for the signitive relation and its institution in *The Critique of Pure Reason*. What is called logic is the visible face of *legein* and the signitive relation is its infrastructure. Logic becomes semi-naturalized, and enters at the ensemblistic-identitarian level. The signitive relation exists in and through an indeterminate totality of rules and categories: Castoriadis proceeds to show the indissociability of these aspects of *legein* from each other and their reciprocal inherence (pp. 252ff). In the universe of *legein*, the signitive relation functions in and through a network of indeterminate totality of reciprocal references. It implies the operative schema of value (standing for something) in an allusion to the Marxian terms of exchange and use-value, and thus—to use a different language—the distinction of *Sein* and *Sollen*. The signitive relation proposes an equivalence, that is, exchange value. Its use-value encroaches on *teukhein*, in serving for *um . . . zu.* In terms of Castoriadis's critique of reason, at this very elementary level, it can begin to be argued that *Sein/Sollen* are mutually articulated or interrelated. Critiquing the idea of the evolutionary appearance of language, Castoriadis argues against a gradual emergence of language and the impossibility of conceiving it as such; instead he argues for it as a sudden and total emergence.

The signitive relation "circularly implies the operative schema of value" in two different forms: the first is *standing for . . . (being valued as . . .)* (p. 253). In *legein*, if a sign can be apprehended as *this* sign, it consequently has the same value of all other occurrences of *that* sign at a given level (and with respect to . . .), and can subsequently be substituted and exchanged for one another: "Equivalence appears as absolute equivalence or perfect substitutability between all the material realizations of a sign provided that these are at least minimally discernable" (p. 253). Second, the signitive relation implies the operative schema of *serving for . . . being valued as . . . (serving a given end, um . . . zu)*, or "use value": This refers to its combinatory value. *Legein* always consists of a system of signs at different levels; signs function through their combination at a given level. In considering *legein* as code, the possible combinations are definite and finite; in considering *legein* as *langue*, then possible combinations are not circumscribed nor absolutely determined, nor finite nor infinite, but rather indefinite. These two forms of the operative schema are indissociable and reciprocal, and exist/are instituted—that is, as the schema of value—simultaneously with the institution of *legein*, "for there is a separation between the abstract-material basis of *legein* from everything else, positing that a given ensemble of occurrences are not "natural events" but have the value of signs: They all stand for . . . they are equivalent in so far as they are signs and not events, and they all serve for . . . can be used for designation" (p. 254). Such schemata—*carrying over, iteration, composition, reciprocal inherence*—comprise a more or less hierarchical network of signs/combinations of signs and various orders and are instituted in and through *legein*, "corresponding to an identitary pseudo-world, coded by these signs and formed by distinct and definite 'objects' and by the distinct and definite "relations" between these 'objects'" (p. 255).

Inherited thought is but a particular kind of elaboration of the logic-ontology of the norms and necessities of *legein*, as all that can have value is that which can be made distinct and definite. In this context, existence and value cannot be distinguished. Yet paradoxically in the inherited tradition, the norm of *legein* as *logon didonai*, cannot be turned in upon itself to give an account of *logon didonai* as the nuclear scheme of *legein*. Inherited philosophy, although continuously elaborating upon *legein*, occults "the *legein* itself" and its own relation to it. For philosophy cannot give an account of, nor take into account, the key schema of *legein*, of the signitive relation, but instead acts as if its ontologies (of things, ideas, the subject) were not mediated by *legein*, that is as if *legein* were a "totally transparent optical medium or a perfectly neutral instrument" (p. 259). In the same way, inherited philosophy needs to also occlude the "end point that the institution of *legein* constitutes for its work—since philosophy knows only the contingent and the necessary, and *legein*, which is neither 'contingent' nor 'necessary,' is that on the basis of which alone necessity and contingence can have any meaning at all" (p. 258). *Legein*, then, as a primordial institution, cannot be grasped by identitary logic, for it (the institution) is "neither necessary nor contingent, since its emergence is not determined but is that on the basis of which, in which and by means of which alone something determined exists." The signitive relation—representation (*Vertreten*)—is irreducible and necessary and is as such "arbitrary" or *nomic*. Determinacy as an ultimate norm is thereby abolished.

Legein involves an essential part of reflexive categories and concepts, but it cannot be constructed on the basis of these. Although the understanding is implied in *legein* and cannot be separated from it, it is only a part of *legein*; that is, *legein* cannot be reduced to it. The institution of *legein* is the implicit institution of understanding and of the signitive relation, but the understanding cannot construct nor produce the signitive relation. The implementation of the categories of the understanding is not possible external to the signitive relation: "Because there is no thinking subject, no thought without language" (p. 259). Here, Castoriadis specifically addresses Kant's transcendental philosophy. From a transcendental perspective, if the object is to exist/be constituted, it requires an initial "genericization/symbolization" of the object (of that which is not yet an object) in relation to "itself." Likewise, no object "is" (constituted) if it is not caught up in relations of causation and reciprocal action, which imply other objects, gradually extending to include the totality of phenomena. Either this totality is present each time "in person" whenever I think of an object—which is absurd—or it is there without being there, and, in particular, it is re-presented there; something that is not it is posited for it and as it "in its place"(p. 259).

As an element of "*legein*," the understanding is instituted. For Kant the understanding is "the faculty of binding according to rules"; yet there are no rules outside the institution. It is the institution that makes for the possibility of rules, and rules are implied by and posited with the institution. In the same way, the categories are also the operative schema of *teukhein*, and are the "results" of a *teukhein*: "Thinking in accordance with categories is making (something) be . . ." (p. 260).

If *legein* is the *Urform* of theoretical reason (as *logon didonaî*),[37] *teukhein* is the *Urform* of practical reason: It is the relation of finality, that is, the realization of possibilities.[38] *Legein* and *teukhein* overlap to a very great extent. In a sense, *teukhein* is a *legein* and vice versa: They refer to and imply each other. Yet, each has a singular characteristic that is absent in the other: In *legein* there is the *signitive* relation, whereas in *teukhein* the *transformative* relation is present. *Teukhein*, as the primordial institution of "doing" in its identitarian aspects, refers to "assembling-adjusting-fabricating-constructing" (p. 260). Instrumentality and finality are characteristic of its mode of being; in this vein, *technique* is a particular development of *teukhein*.[39] If the signitive relation is indicative of *legein*, the transformative relation is characteristic of *teukhein*: *Teukhein* makes something be that is not (p. 262). The *quid pro quo* is something *in view of* something else, not *in place of* something else. Thus, at the root of *legein*, the creativity of action at its most elementary form is found. *Teukhein* brings into being the realm of explicit possibilities as action (the schema of possibility), when we think in terms of things that can be done as a transformative aspect of possibility and impossibility:

> It is in and through the interweaving of society the interweaving of the possible and the impossible that society as a whole and every society in particular constitutes the "real" and its own "real." Reality is not only as has been repeated since Dilthey, "that which resists"; it is just as much, and indissociably, that which can be transformed. (p. 262)

Legein established the institution of reality as the possible/impossible. In this way, reality is socially instituted, whereas as possible/impossible it is a secondary distinction in *legein* (as a code) of obligatory/impossible, which is not so much an impossibility but an exclusion. With *teukhein*, however, it is a "genuine bipartition," in which the "real" exists in bifurcation (p. 263). Within this, the possible is posited as determined: "that which is, in each case, possible, and that which is not is definite and distinct," as well as with the means of transforming the possible into the actual as determined by the presence or absence of its power-to-be.

The imagination is latently present in *teukhein* (as it was in the signitive relation of *legein*) in its transformative relation to *legein*. Both can be transfigured into phantasms, for example, *teukhein* via technique in an imaginative relation of finality (itself pointing to the creativity of finality). Moreover, *teukhein* exists only as the work of the social imaginary, as an *eidos*, in order for it to be real. This finds its parallel as the imagination in the individual, as "the representation of that which, possibly, will be, in other words, the power-to-posit as capable-of-being that which is not" (p. 264). *Legein* then embodies and brings into being the ensemblist-identitary dimension of language/social representing, *teukhein* that of social doing. At its limits, *legein* points to the incoherence of the "pure formal system closed up on itself (p. 264); at its limits *teukhein* points to technique for its own sake, as in the capitalist imaginary—"Technique *stands* today *for* the pure social delirium presentifying the phantasy of omnipotence, a delirium which *is* in large part the 'reality' and the 'rationality' (with but even more without quotation marks) of modern capitalism" (p. 265)—but this positing itself is an imaginary institution.

Legein and *teukhein* each exhibits two aspects: Objective reflexivity and an identitary dimension (pp. 266–68). Regarding objective reflexivity, *legein* and *teukhein* presuppose themselves in the inescapable circularity of the circle of creation. The identitary dimension is also inescapable: *Legein* and *teukhein* can only exist by referring to terms that are singular/unique. Finally, regarding the *Kategorienlehre*, a Kantian connotation reappears in Castoriadis's critique of genetic neo-Darwinism (p. 268). In a nutshell, Castoriadis argues that instead of Darwinian approaches, variables are to be thought of as being transmitted by historical societies in their institution; the institution is in this context interpreted as a radicalization of the transcendental *Ich* as being capable of accompanying all *Vorstellungen*.

Finally, Castoriadis looks to the historicity of *legein* and *teukhein*. There is the possibility for greater "progress" in the material base of *teukhein* than in the "invariance" of the abstract-material base of *legein* as language. All this presumes that *legein* and *teukhein* are historical: They alter themselves. *Legein* and *teukhein* can only be thought of as institutions. The signitive and transformative relations distinguish *legein* and *teukhein* from each other; combined, these two aspects separate *legein* and *teukhein* from their manifestations in nature. It recalls the institution of a collectivity *as something*, which always already entails a magma of imaginary significations (p. 269). The living being, on the other hand, is nothing other than its *legein-teukhein*, as an identitarian-ensemble. What all this means for Castoriadis is that *legein* and *teukhein* are "absolute" creations of the social-historical. The *legein-teukhein* of the living being is characterized by functional closure, whereas the social-historical institution of *legein* and *teukhein* is "potentially the means of an unlimited opening onto what, at the start, was not taken into account in its organization." It is always possible for new "things," "*eide*," and "modes of being" to emerge. In this context, *legein* and *teukhein* "are intrinsically extensible and transformable" (p. 270) as an ontological explosion of meaning and possibilities, in what is a double and radical innovation of two new realms of being.

In elucidating a regional ontology of the social-historical, Castoriadis became entangled in elements of epistemology, whose aspects were not always fully visible on the horizon. The ghost of Kant appeared, and, in addressing the proto-institutions of *legein* and *teukhein*, Castoriadis began to develop a critique of elementary reason. Yet, in so doing, Castoriadis did not lose sight of its ontological basis: The Kant to whom Castoriadis appeals is mediated by Heidegger's *Kantbuch*. In this vein, the imagination, although latent (this more so for *teukhein* than for *legein*) is clearly posited at the root of reason. It thus bridges Enlightenment and Romantic currents of cultural modernity. But it is not until Castoriadis moves more to the thematic of the third *Critique* that the synthesis deepens further; he begins to move in that direction by focusing on Kant's "happy accident" that he first adumbrated in his early paper on Merleau-Ponty (SU). At first glance, and as signaled by Castoriadis in the chapter on the social-historical, *legein* and *teukhein*—as the means by which ensemblistic-identitarian logic is elaborated—would seem to have an indelible hold on the social-historical, despite it being the very mode of being purporting to elude their grasp. On closer inspection, however, they paradoxically point to the social-historical as a mode of being *nomô* (that is, as human institution) as creation and institution of form. In this way Castoriadis's critique of elementary reason challenges both the egological and constitutive aspects to Kantian approaches: Reason is instituted. The emphasis on *legein* and signification in language points to a gradual fading of the being of doing from Castoriadis's primary philosophical agenda; illustrated, for example, in that most of the elucidation of the two elementary institutions was devoted to *legein*. Yet *teukhein*, in many respects, is the more progressive of the two. Castoriadis began, too, to be confronted with the border zones between nature and the social: how to answer the problem of the "natural" or "animal" aspects of anthropos? The main point of difference between the social-historical and nature is the appearance—or institution—of signification in the former. A strong Merleau-Pontian element emerges in Castoriadis's discussion of *legein*—the signitive relation in particular—as a primordial institution that is part of, but not reducible to, language.

In summary, within the horizon of his elucidation, two intentional and two unintentional elements to his articulation of *legein* and *teukhein* may be distinguished. The first was an exploration of institutional infrastructures, where elementary mechanisms are found to be always and everywhere at work, and where the elementary forms of institutions and creativity are isolated from the ensemblistic-identitarian dimensions. The second aspect was an elucidation of elementary institutions as elementary forms of rationality, and here he begins to articulate the imagination as the other of reason. Three less intentional aspects were also discernible. First, the analysis of institutions sees him fall into epistemological entanglements as the Kantian dimension came into view. Second, the being of "meaning" gradually eclipsed the being of "doing" in his elucidation. Finally, the tensions apparent at the interface of the social and the natural begin to mount. In introducing the *Verlegenheitsbegriff* of *Anlehnung*, he attempted to elucidate a connection of selective leaning on as creation; yet this posed more questions than it solved. I noted, too, that although Castoriadis began to build bridges between nature and the social-historical—in contrast to the radical dualism of Kant—the living being was reduced to its ensemblistic-identitarian aspects. The radicalization of creation is yet to appear on the horizon, although partial openings can be discerned. The exploration of the border regions between anthropos and nature does not end with the living being. The next chapter emphasizes Castoriadis's approach to the radical imagination and interpretation of the psyche as being more than nature but not yet fully human. As such, the psyche is *between nomos* and *physis*.

Anthropological Aspects of Subjectivity

The Radical Imagination

Castoriadis's philosophical anthropology of the subject is found in the chapter of the *IIS* called "The Social-Historical Institution: Individuals and Things." Here an elaboration of the psyche as radical imagination is placed in the foreground.[1] The imagination was an incipient theme common to Kant, Freud, and the phenomenological movement, but with Castoriadis it was radicalized to become the very cornerstone of subjectivity and self-hood. In some ways, parallels with the chapter on *legein* and *teukhein* are discernable in that both chapters investigate the borderlands between the social and the natural.[2] At first glance, a focus on the mode of being of the singular psyche might seem out of place in a reflection on the social-historical, yet from its beginnings psychoanalysis also incorporated an endeavor to comprehend society, history, and civilization.[3] In this vein, Castoriadis's foregrounding of the psyche is not a move away from the social-historical. Instead, the psyche is articulated primarily as the basis for addressing philosophical and anthropological aspects of subjectivity by way of the radical imagination, and thus to open a complementary perspective on the social-historical.[4] The move to elucidate the mode of being of the psyche marks a split in the creative imagination: For Castoriadis, it consists of the two, mutually irreducible poles of the radical imagination of the psyche, on the one hand, and the radical imaginary of the social-historical, on the other. Connecting them, as will be discussed, is Castoriadis's specific notion of *sublimation as socialization.* The chapter on the psyche continues the Kantian motif; here we see Castoriadis interrogating Kant and proceeding to deeper layers and questions of subjectivity. Overall, Castoriadis situates himself between phenomenological and structuralist approaches to subjectivity. Like the structuralists and poststructuralists (although in varying ways) before him, he, too, takes off from Freud; or more strongly, he leans on Freud to develop his own thoughts.

Castoriadis approaches subjectivity through the lens of psychoanalysis, and builds on Freud's explicit as well as implicit legacy. Castoriadis's analysis of the psyche seeks to show that the creative imagination is not only at the very center of the institution of the social-historical, it is also the basis of subjectivity. For Castoriadis, however, the philosophical interpretation of subjectivity had to begin with the psyche rather than the individual; the individual in this sense is always the "fabricated social individual" located betwixt the psyche and society.[5] His critical engagement with structuralist debates continues to be apparent, but this time the emphasis shifts from Lévi-Strauss to Lacan. Castoriadis proposes a reinterpretation of Freud and psychoanalysis, yet in these respects he is somewhat selective and brief. There is no attempt to ground his theory in clinical experience, nor is there any sustained attempt to link his theory to Lacan.[6] It is the only part of his philosophical elucidation that properly "leans on" another modern discipline (that is, psychoanalysis), but Castoriadis's argument does not ultimately depend on the psychoanalytic universe. Nonetheless, psychoanalysis is used as a theoretical launching pad from which Castoriadis builds a polarizing model of psyche and society, in which they are not only mutually irreducible but in a fundamental sense also in the end inaccessible to each other. For Castoriadis, "society" is characterized by social-historical modes of being that are unreachable by inherited methodologies. The psyche, on the other hand, is part of nature, but because of its defunctionalized character it is simultaneously *more* than nature. Despite the polarization of the radical imagination and the radical imaginary, Castoriadis also finds points of mutual interplay—for example, some psychical drives are better understood to be social-historical institutions.

Castoriadis's main argument proceeds along two paths: The first reflects on the construction of the psychic monad and its implications for subjectivity; the second considers the social-historical content of sublimation (in the triadic phase, the monadic closure is broken and its unity is now in the background), and how the two aspects connect. Another way of approaching this is to look at the mode of being of the unconscious as the flux of representations of the radical imagination and its link to a radically other mode of being: social-historical signification. The first approach is transcendental, in a broad sense, in that it critically examines the presuppositions and preconditions of subjectivity. Simultaneously it reveals a Kantian aspect to Freud in that Castoriadis posits the monad as a precondition of subjectivity and rationality—that is, he uncovers the primal unconscious as deeper even than the Freudian unconscious. The second path considers the social-historical and the social-historical content of sublimation, as the diversity of human meaning in its fullness can neither be contained nor produced from the psychical monad. Here it is important to Castoriadis's theory that not only are the psyche and the social-historical irreducible, but also inaccessible to each other.

We are made aware of the link between the social-historical and the psyche by the chapter title: "The Social-Historical Institution: Individuals and Things"; the focus will be on how individuals and things emerge as such—and acquire meaning as such—in the space demarcated by the psyche and the social-historical. Castoriadis opens the chapter with a recapitulation of his critique of ensemblistic-identitarian logic that he developed in the previous chapter: All modes of being are only partially congruent to its organization (p. 273). A reiteration of his critique of Kant's Copernican turn is discernable, the limits of which are highlighted by the reference to a "happy accident" in the third *Critique*, as Castoriadis is clear that the preconditions of knowledge do not simply lie on the side of the constructing, transcendental subject. On the contrary, the world lends itself to organization, although as shall be made clearer in subsequent discussion, Castoriadis balks at postulating a similar link between the world and signification, that is, a notion of the world as amenable to meaning or, perhaps better, as *sinnfähig*. Furthermore, when Castoriadis continues his opening discussion of the partial grasp of ensemblistic-identitarian logic, with an allusion to the situation in physics, and suggests that "The questions and the aporias with which contemporary physics struggles refer to a mode of being underlying the physical entity, a mode that cannot be grasped by means of identitary logic" (p. 273), an implicit reference to what will later become the more fully fledged radical *physis* and magmatic nature becomes discernable, especially in regard to the link between ontology and epistemology. He does not elaborate further at this point, however, moving instead to the more "acute" regions where this may be felt: to anthropic being, in the first instance, and, to the psyche, in particular.

Before he addresses the psyche proper, Castoriadis first makes some preliminary remarks on the being of the world, albeit limited to the world of significations as a mode of being that eludes the grasp of identitarian-ensemblistic logic (p. 274). Here it is pertinent to reiterate that the "being of the world" is an important if submerged theme in his philosophical elucidation. The "world as a shared horizon," to draw on Johann Arnason's turn of phrase, is ambiguous for Castoriadis's thought, especially in the 1975 section of the *IIS*, and, indeed, remains so. Nevertheless, Castoriadis's continual return to Kant's observation of the "happy accident," and subsequent criticism that "to be organized" must also signify "to be organizable," indicates an implicit—and ongoing—concern with the being of the world.[7] In the *IIS*, Castoriadis considered only one aspect of the world: the social-historical world of significations. Later during the period where he was more preoccupied with the notion of "*physis*," especially during the 1980s, the concept of the world metamorphoses into a plurality of worlds, and within his later polyregional ontology of the "*for-itself*," the creation of an *Eigenwelt* is considered inherent to all of its levels and modes.[8] However, the problematic of the world *qua* world remains in the shadow of the social-historical world of signification. Castoriadis already moves in this direction in the chapter on the psyche. In his view, the psyche is a monad totally closed upon itself; its ontological condition neither includes openness toward nor connection with the world. In this sense, the monad exists in a strange kind of limbo, as the being of the world can only be encountered in the first instance as a *social world*. While there is a tradition in psychoanalysis in which the psyche is seen as enclosed upon itself, the "monad" proper draws on Pythagorean and Platonic sources: The One that is Everything. Although the image of the "natural world" is present in the *IIS* (and its characteristic of being "organizable"), its being is only discussed in the margins of the more systematic articulation of the being of the social-historical world. The monad escapes ensemblistic-identitarian logic and brings us into direct contact with magmatic modes of being and with a deeper layer of reality. It may be understood as a proto-subject and a microcosm; *physis* in miniature (although it is in another sense more than *physis*). It has emancipated itself from the constraints of the living being and reproduces the totality of *physis* as closed upon itself.

The Unconscious, Representation, and the Monad

Castoriadis reiterates that the difference between the modes of being of the psyche (representations) and the social-historical (significations) are radically other (p. 274). Then he proceeds to discuss representations in general, and relativizes the boundary between the conscious and unconscious. He takes a detour through the unconscious, sensitizing us to its mode of being, that is, *representation*. The mode of being of representations for Castoriadis is—as with signification—irreducible to identitarian-ensemblistic categories. Indeed, it is the mode of being in which identitarian-ensemblistic logic has the least grasp. The mode of being of the unconscious holds a preeminent place for Castoriadis, and the image of

Heraclitus's ever flowing, ever altering river finds its epitome in Castoriadis's understanding of the psychic flux. The radical imagination is conceived as the psychic flux of representations, and ensemblistic-identitarian logic (and accompanying ontology) finds itself practically useless there: "The unconscious, Freud wrote, is unaware of time and of contradiction" (p. 274). An identitary order and logic does not exist for the mode of being of unconscious representation and the necessity of interpreting the unconscious through linguistic terms and relations should not obscure this fact. Unaware of its own mortality, the unconscious is a magma not only of representations, but also of affects and intentions (Interestingly, Castoriadis first introduced his idea of the magma in the 1968 paper ETSS in specific reference to the psyche).[9] Castoriadis strongly repudiates Lacan's suggestion of the importance of metonymy and metaphor and his positing of the unconscious as linguistically structured. Rather, metonymy and metaphor, as modes of waking language, originate from the mode of being of the unconscious (p. 275). This represents a development in Castoriadis's thought from ETSS, where he embraced the metonymic and metaphoric qualities of the psyche, and the symbolic aspect had a much greater presence. More generally speaking, Castoriadis disputes Lacan's depiction of the unconscious as being structured as a language: For Castoriadis, the psyche is radically different from language as representations appear neither as distinct nor definite.

Psychoanalysis provides us with a model of the mind. Castoriadis radicalizes this by positing something deeper than the Freudian unconscious: The primal monad. His view of representations as the real content of the psyche has affinities with the phenomenological, especially Husserl's critique of Kant.[10] Castoriadis makes this point in an even more radical sense than Husserl: The idea of the psyche as made up of representations is radically different from the over-ordered Kantian mind. Castoriadis can be understood as trying to make philosophical sense of "the stream of consciousness"—but by beginning at the level of the unconscious. His discussion of representations, in a reference to the first half of the *IIS*, in the 1965 chapter on the "Imaginary and the Institution" (p. 139), revives the distinction between "perceived" and "rational": Representations are neither perfectly rational nor simple perceptions. An implicit reference to Merleau-Ponty and his concept of perception is clearly discernible.[11] The image and representation are complementary; it is through representations that the imagination expresses itself. Representations are both indeterminate and creative. Yet despite the thoroughgoing inability of ensemblistic-identitary logic to grasp the being of representation, mathematical metaphors creep into Castoriadis's analysis. Following Cantor,

Castoriadis argues that representation is an "inconsistent multiplicity" (p. 277)—a term reprised from his 1968 paper (ETSS 32)—as a mode of being that is simultaneously singular and manifold, where representation is neither "indifferent nor decisive" by ensemblistic-identitarian logic (p. 277 and ETSS 32). The earlier paper makes clearer that the elements of *legein*—for example, "impossible, necessary"—are irrelevant in the psychic domain.

Identitary logic, which is at this point solidly anchored in the psychical realm, loses its grip when the social-historical and the world of imaginary significations are considered. This situation holds also for the social-historical institution of the individual, that is, "the transformation of the psychical monad into the social individual for whom there exist other individuals, objects, a world, a society, institutions—things none of which, originally, has meaning or existence for the psyche" (p. 274). Castoriadis establishes the psyche as monadic in contrast to Freudian formulations; he traces its journey from an originary completeness, via socialization to the social individual. Representation is not only both one and many, but furthermore, it is a being where such designations/relations are neither "decisive nor indifferent" (p. 277). The meaning of a representation and meaning in general is located also in the psyche and then *only* as a representation, which, although in the tradition of the real/rational interpretation, the imaginary mode of being is reduced/eliminated. The mode of being of the unconscious, as exemplified by dream-thoughts, remains without a conclusion, undetermined, and indefinite. They are meanings—or rather, proto-meanings—in a magma; meanings which cannot be distinguished following the schema of identitary logic (p. 280).

Representation originates in the psyche—in the radical imagination—and cannot be explained according to "real" factors. For Castoriadis, Freud's essential discovery was the imaginary element of the psyche, even though Freud himself did not refer to the imagination, and his positivist presuppositions—translated into a search for the positive reality of the psyche—prevented him from grasping the significance of his own insight. Yet the role of the imagination reappears in his recognition of the central importance and relative independence of fantasy for the psyche (p. 282). It is inherent to psychic life, but its relation to other elements of psychic life remained to be explained, but, within the limits of traditional thought, such explanations are doomed to failure, as they look for the origin of representation external to representation itself, that is, they look to inherited methodologies and ontologies. The psyche, however, is the very thing under investigation: "The emergence of representations accompanied by an affect and inserted into an intentional process" (p. 282).

That is, there is no real and external (or internal) referent for representations; they emerge from the psyche itself as a flux of creative representations. It is a completely new mode of being that creates itself.

Castoriadis takes us through possible ways of understanding the origin of representations. The first under consideration is the *Trieb*, or *drive*. Drives are manifest only as representations, but even postulating a bridge between the psyche and the soma cannot provide an account of the form or content of the representation in affects. From this Castoriadis concludes that the psyche is itself "the capacity to produce an 'initial' representation, the capacity of putting into image or making an image (*Bildung* and *Einbildung*)" (p. 282). This links into his fusion of Kantian and Aristotelian approaches to the imagination (as pointed to in the previous chapter). The source material and the organization of this representation, however, still need explanation. The psyche has the (at least minimal) capacity to organize into an experience what would otherwise simply remain a chaos of impressions. The psyche is formation and imagination on a radical scale. Castoriadis argues that psychical life's existence depends on this original capacity of the psyche to not only cause representations, but also, an originary representation that further "contains within itself the possibility of organizing all representations—something that is formed and forming, a figure that would be the seed of the schemata of figuration" (p. 283). It is the "radical imagination that makes a 'first' representation arise out of a nothingness of representation, that is to say, out of nothing" (p. 83). This is the first time in the *IIS* that Castoriadis refers to, even if somewhat obliquely, his central notion of creation as *ex nihilo*. In fact, he had already referred to it explicitly in the earlier ETSS (p. 25). Yet, this is somewhat misleading, for, as a monad, creation cannot be *out of nothing*, but can only be *out of itself* and nothing else. Here it is worth mentioning that Castoriadis later makes a point of emphasizing the dyadic context as essential for creation in an explicit critique of inherited traditions—such as the Pythagorean and, in this context for Castoriadis, also the Platonic—of the unity of the "one,"[12] since it is only with the invention of the dyad that alterity and otherness can first be spoken: Within the "one" there can only be identity and the same.[13]

Castoriadis goes on to demonstrate that these ideas were implicitly present in Freud's thought. Freud's "originary phantasmatization" becomes, in Castoriadis's hands, the radical imagination, preceding and presiding over the organization of drives. It is at the primal level of fantasizing that the psyche has the capacity to produce *out of nothing* something that is meaningful for it (p. 285); it takes precedence to drives. Yet Castoriadis notes that thinkers from Klein (1965), to Laplanche and

Pontalis (1964), have been unable to distinguish between the constituted and the constituting phantasy-phantasmatization: The original psychical subject is the primordial phantasy that is "at once the representation and the investment of a Self that is All" (p. 287). Finally, Castoriadis takes up Freud's distinction of the "reality principle" and "hallucination" (which also implies the "real"): The mother's breast, or its absence, and the ensuing fantasy that posits its image as "real."

Castoriadis begins to build toward his notion of the psyche as monad. In tracing an originary state and primal phantasy, Castoriadis argues that the original psychic state must also exist as representation. Some accounts characterize phantasmatic formations as potential/actual distortions of the real, which leads to an antinomy of "the real"; it is posited as the capacity "to produce out of nothing something that possesses a meaning for it" (p. 285). Other theorists have tried to trace a primal phantasy, too: Castoriadis mentions Laplanche and Pontalis in this regard (p. 286), and gives them credit for realizing that in such a phantasy there is no distinction between subject and nonsubject. The originary state of the psyche aims at coinciding with the total scene; the originary psychical subject is the primordial "phantasy," "at once the representation and the investment of a Self that is All" (p. 287).

More orthodox Lacanian accounts of the subject (and society) posit the imaginary formations as a "response" to a situation (of the subject or of society) that would already clearly be defined outside of any imaginary component, on the basis of "real" (or "structural") givens (p. 288). These accounts stress the Lacanian (desiring) subject's quest for the initial lost object and originary split within the subject. In all these cases, the function imputed to the imaginary is that of replacing or covering over this gaping hole at the very core of the subject's being, rather than seeing the imaginary as creative of (psychical) reality itself, that is as positing itself as a desiring subject that simultaneously constitutes itself as desiring subject by constituting an object as desirable. *Anlehnung* (*anaclasis*) characterizes the original relation between psyche to the biological-corporeal reality of the subject, which, as seen in the previous chapter on *legein* and *teukhein*, Castoriadis transposed to the social-historical leaning on the first natural stratum where the relation between the natural and imaginary strata is interpreted as one of creation rather than one of determinacy. Hence the psyche takes up the somatic data and "takes them into account." Fantasying as the emergence of representation (and its alteration) evinces the radical imagination as creation; that is, not caused by an "object." The psyche makes something be, and also, in the same moment, can make it be as *lack,* as a presentification-figuration (p. 290). The idea of absence or lack—the absent breast—points us back to an originary mode of psychical being, as "representing-representation to which nothing is "missing," to an aim-intention-tendency of figuring-presentifying (in itself) through representation which is always realized" (p. 290). At the level of the originary unconscious, "to say that there is an intention, an aim, a "desire" is to say *ipso facto* that there is a representation which is this intention as something realized, in the sole reality which exists" (p. 291).

Castoriadis addresses Freud's conviction that in the psyche there is "no index of reality" for the unconscious (p. 291). As such it belongs to another region of being: The radical imagination brings itself into being and "makes be that which exists nowhere else and which, for us, is the condition for anything at all to be able to exist" (p. 292). Psychical reality comprises representations. Psychical reality consists of representations that connect up. Evoking Kant, Castoriadis recognizes—with Freud—that there are rules that organize the representations and their relations, but they are not ensemblistic-identitarian. The first posits that there is nothing gratuitous in that the realization of unconscious intentions is ever present (p. 292). Second, connecting representations is a charging of affectivity. In this way, the question of the unconscious psyche and its reality is also the question of the origin of representation, the origin of relation, and the origin of the pleasure principle as an intention aiming at an affect. But unconscious representation consists in the ultimate indistinction of separate moments. In relation to the unconscious, concepts/ elements/processes such as "reality," "external," "rationality," and "truth" have no meaning whatsoever: Neither then "reality testing," nor representation of words as words that convey some kind of rationality. Moreover, and important for his later trajectory, Castoriadis argues that there can be no distinguishing of "internal" and "external," as is the case with the later "subjective instance" of the *for-itself* and the creation of an *Eigenwelt* and an internality.[14] Instead there can only be representation, prior to all such distinctions, of "*everything* (as) *self*, of *self* (as) *everything*" as the only reality of the psyche (p. 293), but strangely, this "self" cannot be seen as part of the "subjective instance" for this would require an internality. For Castoriadis it is autistic rather than primary narcissism as it excludes any sense of self-reflexivity, which finally points to a proto-meaning as anchored in the unlimited pleasure derived from the omnipotent and omniscient mode of being of the self-enclosed monad.

For Castoriadis, the core of the psyche's being is monadic. In its originary "state" and "organization," the subject is entirely self-referential: No distinction is made between it and the "world," or rather the "world" is at the same time self, proto-subject, and proto-world (p. 294). The triadic aspect—representation, affection, intention—is at this point an undivided affect, whose "being is meaning" (p. 294). Recent discussion, however—in particular, Gauchet (2002)—has cast doubt on the polar model of the (neo)Freudian monadic psyche as unaware of the self and its limits to an opening toward reality. Gauchet argues, instead, that the psyche must be understood as in some way ontologically open to the world, which in turn coexists in tension with trends toward closure and "the blurring of personal boundaries" (Gauchet 2002:10).[15] Interestingly, a little later in the *IIS* (p. 335), there is an ambiguous opening within Castoriadis's own thought that might facilitate an internal relativization of his elaboration of the psychical monad. There he says that "the psyche doubtless contains as potentiality its opening up to the world" (p. 335). Castoriadis also problematizes the status of the monadic psyche as subject. At this point, recall that the terms "subject" and "social individual" are not yet explicitly differentiated. How can there be "meaning" for a Self that is All, that is, for a being that neither opens onto the world nor to other "selves" (social or psychical), for a being that is not yet a subjective instance but a self-enclosed totality? How can there be a meaning that is not socially instituted (perhaps the idea of "proto-meaning" better characterizes this region of being), or at least a "meaning" that would signify its non-social status? To distinguish at this stage between representation and "perception" or "sensation" is impossible. Instead the subject at this juncture is conceived as "totalitarian inclusion," autistic in the sense of undivided; the subject is in an undifferentiated, monadic state. In this way, the subject is not only the totality of the subjects in and the organization of the scene: it is the scene of the fantasy element of an initial "state." The psyche suffers the breakup of its monadic "state" imposed upon it—in the triadic phase—by the "object," the other and its own body: "This loss of self, this split in relation to the self, is the first work imposed on the psyche by the fact of its being included in the world" (p. 297).

Sublimation and the Social Institution of the Real

The social institution of the individual (i.e., the socialization of the psyche) is inseparable from the two histories of psychogenesis and sociogenesis. It is in this psychical history that the psyche alters itself, and participates in the social-historical world. This process is dependent on both the psyche's own creativity and "the history of society's imposition on the psyche of a mode of being which the psyche can never generate out of itself and which produces-creates the social individual" (p. 300).

The social individual emerges as the combination of the "always impossible and always realized" of a private and of a common/public world. How do things, individuals, a world, a society exist for a psyche, which is in no way "predestined by nature" for them? Reality is not given, but constituted, together with the subject; or, rather, reality as socially instituted reality irrevocably confronts the subject. At this stage of the socialization process, the subject is not yet conversant with "significations." The significance of the Oedipus situation—via the confrontation with the institution of signification, and the institution as the ground of signification (and vice versa)—is the way by which this is achieved. In other words, it is necessary and sufficient that the child be referred to the *institution* of signification and to signification as (anonymously) instituted. In this way, "only the institution of society can bring the psyche out of its originary monadic madness" (p. 309). Proto-meaning will continue to be important in the unconscious, but over and above this, the establishment of the "reality ego" opens for the subject access to the horizons of meaning and signification, where the two poles of meaning encounter each other and bring the other into the being of the world.

In the context of the current work, the key element of Castoriadis's elucidation of the psyche is his approach to sublimation and the psyche.[16] Sublimation is the "socialization of the psyche considered as a psychical process" (p. 311). In brief, Castoriadis rethinks Freud's somewhat underdeveloped notion of sublimation. It is the violent invasion of the forms of the instituting radical imaginary—and its social meanings as imaginary significations—into the psychic flux of representations as radical imagination, and into its region of proto-meaning, such that, as Arnason argues "proto-meaning becomes an inexhaustible source of surplus meaning which can be transmuted into diverse forms in different domains of culture" (Arnason 2000, p. 9). Each pole of the creative imagination comes into play: Two versions of "meaning" are activated. Sublimation then is the establishment of the intersection between the private and common worlds respectively. In this way, escape from a public reality into a private world (of psychosis) is always *ipso facto* flight from reality that is socially instituted, and not "naturally" given. The process of sublimation replaces furthermore the psyche's "private" objects of cathexis with socially instituted objects and meanings, with "common language" and "social doing" illustrative of this process.

Although Freud recognized the social nature of reality in *Totem and Taboo*, he did not connect it to the problematic of sublimation. Castoriadis's interpretation of sublimation, however, is not primarily focused on the Freudian account of the desexualization of drives. He sees it as the founding of an intersection between the two modes and regions of being; the psyche must now take its objects in *another* mode of being and relations than previously. Here Castoriadis evokes the magma again, and it is worth quoting him in full:

> Thus it is henceforth another object, because it has another signification, even if it is "the same" physically and even if, for the psyche, this separation is never truly realized and the "successive layers of lava" corresponding to the successive formations of the object are not only shot through with volcanic openings but are almost never entirely solidified. (p. 313)

For Castoriadis this change of object heralds the "making be" of individuals and things for the subject: "Objects" no longer exist for the psyche. For example, the representation of "mother" holds in this way as a magma for the psyche. Sublimation and repression are not mutually exclusive but exist in different modalities and charges: The sublimated "tender mother" coexists with repressed desire for the mother as an erotic object.

Once the social individual has been constructed, pleasure ceases to be "organ pleasure" and becomes representational pleasure. It transforms both its object and source, paradoxically reminiscent of the originary context in which for the psyche pleasure *qua* pleasure was representation (p. 315). The social individual is created by creating herself—at once objectively, through common states of affairs and relations, and subjectively in that these things and individuals are for herself. When taken by itself, the psychogenetic process is insufficient to account for the formation of the social-individual and to resort to biologically determined accounts is similarly unhelpful; each disguises the role of the social-historical (in its social and historical aspects). The social-historical form of capitalism, to use Castoriadis's example (p. 318), could not survive without the daily reproduction of "capitalists" and "proletarians" instead of "peasants" and "feudal lords." The psyche, however, cannot produce the "capitalist" world of significations from itself. In this way, being a "capitalist" individual and all that this involves would only be a phantasy or delirium, if it were not able to be realized as a social actuality, and psychotic if their respective processes of sublimation did not push them to become walking fragments of the institution of society. In contrast, however, the psyche as radical imagination forms the positive condition of the existence and the functioning of society; the constitution of the social individual cannot ever abolish the psyche's creativity as "the representative flux as the continuous emergence of other representations" (p. 321). That is, there is always representation, and, as a magma, the psyche's mode of being is not completely graspable by us. The emergence of otherness as representative flux is always both temporalization and spatialization. In an allusion to Kant, Castoriadis tells us that there is no thought without representation; thinking is always necessarily putting representations into motion, albeit, in certain directions and according to certain rules.

The inherited tradition has occluded the being of representation; it has been thematized in inadequate ways or relegated to the faculty of intuition, thought, or perception as in the Kantian and phenomenological traditions. Its being as radical imagination remained unrecognized; it eluded the grasp of traditional onto-logics (p. 330). Representation shatters the determinist imaginary of Western thought. The problem has been that representation has not been considered for itself but has been seen in regard to truth or knowledge or access to the being regarded as determined by an elsewhere. It has been interpreted as a copy—generally defective in some way, an image, and a perpetual source of error. It is thought via "the subject" and "the thing" and not in terms of its own organization: "It then becomes a set and stable 'spectacle,' a painting hung 'within' the subject, a defective tracing of the 'thing,' a weak ended and retained perception" (p. 331). It is rather the "incessant flux" in which things can and must be given, and then is in excess of every posited figure. It is what makes the invisible radical imagination visible as "immanent transcendence" (p. 331); representation is the very means through which a world emerges, not an impoverished image.

Perception and things emerge in the history of the subject. Contrary to psychological and egological approaches, perception is socially instituted and cannot be approached solely from ideogenetic contexts (p. 334). It is so in general, and specifically each time as *this particular* institution within *this particular* magma of imaginary significations: The individual is not transcultural; or rather, there is no transcultural individual.[17] Perception is not just "social vision"; it is possible only within language (language itself can only be thought of as a transcendental—as a qualified not "pure"—condition of perception) and hence is caught up in significations of meaning.[18] Imaginary significations animate and inhabit "things" and give them their meaningful content: "We are unable to think of an individual perception essentially independent of the social institution of the individual, of the thing, of the world" (p. 355). Castoriadis turns to critique the schematism of Kant's Transcendental Aesthetic (p. 337). Social *legein* produces operative modalities of representation, but they are borne—in an unmotivated way—by the two poles of the creative imagination. If the imagination is the other of reason, then representation is its mode of being as "pure intuition" by making a figure emerge and presenting it as the source of all logical operations and to their "respective *place* in a 'space' and in a 'time'" (p. 337). In a reiteration of a point made in his discussion of the *Timaeus*, Castoriadis characterizes Kant's space and time as but mere particulars of a receptacle and as independent of all content. What traditional thought has overlooked is the emergence of otherness, which can only exist as the incessant creation of other figures. "Pure" space and time can only be so for a second-order reflexive separation. The egological aspect of Kant's critical philosophy is moreover subverted by the irreducibly social-historical nature of language, whose assumed absence makes the transcendental subject incoherent in communicating to itself.

It is interesting—and significant—to note that the being of the world crops up here, toward the end of the *IIS* chapter on the psyche (pp. 333–34). The world appears between the poles of the psyche, the social-historical, and their mutual encounter at the nexus of the social-individual. To have access to a world means that the subject is—both "transcendentally and ontologically"—within language in general, as well as within a particular language.[19] The world horizon, like "things," is itself a social-historical institution in need of perpetual questioning and articulation as creations of the radical imaginary. But, the subject is not reducible to a social-historical institution; it is, as has been shown, also anchored in the psyche: The social individual always exceeds the social-historical institution,

> so that psychology . . . is the logical-transcendental condition for all ontology for all reflection on things and the world, on beings and being. A world and things (and a logic) are possible only to the extent that there is a psyche and the madness of the psyche. (p. 336)

Here Castoriadis seems to vacillate between the language as social-historical and the psyche-subject as the "true transcendental" of the world. Despite Castoriadis's general emphasis on the social-historical, he often seems to lend more weight to psychological phenomena, to which the discussion of *Anlehnung* in the previous chapter also alluded. The final few sentences of this particular *IIS* section are rich with the presence of Merleau-Ponty's later thought (p. 336).[20] Castoriadis refers implicitly to contexts of the visible and the invisible, of the given caught up in the not given "in an undefinable host of shadows which, far from constituting that which simply 'could not exist' each have a peculiar tenor other than *that which* is seen" (p. 336). "Thickness" and "depth" exist outside only because they are also inside. The imaginary—in its two irreducible poles—is the transcendental condition of the real.[21]

For Merleau-Ponty, the ultimate ground is the world as horizon of horizons, that is, the ultimate context for all experience, or the ultimate *Sinneszusammenhang*. This sense is closely related to the world as the domain of cultural articulation, and the subject as being-in-the-world.[22] As mentioned, the world horizon appears here, but again, remains undeveloped. The social individual exists in a relation of openness and closure between the psyche and the subject, but it is ontologically always already open to the horizon of the world, and *opening* the horizon of the world in the sense of "doing." Castoriadis closes his early paper on Merleau-Ponty (SU), with these words:

> The circularity of the singular being, or this singularity of the circular being, which is bound with the circularity of what there is in a circle not superimposable upon itself, presents us with a reversibility conditional upon an irreversible relationship, that between mind and world, which brings it about that the spirit is in the world, but as the other. The subject is not an opening in the sense of a window or a hole in the wall. "The open, in the sense of a hole, that is Sartre, is Bergson, is negativism or ultra-positivism (Bergson)—indiscernible. There is no *nichtiges Nichts*" (VI 196). It is opening, then, in the sense of the work of opening, constantly renewed inauguration, performance of the primitive spirit, the spirit of praxis. Or, in other words: the subject is that which opens. (SU 143–44)

Returning to the text of the *IIS*, in the closing paragraphs of the chapter on the psyche, if it is the being of the subject which "opens" the world, then it is the being of the social-historical that provides the primordial opening: "To say that it is only in and through the institution of society that there is an opening up to the world does not block this opening—in a sense it even widens it" (p. 338). The *overlap* and *coexistence* yet mutual *irreducibility* of private and common worlds makes the world and the question of its being emerge in the first place: Neither path of enquiry can be done away with. In contrast to traditional thought, the mode of being of representation and the world are not in opposition. In an implicit opening onto civilizational themes and intercivilizational encounters—as long term, historically meaningful patterning of the world—each social-historical world as a *kosmos idios* creates its own world, and "accepts that of others when it encounters it only by including it in its own, reabsorbing it, digesting it in one way or another—in order to recognize that in and through their different, particular worlds, and only in this way, is a world created or does it exist as a world" (p. 339).

The being of the subject that "opens" the world is surely the subject in the narrow sense of the autonomous subject who puts the instituted world into question. What of the social individual? The implications of the "social individual" or "the socially fabricated individual" are not fully explored by Castoriadis. In the 1980s, as we shall see, he speaks of the autonomous subject as a separate level of *for-itself* from the really existing "social-individual." As such, the "subject" for Castoriadis is one that can lucidly and self-reflectively question the existing, social institution; the subject can "open" the world. In this vein, the social individual would seem to tend toward a heteronomous instance of subjectivity. As we saw, moreover, in the previous chapter on the proto-institutions of *legein* and *teukhein*, the social-individual was characterized by Castoriadis as a *teukhein*, which is fabricated in view of a particular end. Castoriadis elucidated subjectivity as part of the being of "doing" (*teukhein*) and not "signification" (*legein*). In this vein, the psyche—and psychoanalysis—is primarily seen as a poietic-political *activity*. The being of doing has been transmuted from its original place in the social-historical to the realm of subjectivity. The social-historical as the anonymous collective, cannot be understood primarily in terms of subjectivity as lucid activity, rather it is the anonymous temporalization of the magma of self-altering significations and, although it is anthropic, it is not human. The social individual is "human," but not necessarily autonomous.

In opposition to the psychoanalytical reductionism of some interpretations, Castoriadis's elucidation of the psyche has taken us from one pole of the creative imagination to the other: From radical imagination to radical imaginary. They are irreducible to each other. As such, there is a certain *imbalance* between them: It is easier to portray the idea of *ex nihilo* on the level of the psyche, and easier to portray meaning at the level of the social-historical.[23] Castoriadis does want to posit meaning at the level of the psyche, however, and also wants to argue for creation *ex nihilo* at the level of the social-historical. In some ways, this indicates an uneasiness between the two levels of thinking, for the creation he has in mind is primarily creation of new meanings. That being so, there are reasons to expect a reorientation of the whole thematic, and indeed, this will be encountered with the later rethinking of *physis* as creative. Between the psyche and the social-historical, then—and enveloping them—there is the hovering being of the world. On Castoriadis's account, the psychic monad as a deeper, more primal layer than the Freudian unconscious is characterized by the flux of representations as radical imagination. Representations form a kind of proto-meaning for the psyche, which, through the process of sublimation, encounters the other, irreducible dimension of meaning: social-historical meaning as signification. Sublimation is just that: The sometimes violent encounter of the radical imagination and the radical imaginary from whose ashes the social-individual as subject and the being of the world emerge as meaningful. The present chapter has primarily addressed one dimension of meaning—that of the radical imagination and representations. The following chapter focuses on the more clearly elaborated pole of meaning in its full sense: the radical imaginary and social imaginary significations. This will provide an opportunity to build a broader perspective on the problematic of meaning and the world horizon, and their respective places in Castoriadis's thought.

4

Hermeneutical Horizons of Meaning

Merleau-Ponty famously wrote, "because we are in the world, we are *con-demned to meaning*" (1962, p. xix). Castoriadis would seem to agree, at least in the writings predating his ontological turn. For example, his 1971 homage to Merleau-Ponty—"The Sayable and the Unsayable"—discloses a rich meditation on the importance of the world in the formation of sociocultural meaning (SU). With the onset of his ontological turn, how-ever, Castoriadis increasingly recasts his elaboration of *meaning*, not only in terms of its sociality but also—and most especially—with respect to its world relation. More and more, Castoriadis understands the human condemnation to meaning along ontological lines that bypasses the phe-nomenological insight that we are always already *in*-the-world. Castori-adis continues to elaborate meaning as fundamental to the human condition, but it is increasingly cast in ontological terms, where the social-historical creates *ex nihilo* "its world as *the* world" (p. 359; emphasis added).[1] Ricoeur and Merleau-Ponty, each in his own way, accepted that latent meaning contexts provided the infrastructure of world articulation; this was obscured in Castoriadis's thought. Ricoeur's account of meaning incorporated an analysis of understanding (along Heideggerian lines as a way of *being-in-the-world*), but Castoriadis resisted this conception. By way of contrast, although it could be argued that where Merleau-Ponty hesitated at the ontological implications of the imaginary element (and the creative imagination, more generally), Castoriadis embraced them.[2] Unlike Merleau-Ponty, the problematic of the world tends to be more ambiguous and underdeveloped in Castoriadis's thought. This holds implications for his overall ontology. Thus even though Castoriadis does find us "condemned to meaning," the Merleau-Pontian echo is not only an affirmation, but a twofold point of difference as well. In the first instance, the phenomenological problematic of the world appears as an omnipresent, albeit subterranean theme in Castoriadis's thought. In the wake of his ontological turn, the "role" of the world—and the human condition—is reconfigured along ontological lines as *magma* that both exceeds and marginalizes the phenomenological context of our *being-in-the-world*.[3] In the second instance, Castoriadis's most important contribution to an elaboration of meaning, as will become clear, is his link to the creative imagination, in general, and to the *transsubjective* (or *asubjective*, in Patočka's terminology) contexts of the radical imaginary, in particular.

In the final chapter of the *IIS*—the topic of the present chapter— Castoriadis focuses on the being of social imaginary significations, which, despite his protestations to the contrary, incorporates an interpretative element to creation, as well as an a creative element to interpretation. Over the course of the present chapter, I reconstruct two moves: the ontologization of the world, and an implicit hermeneutical turn in Castoriadis's thought.[4] As we have seen, Castoriadis considers the creative imagination along two axes: the radical imagination and the radical imaginary. The radical imagination is the mode of being of the psyche and it provided the focus of the previous chapter, whereas the present chapter—which marks the final stage of our journey through *nomos*—elucidates the radical imaginary as an aspect of the social-historical. It opens, more specifically, onto Castoriadis's theory of meaning, which he links to the creative imagination and elaborates as an account of "social imaginary significations." Here we find ourselves confronted with the dual mode of social imaginary significations: their immanence within language as a social institution, on the one hand, and their mode of world forming, on the other. Compared to the previous *IIS* chapters, the final chapter is more unsystematic in character. Not only is it considerably shorter, it also reads as a series of exploratory moves in different directions that signal various future avenues of thought, or elucidations still to be completed. The endnotes, too, are sparse, a further indication of the lack of organization with which Castoriadis approached this chapter. The chapter is no less interesting for all that, however, with labyrinthine paths emerging and, in turn, diverging. Of most interest are three currents hitherto more or less marginal to Castoriadis's work: The first concerns the interpretative element to creation (and the creative element to interpretation), where, ironically, Castoriadis's observations regarding Merleau-Ponty's hesitations in approaching the being of the imaginary seem apt in light of Castoriadis's own reservations about interpretation;[5] the second concerns the ontologization of the world; and the final rejoins earlier questions concerning a general ontology and the reemergence of *à-être* in Castoriadis's thought.

Despite the generally unsystematic approach to the chapter on imaginary significations, Castoriadis's opening question is systematic in itself. He asks, "Can we go beyond a merely negative ontology and criticisms of the limitations of identity logic?" (p. 341). Not only does this indicate a shift toward emphasizing a more positive elucidation of his philosophical project, it also resurrects the ontological agenda first signaled in the earlier *IIS* chapter on the social-historical. Yet Castoriadis's progression beyond a negative ontology is somewhat mixed. In that it begins to expand its concerns beyond the human to non-anthropic regions of being, and to herald preliminary figurations of his more general ontology of *à-être* and subsequent ontological shift, the final chapter of the *IIS* bridges the problematics of *nomos* and creative *physis* (and thus also the first and second sections of the present study). Central to Castoriadis's later general ontology is the idea of being as heterogeneous, and as heterogeneously multi-layered; long present in Castoriadis's thought, it now reappears in the final *IIS* chapter. Finally, a consistent theme that appears in various guises throughout this chapter is the notion of being as the interplay of determinacy and indeterminacy, whether as *chaos* and *kosmos,* or as *peras* and *apeiron* (see GMPI).

The Ontologization of Magmas

Castoriadis's first move in responding to the question of the limits of negative ontology is to reintroduce the *magma* metaphor. As observed in the previous chapter, Castoriadis originally introduced the term "magma" in 1968 (ESS), where it seemed to epitomize the mode of being of the psyche as radical imagination.[6] As discussed in Chapter 1, the magma first appears in the *IIS* in the chapter on the social-historical, by which time Castoriadis had expanded its reach beyond the psychical region to include the social-historical and the imaginary regions as well, but, it is to be noted, he continued to restrict it to modes of anthropic being. In the *IIS* chapter on *legein* and *teukhein*, as well as in the chapter on the psyche, Castoriadis did not so much *denote* the magma metaphor, as *evoke* it indirectly through thick symbolic description indicative of its origins as a geological term.[7] Returning to the magma in the final chapter of the *IIS*, Castoriadis now proceeds in the first instance to broaden its scope of ontological reference beyond anthropic modes of being, rather than to more completely and positively elucidate its mode of being, which might have been warranted by his questioning the limits of negative ontology. He begins with a list of "new" domains of enquiry that challenge the grasp of identitarian logic, and which has expanded to include nonhuman regions of being as well, with cosmology and the auto-organization of living organisms chief among them. I observed in Chapters 1 and 2 of this book that the respective problematics of cosmology and the new biology were present in Castoriadis's thought as far back as MSPI, as well as in the *IIS*, as if promising incipient areas ripe for further exploration.[8] Here they begin to be configured more explicitly, and their relevance for an interrogation of the contemporary scientific context—that is, in regard to the status of objective knowledge in its various domains—is more evident. These expanded regions of magmatic activity begin to suggest a move toward a rethinking of the being of nature and opening up toward Castoriadis's later, transregional ontology of *physis* beyond social imaginary significations that will be the central focus in Part II of this study.

At this stage, Castoriadis indicates his opposition to the imposition of a unifying and universalizing logic-ontology on the diversity of magma in what would essentially become a transregional or general ontology (p. 341).[9] Instead he continues to emphasize the ultimate regionality of these significations and modes of being. On the other hand, although Castoriadis stresses the importance of regional ontologies, it is clear that at this juncture of the *IIS*, the magma encompasses at least a polyregional, if not yet clearly a transregional mode of being. This is despite its original emergence in conjunction with a very specific and singular mode of being: the dream. All in all, the mode of being of the radical imagination is however a mode of being *sui generis* in that, as I noted in the previous chapter, it is more than nature, yet not fully human.

Castoriadis now begins to link magmas to the long held Greek intuition that being is neither chaos nor kosmos, but a partially ordered, partially indeterminate mode of being (p. 341). In GMPI he observes:

> There was among the Ancients an implicit ontology, as found in the oppositions between *Chaos* and *Kosmos* and between *phusis* and *nomos,* Being is as such chaos—both in the sense of void (*chaino*) and in the sense of a jumble defying all definition—as it is *kosmos*, namely, visible and beautiful arrangement. Being, however, in no way is wholly "rational"; such an idea was excluded from the Greek conception of things, even in Plato. (p. 98)

As I noted in previous chapters, Castoriadis had intermittently drawn on the image of the interplay of chaos and kosmos, but he was not so explicit in respect to how this manifested in the natural substratum. Here in the final *IIS* chapter—as earlier—kosmos is elucidated as an order of meaning, which in this last *IIS* chapter is linked more clearly with trans-subjective contexts of culture and institution, in contrast to a world cons-tituting transcendental subject (p. 341). Yet despite Castoriadis moving to posit magmas in nature beyond the grasp of ensemblistic-identitarian logic, the metaphor of chaos implicitly carries with it residues of the "two world" tension mentioned above: If being were completely chaotic it would be neither amenable to organization (a point to which Castoriadis consistently draws attention when referring to ensemblistic-identitarian logic) as natural, nor formable (by social imaginary significations) as meaningful. Although it is apparent that Castoriadis increasingly regarded various regions of nature, too, as magmatic, the Enlightenment vision of a meaningless nature and meaning-conferring subject still holds sway in his thought; whatever "the being of nature" (the all encompassing if somewhat vague "first natural stratum") might be, it is malleable and *ontologically altered* by the forming power of imaginary significations and the self-instituting world. In this imagining of the first natural stratum, Castoriadis seems to imply a notion of Aristotelian *hyle* as the substratum upon which form can be imposed; nature as magma is not yet thought of in terms that could be aligned with a radical interpretation of *physis*.

The discussion of the meaning of being as situated between chaos and determinacy ends abruptly (p. 343). Without warning, Castoriadis em-barks upon a new section dealing with the magma proper. Here he begins to partially convert the notion of magma from a negative theory into a positively articulated one, which is somewhat reminiscent of Kant's strat-egy and changing characterization of the noumenal realm: In the *Critique of Pure Reason* it was understood as a negative limit, but was transformed into a positive source of knowledge for the *Critique of Practical Reason*. The first sentence of this new section is clearly Husserlian in tone, and echoes his call to return "To the things themselves."[10] Castoriadis's ver-sion goes as follows: "What we seek to understand is the mode of being of what gives itself before identitary or ensemblist logic is imposed; what gives itself in this way in this mode of being, we are calling a magma" (p. 343). The language, too, is now very different from the beginning of the chapter, shifting from the tone of scientific discovery and of qualifying scientific validity to a remembrance of the *Lebenswelt*, or Husserl's earlier and related, and arguably more important, notion of *Horizon*.[11] Castori-adis reintroduces the magma metaphor as a way of describing some-thing—or a mode of being—that presents itself to us before categories are imposed. Whereas in the first section of this *IIS* chapter he repudiated the idea of a single new logic that might lead to a transregional ontology, here he makes the first step to postulating an overarching logic (such as the magma).

Castoriadis offers three disparate statements about the magma. First, the notion of magma cannot be defined within received language. Second, he backtracks (p. 343) to offer a definition that "may not be unhelpful" (p. 343). Here the magma appears ambiguously, couched in ostensibly positive terminology, yet adumbrated as a negative counterimage to an identitarian-ensemblist set: "A magma is that from which one can extract (or in which one can construct) an indefinite number of ensemblist organizations but which can never be reconstituted (ideally) by a (finite or infinite) ensemblist compositions of these organizations" (p. 343). Finally, he moves to give an "intuitive description"—that is, drawing on oblique and symbolic language—of the magma metaphor where the magma reveals itself to be a description via language and the virtual totalities of significations that explicitly relies on an "accumulation of contradictory metaphors" (p. 344). Within this context, the idea of magma enables an ongoing interplay between indeterminacy and determinacy as a more positive version of the idea of being as *neither chaos nor order* previously introduced at the beginning of the chapter. Castoriadis concretizes the notion of magma by appealing to language in the next section "significations in Language" (p. 345), which, in drawing on the notion of everyday *Zuhandenheit*, will be essentially a phenomenology of language. In looking back on the progress of the chapter, we will see that Castoriadis ventured briefly toward a general ontology of the magma, but in the end, it ultimately served as a prolegomena to a discussion on language, itself acting as a bridge to his theory of meaning.

Meaning in Language

To be in language is simultaneously to accept to be in signification. This means to be in the midst of something that can never fully be brought under control or closed: There is always an excess of language (p. 350). Castoriadis's introduction of "language" as a theme is a new move in the *IIS*.[12] In this context, it is apposite to query where it is placed in relation to the social-historical and the psyche. Language, in Castoriadian terms, is neither reducible to the social-historical nor to the psyche; in contrast to the Lacanian perspective, it has an in-between status. The elucidation draws on examples from the lifeworld. Castoriadis argues that the unending emergence of new signifieds points to the living—that is historical, diachronic—nature of language, rather than to its synchronic aspects:

"The bundle of such referrals is therefore open." Yet, the identitary aspect is also included: "The word also refers to its referent or referents" (p. 345).

Here Castoriadis offers us a condensed theory of meaning through relativization of three dichotomies that prevail in conventional theories. He claims that each distinction has unwittingly confused the question and has therewith occluded the being of signification. They have further confused identitary *meaning*—which for Castoriadis would be an oxymoron—with its identitary *usage* (see p. 347) in that they each overdraw the demarcation between determination and indetermination and obscure the interplay between them. To illustrate his point further, Castoriadis again draws on the realm of lived experience. He notes that although, for example, computers and linguists alike would struggle with the complex processes and operations of significations and the open-ended possibility of determinations in language, in actual fact ordinary people—the example used by Castoriadis is "an illiterate fisherman" (p. 347)—can and do live with this interplay (in a pragmatic fashion that involves contexts of action). Each of Castoriadis's analyses offers a quick and preliminary sketch but not any sustained engagement with the theoretical issues to hand. The first relativizes the "naming" theory of meaning and the structuralist perspective, which rejects a direct relation between the word and thing, leaving a system of differences (pp. 345–47). Castoriadis rejects both sides of this dichotomy, and interprets signification to be a privileged referent simultaneously intertwined with an open "bundle of referrals" (pp. 345, 347).

The second dichotomy addressed by Castoriadis is the Fregian distinction of "*Sinn*" and "*Bedeutung*," understood as "inherent meaning" and "external referent" or "connotation" and "denotation" (pp. 347–48; see also Frege 1892).[13] However, the idea of the connotative aspects as optional and arbitrary, versus the firmly demarcated core of the referent, proves to be misleading, as there is an identitary use of meaning, that is, a point at which we choose on pragmatic grounds to draw the line between the two. Protestations to the contrary, Frege's distinction presupposes a very traditional metaphysics: that there is an Absolute Thing as ultimate, self-contained, and separate. Castoriadis here observes an Aristotelian infrastructure of the self-contained thing in itself as the enigmatic *ousia*. There exists a whole indeterminate network of relations and involvement between the two aspects: There is no determinate substratum, and there cannot be a connotation without reference to a denotation. Yet, similar to his critique of functionalism, in particular of Malinowski, Castoriadis does not develop these insights further to engage with more sophisticated versions of functionalism; he does not go beyond Frege to discuss further developments in analytical philosophy. There are other parallels to Frege's *Sinn* and *Bedeutung* to be found, most especially, for example, in phenomenology with Husserl's interest in the intentionality of meaning: Intentionality is always intentionality toward something.[14] In this way, meaning is a phenomenon that brings us forth toward the world. This has been taken up in different ways by phenomenological thinkers, for example, where Husserl emphasized intentionality toward the world, Heidegger emphasized our always already being-in-the-world. Yet Castoriadis neither discusses the intentionality of meaning, nor its radicalization in post-Husserlian, particularly Merleau-Pontian phenomenology.

Castoriadis's final *Destruktion* of conventional accounts of meaning is aimed at currents in literary theory and addresses the dichotomy of "proper" and "figurative" meaning (pp. 348–49). Instead of relativizing the two sides of the dichotomy, Castoriadis asserts that "[e]very expression is essentially tropic" (p. 348), and thereby privileges the figurative dimension. However, this also points to the inherently symbolic nature of meaning, on the one hand, and its openness (to the world), on the other. He thus suggests the possible relativization of his own distinction between ensemblistic-identitarian and signitive forms of meaning, which—although he points to their overlap—remain radically separate when it comes to the being of the world and its (ensidic) elaboration. A fourth feature to note about Castoriadis's discussion concerns the absence of the performative dimension of meaning-as-doing. This is exceptionally curious given his interest, proclaimed at the beginning of the second half of the *IIS,* in the importance of elucidating the being of social-historical "doing" as *making-be.* The importance of the being of "doing" as part of language was a theme present in the early SU but has now all but disappeared. This final (absent) distinction came to prominence with the later Wittgenstein (1953) and his idea of *Sprachspiele,*[15] and from another angle, the theory of speech acts as developed by Austin and then Searle.[16] Meaning is to be found in the ways that people use language or "do things by words."

Castoriadis proceeds to open two parentheses. The first addresses the practice of "sophistry" (p. 349), and here he limits himself to ancient Greek interlocutors. For Castoriadis, as with the metaphysical tradition, albeit in a different way, sophistry refers to the self-destructive use of language through the "implacable use of identitary logic" (p. 349), which precludes a single "referent" being embedded in diverse contexts of meaning (and hence not reducible to a unitary meaning): It embraces "truth as tautology" (p. 350).[17] There is, he asserts, a self-destructive potential inherent in language: He summarizes it as the demand within discourse itself for determinacy and its ultimate requirement for tautology (p. 350). The use of language is seen as a perpetual balancing act where absolute protection against destruction of coherent discourse cannot be guaranteed; whoever takes that path will also destroy himself as a speaker in the process. The second parenthesis is predicated on the distinction between punctual and contextual meaning. It warns against the isolation of the identitary-ensemblist dimension of language in a distinguishing between denotative and contextual functions. For Castoriadis, however, there is no strict separation between language as code and the contexts that go beyond that code. In this vein, it is interesting to note that he seems to think that "context" is too trivial an expression which cannot properly evoke the interplay between the two sides of signification: *peras* and *apeiron*.[18] However, it is essential for language that that due space is given to the wider interplay of determinacy and indeterminacy that backgrounds its figurations of meaning.

To sum up: The initial question that Castoriadis poses in this chapter on social imaginary significations concerns moving beyond the limitations of negative ontology. The first step comprised an identification of a whole series of fields where inherited thought was manifestly inadequate. These fields now begin to extend beyond anthropic into natural modes of being as well. Castoriadis highlights the essential regionality of significations: Not only is the elaboration of more regional ontologies required, so, too, is a dialogue between the elucidations of the various regions, as well as with philosophical questions. Castoriadis is cautious about any general ontology, yet he begins to implicitly consider the idea of a general ontology with the extending reaches of magmatic modes of being. Nonetheless, in his view, a general ontology would be premature; instead there needs to be a serious of heterogeneous, regional ontologies. There is, at first glance, no direct connection in this *IIS* chapter between subsections ("Significations in Language" and "Social Imaginary Significations and 'Reality'") as Castoriadis's claims concerning language and signification have no obvious bearing on what he goes on to argue about social imaginary significations. In this way, it can be said that the second section seems to serve the purpose of anchoring the notion of magma. Here Castoriadis moves to take the first steps toward reconceptualizing language and laying the foundation for a new philosophy of language; this supports the view that this final *IIS* chapter consists of a series of exploratory moves neither closely nor systematically linked.

Meaning and the World: A First Approach

Although there is no explicit connection, Castoriadis's prior elucidation of meaning is presupposed as a kind of tacit background to the final part of the *IIS* chapter where Castoriadis turns to address the being of signific-cation proper. This section spirals out in different directions, too. Three can be identified in particular: The first addresses the relation between social imaginary significations and nature; the second looks at the more intimate relations between imaginary significations and "social objects"; and the third draws attention to the world.[19]

In addressing the relation between social imaginary significations and nature, Castoriadis recapitulates the idea of *Anlehnung* and its presence in the social-historical region (pp. 353–54). The relation between the first natural stratum and social imaginary significations is neither causal nor instrumental. We are dependent on it but recreate it in our social image. Here we can see that the images of *peras* and *apeiron*—and their inter-play—reappear, albeit in a different context. Although Castoriadis aban-dons the notion of *Anlehnung* when he moves to consider social objects, an alternative does not emerge. It could be speculated that such an alter-native would need to include an interpretative dimension and, as such, was unattractive for Castoriadis's main purposes. Instead, the sudden re-emergence of the world as an integral part of the social-historical is dis-cernable. It is not just that signification is the mode of being of the social-historical, but that significations create a world "and nothing exists as so-cial-historical which is not signification, caught up in and referred to an instituted world of significations" (p. 354). Thus two aspects to the social-historical can be found: Creation of significations in language, and the creation of signification in—and as—a world. This would seem to sup-port Arnason's (1988a) argument that sociality (*Sozialität*) and world rela-tion (*Weltbezug*) are to be regarded as the two primary aspects of meaning, yet Castoriadis brings a perspective that is quite distinct from Arnason's more phenomenologically oriented approach.

On Castoriadis's account, the social-historical creation of a world of significations truncates—or, in his stronger statements, rejects—the sense of the social-historical encounter with, and articulation of, the broader world horizon. Or, rather, he implicitly maintains that the world in some way encounters the social-historical through the process of *Anlehnung*, that is, only the ensidic level, by which it is ontologically altered (p. 354). Given that the ontological alteration of the first natural stratum by the social-historical has no equivalent in the psychical realm—the "leaning on" by the psyche does not ontologically alter the first natural stratum—it is questionable whether *Anlehnung* can be transposed so unproblematically from one region to another. Instead of *Anlehnung*, we should think of a mutual *encounter* of the social-historical and the world, with the implication that this not be reduced to the social-historical's identitary elaboration and organization of the world. Why then does Castoriadis retain the term *Anlehnung*? One possible interpretation would be to see the interplay between the social-historical and the first natural stratum as a translation of the Marxian idea of the metabolism between anthropos and nature: labor as the production of useful objects. This too brings into play the relation between determinacy and indeterminacy. The reemergence of the world also points us to preliminary directions developed later toward a multiregional ontology of the *for-itself*, for which, in each niveau, the creation of an *Eigenwelt* proper to that particular level of being is crucial for the organization of this world—and here Castoriadis consistently, if implicitly, distinguishes between the ensemblistic organization of the world as it leans on the first natural stratum, and the signification of the world as endowed with meaning.

Second, when the being of social objects is encountered, the sense of *s'étayer* is no longer pertinent, as it is something more intimate and internal, whereas the idea of *Anlehnung* suggests an external relation. Castoriadis polemicizes here against two targets: Marx and Durkheim. With respect to Marx, Castoriadis's critique is illuminating but unsurprising and reflects his still unfinished settling of accounts with Marx. In this context, Castoriadis highlights the institutional side of signification and takes up his interpretation of Marx's technological determinism. Castoriadis stands Marx on his head (as Marx did Hegel), where, for Castoriadis, the organization of society gives meaning to technological development and not vice versa. Although Castoriadis allows some forms of determinacy, he limits others and tends to overstate his critique of inherited thought. In a reference to Durkheim, Castoriadis contests the idea of "social facts" as "things" as they are too meaning-dependent and meaning-imbued for that to be useful. Yet neither does Castoriadis tell us the whole story. For in a certain sense, social facts are indeed "things" in that there needs to be a certain kind of material support for them, a certain *Dinghaftigkeit*: "Things" are transmuted into social facts.

Castoriadis now shifts to another context, this time, to the institution of the *world* as such. Before discussing Castoriadis's approach to the world in the 1975 section of the *IIS*, however, it is worth looking at his earlier adumbration of the world in the *IIS*. Castoriadis had previously discussed the idea of the imaginary institution of the world in the final chapter of the 1964–65 section: "The Institution and the Imaginary: A First Approach" (especially pp. 149–55). There are two parallels that can be noted with the appearance of the world in the 1964–65 and 1975 sections of the *IIS*. First, the world appears as a central, indeed, necessary aspect or complement to imaginary significations: Social imaginary significations do not create a matrix of meanings that are eternally *becoming* without crystallizing into form, nor do they create just any kind of form, rather, they create each time a concrete world of meaning.[20] Second, both the earlier (1964–65) and later (1975) discussions reveal a fundamental ambiguity with respect to the world, especially in its "division" into a "natural" and a "social" world.[21] In the 1975 section of the *IIS*, the world *qua* social world tends to take precedence over the broader world *qua* world (or from a different perspective, the world as a meta-horizon). These two aspects of the world (each of which presupposes the world as a horizon of meaning) open onto broader contexts of the self-revealing/self-manifesting/self-creating aspects of being than consideration of the so called the natural world alone.

However, the ambiguity of Castoriadis's earlier (1964–65) approach to the world is different from that of the 1975 section of the *IIS*. In 1964–65, Castoriadis tells us that the social-historical,

> defines and [elaborates] an image of the natural world, of the universe in which it lives, attempting in every instance to make of it a signifying whole, in which a place has to be made not only for the natural objects and beings important for the life of the collectivity, but also of the collectivity itself, establishing, finally, a certain "world-order." (p. 149)[22]

Here the move toward the ontological role of imaginary significations in creating the world is not *apriori* to the world, in general, nor to the natural world, in particular, and in this way opens onto a twofold ambiguity. First, it is unclear whether the "world order" is ultimately social (as *nomos*) or natural (as *physis*, and hence incorporating both the social and the natural as part of a cosmic order). Second, as the world is *apriori*, it is not clear from Castoriadis's formulation to what extent the social image of the world is meant to be a reflection of the natural universe, as Castoriadis only uses the term "universe" to refer to the natural kosmos as a whole. At this point, the "ontological alteration of the first natural stratum" by the social-historical is not yet fully visible in his thought. From the above quotation, I also note that phenomenological resonances were still present for Castoriadis: Our mode of being is, as Heidegger has shown, to be *in-the-world* (*in-der-Welt-sein*) and, in a greater sense again, as Merleau-Ponty has explicated, not merely *"in"* but also *of the world* (*au monde*). This is amplified further in a note that follows from Castoriadis's observations (p. 149) concerning the mutual entwining of "world-image" and "self-image" (which Castoriadis still directly related to the being of social doing) that implies a relation *to* and *in* the world: "This is actually a tautology, for one cannot see how society could "represent" itself without *situating itself* in the world; and it is evident that all religions insert humanity in one way or another in a system to which the gods and the world also belong" (n. 55, p. 392).

The Imaginary Creation of the World

Ten years later, in the 1975 section of the *IIS*, Castoriadis elucidates the interplay of social imaginary significations and the world somewhat differently:

> The institution of society is in each case the institution of a magma of social imaginary significations, which we can and must call a *world* of significations. For it is one and the same thing to say that society institutes the world in each case as its world or its world as the world and to say that it institutes itself in instituting the world of significations that is its own, in correlation to which, alone, a world can and does exist for it. (p. 359)

To assert, however, that the social-historical creates *the world as its own* is not equivalent to the statement that the social-historical creates *its world as the world*. In the first instance, the world appears as prior: The social-historical encounters and elaborates it via creative interpretation as "our world." It is, to draw on Merleau-Ponty, to put the wider world into form, to articulate it (*mise en forme du monde*). In the second instance, "our" world is absolutized and the ontological difference between the social-historical world and the world *qua* world is masked.[23] In so far as Castoriadis connects the two formulations, however, an initial turn is given to the whole discussion of the institution of the world, reduced here to the self-contained and comparatively closed character of the social world as imaginary significations.

The image of a relatively closed social-imaginary world is furthermore in tension with his idea of meaning as an ultimately open-ended context. To reiterate, Castoriadis highlights but one aspect of the world as a context of meaning. He does not properly engage with the other aspect of the phenomenological-hermeneutical tradition of theorizing the world of lived experience, where the world is envisaged as an open-ended unity of the horizons of experience, and as such can be considered a *shared, intercultural horizon*. Instead he collapses the world as a dimension of experience into the world as a dimension of the ensidic organization of the world. In this he follows conventional scientific approaches to the world, on the one hand, while implicitly accepting that "meaning" lies on the side of the sovereign subject—or in this case, the sovereign social-historical—on the other. Yet, as Johann Arnason has pointed out (1989c), modern forms of rationality, which ostensibly empty the world of meaning, are still embedded in webs of meaning and signification, albeit of the self-negating variety. This aspect is neglected by Castoriadis and has implications for his overall elucidation of the world, meaning and the social-historical. Castoriadis, moreover, curtails the creative aspect of interpretation, such that it becomes creation of the world *ex nihilo*, for interpretation as such is possible only with *experience*. Thus the concept of the "world" is reduced to the totality of significations, and inclusion of the experiential aspect of the world as the transcultural and external horizon of meaning is absent.

Before proceeding with the reconstruction of this final *IIS* chapter, let us turn to the interlocutor who has most explicitly criticized Castoriadis for sidestepping the world as a *phenomenological* problematic: Johann P. Arnason. Where Castoriadis's elaboration of the world takes an ontological direction after his "first approach" to "the institution and the imaginary" in the 1964–65 section of the *IIS*, Arnason proceeds along a phenomenological-hermeneutical path to offer a *culturological* alternative to the institution and the imaginary that explicitly avoids ontological terrain.[24]

Excursus: Johann P. Arnason's Phenomenology

Icelandic sociologist and philosopher Johann P. Arnason is known for his work on multiple modernities and civilizational analysis. With S. N. Eisenstadt, Arnason is a major contributor to these unfolding debates, which have taken place within overlapping currents of social theory and historical sociology over the last quarter of a century or so.[25] Arnason's distinctive contribution to phenomenological-hermeneutical debates has been a neglected aspect in the reception of his work, however. More precisely, Arnason elaborates a distinctive rereading of the sociological classics (first Marx and phenomenological Marxism, but later Weber and Durkheim, as well), which he combines with a sustained encounter with phenomenological-hermeneutical sources, primarily Merleau-Ponty and Castoriadis, in the first instance, but also Ricoeur and, more recently, Jan Patočka.[26]

As with Alfred Schütz (1967), Arnason's phenomenological approach can be situated within social philosophy and sociology; both emphasize Husserl's articulation of the "lifeworld" as the key to phenomenological investigation, and draw on Max Weber's thought in central ways. There the comparison stops, however: Whereas Schütz was concerned with an analysis of everyday life, Arnason focuses on the sociopolitical institution of the cultural world along civilizational constellations and, most salient for our current purposes, where Schütz focused on the intersubjective level of analysis, Arnason shifts the focus to the transsubjective—or cultural—level of investigation.

For present purposes, six problematics can be considered central to Arnason's phenomenology. First, he identifies the emergent current of post-transcendental phenomenology as the most promising way forward for sociocultural analysis. Second, Arnason emphasizes the importance of the ongoing elaboration of the world horizon to the phenomenological legacy. For Arnason, cultural articulations of the world set up the imaginary infrastructure—or, in Castoriadis's terms, a magma of social imaginary significations—for each cultural (or civilizational) constellation. In turn, the spectrum of cultural articulations of the world makes possible the varieties of the human condition as modes of being-in-the-world. Third, cultural articulations of the world emphasize the importance of meaning. Arnason's theory of meaning focuses on transsubjective constellations that emphasize its imaginary and figurative dimensions. Cultural meaning is both self-interpreting and world-interpreting and thus introduces, fourth, an irreducible hermeneutical dimension to the human condition, which, fifth, offers an elaboration of culture that goes beyond sociocentric confines. Finally, cultural articulations of the world reveal the world as a transsubjective (and transobjective) horizon, rather than as an intersubjective domain, as the more conventional notion would have it.[27]

For Arnason, the advent of the world horizon as philosophical problematic points to an emergent field of phenomenological enquiry, which he termed "post-transcendental." He first coined the expression "post-transcendental-phenomenology" as part of his critical response to Habermas's assertion that, in contrast to twentieth-century currents of Marxism, structuralism and analytic philosophy, "the phenomenologists have not yet arrived at their 'postism'" (Habermas, cited in Arnason 1993, p. 82). Habermas ultimately relegates phenomenology to a position of historical curiosity rather than seeing in it a vital current of thought with the capacity to transform itself beyond its original context. In emphasizing the increasing significance of the world horizon as a phenomenological problematic in its own right, however, Arnason develops an alternative perspective that draws centrally on Merleau-Ponty. Arnason's rendering of Merleau-Ponty's *mise en forme du monde* as "cultural articulations of the world" is fundamental to his elaboration of the post-transcendental turn as part of the richness of phenomenology's capacity to transform itself beyond the limitations of a philosophy of consciousness. His excavation of "post-transcendental" currents in phenomenology begins with the later Husserl, and its transformation by Heidegger, with their respective emphases on "the world" (albeit from different perspectives). Arnason interprets the world problematic as a further development of the Husserlian concept of *horizon* (and has not participated in the recent emphasis on "life" dimension of the "lifeworld" in phenomenological debates). In Arnason's view post-transcendental currents first come to their clearest expression in third generation phenomenological thought, especially Merleau-Ponty, Levinas, Patočka, and, later (post-phenomenological) thinkers such as Castoriadis, Lefort, Taylor, and Richir.[28] Arnason's approach to phenomenology takes its cue from Merleau-Ponty in the *Phenomenology of Perception* (1962, p. viii), and sees it as a historical "movement" that first takes clear expression in Hegel's search for the objective spirit of particular cultural formations, extends across to Nietzsche, before reemerging with its "self-labeling" turn in the twentieth century. So understood, phenomenology will be self-diversifying as well as continuing to incorporate more or less enduring emphases and elements.

Arnason's hermeneutical phenomenology presents a *culturological* alternative to the ontological turn in phenomenology (most especially the Merleau-Pontian and Castoriadian versions). His use of this term has been unsystematic, and it is used sometimes in contrast to, sometimes as synonymous with "culturalist." Increasingly, however, he wants to distinguish "culturological" from "culturalist" approaches, with the former much more explicitly focused on historical diversity while the latter is seen as more typological (with a tendency to ahistoricality). His work reconstructs openings onto culturological contexts in, most especially, the thought of Merleau-Ponty, Castoriadis, Patočka, and Weber. Here he wants to emphasize the world as a transsubjective—that is, cultural—context that is irreducible to subjective or intersubjective domains of analysis. As mentioned, Merleau-Ponty's notion of *mise en forme du monde*—which Arnason generally renders as "articulations of the world"—is pivotal to the development of his phenomenological investigations. For Arnason the enigmatic and underdetermined metacontext of the world horizon can only be understood in the diversity of its historical cultural articulations, which each time opens onto a partially structured field in which the conflict of interpretations become visible. Thus Arnason elaborates the world horizon as an underdetermined unity that can, paradoxically, only be expressed as a plurality: To grasp the plurality of the world, concrete historical analyses are needed.[29] In this way, a culturological approach to phenomenology emphasizes the variety of human historical trajectories, and incorporates a cultural hermeneutics in tandem with historical analyses, particularly, in Arnason's case, of processes of state formation within civilizational contexts.

For Arnason, the problematic of "culture"—as an autonomous element of the human condition, neither reducible to "the social" nor to an aspect of the social—is to be approached hermeneutically.[30] In this way, his approach to post-transcendental phenomenology focuses on "cultural articulations of the world" through a distinctive fusion of the phenomenological problematic of the *world as a shared horizon*, and the hermeneutical problematic of *culture* as a transsubjective context. In an innovative reading of Weber and Merleau-Ponty, "culture" for Arnason is to be understood as "the complexes of relations between man and world" (1982, p. 2). It compares the cultural contexts of world articulation with Weber's early interpretation of culture as ways of lending meaning and significance to the world. More broadly, it emphasizes Arnason's distinctive elaboration of the historical-anthropological notion of culture that goes beyond conventional sociocentric understandings. Concomitantly, he elaborates a decentered anthropology: Not only is the human condition one of "self interpretation," it is, just as fundamentally, one of "world interpretation."

Arnason critiques Castoriadis's neglect of the phenomenological problematic of the world,[31] but nonetheless finds in Castoriadis's innovative connection between the creative imagination and meaning—summed up in the concept of "social imaginary significations"—an important stimulus to his own elaboration of culture. On Arnason's account, Castoriadis overemphasized the "ontological" and "creative" dimension of imaginary significations, to the detriment of the "interpretative," which is, in turn, connected to Castoriadis's marginalization of the problematic of the "world" as a metacontext. In contrast, Arnason highlights the interpretative dimension of creation, and of cultural articulations of the world, and reconstructs the interpretative element of Castoriadis's elucidations of imaginary significations.[32] In this vein, Arnason relativizes Castoriadis's strong notion of human creation as *ex nihilo*. Instead, Arnason's highlights the interpretative dimension of creation—and the creative dimension of interpretation—and prefers the term "creative interpretation." In so doing, he argues that human creation is not *absolute*, as it was for Castoriadis, but *contextual*, that is, interpretative, cultural, and historical.

One consequence of bypassing the phenomenological tradition of "the world horizon" is that, at least within Castoriadis's framework, the social-historical institution of the world becomes a "functional" aspect of the institution of society *as such* rather than as an ongoing confrontation between the social-historical and the world as an open-ended horizon of horizons (as was the case with Merleau-Ponty, for example). In this functionalist moment, the world for Castoriadis seems to serve to integrate society: It holds it together (p. 359). That a functionalist moment creeps into Castoriadis's theory of meaning is paradoxical, given that the social-historical as radical imaginary was meant to be nonfunctional and/or transfunctional. Castoriadis links the idea of the world to the *ecceity* as the mode of co-belonging that is part of the distinctive institutions of a particular society as a response to the question of the ways in which continuity is instituted in other societies.[33] So conceived, the "world" can neutralize transcendence (for example—and especially—religious forms of transcendence), in that the question, "Is there something essentially religious toward the world?" remains unasked. Instead, the changing forms of difference between the everyday and the transcendental (or, as S. N. Eisenstadt prefers, the mundane and the transcendental, or from a Merleau-Pontian perspective, the visible and the invisible) are social-historical creations and do not—and cannot—refer to a transcultural experiential dimension of the world as such. There is, however, a twist to this: We need to look at the whole cultural world, as modes of identity can change between one institution and another. As an example, Castoriadis refers to Athens, Corinth, and Sparta as neither reducible to "parts" of the ancient Greek world of citizen states, nor instances of the "concept" of the Greek city "any more than they are societies other than ancient Greek society. Rather they represent a mode of co-belonging of ancient Greek society "proper to the institution of this society" (pp. 359–60).

Castoriadis proceeds to enquire into the reasons why society institutes itself in instituting a world of significations. In his discussion, however, he addresses (or rather revises) only the idea of *signification* as an essential component in connection with language and *legein* and *teukhein*, and does not address the concept of *world* as such. Overall, we can see that Castoriadis tends to sidestep the ongoing problematic of the world. Instead, he addresses the problematic of social imaginary significations somewhat in a void; that is to say, and from another angle, Castoriadis, like Husserl, brackets the world. Although Castoriadis has, for the time being at least, managed to exorcise the world, as we shall see it reemerges and permeates his ontological reflections, although staying within the shadows. Castoriadis links his discussion of social imaginary significations and its relation to *legein* and *teukhein* and their respective underlying circularity and mutual implication (p. 360). Society does not "first" posit ends: Society and its "ends" are there simultaneously in what Castoriadis was to call the "circle of creation" (*IIS* p. 361).[34] "Society" is there *all at once*: The infrastructure implies the whole web of signification. As such, it is an inextricably interconnected web such that subsystems or causes/effects cannot be clearly demarcated. Nonetheless, Castoriadis does not explicitly acknowledge that the circle of creation is always already a hermeneutical circle: *We are always already inside the web of signification.* The only way forward is to gradually deepen our understanding of the ways in which things presuppose each other.

Castoriadis now adopts a very interesting move. Hitherto he addressed those kinds of significations that are, in his words, "second-order or derived" (p. 361). He now begins to discuss primary imaginary significations, that is, those that have no world referent. In these cases, consideration of *legein* and *teukhein* are only helpful in the last instance: The two proto-institutions are only operational with significations that have a world referent. For Castoriadis, primary imaginary significations most fully epitomize the mode of being of the social-historical. Central imaginary significations—as the core nucleus of meaning for each social-historical constellation—have no objects; they have no *world referent*. Instead, they "*create* objects *ex nihilo*; they organize the world (as the world "external" to society, as the social world, and as the mutual inherence of each of them)" (p. 361). Here Castoriadis introduces the term creation *ex nihilo* for the first time in the 1975 section of the *IIS* (although it was implicitly referred to in the previous chapter, and explicitly first mentioned in the early 1968 paper ETSS). Creation *ex nihilo* is unequivocally linked to the creation of the social-historical world of signification of/by first-order significations. Central significations carry a special status for Castoriadis in that they have no world referent, do not lean on the proto-institutions of *legein* and *teukhein*, and are accordingly entirely generative. For example, to create a core signification, such as "God," is meant to point to a manifestation of creation *ex nihilo* as having no reference to the world, as core significations are conceived as fully imaginary and purely generative. As seen from the above quotation, the world nevertheless persists as a shadowy presence; it would seem from the formulation that the "external world" is created as such by social-historical significations. The world is created as "external," instead of the existing world horizon emerging as "externalized" from the social-historical elaboration of its encounter with it. On the other hand, as indicated above, the world as clearly separable into ensemblistic-identitarian and imaginary dimensions is not a transcultural phenomenon and assumes the separability of the mathematical (as rationalizable) from the imaginary (as the bearing and bestowing meaning); it is in fact peculiar to the conditions of modernity.[35] Continued tension is evident in the bifurcation of the world in its natural and social versions, as well as in the disappearance of a sense of the sacred from the world.

Castoriadis's creative imagination is a radicalization of Kant's productive *Einbildungskraft*, and of varieties of the productive imagination in modernity, more generally. However, Castoriadis's version did not generally incorporate other aspects of the imagination, for example, the symbolic or the receptive. In other words, it is always purely imaginary creations that have the most impact for Castoriadis, that is, creations that have no referent to the "real" world and that can be said to be *ex nihilo*. As such, Castoriadis's account of the creative imagination did not incorporate those aspects that might also emphasize the interpretative element. The most telling example here, as we have seen, is the signification of "God" as an imaginary creation; in no way can it be said to even "lean on" the world (although Castoriadis reveals a sociocentric bias to the conceptualization of the sacred or, more narrowly, "God." I return to this). Castoriadis's notion of the creative imagination and its ontological role fuse Kant's first and third *Critiques*—the creative imagination combines the (varying) ontological role that it plays in the first *Critique* as the root of reason, with the radical creative and generative role of the imagination in the third *Critique*. In addition, the social-historical mode of being of the radical imaginary has deep affinities with the aesthetic creation of the third *Critique*. Castoriadis generally privileges those creations that he can call purely "imaginary"; often his examples are explicitly taken from the realm of art, and the aesthetic realm, more generally. In this manner, Castoriadis blocks engagement with other ways of encountering the world. In the context of the third *Critique* as one of his departure points, the Fichtean aspect is very marked. In the *Wissenschaftslehre*, Fichte tells us that "all reality is brought forth solely by imagination" (Fichte 1982, p. 59), on which Castoriadis draws for his own elucidation of the imaginary creation of social-historical worlds.[36] Castoriadis had earlier in the 1965 *IIS* section noted the importance of the imagination in its "unfoundability" for Fichte, from which Fichte later retreated (n. 53, pp. 391–92). In this vein, it is apposite to note that it is only post-*IIS* that Castoriadis's qualification of the *ex nihilo* but not *cum* or *in nihilo* occurs.

In Castoriadis's view, the social imaginary signification of "God" exemplifies the mode of being of the social-historical as *creatio ex nihilo* (pp.

361–62). He argues that "the word God has no referent other than the signification God, as it is posited in each case by the society in question" (p. 362). It is, however, somewhat disingenuous to start with the phenomenon of monotheism. If polytheism or archaic religion were the starting point (as was the case with Durkheim), then the distinction of the "sacred" and the "profane" would become necessary prior to the creation of "gods," and the discussion of the world (and experience) would be accordingly quite different.[37] For Durkheim, the self-experience of society is important: Individuals have religious experience within a broader collective as social beings. Apart from the resonances with the Fregian debate, here Castoriadis attempts to circumvent Durkheim: The creation of God *ex nihilo* does not "lean on" the world of lived experience, nor, on Castoriadis's account, does it draw on a tradition of meaning. It is created *out of nothing*.[38] For Durkheim the division of the sacred and profane transpires prior to the creation of "God" (as a *version* of the sacred); Castoriadis, on the other hand, posits "God" first, from which the division of the sacred and profane is derived (p. 362). Castoriadis wants to demonstrate that a primary signification—for example, "God"—is not attached to something "separate"—or only in a derivative and "trivial" way—but is the *generator* of meanings. Nevertheless, for Durkheim, the sacred need not be a personal or a world-fabricating God; for him, the sacred can lean on an experiential or "lived" sense. In this context, Durkheim emphasizes the existence of those religions without a god, for instance, early Buddhism. Nevertheless, the later Durkheim truncates this avenue of thought as well: In the final analysis, the sacred is elaborated as society in disguise, therewith smuggling in a hidden referent into the scenario (Durkheim 1965). The sacred and profane distinction also begins to manifest as a social imaginary signification in which the world appears as a referent, not just as the world as entirely created by social imaginary significations. The phenomenology of religion has shown that the sacred and profane can be considered as more or less transcultural and transhistorical as a way of world-forming; and they survive into nonreligious modes of thought.[39] In this way, Durkheim's distinction of the sacred and profane can be given an added phenomenological sense. As indicated above, that Castoriadis commences with monotheism can be considered an intended stratagem on his part. In his discussion of the signification of *God*, Castoriadis brackets out the question of religious experience to which the social imaginary significations refer. More broadly, it can be argued that Castoriadis's previous attempt to bracket the world emerges from ignoring the experiential aspect of the world in his philosophy after his shift to ontology.[40]

Castoriadis abandons the analysis of the signification of God somewhat abruptly, and proceeds to another level of enquiry: The economy (*l'économique*).[41] *L'économique* is a signification superimposed in the differentiation of institutional spheres (or the division of labor). *L'économique* is neither given in a quasi-naturalist way as Marx would have it, nor is it an arbitrary distinction invented through a whim by economists. It is neither necessary nor contingent, as Castoriadis would later refer to our social-historical condition in the Preface to *CL* (written in November 1977, that is, shortly after the *IIS*) but emerges in the history of imaginary significations and the imprint on—or crystallization within—social life. The imaginary of *l'économique* is a historical phenomenon emerging in historical time, yet Castoriadis argues that transhistorical versions of this argument are unsuccessful. But it is problematic to argue that only some civilizational constellations institute an imaginary of *l'économique*, as they still refer to basic aspects of the human condition. In this sense, Castoriadis may have underestimated the importance—and interest—of common features within the social-historical field, some of which address, for example, the anthropological necessity of social production and reproduction through the transformation of nature.[42] Although there are always significations internal to a particular social-historical constellation, there is still common ground between them. All in all, it can be argued that, when it comes to elucidating the social-historical, concrete modes of interaction with nature and their anthropological implications are undertheorized in Castoriadis's thought. However, Castoriadis does include a signpost that would seem to point in that direction and would seem to admit the significance of something transcultural (p. 363). He mentions both Aristotle and Montchrestien (a late classical thinker, and an early modern thinker, respectively) as glimpsing the possibility of separating the economic sphere that was well ahead of institutional practice of the social-historical. This might seem to point to some kind of Heideggerian moment of transcultural "clearing."[43] Castoriadis argues that the economy, too, as a central social imaginary signification, is a creation *ex nihilo*. It cannot be understood on the basis of differentiation of something that existed prior: The economy as a separate sphere did not exist prior to capitalism. There is no sense of *Anlehnung* here, not on the first natural stratum, the kosmos, or instituted forms of the social-historical.

In his brief summary of this *IIS* subsection, Castoriadis somewhat arbitrarily severs central social imaginary significations from experiential contexts and the world, while simultaneously positing his ideas of social imaginary significations as an alternative to Weber and Durkheim. For Castoriadis, social imaginary significations can neither be understood as collective representations *à la* Durkheim, nor as intended meanings as per Weber. Instead, meaning happens even when not intended: It is part and parcel of our ontological condition. In the first sentence of this section, he reiterates the Husserlian opening of this (*IIS*) chapter and, despite his explicit reservations to the contrary, reveals his continuing recourse to phenomenological frameworks of thought:

> Social imaginary significations place us in the presence of a mode of being which is primary, originary, irreducible, one which we must, again here, reflect upon in terms of itself without submitting it in advance to the logical-ontological schemata already available elsewhere. (p. 364)

The second paragraph continues the Husserlian engagement. Here, Castoriadis argues that core significations are not the *noemata* of a *noesis*; rather it is imaginary significations that make the *noema* and *noesis* possible in the first place. His observation that social imaginary significations are not reducible to a subject (whether individual or collective), returns Castoriadis to his ongoing, yet somewhat fragmentary critique of Durkheim and Lévi-Strauss and the inadequacy of the terms "collective representation" or "social representation." However, although Castoriadis shifts in his discussion from the early to the later Durkheim, he does not properly distinguish between them. This is inadequate for the purposes of his critique of which focuses primarily on the early Durkheim of *The Division of Labor* (pp. 365–66). In the second paragraph Castoriadis addresses the "world of instituted significations"; here again, he critiques Durkheim and makes a sharp distinction between *signification* and *representation*. Castoriadis argues that Durkheim's collective *conscience* comprises the images in common with individual representations, yet, again, he does not clearly distinguish between Durkheim's shift from the idea of a collective *conscience* to the later problematic of collective *representations*.[44] There are different components to social imaginary significations; without using the term Castoriadis appears to be characterizing the *anonymous collective* as a web of significations. Overall, however, Castoriadis's discussion of Durkheim seems curtailed, but there are nonetheless several suggestive overlaps between the later Durkheim and Castoriadis's notion of social imaginary significations that, although beyond the scope of this study, would be very interesting to pursue further. A discussion of their respective approaches to religion and the social would also be interesting, especially in light of Gauchet's analyses (1999). Castoriadis does not further elaborate on the "anonymous collective" of his own elucidation, by means of which central social imaginary significations are created/instituted.

Castoriadis turns to consider Weber. He argues that Weber reduces the entire gamut of meaning to subjectively intended meaning. Social imaginary significations cannot, however, be reduced to this. Although he does not say it explicitly, it is assumed that Weber's framework of subjective meaning is biased against the "objective spirit," as it exists only in the minds of individuals and therefore is cut off from the trans-subjective, social-historical web of meaning and signification, which tends to dehistoricize meaning as it is removed from any broader context. Then, in a shift of emphasis, Castoriadis criticizes Weber's ideal types for dehistoricizing, which, as I suggested earlier, seems to be the case for Castoriadis's own thought as well.[45] Neither does Castoriadis make explicit the unstated sense of Hegel's objective spirit at work in his account.[46] Nonetheless, Castoriadis seems to be onto something: If we need to construct ideal types, there also needs to be recognition that these are embedded in whole complexes of epochs and historical meanings (historicity) of significations (p. 368); that is, a "culturalist" approach still relies on "culturological" contexts of elaboration. Durkheim and Weber had already partially discovered the hermeneutical dimension of meaning to a greater extent than Castoriadis admits but it is also true that his critique of them reflects an implicit discovery of hermeneutical aspects of social imaginary significations.[47]

In concluding his discussion of Durkheim, Castoriadis observes that social imaginary significations are the "conditions for the representable and the do-able" (p. 367). They emerge as the preconditions for subjective representations which are at most semiconscious: They do not impose a monolithic meaning on the subject, but rather open onto a limited field of possible meanings which must be interpreted and construed by the subject. The hermeneutical infrastructure continues in his discussion of Weber where, to lean on Gadamer: *Sinn ist auch dort vorhanden wo er nicht intentional vollzogen wird*. Meaning is not to be confused with intentional meanings of the (interior) subject, nor ideal typical, brought into play by an externality, rather meaning is operative within (trans)subjective contexts without being fully intended. Meaning as the instituted magma of imaginary significations is again seen as the precondition for subjective meaning: Subjects interpret and transform implicit and latent meanings into explicit and intended meanings realized by the subject. Social imaginary significations are latently operative: They give direction and consistency to the self-altering social-historical world (pp. 367–68).

The final section of this *IIS* chapter is entitled "Radical Imaginary, Instituting Society, Instituted Society" (pp. 369–73). It is meant as a complete summing up of the *IIS*, and is the only place in the *IIS* where its themes are linked together. Instead of a recapitulation, however, new directions appear, and further gaps and loose ends emerge. Castoriadis tells us:

> Within *à-être*, the radical imaginary emerges as otherness and as the perpetual [origination] of otherness, which figures and figures itself, exists in figuring and in figuring itself, the creation of "images" which are what they are and as they are as figurations or presentifications of significations or meanings. (p. 369)[48]

In the preceding quotation, for example, insofar as figures figure themselves and present a meaning, questions of the symbolic dimension reappear. This echoes the 1965 section of the *IIS* where Castoriadis suggests that symbolic "figures"—as a "second imaginary"—are that which "render society visible to itself" (p. 130). The symbolic and the imaginary are deeply entwined: If the imaginary institutes the world, the symbolic comprises the world's "ultimate elements" (p. 130) and syntheses of such elements appear as "partial totalities" (p. 130) reminiscent of Weber's "world orders." From the 1975 section of the *IIS* onward, Castoriadis, unlike, for example, Ricoeur, generally plays down the significance of the symbolic realm, seeing its roots in the imaginary as more fundamental to theorize. Indeed, in the final chapter of the 1965 section of the *IIS*, Castoriadis, in positing the imaginary as prior to the symbolic, thought that that was the end of the matter. But did the symbolic ever really disappear? In this 1975 *IIS* section, as I have shown, Castoriadis approaches his key concepts of being through reliance on symbolic description—be it in reference to the magma or *à-être*—as indirect metaphors and neologisms. The 1965 section would seem to suggest the ongoing need for elucidation of the symbolic, especially in terms of its relation to the imaginary—"The deep and obscure relations between the symbolic and the imaginary appear as soon as one reflects on the following fact: The imaginary has to use the symbolic not only to 'express itself' . . . but to 'exist,' to pass from the virtual to anything more than this" (p. 127)—on the one hand, and also in terms of the hermeneutic preconditions of creation onto which it opens. If our ontological condition is to be condemned to meaning, then it would seem to involve two reciprocal aspects and layers: the imaginary and the symbolic. The imaginary as the primordial or transcendental relation to the world is entwined with the symbolic as an element of and within the world.

Returning again to our focus on the final chapter of the *IIS*, the next paragraph takes up the relation of reception/alteration between the social historical and the first natural stratum (p. 369). Here a different sense of creation, one that incorporates interpretative aspects, begins to appear. After pointing to the radical imaginary as instituting society, Castoriadis writes: "The institution of society by instituting society leans on the first natural stratum of the given—and is always found (down to an unfathomable point of origin) in a relation of reception/alteration with what had already been instituted" (p. 369). Something is given—a Fichtean *Anstoss*, an encounter with the being of the world—that is received, and that must be interpreted for it to be altered, that is, created anew. Castoriadis had previously stated that core imaginary significations, which are created *ex nihilo*, are purely generative. He had elaborated a chasm between them and the experiential dimension of the world—in its multiple aspects—as well as the instituted historical constellations of meaning/interpretation, that is a civilizational component. Second, Castoriadis seems to be giving some credence to the idea of the interaction of *instituting* and *instituted* society (there is a sense of a sometimes violent encounter) in that the new institutions of necessity take into account the already instituted. An emerging analogy with *natura naturans/natura naturata* is beginning to surface here, which will become increasingly important to his later thought. A complex relation of the self-creating natural form, the reception/interpretation of that natural form by the social-historical—which brings it into the domain of culture and is such no longer reducible to a purely natural form—is discernible. There is possibly greater scope than Castoriadis allows for this more complex moment of alteration and reception, but it is not taken up, especially in the case of core or central social imaginary significations for which he reserves his strongest sense of *creatio ex nihilo*.[49]

Castoriadis introduces the idea of *instrumentation*—"in two basic institutions" (p. 370)—as the means by which the institution of a magma of significations is at all possible by instituting society. He does not, however, properly explain what is meant by this idea. Perhaps he believes it is implicit in the proto-institutions of *legein* and *teukhein*, which are the "two basic institutions" referred to. The point here to reprise—as in Chapter 2—concerns the ambiguity of the "ensemblist-identitary" dimension of *legein* and *teukhein* as well as its shadowy presence in nature. It is interesting to juxtapose this sense of instrumentation of the magma of significations (and its being brought into being via instrumentation) against the idea of "figurating-presentifying of the magma of significations which this institution brings each time into being" (p. 370) to track the changing relationship between the two. What is instituted each time is the institution of the world, says Castoriadis, "as the world of and for that society, and as the organization-articulation of the society itself" (p. 370). Here the world makes a return. Again, however, it seems phantomesque. For still Castoriadis cannot seem to fully recognize that the institution of the world "of and for" a particular society is also an interpretation of the (broader) world, which transcends each particular society's articulation of it. Indeed, each social-historical constellation institutes its place within the wider world and concomitantly the wider world as a shared cultural horizon of interpretation. We start to get an indication of what Castoriadis means by the "*world*" in the following paragraph:

> This institution is the institution of a world in the sense that it can and must enclose everything, that, through and in it, everything must in principle, be sayable and representable and that everything must be totally caught up in the network of significations, everything must have meaning. (pp. 370–71)

To draw on a well-known metaphor, Castoriadis seems to work with an image of a "closed world" rather than an "infinite universe." The "world" to which he refers is ultimately a social "referent" not leaning on the kosmos in the wider sense at all, which is quite different from the 1965 first approach to the imagined world. It could also be seen as a preliminary prefiguring of the idea of the *Eigenwelt* that was to become increasingly important to his thought, especially that of the living being.[50] Although a rupture appears between the animal and human psyche that manifests in the defunctionalization of the human, and, hence, the creation of an opening for the instituting capacity of social-historical signification, the institution of the anthropic world seems as closed as the *Eigenwelt* of the living being; indeed it is tempting to go a step further and compare it to the closed world of the psychotic, which, as Castoriadis points out, is logical within its own terms, but bears no reference to the real world. The world as such returns, but in a strictly negative shape:

> The manner in which everything, each time, has meaning, and the meaning it has is rooted in the core of the imaginary significations of the society considered. But this overlapping is never guaranteed: what escapes it, at times almost indifferent, can be and is of the utmost seriousness. What escapes it is the enigma of the world as such, which stands behind the common social world, as *à-être,* that is to say, as an inexhaustible supply of otherness, and as an irreducible challenge to every established signification. What escapes it as well

is the very being of society as instituting, that is to say, ultimately, society as the source and origin of otherness, or perpetual self-alteration. (p. 371)

As is apparent, the world as a negative figuring of "an inexhaustible supply of otherness" (p. 371) is linked explicitly to *à-être*. However, what Castoriadis misses here is that each society institutes the world in a concrete, positive sense imposed on a broader horizon, common to the human field as a whole. Approaching this from another angle, part of the problem with the phantom "world" in the *IIS* is that, as the quotation above shows, Castoriadis has not systematically approached the idea of the world as *à-être* as being—distinct from "the social world." Hence, the idea of the world remains a contradictory and subterranean presence in his thought. Some of this could be attributed to the ongoing and shifting balance of tensions between Romantic and Enlightenment images of "world orders" and "worldhood" in his thought.[51]

In turning to consider the problematic of the creation of social-historical worlds of meaning as *ex nihilo*, Castoriadis found himself confronted with equally pressing questions, especially the convergence of the phenomenological context of the world and the hermeneutic problematic of interpretation. The convergence of these two problematics led to a more general problematic of *world articulation*—to draw on Merleau-Ponty's image of *mise en forme du monde*—in its overlapping aspects of interpretation and creation. When the problematic of the world horizon was considered more carefully, and the implications of interpretative creation for the social-historical articulation of the world became clearer, however, Castoriadis's notion of creation *ex nihilo* requires further scrutiny.

The Return of *à-être*

Castoriadis opened this subsection with a reference to the *à-être*: Here it half returns. Its source of otherness makes it translatable as creative *physis*. Although, at the beginning of this final *IIS* chapter, Castoriadis began to extend magmata to non-anthropic modes of being, at this concluding point of the chapter, *à-être* remains subterranean to the theme of anthropic being as a unique region of being and is neither systematized nor explained further. As will become evident, the *à-être* stands behind the common social world, which, as shall be shown in the next part of this book, becomes overshadowed by creative *physis*. That is, Castoriadis singles out but one aspect of the world as *à-être*—other aspects to consider include the world as an open-ended unity of horizons, and attention to the modes of experience and interpretation, and experience and signification.[52]

Where does this leave us? The originality of Castoriadis's approach to imaginary significations was to link meaning to the creative imagination in its dual aspects of the radical imagination and the radical imaginary. However, meaning in the full sense appears not in the psychical domain but in the social-historical. It involves significations rather than representations and as such is collectively instituted. In this vein, ontological alteration of the first natural stratum is a social-historical phenomenon, not a psychical phenomenon. The radical imaginary creates a world of significations as the infrastructure for its ongoing social-historical interpretation and elaboration, as well as "social doing" as overlapping aspects of interpretative creation. Yet there lurks a more complex, albeit incomplete, picture of the being of meaning in the *IIS* as well, that emerges when the latent potentialities and various loose threads are brought together.

Social-historical meaning emerges historically, through confrontation with and elaboration of various "interpretative challenges" that are encountered along the way. In this vein, the instauration of the project of autonomy in ancient Greece was not as straightforward as Castoriadis would have it: It could just as well be interpreted as emerging through *two* revolutions, not one (Arnason 2000). Gadamer's (1998, pp. 17–18) observation, in discussing pre-Socratic thought as the beginning of philosophy, on the "meaning of beginning" (*Anfang*) could perhaps be helpful here: Although there are many interrelated meanings of "beginning" in interpreting history, one stands out for Gadamer as the most useful, and relevant in the context of emphasizing the interpretative and contextual aspects to creation. He suggests considering the "meaning of beginning" (*Anfang*) not as that which is incipient (*Anfangenden*), but from incipience (*Anfänglichkeit* or *Anfänglichsein*). For him, *Anfänglichsein* refers to "something that is not yet determined in this or that sense, not yet determined in the direction of this or that end, and not yet determined appropriate for this or that representation" (Gadamer 1997, p. 17). Or, as Castoriadis tells us in his discussion with Ricoeur, a "potential potentiality": It is created and instituted as such only in interpretation and reactivation of latent-meaning contexts.[53] What is "potentially there" is not there since all time, but emerges—becomes amenable to meaning—only within specific interpretative contexts in specific social-historical constellations. It is not yet "something," but neither is it "nothing at all." In terms of the creation of the *polis*, Cleisthenes set something in motion (as Solon had done before him), but its end was not determined, and its emergence involved reactivation and interpretative creation of historical contexts of meaning. In fact, a variety of different interpretative creations of the *polis* emerged—Sparta and Athens are the best known—such that it is better to speak of a (contested) field of *poleis* (and in that vein, a broad field of the autonomist imaginary). History as *kosmos*—an order always to be invested with meaning—involves interpretation, not just creation: We need to creatively interpret history in order to lend meaning to or, more broadly, to make sense of our actions in the present, and to relate the aspects of interpreted continuity between past and present, temporal distance notwithstanding.

Where does the notion of interpretative creation leave Castoriadis's creation *ex nihilo*? Castoriadis insists that social-historical creation (of the world) is *out of nothing*. By this he means an absolute and radical creation that leaves little room for circumscribing factors.[54] The idea of creation *ex nihilo* was meant to provide an alternative model to that of determinacy: The two modes are radically separate for Castoriadis. Within these parameters, that is, assuming that the social-historical creates itself as a self-altering world of *meaning*, the "out of nothing"—in the sense of "neither producible nor deducible" from the already given—is an important aspect of creation. Creation is not amenable to determinism. However, it is not the sole aspect. In his later writings, Castoriadis recognizes that there is something more that happens in the moment/process of self-creation, and qualifies the *ex nihilo* by adding that this does not simultaneously mean "*in* or *cum nihilo*." He conceives the creation "in something" and "with something" as a "conditioning" by what is already there—be that the first natural stratum or the existing social-historical world as always already instituted—and he carefully delineates "conditioning" from "determining" (TC). Yet, "conditioning" does not for Castoriadis evoke "interpretation" or "interpretative contexts" (the "with" of creation, for example, tends to be skewed toward instrumentalist notions). To introduce an interpretative moment to creation—and a creative moment to interpretation—is to take it in a different direction altogether.

In an unpublished radio discussion from 1987, Ricoeur and Castoriadis discuss their differing approaches to "production from something to something" and "creation out of nothing." For Ricoeur, creation proper is something reserved for God. Human production—in the pre-Fichtean sense—is still creation, but it is not out of nothing.[55] It is a production of new syntheses of new configurations not reducible to a simple recombination of the already existing. The emergence of a new form sees the interpretative creation of a not fully closed (determined) meaning constellation materialize from another not fully formed (closed upon itself) meaning constellation. Being as *à-être* evokes the sense of forms never so fully closed as to prevent the emergence of new forms. Thus *kosmoi* as social-historical worlds of meaning are situated betwixt "a fully determined something" and a "completely chaotic nothing." The significance of meaning is that it is both explicit and latent. A particular meaning emerges only in specific historical contexts; it is reinterpreted both in terms of its historical emergence and significance, as well as spilling outward and opening up into the reinterpretations, decline, and uncertain reactivation and creative reinterpretations (of the emerging or distant future-as-present). To speak of historical meaning is to imagine an incipient hue of the always becoming-meaningful.

Creation is not only conditioned, it is also contextual. There are always *contexts* in which creation occurs and interpretative challenges to which creations of new forms respond; in this way, "conditioned by" simply sidesteps the issue at hand. If there is a context to creation, then, inevitably, the interpretative aspects to creation demand elucidation. In this vein, Castoriadis's reluctance to plunge into the waters of elucidating *interpretation as creative* remains curious. Very occasionally, Castoriadis, in speaking of the interpretative context of creation (like Freud, who, as Castoriadis liked to point out, always spoke of the imagination but without ever uttering its name, so, too, is there a similar situation with Castoriadis and interpretation), speaks of a *re-creation*.[56] But what is re-creation if not an interpretation—creative interpretation or interpretative creation—of an existing creation? He certainly does not mean it to be mere repetition or mimicry. What is philosophical elucidation if not interpretation, and interpretative creation at that? If our ontological condition "condemns us to meaning," it also condemns us to the porousness of meaning and the subsequent need for its ongoing interpretation and re-creation as interpretative creation. Thus, the strong idea of creation needs to take into account that new creations involve responses—or, more baldly, *are* responses—to interpretative challenges of particular social-historical constellations as contextual creation.[57] Interpretation as creative—and creation as interpretative—is part and parcel of our human condition; as such, due care is needed to incorporate an elucidation of this mode of being into our interpretative frameworks, be they ontological, epistemological, or sociological.

The kosmos is always a social-historical world—that is, order—of meaning woven into the chaos. Yet, as Merleau-Ponty's idea of *mise en forme du monde* evokes, world articulation is twofold. It is not just that we create a world, but also that we encounter it in its various fragments, regions, and aspects; it thus becomes involved in interpretation. Castoriadis is more ambivalent, however, about this last, overlapping aspect. An articulation of the world always already involves its interpretation (in both its social and natural aspects), for we always find ourselves in a given world. As mentioned in the earlier Introduction to *Nomos*, the interpretative aspect of world articulation—or world shaping—is not for Castoriadis *la philosophie*, but *le philosophique*. Indeed, Castoriadis emphatically denies the world interpreting aspect of the social-historical (and by extension, *le philosophique*):

> How is the world *tout court*, since there effectively is this indefinite variety of worlds proper to each society? The response is: The world lends itself to (is compatible with) all these SIS and privileges none. That means: The world *tout court* is senseless, devoid of signification . . . The result is that, *at this level*, all "hermeneutical" discussion, every attempt to see in the creation of SIS "interpretations" of the world, has no ground to stand on. (DD 364–65)[58]

For Castoriadis, the world-creating modality of the social-historical is the other side of the coin to his rejection of transcendent, that is extrasocial, sources of meaning embedded in the kosmos; it is that which distinguishes the Greek tradition from the monotheistic. As the preceding quotation shows, Castoriadis rejects the idea that the world is intrinsically meaningful, or that it embodies an extrasocial order of meaning. He links such "world interpreting" approaches to hermeneutics. As has been argued, Castoriadis was no friend of hermeneutics: He seemed to associate it variously with the monotheistic traditions of interpretations of sacred texts in search of a revealed and absolute Truth (thus for Castoriadis hermeneutics did not ascribe to the meaning of *la philosophie* as explicit questioning and problematization) or the Heideggerian sense of the unveiling of Being. For him, hermeneutics neither questions nor problematizes the world: It does not contain that essential moment of critique as *la philosophie*. For Castoriadis, hermeneutics was in effect a negation of modes of being *nomô* in its attempts to unearth an internal meaning to the text or of history. He tended not to engage with the philosophical turn of hermeneutics (and its counterpart: the hermeneutic turn of philosophy) in a serious way; his interpretation of hermeneutics was itself a caricature.[59] Yet closer consideration of the interpretative aspects of world articulation cannot be merely consigned to a negation of *nomos*, nor to a heteronomous reproduction of the existing, instituted world. Interpretation is not only creative, it also problematizes. Putting the world into question need not always take an explicit form. With the polysemy of meaning, multiple interpretations of a "text" or "event" are inevitable. In that these will inevitably conflict, a field of tensions is both encountered and reconfigured. A historical field of conflicting interpretations is inherently problematizing and interrogative, both in terms of an intrafield of interpretations, and of the interfields of wider scope.

In the course of this chapter, I have inventoried several key elements of the being of meaning: the magma metaphor at the beginning of the chapter and its transformation to *à-être* by the end of the chapter; the radical imaginary; the world *qua* world, and the world in its social and natural aspects; the symbolic as it is enigmatically related to both the being of the world and to the radical imaginary in a more reciprocal relation than Castoriadis explicitly argued; and Castoriadis's implicit shift toward the acknowledgment of the being of interpretation and its essential role in creation. The being of meaning is multilayered and begins to look, in building on the labyrinth metaphor, more like a series of catacombs: The crisscrossing of underground tunnels that lead us to places as yet unknown. At the beginning of this chapter, I alluded to Ricoeur's incorporation of the Heideggerian element of understanding as our ontological way of being in-the-world, and to Castoriadis's resistance to that incorporation, as well as (especially) Merleau-Ponty's emphasis on world articulation. Now I am in a better position to move toward a preliminary figuration of this schema within Castoriadis's thought.

At the end of the *IIS*, it is apparent that Castoriadis does move toward an implicit embracing (and radicalizing) of the philosophical hermeneutical turn where the being of interpretation becomes integral to the interrelations between world creation and imaginary meaning. Not only are imaginary significations, as generators of social-historical orientations of meaning-constellations in the creation of the world, themselves in need of interpretation, this interpretation can only proceed indirectly through symbols. Putting aside the question of the social-historical encounter with the being of the world in terms of imaginary significations and the world-as-referent, our symbolic access to imaginary significations—not just in terms of the symbolism of concrete institutions, but within language too "all expressions are essentially tropic"—would seem to suggest our necessarily multilayered way of being-in-the-world.[60] In contrast to Merleau-Ponty, for Castoriadis the being of the world has hitherto remained an essentially negative image in his thought; yet because of this, its surplus of meaning more clearly structure the background horizon.[61] What has become clear, however, is that it is not just the imaginary that has an essential relationship to the world, but also the symbolic and their overlapping connection is more reciprocal than Castoriadis gives credence. The world however continues to reappear in changing guises in Castoriadis's thought, as we shall see as we begin to track his shift toward a general ontology of creative *physis* in Part II of this study.

This completes the elaboration of Castoriadis's long journey through *nomos* and his elucidation of its ontological preconditions. So far I have approached the *IIS*—limited to the 1975 section—chapter by chapter. The approach has drawn on the tenets of hermeneutical reconstruction to interpret its explicit, as well as its more latent, contexts to better amplify and problematize key aspects of Castoriadis's thought. The chapters were treated as successive and loosely interwoven philosophical elucidations of fundamental aspects of the human condition (with the exception of religion): ontological, epistemological, philosophical, and anthropological respectively. In this context, this concluding chapter can be characterized as a meditation in philosophical hermeneutics, as, in elucidating the being of the radical imaginary, Castoriadis concomitantly presented his theory of meaning, and in so doing, could not but move to hermeneutic concerns. Although Castoriadis attempted to circumvent the issue of interpretation as it relates to creation, meaning, and the symbolic and the world, he nonetheless found himself in the thick of it, and, despite his protestations to the contrary, his elucidation of social imaginary significations incorporated an implicit shift toward hermeneutical contexts. The chapter is haunted by the problematic of the world, yet Castoriadis seems reluctant to explore the rich resources that the various developments of this theme within phenomenology offered. As we have seen, the world turns out to be half-acknowledged and half-exorcized in his thought, and, as such remains phantomesque in his elucidation. Unsurprisingly, tension emerges in his elucidation of the world in its overlap with—and distinction between—the social-historical world and the natural world upon which it leans. Yet, from another angle, this tension is unsurprising and can be interpreted as a manifestation of ongoing interpretative conflicts between Romantic and Enlightenment cultural currents that structure modernity's field of tensions, here specifically in the general trends evident in their respective conceptions of the world.

The journey through the *IIS* revealed interlacing aspects of the human condition, but the *human condition* was not always already tackled as explicitly *in*-the-world. We move now to discuss anthropic being in relation to its place in the natural world and beyond. In the next section of the book, I consider Castoriadis's shift toward a general ontology of radical *physis* that was incipient until the late 1970s in this thought. We find that the interlacing between the Romantic and Enlightenment constellations, in their conflicting articulations of the world and its various aspects and modalities, continue to be realigned in Castoriadis's thought. As we pause at the threshold of Castoriadis's ontology of creative *physis*, I note his post-*IIS* preface to *Crossroads in the Labyrinth* (which is to be interpreted as another internal transition in his thought) and ponder his new vision (and metaphor) for philosophizing: Unlike Plato, we seek not to exit the cave but to enter the labyrinth. As we do so, we are confronted with innumerable intersecting tunnels of meaning that propel us in a myriad of directions. In Part II of this book, we follow those that lead into regions of the natural world.

Physis

It is not stones and trees that matter to me, but men in the city, said the philosopher. Ultimately it proved impossible for him to remain faithful to this dictum. For in reflecting upon men in the city he was led to assign them a place in the world and to recognize their substantial kinship with stones and trees.

—**MSPI 145**

We shall therefore say . . . that this is *physis* which has in itself principle and origin of form. This amounts to saying: that is *physis* which has in itself principle and origin of creation—since the sole creation that is of import is that of forms.

—**PA 335**

Introduction to Part II

Physis *and the Romanticist Imaginary of Nature*

As was evident by the final chapter of the *IIS*, Castoriadis had begun to extend the scope of magmas beyond the human realm and into nature. Not surprisingly, this expansion wrought changes in his overall philosophical reflections, in particular to his rethinking of the ontological significance of the creativity of nature, on the one hand, and the lines of continuity and discontinuity between human and nonhuman nature, on the other. As with his rethinking of the being of human institution (*nomos*) after his break with Marx, Castoriadis returned to the ancient Greeks—most explicitly to Aristotle, but also to the pre-Socratics, and to the Hesiodian notion of *chaos*—to reflect more fully on the ontological modes of magmas in nature. This time, however, his focus was not so much *nomos* but *physis*. In particular, he began to foreground the creative aspects of *physis*, whereas earlier he had tended to view it in more normative terms, at least as far as the human world was concerned.[1] Yet, as will become clear, although he increasingly emphasized the imaginary of *physis*, Castoriadis did not abandon the productive tension and configuration of the *nomos* and *physis* problematic. From another angle, we could say that he did not abandon his preoccupation with the human, political world as the "creative imaginary institution" of *nomos* to *replace* it with a reconsideration of the creativity of *physis*; instead, he brought a more sustained reflection on the creative aspects of nature into the wider field of his philosophical concerns. Drawing out the implications of these changes forms the focus of the second half of this study.

Can Castoriadis's rethinking of *physis* be reconciled with the herme-neutic of modernity that was signaled in the General Introduction of this book? Recalling Johann P. Arnason's pioneering reflections on the cultural horizons of modernity might be helpful at this point. Arnason's cultural hermeneutics articulates modernity not as a "project" (as did Habermas), but as a "field of tensions" involving a historically changing, partially structured conflict of interpretations that emerge from the competing world articulations variously offered by Romanticism and the Enlightenment. Within his thought, Romanticism and the Enlightenment are not reduced to intellectual or historical movements, but are elaborated more broadly as *cultural currents* that are constitutive of modernity's field of tensions. Arnason's theory of cultural modernity insists moreover on the centrality of two other aspects: First, and most relevant for our current purposes, that the constitution of cultural modernity includes a rediscovery and reworking of classical sources; and, second, that the elaboration of "constitutive" (not just "significant") cultural others and "other-nesses," both intracultural and intercultural, are fundamental to its self-institution (Arnason 1996).

But can Castoriadis's return to classical sources be situated within modern constellations? In rethinking nature, the main problematic concerns its bifurcation in modernity. In his Tarner lecture, Whitehead (1921, pp. 26ff) speaks of the bifurcation of nature into the objective quantities of physical nature and the subjective qualities of perceived nature. Four nodal points for discussion are identified: causality, time, space, and appearance. Castoriadis, too, addresses these themes in innovative ways, with some fruitful overlap with a Whiteheadian perspective. Castoriadis relativizes the radical distinction between the object and the subject through a criticism of Kant's reluctant confession in the third *Critique* of a "*glücklicher Zufall*": On Castoriadis's account, for the world to be able to be organized by us, means that it is ontologically organizable. However, he takes the subjective aspects of organizable nature, and uses this as a springboard to critique the determinacy-as-causality argument. He does so by radicalizing the concept of nature as the ontological capacity of not only human but also nonhuman or natural modes of being to create their own world of (proto)meaning as a new stratum of reality.

Castoriadis's rethinking and radicalization of *physis*, which was most evident during the 1980s, signals not only a return to ancient Greek sources, but to a critical reconsideration of the modern Romantic idea of nature (or of the *Romanticist imaginary of nature*). The rediscovery of the other, exceedingly creative dimension to *physis,* places Castoriadis within the discontinuous modern tradition of *natura naturans/natura naturata*, as well as within the field of *Naturphilosophie*; these two currents of thought overlapped in various contexts, and emphasized nature as self-creative. The self-creative dimension of nature was most clearly foregrounded by the German *Frühromantiker* as part of a more expansive *naturphilosophical* horizon. Castoriadis's shift to creative *physis* is to be situated within this setting; his later meditations find rich nodes of contact with what might be termed a *critical Naturphilosophie*. Castoriadis's *Naturphilosophie* could also be linked to later currents of thinking about nature and the kosmos— especially as a critique of the hegemony of modern forms of reason or rationality and/or mechanistic views of the natural world—such as those found in successive stages of Romantic thought up to and including the late stage to be found in *Lebensphilosophie*, but, it is important to stress, without the "Romantic excess" to which these currents were prone, be that philosophically or politically.

Naturphilosophie is a distinctively German intellectual endeavor. It was very much identified with the German Romantics (especially the *Frühromantiker*).[2] There is neither an English nor French equivalent to the term. Schelling is centrally associated with it, but an important precursor can be found in Goethe.[3] Goethe and Schelling have each bequeathed a different lineage of reflections on nature to Western traditions of thought, especially phenomenological currents. Goethe's morphological approach has been influential in the phenomenology of nature generally, and Klagesian phenomenology in particular.[4] It is fair to say, however, that Schelling's influence, at least recently, has been more significant: Significantly, Merleau-Ponty devotes an important discussion to Schelling's work in his seminars on nature, and post–Merleau-Pontian strands of thought have developed these insights further.[5]

Naturphilosophie refers to a trend that did not so much reject science *tout court* as reject the Galilean (and Kantian) program of science and its ahistorical precepts. *Naturphilosophie* set out to reinstate the comprehensiveness of a total science (Gusdorf 1985, p. 14). On these accounts, science is understood as part of philosophy and is ultimately reabsorbed into its fold. In this way, *Naturphilosophie* attempts to bridge the gulf opened by the Enlightenment between subject and object, internal and external nature, mind and body, and so forth. *Naturphilosophie* implies a refusal, moreover, to radically separate humanity from the kosmos in which it dwells; rather, it aspires to restore a "new alliance"—a meaningful alliance—between the two.[6] *Naturphilosophie* is not content to regard the world of appearances and surfaces of things; instead it seeks to discern visible roots in the invisible, in the very act of "knowing" or "grasping" the kosmos, often occurring at the nexus of poetic and religious motifs and themes. In this vein, it envelops both a philosophical anthropology and philosophy of nature, while underscoring modes of continuity between the two:

> *Naturphilosophie* wants to be neither a philosophy of spirit, nor a materialist philosophy, nor a philosophy of reason or of God, but at once all of that and something else besides, a way of thinking about the world, but not possession and reduction of the world to thought, thought in the world, situated in the world, disinclined to self-closure, in a state of subordination, obliged to call premonition, divination to the aid of reason. (Gusdorf 1985, p. 38; my translation)

Pursuant to the above passage, it is a truism to note that some varieties of *Naturphilosophie* tended to excess. Three trends can be identified. First, they could be too directly rooted in religious traditions, such that strong theosophical undertones blurred the boundaries between theology and philosophy. Second, the idea of creative nature could involve assumptions with things not so easily compatible with nature, such that illegitimate links were made to natural science. Third, *Naturphilosophie* was also meant to apply to nonrational modes of cognition, such as intuition and *Einfühlung*. That being said, the complete rejection of Romantic contexts and *Naturphilosophie* needs to be reconsidered. *Naturphilosophie* was not so much a dismissal of science or rationality, as an attempt to respond to the interpretative challenges posed by the wholesale reduction of ontological meaninglessness and lifelessness emerging from some strands of Enlightenment thought, and the attempt to recreate contexts of meaning as part of a critical response. In this respect, too, Castoriadis's interpretation of creative nature as a critical reconsideration of the Romantic imaginary of nature can be understood as a critique of the excesses of Enlightenment visions of nature as generally inert and emptied of meaning, or, from a different perspective, of the excesses of an overly rational and rationalized world. Castoriadis's characterization of the creative imagination—to draw on his generic term—is in this vein to be understood not so much as a nonrational but as a transrational element.

The second approach that is fundamental to interpreting the Romanticist imaginary of nature is the intermittent tradition of *natura naturans/ natura naturata*. *Natura naturans/natura naturata* generally emphasizes the creative powers of nature (*naturans*) as opposed to the relatively stable results of its creation (*naturata*) (which is the traditional object of mechanistic science). *Natura naturans/natura naturata* hearkens back to the medieval Arabic tradition and the rediscovery and translation of Aristotle's works

(Hedwig 1984; Siebeck 1890); Vincent de Beauvais is credited with its first usage in a Western context in his *Speculum maius* (1244). As a philosophical concept, it started to gather momentum with Bruno and the Renaissance neo-Platonists (Védrine 1967), but it was in early modernity with Spinoza ("*Deus sive natura*") that it took on greater importance. In the process controversy emerged—the so-called Pantheistic debate—that was to subsequently inform Kant and his circle (Lenoble 1953, Guyer 2000, Ameriks 2000). Although he drew on Spinoza, Schelling's interpretation went in a different direction; his departure point was Section 76 of Kant's third *Critique*, as well as the role of the productive imagination in Kant's first *Critique* (both first and second editions). For Schelling, the (transcendental) imagination was, like the nature of *naturans* and *naturata*, in constant tension and *Schweben qua* synthetic activity that also appears in nature.[7] Nature itself was conceived as an organism and Schelling's thought can thus be characterized as more of an ontology of *becoming* than an ontology of *being*. In bridging ontology and epistemology, Spinoza's *deus sive natura* became Schelling's Absolute. Mechanical movement, which, unlike when taken up by Galilean and Newtonian science, was considered to be secondary movement; the primordial surging forth of the fundamental forces of nature herself was primary. For Schelling, *Naturphilosophie* promised the unity of nature (as ontology) and of thought, thereby bridging the opposition between subject and object.

Mention should be made at this juncture of Merleau-Ponty whose later thought also evinced an ontological shift emerging in good part from a rethinking of the Romantic idea of nature. The parallels between the later philosophy of Merleau-Ponty and Castoriadis are striking, as are their points of disparity. Each wishes to retrieve a "second" or "alternative" meaning to nature: As Merleau-Ponty puts it, a "primordial, nonlexical" meaning, that is, the primordial as "the nonconstructed, the noninstituted." For him nature is an "enigmatic object, an object that is not an object at all" (2003, pp. 3–4). One crucial point of difference relevant to the present study is that Merleau-Ponty's conception of *être au monde* incorporates an experiential aspect, that, while present in Castoriadis's pre-ontological thought (for example, in his 1971 homage to Merleau-Ponty, "The Sayable and the Unsayable"), is absent in his later work. Central to their respective approaches is a rethinking of the Romanticist imaginary of nature. As stated in the General Introduction to this book, Castoriadis's rethinking of the philosophical idea of nature has been marginal to the critical reception of his work; this is not the case, however, with Merleau-Ponty. Since the publication (and subsequent English-language translation) of his seminars on nature (2003), research into this aspect of his thought, and the impact it had on the ontology of *The Visible and the Invisible,* is well underway.[8] Merleau-Ponty's reconsideration of the Romantic idea of nature, as evidenced in his lecture-courses on nature, was more or less contemporaneous with his shift toward the more post-phenomenological ontology of *The Visible and Invisible.* More specifically, Merleau-Ponty's rethinking of the Romantic idea of nature acts as a critical response to the dominant place that the Cartesian view still holds in Western thought today. His rethinking of Romantic nature traces an unusual lineage: Schelling, Bergson, and Husserl. Merleau-Ponty's reconstruction of Bergson's thought emphasizes aspects of negativity and nothingness as part of being.

He interprets Bergson's perspective on nature as incorporating an ingredient of the possible. Merleau-Ponty argues that Husserl's problem of transcendental idealism was shared with Schelling, and that links can be made to the pre-philosophical *primordial* in his thought, as well as to his later inclination to recognize nature as all-embracing. Merleau-Ponty compares Schelling to Kant, Fichte, and Leibniz. He interprets Schelling's nature as an attempt to "retrieve the pre-reflexive beyond idealism" (Merleau-Ponty 2003, p. 51) and he finds hermeneutical resources for his own ontology of brute or savage being in the "barbaric rest" of Schelling's *Abgrund* of the *naturans* as the "pure, unmotivated surging forth" (Merleau-Ponty 2003, p. 37).[9] Merleau-Ponty highlights the productive tension between *naturans* and *naturata* in Schelling, as well as the continuity between human and nonhuman modes of being that it makes possible.

Finally, it seems important to note the many points of inspiration that Merleau-Ponty finds in Whitehead's conception of nature (2003).[10] After considering the Romantic idea of nature, Merleau-Ponty goes on to interrogate scientific notions of nature. He is very sympathetic to Whitehead's position, and devotes a whole lecture to its elucidation. Whitehead, as is well known, takes Heraclitus's "ever becoming" flux as his starting point. He envisages nature as process of events or activity of becoming of overlapping immanence and transcendence which we can only experience in its concrescence but which is never therewith exhausted (1929). Nature for the later Whitehead is not to be divided into an absolute temporality and spatiality, but is rather a "spatio-temporal unfurling"; in turn, this resonates with Castoriadis's later notion of creative *physis*, especially in the sense of its overlapping cosmological and ontological aspects (although Castoriadis always marginalized "the spatial" aspect in his thought). These trends link to the Whiteheadian impulse toward a critical, philosophical interpretation of scientific visions of the world that are to be enriched by quasi-speculative philosophical world articulations.[11]

Unlike many of the interpretations found in the Merleau-Ponty literature that emphasize the lived body (*Leib*) and intercorporeality as the pivotal site of interrogation, a more unorthodox interpretation of his philosophical trajectory is especially relevant for our purposes. Arnason (1988a, 1993) and Rechter (2007) each argue that in moving beyond the mode of perception, an incipient cultural turn is visible in Merleau-Ponty's later work. Here, theoretical weight is given to the institution of the world as a meta-horizon, and as a transsubjective (and transobjective) context. Following Arnason (1993), it emphasizes the "true transcendental" as the entwining of nature and culture, as Merleau-Ponty put it in his unfinished working notes—as the institution of meaning constellations—as *Ur-Stiftung*. Clear parallels between Merleau-Ponty as a cultural philosopher can be made with the interpretation of Castoriadis's later ontology, as presented in this study.[12]

Castoriadis's rethinking of the idea of nature and objective knowledge, his shift to a more Romantic conception of nature as creative, and the development of his regional ontologies of the living being and cosmology, are basic to the philosophical aspects of the project of autonomy. It involves an interrogation of the image of nature that underlies the cultural project of the infinite pursuit of "rational mastery" as embodied in capitalism, bureaucratic structures, and capitalist science (as one side of the dual imaginary institution of modernity). Castoriadis's encounter with the Romanticist imaginary of nature is sustained. From this engagement a critical reevaluation of its Aristotelian and pre-Socratic roots, and engagement with its sociopolitical dimension through the rise of the environmental social movement (1981, 2010a, 2010b), in which he sees a contemporary upsurge of the autonomist moment, emerges. As such, it also indicates a deepening sense of the interplay between Romantic and Enlightenment outlooks in his thought, although he did not particularly acknowledge this aspect.[13] This is particularly evident in the critique of the Enlightenment imaginary of nature as embedded in scientific and capitalist attempts to infinitely master, measure and quantify it, as argued by various versions of the ecological movement, of which Castoriadis sympathetically writes.[14] Not only does the ecological movement seek to set limits on the boundless pursuit of rational mastery, it simultaneously reembeds nature and the world in reconfigured meaning constellations. Castoriadis explicitly links the reinterpretation of nature to the reactivation of Aristotelian *physis* (PA), as part of a radicalized version of *natura naturans/natura naturata*.

As noted in the epigraph to the first section of this study, Castoriadis observed in a major 1974 essay that "no ontological place" had been found for *nomos*. A little more than a decade later he wrote that *nomos* "gives full meaning to the term and project of autonomy." Although both these comments are directed against the historical centrality of *physis* for Western philosophical thought, closer examination of each of these essays demonstrate a marked shift in his elucidation of *physis*. In the earlier essay, Castoriadis criticized the ways in which philosophy had drawn on *physis* at the expense of *nomos*; that is, to obscure the order of *nomos* as a self-instituting, human order. Specifically, in his early thought, the order of *physis* was reduced to nature as a "natural norm," a "natural law" in so far as it might—or might not—be encountered by anthropos. The later essay reveals a rethinking of the creative element of *physis*, not only as it manifested itself and impacted the *human* domain, but nonhuman nature, too. Although Castoriadis rethought the interplay of *nomos* and *physis*, and broadens the scope of *physis*, as we shall see, he still regarded "*nomos*" as a distinctively human, that is, sociopolitical order. As elaborated in the following chapters, Castoriadis's shift toward a transregional ontology of creative *physis,* and his critical reactivation of Romantic sources, do not signal the reduction of the *social* to *naturalistic* explanations, nor is the social conceived as the outcome of cosmic processes. Indeed, the reverse is true: An ontological perspective that pictures the world as a partial and discontinuous organization of beings, and that considers the successive strata of development as emergent forms of self-organization, is able to incorporate the social-historical domain in a cosmic context without reducing it to natural or quasi-religious impulses that would thereby disallow its novelty.

5

The Rediscovery of *Physis*

If Castoriadis focused on an elucidation of a regional ontology of *nomos* during the 1970s, from the 1980s a shift becomes apparent in his thought as his writings become more infused with a growing realization of the importance of the creativity of *physis*. For convenience, we can date this with the publication of his 1980 review of Varela's *Principles of Biological Autonomy* (1979). More broadly, by the end of the 1970s and the beginning of the 1980s Castoriadis shows a growing awareness of the importance of rethinking nature in relation not only to the political but also to the philosophical aspects of autonomy. In this vein, although it is apposite to note that Castoriadis's debate with Cohn-Bendit on "ecology and autonomy" took place in 1980, the impetus to rethink nature appears to have occurred slightly earlier with Morin's *La nature de la nature* (1977).[1] Castoriadis wrote a review of *La nature de la nature* in which his questioning of the scientific worldview begins to appear in tandem with a reevaluation of the Aristotelian notion of *physis*.[2]

In retrospect, the clearest published suggestion of an emerging shift toward a general ontology of *physis* as creativity occurs in Castoriadis's second meditation on Merleau-Ponty's thought—"Merleau-Ponty and the Weight of the Ontological Tradition"—which he composed just after the *IIS* in 1978.[3] The essay highlights the overall centrality of the imagination and radical creation as anthropic modes of being, even though, in Castoriadis's view, Merleau-Ponty ultimately remained caught in the impasses of the inherited ontological tradition and could not fully embrace the radicalism of the imaginary element. In the same paper, however, we find Castoriadis's earliest published indication of the shift toward rethinking the creativity of nature and the consequent move toward a general ontology of *physis* (and its continued interplay with his regional ontology of *nomos*). To my knowledge, this is the only place in his oeuvre where he explicitly brings together the idea of creative *physis* (which in that particular instance he terms "*hyperphysis*") and the notion of *à-être* as a polyregional or transregional understanding of being ("to be"). Even though he does not elaborate their connection at length, his discussion of a "*hyperphysis*" in relation to the social-historical and beyond is a clear indication of his roads through and beyond *nomos,* and indicates a transitional interpretation that falls between his earlier interpretation in VEJP and the later PA (which I discuss later). It is worth quoting him in full:

> If, therefore, we want to think "the polymorphism of the wild Being" in relation to the being of the social-historical sphere and as something other than an external description; if we want, starting from the mode of being of this being (*étant*) that is the social-historical, to shed further light on the signification of to be, we ought to say that in truth this signification is: to-be (*à-être*). But then, also what Merleau-Ponty calls Being—namely, the reciprocal inherence of "that which" is and of "the manner in which" it is—can no longer be thought as Being-given, Being-achieved, Being-determined, but as continued creation, perpetual origination, which concerns not only "concrete existents," and is not reproduction of other exemplars of the same, but also and essentially the forms, the *eide*, the relationships, the types, the generalities, which we are therefore unable in any way to exhaust within the horizon of any sort of determinacy whatsoever, be it real or rational, and which we see at work in its most eminent manner in human history. But then, neither can we say without equivocation that "everything is natural in us": to call "natural" the obligatory perception of another as traffic cop, Secretary General of the CPSU, or representative of Christ on Earth is to force the meaning of words. We can say that everything is natural in us (and outside us) on the condition that we no longer refer to a *phusis*, the production of what is in the repetition of what has been according to given norms, but rather to a *hyperphusis* as an engendering irreducible to the engendered, ontological genesis, emergence of *other* types, *other* relations, *other* norms. (1993: 24, emphasis in the original)

This rethinking of *physis* entails a rediscovery of its creative element, and occurs as part of Castoriadis's radicalization of the classic Aristotelian formulation of *physis* as internal qualitative movement and change (*alloiosis*) to creative emergence.[4] As indicated above, the problematic of radical *physis* converges with Castoriadis's neologism for being that was encountered in Part I of this book: *à-être* as an *incessant always-becoming-being*. With Castoriadis's increasing emphasis on radical *physis*, ontological creation of form expands from its confines to anthropic regions of being to now incorporate non-anthropic modes and regions of being as well.[5] As such, to continue to characterize Castoriadis's philosophical elucidation in terms of an ontology of *nomos* becomes somewhat misleading; instead what is to be noted during the course of the 1980s is the emergence of a shift from regional *nomos* to transregional *physis*, not as a replacement of one by the other, but rather as an interlacing of the two orders. Thus, unlike the being of the world, which was absorbed into the *à-être* stratosphere (as discussed earlier in Chapter 4), the shift to transregional *physis* does not signal the reduction of *nomos* to *physis* and the productive tension between them is maintained. The interplay of *physis* and *nomos* forms the *circle of physis and nomos*, or what Castoriadis called post-*IIS*, "the primitive circle of creation" (ISR), albeit with slightly different connotations,[6] where, as previously mentioned, *physis* shifts from being interpreted primarily in opposition to *nomos* to being the enabling ground of *nomos*, as well as one of its endpoints. Indeed, the shift to creative *physis* can be characterized as a reinterpretation and relocation of Heidegger's *ontological difference*: *Physis* as creative emergence appears as a transregional aspect of being, which deploys itself as it creates itself heterogeneously as diverse—but each time specific—regions of being (such as the *nomos* of the social-historical).[7]

As seen in the first section of the book, Castoriadis's early ontological concern foregrounded human modes of being, with the order of *physis* figuring in opposition to the order of *nomos*. Castoriadis's later approach to rethinking *physis* is distinctive in that he connects a critique of modern scientific knowledge, and its metaphysical presuppositions, to a reactivation of Greek social imaginaries by way of *naturphilosophical* themes, and the 1980s debates on the idea of autopoiesis. Although for Castoriadis these began as distinct aspects, overall they converged and overlapped in this thought. Within this context, Castoriadis begins to elucidate two more *regional* ontologies: a philosophy of the living being and a philosophical cosmology, respectively. As was the case with the interlocking modes of anthropic being, however, each of the new regional ontologies exceeds strictly regional boundaries. First, the living being is elucidated as part of the polyregional ontology of the being *for-itself*, which crosses the intersection of the natural and the social, of *physis* and *nomos*.[8] Second, as we shall see, the philosophical cosmology spills over into Castoriadis's general ontology of creative *physis* as *à-être*.

In his later writings, the tensions evident in Castoriadis's approach to the "world horizon" start to become more apparent. As discussed in the final chapter of the *nomos* section, there is a persistent ambiguity in Castoriadis's notion of the world. Although envisaged as an all-encompassing horizon, it sometimes seems to refer more to a cultural world as instituted by imaginary significations. At other times, it referred to a natural world as either the sum of all natural entities, or the mathematical—that is, rationalizable—world of the first natural stratum. This is, moreover, entwined with the idea of the first natural stratum as the region of being most amenable to ensidic elaboration.[9] Further, as I suggested in Chapter 4, the problematic of the world becomes increasingly presented in truncated form and absorbed into the problematic of radical *physis* as *à-être*.[10] As Castoriadis's critical interpretation of the Romantic imaginary of nature and his articulation of *naturphilosophical* issues progressed over the course of the 1980s, it becomes apparent that Castoriadis begins to take greater account of the being of the natural world, which had previously been more or less restricted to the first natural stratum, especially in regard to the polyregional ontology of the *for-itself*.[11] The *IIS* focused on delineating the social-historical as a creative mode of being from the more strongly ensemblistic-identitarian amenable regions of natural being; it thus primarily addressed the boundary between the psyche and the social-historical. In his later works, Castoriadis turned to the natural world—including the first natural stratum—to rethink its ontological implications, especially in relation to the social-historical. In this vein, it is worth noting, that in his later works Castoriadis tended to drop reference to *Anlehnung*. Instead of *Anlehnung*, it is more useful to think of an encounter with the world. The move toward radical *physis* and, concomitantly, the circle of *nomos* and *physis*, takes up where *Anlehnung* left off.

Castoriadis's path to *naturphilosophical* concerns—especially regarding the problematic of radical *physis*—was circuitous. Unlike Merleau-Ponty, Castoriadis did not undertake a sustained rethinking of the philosophical idea of nature as his path to ontology, nor did he pursue an enduring dialogue with the philosophical tradition of conceiving nature, as Merleau-Ponty did.[12] Instead he came to reconsider the underlying imaginary of nature as a result of his engagement with the idea of autopoiesis on two overlapping levels: first, through a reconsideration of Greek sources; and, second, via an encounter with the idea of autopoiesis as it emerged within (especially francophone) scientific contexts, which formed part of his reevaluation of scientific knowledge. In the early 1980s,

Castoriadis returned to ancient Greek sources and imaginary schema to further his thinking on the idea of being as self-creating, that is, as literally autopoietic. The neologism of autopoiesis provides openings for Castoriadis for a potential reactivation of ancient Greek imaginary schemas for elucidating being. "Auto" meaning, "of and by itself" and "poiesis," meaning "creative production," or for Castoriadis, "radical creation," lends Castoriadis points of support to elucidate being in general as *à-être*, "self-creating," or literally, "autopoietic." Although Castoriadis finds inspiration in Aristotle for his reconsideration of *physis*, there is, more so than with his engagement with *nomos*, an evident reinvigoration of archaic sources for support, in particular, pre-Socratic notions of *physis* as an element of being *qua* being; and Hesiod's notion of chaos (as *void* and as *abyss*), in particular in regard to its interlacing with the ordering of kosmos as an overall image of being.[13] Earlier indications of this aspect to Castoriadis's work in the *IIS* (both the 1965 and 1975 sections) were foreshadowed, but now his emphasis is not just on the social-historical as a meaning-creating order, but also on the chaotic element of being as challenging the specifically modern—particularly modern scientific—notion of the world (or being) as not only amenable to reason/logos, but exhausted by it (ISCS). Castoriadis's encounter with autopoiesis coincides with a deeper immersion in Greek sources. Pre-Socratic visions of self-animated being; archaic insights (from Hesiod's poetic ontology) of *creatio ex nihilo*; the meaning of being as an interplay of chaos and kosmos (that is, the idea that being is neither fully ordered nor fully rational in the way that inherited science and philosophy presume); and a rediscovery of the creative aspects of *physis,* especially as articulated in its classic form by Aristotle, all provide impetus to his onto-cosmological thought, as a philosophical interpretations of world order.[14]

Second, coinciding with this phase of Castoriadis's trajectory was the emergence and increasing importance of the idea of "autopoiesis" for a diverse range of especially natural scientific disciplines, particularly in francophone contexts. Building on the elaborations of von Neumann in the 1940s, autopoiesis is a term first coined by Chilean biologists Varela and Maturana in 1973.[15] The idea of autopoiesis does not lend itself to a unitary framework, rather it is but one of a number of heterogeneous trends within a contested and interdisciplinary field that ranges from cybernetics, psychology and biology, to physics, chemistry, and mathematics. It comprises overlapping and sometimes conflicting approaches—and interpretations of approaches—such as self-organization theory, complexity theory, systems theory, chaos theory, and so forth. The problematic of autopoiesis signals a great advance on mechanistic visions of, and approaches to nature, and to "living systems" in particular, which have long been conceived as an effect of mechanistic conditions.[16] Castoriadis's location within the autopoietic field is ambiguous. On the one hand, he has consistently questioned those theoretical directions emerging from cybernetics and information theory (for example, as in the early MSPI). In this vein, one of his enduring criticisms of several strands of "complexity" theory was that they still drew on an onto-logic of determinacy, within which ontological creation and the emergence of alterity could not be adequately acknowledged. On the other hand, he was a participant in debating these broad questions in many of the Cerisy Colloques, in at least one important discussion group (hosted by CNRS), and, finally, in his dialogue and engagement with Varela, who was perhaps the best-known proponent of the autopoietic approach. Indeed, Varela's studies on living systems within the context of immunology were of inspiration to Castoriadis's own reflections on the living being.[17] In an interview with Isabelle Stengers, Varela himself distinguishes autopoietic theory, in the narrow sense, from the more mathematically oriented, self-organization theories of, for example, Henri Atlan (for example, 1979, 1998; and 1983, coauthored with Milgram).[18]

Creative *Physis*

Although there are some early indications of Castoriadis's preliminary concerns with creative *physis* that precede the *IIS*—see especially, MSPI—the growing interest in *physis* was set aside in the 1970s when Castoriadis engaged in his most systematic philosophical work on anthropic modes of being; at that point it is better interpreted as a sideline to his primary theoretical preoccupations. However, from the early 1980s—and increasingly visible from the mid-1980s—Castoriadis began to rediscover the creative aspect to *physis* that he had overlooked in the earlier elucidations that had emphasized the singularity of *nomos* as a creative mode of being in opposition to *physis*.

I now turn to a 1983 archival document, "Autonomie et complexité" (AC), as a primary text for interpretation, as well as "Imaginaire social et changement scientifique" (ISCS) and "*Physis* and Autonomy" (PA) for amplification.[19] The importance of AC lies in its depiction of a comprehensive, even if preliminary, overview of Castoriadis's shift toward creative *physis* and the overlapping *naturphilosophical* contexts whence it emerges. Castoriadis's encounter with the autopoietic field occurred on four different but intertwining levels: First, a philosophical elucidation and radicalization of Varela and Maturana's neologism "autopoiesis" that took greater account of its ancient Greek sources and imaginary schema; second, a reconsideration of the objectivity of knowledge, especially in terms of the entwining of subject and object, and as this applies to the idea of increasing order or increased complexity (I take this up in the next chapter when discussing his critique of objective knowledge); third, a review of the living being—that is, autopoiesis in the narrow sense—and ongoing discussion with Varela regarding the limits of autonomy (the thematic of Chapter 7); and finally, a rethinking of cosmology (I address this in Chapter 8), particularly in regard to the "spectre of the spatialization of time that haunts physics." These converge with his rethinking of *physis* as part of his *naturphilosophical* radicalization of autonomy.

AC comprises a report of the third meeting of the "Groupe de Réflexion Interdisciplinaire," on March 17, 1983.[20] The topic for discussion was "Autonomie et complexité."[21] Two texts had been circulated among the participants: Atlan and Milgram's "Probabilistic Automata as a Model for Epigenesis for Cellular Networks" and the introduction to *Ordres et desordres* (1982) by Jean-Pierre Dupuy.[22] Castoriadis's introductory intervention comprises a significant part of the reported meeting. Castoriadis opens the debate with a series of notations that address the philosophical implications of the theme for discussion—autonomy and complexity—rather than the agreed upon texts for reading and discussion. He begins with the theme of the "*auto.*"[23] He notes its widespread use as a substantive prefix: autonomy, auto-organization, *autopoiesis* (in reference to Varela and Maturana), but questions whether there is a genuine connection between all of them. He asks if there can be said to be something like a transregional metacategory of the *auto*, or has a transregionality been illicitly included? Castoriadis thus confronts us, albeit implicitly, with the central problematic of *physis* and *nomos* and transregionality: How can *physis* be transregional if *nomos* is still to retain any weight? As well, it points to the crux of his disagreement with Varela: Can we speak of biological autonomy? As is the case with much of his writing, the link between *physis* and *à-être* tends to remain latent. For Castoriadis, it is not possible to speak of *physis* in the human domain without invoking *nomos*, and, indeed, *nomos*—not *physis*—is to be thought as the mode of being of the social-historical. As discussed in Chapter 4, Castoriadis tends to reject an understanding of a transregional category that posits being as homogenous, yet he cannot completely reject the possibility of a transregional characteristic out of hand. Indeed, its presence is increasingly felt in his philosophical reflections, but arguably without the adverse implications that seemed to concern him.

Embarking on a "philosophical-metaphysical" excursus, Castoriadis identifies various social imaginaries that serve to grasp the world within which discussions of the *auto* must *necessarily* occur. He argues that imaginary schemas are as such "onto-cosmological," as each claims to grasp the essence of all that can be said *to be (être)*.[24] Castoriadis divides these imaginaries into two kinds, with the respective meanings of—and importance lent to—the idea of *inertia* or, in contrast, to the idea of *movement*, as distinguishing principles. First, Castoriadis identifies the classical modern imaginary of Western science that has prevailed since Galileo, Descartes, and Newton. The modern scientific imaginary views (natural) being as inert, passive, and extended; it is habitually considered in the most general sense as the cosmological object. In ISCS (p. 174), Castoriadis goes further and points to the prefiguring of inertia as far back as the twelfth century. Later in the AC discussion, Isabelle Stengers contests Castoriadis's argument concerning the scientific imaginary and motion (inertia), arguing instead that in the modern scientific tradition not all images of the world can be reduced to the idea of inertia. In her view, Newton's understanding of the world envisaged nature to be unceasingly animated by God. Stengers is, in the present writer's view, correct to point to the reductionist tendency in Castoriadis's interpretation of imaginary significations, particularly as they pertain to the various strands of monotheism, in general, and to the impact of Christianity on the Western constellation, in particular. Nonetheless, the two images of an animated nature/world differ in that ultimately the Newtonian version is neither self-moving nor self-creating in any of the ways, or with any of the meanings, that are important for Castoriadis in this context; that is, that of the *auto* and that of *creation* in its alterity to production. In ISCS, Castoriadis critiques Plato's Demiurge for the same reasons. A further point is worth mentioning: For Castoriadis, one of the chief characteristics of the Greek vision of being as self-moving and self-creating lies in its contrast to the Christian schema, in which, on Castoriadis's account, natural being is *neither* self-creative *nor* self-moving, but produced and set into motion externally and Divinely by a Creator-Legislator God. His alternative elucidation of being can thus also be interpreted as part of his wider polemic against monotheistic (and therefore heteronomous) traditions and sources, and the importance of reinvigorating classical sources both for the project of autonomy writ large but in particular in its aspect as *la philosophie*.

Castoriadis continues his discussion and suggests that when the "*auto*" is invoked in such contexts, a second imaginary schema is drawn upon: the ancient Greek imaginary, which was given its classic form by Aristotle.

The ancient Greek image of the world and of being suggest that they are characterized by their own dynamism (*dynamisme propre*). It is an animated view of the world, where being is seen as "*auto, mouvement—au sens le plus profond—phusis, c'est-à-dire poussée, naissance, croissance.*" Here *physis*, although still remaining within the constraints of the Aristotelian framework, is seen as the most important sense of qualitative movement with which being itself is endowed. Castoriadis consistently refers to *physis* in terms of "*the push toward*" (*poussée*), and not, as is more common in the French literature, as *the power/force* (*puissance*) *to*.[25] Although here Castoriadis links *physis* to being in its most general sense (drawing on Greek antecedents in the process), as I have already indicated he tended to be ambivalent regarding its transregional nature, suspicious of its homogenizing capacity. In this way, it is important to note that he did not ever systematically elucidate the kinship between transregional, radical *physis* and regional *nomos*; rather, it requires hermeneutical reconstruction. However, as I signaled earlier, the tension between *nomos* and *physis* is not collapsed. What remains more or less latent in Castoriadis's thought, however, is the transregionality of the creative element of *physis*, of which *nomos* is one of its points of culmination.

Castoriadis traces the image of dynamic being to the pre-Socratic founders of philosophy. In AC and in ISCS a particularly clear sense of the plurality of the Greek imaginary context is apparent (Castoriadis seldom makes this aspect plain). In particular he suggests it was central to Heraclitus and Empedocles, as well as to Aristotle (ISCS). Although Castoriadis—contrary to his usual insistence on the discovery of philosophy as consubstantial with the creation of the democratic *polis*—arrays the pre-Socratic thinkers in line with Aristotle, his elucidation of *physis* (and *nomos*, too, for that matter) remains primarily an engagement with Aristotelian *physis*. In respect to movement and *physis*, Castoriadis argues with Aristotle for the qualitative motion of alteration "in that matter acquired another form" (itself regarded as essence) that has been reduced by the moderns to quantitative, local movement (as discussed earlier). In drawing on the Aristotelian distinction between natural being and artifact (*physis* and *techne*), Castoriadis foregrounds the internal push—that is, the dynamic movement—of *physis*.

In clear recognition of the plurality of Greek imaginary schemas, Castoriadis points out that there were two other interpretative patterns that might be seen as alternatives to the Aristotelian and its pre-Socratic antecedents and their vision of being as dynamic in antiquity: the Democritean/Epicurean and the Platonic. The first posits a kind of movement within being as atoms, while including an element of "chance" as the accidental encounters of atoms from which new forms surge forth. In the Platonic model of the *Timaeus*, that which *is*—departing from the fabrication of the demiurge of the world—is the *chora* as a residue of *physis*. The *chora* is both chaos and receptacle of chaos as a mysterious indeterminacy of matter, of form, and of space that is always caught up in disordered motion.[26] There is therefore always movement. Absent, however, is the formative role of chance; instead the demiurge imposes the form. The residue of *physis* in the *chora* is an archaic image of being that persists in various ways throughout the Greek tradition: Traces can be seen even in the idea of *physis* as not fully ordered. Castoriadis envisaging of being as *à-être* falls within this imaginary schema.[27]

Castoriadis then shifts his discussion in AC from the pre-Socratics to contemporary physics, with passing comments on the advent of Christianity and its effect on the imaginary schema. He dates the marginalization of the image of dynamic being with the rise of Christianity. For Castoriadis dynamic being is meant in the strong sense of *self-moving being of and by itself*. As such, in his view, the influence of Christianity proved retrograde: Christian dogma could not grant the world its own self-propelling movement. In turn, this was instrumental in opening a space for the world/matter to be considered inert, that is without auto-movement. On Castoriadis's interpretation, the ontological framework, within which God was seen to endow the (natural) world with a certain quantity of movement and energy in the universe in order for it to move, while simultaneously fixing the eternal laws (of nature), was not really movement (or creation) at all. Castoriadis discerns a connection between this and the gradual return to heteronomy on the level of the social world.

At this point, Castoriadis turns to the domain of physics, focusing particularly on cosmology. He proposes a discontinuity as the very basis of being, observing that postulating a break with the initial symmetry to account for the existence of a universe is inescapable, and that without this break there would have been nothing. Implicitly, Castoriadis draws on an aspect of his emergent philosophy of mathematics that privileges the dyad. Here he concurs with Aristotle, in that only with the advent of the dyad can alterity and creation be thought.[28] In this context, Castoriadis argues that the idea of "passage" from a disordered state to an ordered one presents difficulties. In an extension of his critique of sufficient reason, he argues that although certain types of disorder might be deemed necessary, they are not sufficient to produce a higher-level order (which would simply be an outmoded physics). What is missing is the idea of the "supplement of creation." Thus, for Castoriadis, a "supplement of sufficiency" cannot exist; instead, there is the moment of *autocreation*. On Castoriadis's account, it is necessary therefore to invoke the moment of creation as an irregularity or as the result of chance.[29] This would seem to show that "what is" can propel itself in a particular direction rather than in another. Self-creation and the presupposition of the origin occur even at the physical level. In referring to theories of an ultimate unification, Castoriadis points out that at a certain level (at a temperature of 10^{17} Kelvin) the distinction between the three fundamental forces does not exist. These three forces only appear subsequently, that is they create themselves, and create themselves with what he terms a "local"—as opposed to a "universally" valid—laws governing weak interactions that only appear at a particular moment.[30]

Castoriadis then turns to address the other side of the equation: the living being and the human being. A shift in his thinking, from the organization of the living being as per the *IIS* to the living being's creation of laws, becomes apparent. On his account, the problematic of the living being is incompatible with reductionist frameworks of mechanistic nature. The living being appears at a certain juncture of being, constitutes a specific type of being, while bringing into existence (*fait exister*), that is, creating, certain laws, about which it would be empty to affirm their prior existence. The organism creates them at the same time as it creates itself qua living being (*l'être vivant*), which for Castoriadis amounts to the sense that *physis* pushes itself toward form (*eidos*) in order to be. This also holds for the level of humankind as simultaneously psychic and social-historical. How should the qualitative specificity of each of these levels be then defined? What can be said of the difference between the self-constitution of the living being and that of society? Is it the same type of self-constitution that is in play? How is it possible to characterize these differences other than as phenomenological differences? Do they perhaps lie in qualitative differences of form? These questions remain open for Castoriadis. In the realm of the being *for-itself* (*pour soi*), he posits a radical break between the nonorganic and the organic on the one hand, and the human on the other. Yet it is clear that for Castoriadis the self-creation of laws of the "autonomic" living being at the level of anthropic being is different in kind, not just degree; the tension between *physis* and *nomos*, regional *nomos* and transregional *physis*, emerges particularly clearly in this context.[31]

Castoriadis ends his discussion in AC by broaching the subject of order and disorder from epistemological and ontological perspectives. In the first instance he relates the problematic to the living being and consequent implications for scientific knowledge. Castoriadis points out that to measure the creation of order or complexity that emerges from an encounter—or shock—with noise or disorder presents difficulties in its measurement, for the discernment of "order" or "disorder" cannot be demarcated from the subjective viewpoint of the scientific observer. As will be discussed more fully in the next chapter, all acts of knowledge are the function of two ensembles: that which depends on the observer and that which depends on the observed (as the natural world). The natural world has a certain structure, as Castoriadis admits, but he does not systematically elaborate this thematic in non-ensidizable terms, although glimpses can be discerned in his two regional ontologies of the living being and of physical nature. Castoriadis argues that Atlan and Milgram's ideas, which give the probabilistic automaton upon which the living being is modeled more efficacy than the determinist automaton, nonetheless still lean on determinist affirmations. In closing, Castoriadis introduces the philosophical notion of the being *for-itself* in relation to the living being: The living being constitutes or creates its world by accepting only the information that it decides to integrate as such.[32] It is therefore this closed world (from the point of view of the functioning of the living being, informational and cognitive, for example) that is characteristic of the living being, à propos of which Varela speaks of "biological autonomy" (although, as we shall see in Chapter 7, Castoriadis rejects the notion of biological autonomy).

Absent from Castoriadis's discussion in AC, however, is any mention of the archaic heritage beyond the Greek imaginaries of movement/*physis*; it seems pertinent to point to it here. As Castoriadis recognizes in ISCS (pp. 174–75) the idea of being/world in the ancient Greek imaginary reworked archaic mythological and religious themes.[33] In the first instance, the archaic bequest to ancient Greek thought was the idea of world not as fully ordered but as a combination of chaos and kosmos. We encountered this imaginary schema in the first section of the book, but there it was limited to an order of meaning for the social-historical world. Here Castoriadis moves beyond strictly social-historical limits in his widening problematization of the world: a world that was not fully ordered, a world that is not fully rational (or rationalizable) and thus not completely amenable to the grasp of rational thought. Castoriadis draws on two meanings of chaos in ISCS and in *CQFG*. First is the void in Hesiod's *Theogony* from which he traces the non-Christian version of creation *ex nihilo* as "creation from nothing and by no one" (ISCS): The world surges forth from the void. The world—which Castoriadis tends to absorb into being—is considered not only animated but also *self-animating*, to which, as discussed earlier, Castoriadis contrasts the Judeo-Christian (and Platonic) tradition in which matter is neither self-animating nor self-creating. Castoriadis points to a second meaning of chaos toward the end of the *Theogony*: the idea of an interplay between chaos and kosmos, between disorder and order. It is this interplay that makes science, philosophy, and politics possible. For if the world were fully ordered and fully rational, there would only be a single system of absolute knowledge. If the world were absolutely disordered, fully chaotic, nothing could be articulated or accessible to forms of rationality. For the possibility of rational enquiry to exist, the world must exist as an interlacing of chaos and kosmos, order and disorder. It is evident moreover that the idea of being as an interplay of chaos and kosmos informs Castoriadis's later notions of being as radical *physis qua à-être*.[34] As I have shown during the earlier discussion of the VEJP, Castoriadis has already alluded to the indeterminacy of *physis* in his discussion of *physis* and *hyle*. There seems, however, to be a tension in Castoriadis's articulation of *hyle*. As part of radical *physis*, *hyle* is no longer the substratum that is formed, but one that forms itself. Yet it is further ontologically altered—ontologically formed—by the order of meaning that is imposed by the social-historical. Adding to the complexity here is that commentators have generally interpreted Aristotle's elaboration of *hyle* as a reconfiguration of Plato's *chora*, although the "chaotic residue" of the *chora* for Aristotle, as with Castoriadis, seemed to be embedded in *physis*. As with the earlier VEJP, Castoriadis concludes—but now in stronger terms—that the possibility of knowledge tells us something ontological about the being of the world.

Reconfiguring the *Nomos* and *Physis* Problematic

Although in VEJP Castoriadis had noted—almost in passing—the indeterminacy of *hyle* and *physis* and the potential within *physis* for self-alteration, its radically creative potential was yet to be elaborated. Fifteen years later, the situation had altered. *"Physis* and Autonomy" (1997) is an important essay that has received too little attention in the secondary literature: It provides the most lucid indication of the reconfiguration of the *physis* and *nomos* problematic in Castoriadis's thought and as such provides us with important points of hermeneutical reconstruction. It clearly demonstrates the shift in Castoriadis's rethinking of Aristotelian *physis*, while simultaneously making clear its ongoing interplay with *nomos*.[35] In contrast to the earlier VEJP, but still drawing on Aristotle's classic formulation, Castoriadis radicalizes *physis* beyond the limits of a conventional

Aristotelian framework, and, in so doing, addresses its non-anthropic aspects more fully.

The title of the paper, "*Phusis* and Autonomy," alludes to a slightly earlier discussion by Castoriadis (with Daniel Cohn-Bendit), "From Ecology to Autonomy" (1981). Each relates to the project of autonomy and ecology/nature in different but intersecting ways: The first emphasizes the political aspect; the second shifts to the philosophical dimension and questions the cultural imaginaries underpinning of the scientific worldview, on the one hand, while grappling with the relocation of the Aristotelian *physis* and *nomos* problematic—and consequent implications—into the newly emphasized ontological region of the living being, on the other. As in VEJP, so, too, in PA does Castoriadis posit the following question: Is there a *physis* of *nomos* and a *nomos* of *physis*? In PA, however, he acknowledges that there are two, divergent elements to Aristotelian *physis*, but their divergence "can become for us again today a fruitful new point of departure" (PA 332), that is, a starting point for rethinking the creativity of *physis*. Whereas in VEJP he responded to this through a discussion of Aristotelian *physis* as it affected human *nomos*, now he also continues to appeal to Aristotle and his "profound problematic" of *physis*, but approaches it from a different angle. As in the earlier VEJP, Castoriadis identifies two dimensions to Aristotle's *physis*, but, significantly, these differ in the later text (PA) from his earlier exposition. First, in PA they no longer incorporate a normative dimension; second, while the idea of "teleological" *physis* has been retained (as an aspect of Aristotle's thought), the earlier dimension discussed in VEJP of "actuality" has been dropped in favor of highlighting those aspects of *physis* that open onto contexts of creation.

Castoriadis identifies the first aspect of *physis* as teleological—and ironically points out that these days only "machines" can be said to have "ends" (although such ends are still external to the machine themselves!). However, it is in articulating the second aspect of *physis*—as qualitative movement—that a less than systematic approach to its elucidation, indicative perhaps of PA's original mode as an oral presentation, is more evident. Castoriadis does not elucidate *physis* in its radical form so much by rigorous argumentation as by juxtaposing and evoking the different nuances in Aristotle's statements on *physis* to interpret and radicalize Aristotle's nuances of *physis* to suit his own ends. In this way, *physis* slides, on Castoriadis's account, from Aristotle's statement in *Physics* 2.192b21 "the essence of the things that have in themselves, as such, the principle of movement" to (still citing Aristotle), "*Physis* is the principle of movement existing in the thing itself" to his definition in the metaphysics "*Physis* is the principle in the thing itself" (PA 333). He sums up Aristotle's *physis*: "That is *physis* (or appertains to *physis*) which has in itself, which contains in itself, the origin and the principle of its movement" but recasts it more strongly to reveal the Greek imaginary schema of being as self-moving: "that is *physis*, that is nature, which moves itself of itself (*s'auto-meut*)" (PA 333).

After providing us with his interpretation of Aristotle's *physis*, Castoriadis ostensibly returns to the first aspect—the teleological—although in effect his discussion intertwines the two aspects. In reevaluating its relevance for us today, Castoriadis returns to the ground covered in VEJP, but here he distinguishes more fully between the "*telos*" of the physical from the "ultimate *telos*" of the *nous*. As in VEJP, *physis* continues to be equated with the *eros* of thought; in the earlier paper, it was the determinacy of *eros* within thought that made *physis* thinkable and knowable for us. In the later PA, *physis* as *eros* is not discussed in reference to anthropic being, but in reference to natural modes of being: *Physis* as *eros* in this context is interpreted as "movement toward, pushing toward form, toward the thinkable, toward law, toward *eidos*. *Physis* appears then, as the *pushing-toward-giving-itself-a-form*" (PA 333).

The elucidation continues to be somewhat oblique. Castoriadis summarizes and continues to shift the argument: "There is a pushing of nature toward form; *physis* tends to give itself the most perfect, or (perhaps) the most complex, form possible" (PA 333–34). The idea that *physis* creates the most complex form possible may indicate the de-divinization of the first mover from *theos-nous* (as in VEJP) to the *nous*.[36] Castoriadis then highlights its dynamic and nondeterminist (that is not reducible to an ensemble) character: "*Physis* is the irresistible push of a being . . . that tends to give itself a form in order to be, a law in order to be determinate, that tends to give itself, perhaps, a 'thinkability.' *Physis* would tend to form itself" (PA 334). Hence, Castoriadis highlights, in radicalizing Aristotelian *physis*, that *physis* is self-moving and self-forming; in order *to be* it must give itself its own form. To further illustrate his point, Castoriadis draws on Kant's *Critique of Judgment*, as well as Francisco Varela's thought, to argue that a notion of *teleonomy* would be preferable to *teleology* to elaborate the capacity of living beings to "posit themselves—partially—as their own ends" (PA 334). The convergence between radical *physis* and *à-être* appears very clearly here; the point of Castoriadis's excursus was to demonstrate that the ultimate end of *physis is to form itself in order to-be*, or *à-être*. Castoriadis diverges from Aristotle's interpretation of *physis* in arguing that the form is not predetermined. Castoriadis also directly mentions the *natura naturans/natura naturata* tradition, from which he distances himself, as he thinks such thinkers take on "the imperfect tense of ontological eternity (PA 336). This divergence was not present in the earlier VEJP: Castoriadis explains this further in his examination of Aristotle's second interpretation of *physis*.

Aristotle's second interpretation of *physis*, which differs from the account Castoriadis provided in VEJP, concerns the idea of movement. Unlike Heidegger, Castoriadis focuses on *alloiosis*.[37] He critiques the impoverishment of modern interpretations of nature where the richness of Aristotle's idea of qualitative forms of movement is reduced to a purely mechanical "local movement." Castoriadis draws our attention to the various kinds of movement in Aristotle: local, generation, corruption, and in particular, *alloiosis* as qualitative alteration. Building on his discussion of Aristotle's first aspect of *physis*, Castoriadis interprets *physis* as that which "*has in itself the principle or the origin of its* change—*of its alteration*" (PA 335). Castoriadis attributes the principle of movement as understood by moderns as not only external to the things moved, but external to the "totality of the moved and the movable" as a transcendent principle of God (PA 335). Here it can be seen that Castoriadis retrieves the dynamic sense of nature that is *physis*, and radicalizes it from movement to alteration, to change-in-form, to transformation; "and this last includes the *appearance*, the *emergence*, the *creation* of form." Thus in his completed reading, *physis* for Castoriadis becomes that which has in itself the principle of the creation of form. He contrasts his radicalization of *physis* as the principle of creation of form to Aristotle's determinist account of *physis* as the determined *eidos* linked to *ousia*, or the *to ti en einai*, which Castoriadis now refers to as the "imperfect tense of ontological eternity" (PA 336). Castoriadis concludes that the two aspects to *physis* in Aristotle converge, but that even in Aristotle's thought, this leaves an "enormous residue": humankind. For humankind is not reducible to *physis*, that is, internal, creative movement, but also participates in *nomos*, indeed, it is the order of *nomos* that makes anthropos qua anthropos. As Castoriadis notes, after the rethinking of *alloiosis* what remains is anthropos as "*arkhe ton esomenon*: principle and origin of what will be (*De Interpretatione* 9.1917), that is, as nonpredetermined (in echo of his conclusions of the earlier VEJP). It is only in the human domain that *nomos*—and autonomy—have meaning.

Castoriadis concludes PA with a discussion of "autonomy" in its relation to *physis*, that is, why it pertains only to the human realm. Here he takes issue with Francisco Varela. Although Castoriadis agrees with the idea of the "self-creation of the living being," he does not concur with

Varela's notion of "biological autonomy" for the nonhuman realm because "autonomy" is at root political and can only have meaning for anthropos. Here it is worth quoting him in full:

> We arrive, therefore, at an idea of autonomy that differs radically from simple self-constitution. We conceive autonomy as the capacity, of a society or of an individual, to act deliberately and explicitly in order to modify its law—that is to say, its form. *Nomos* becomes the explicit self-creation of form, which thus makes it appear both as, still, the opposite of *physis*—*and* as one of the latter's points of culmination. (p. 340; emphasis in the original)

Nonetheless, with the rethinking of the living being, and the subsequent elaboration of the polyregional ontology of the *being-for-itself*, which spans the living being as well as anthropic modes of being, the problematic of *physis* and *nomos* is enlarged to include consideration of the living being, even if Castoriadis ultimately retains "*nomos*" as a purely human mode of being (I discuss these matters more fully in Chapter 7). Although maintaining a clear distinction between the human domain and the region of the living being as far as "autonomy" and "*nomos*" went, it is clear that, through a rethinking of *physis*, Castoriadis has come to view both regions as characterized by *physis* in the sense of ontological self-creation: "Beings (*les étants*) have in themselves principle and origin of creation of forms, being (*l'être*) itself is defined by *alloiosis* in the strong sense of the word—self-alteration, self-creation" (PA 336).

Despite Castoriadis's strong connections with contemporary *naturphilosophical* problematics and his rejuvenation of ancient Greek imaginary schemas, his discussion of radical *physis* is unsystematic. To my knowledge, "*Physis* and Autonomy" is the only published essay in which he explicitly addresses it in some detail. Distinct from the development of radical *physis*, yet analogous to it, Castoriadis's neologism *à-être* remained a subterranean presence within his elucidations. It was occasionally broached in the *IIS*, but became more important in his later, post-*IIS* trajectory when he began to consider non-anthropic regions of being. That being said, *à-être*—and creative *physis*—remain but sketchily contoured throughout Castoriadis's trajectory. This could be interpreted as indicative of the lack of systematization with which Castoriadis pursued his later critical *Naturphilosophie*. More probably, it is possible to read it as Castoriadis's ambivalence regarding the juxtaposition of the idea of being as heterogeneous to a transregional characteristic of being—as is visible in the final chapter of the *IIS*—which in some instances could seem to emphasize an ultimately univocal interpretation of being, which would therewith neutralize the importance of *nomos*.

The discussion of selected textual sources in this chapter evinces a major philosophical shift in Castoriadis's conceptualization of the *nomos/physis* problematic. It took place over the course of a decade: from the time of the 1975 VEJP to the 1986 PA. His encounter with the problematic of the *naturphilosophical* contexts of autopoiesis was a decisive factor for his philosophical trajectory. Its influence can be seen on four interconnected levels of his thought: his reconsideration of Greek sources for his later interpretation of transregional being as self-creating; his rethinking of objective knowledge; his ventures into philosophical cosmology; and his reevaluation of the living being, especially in light of his dialogue with Varela. In brief, Castoriadis's engagement with autopoiesis was significant for his shift toward an ontology of creative *physis*. Castoriadis's turn to creative *physis* is distinctive in that it emerges from separate but ultimately conjoined strands of thought; they ultimately converge in his thought, yet they also remain peculiarly unarticulated. As with Merleau-Ponty, Castoriadis's interpretation of *physis* can be read as a critical reappropriation of the Romantic conception of nature, in particular, through a reactivation of the intermittent tradition of *natura naturans/naturata*. However, as I have emphasized, Castoriadis draws strongly on aspects of the Greek—and, in particular, the Aristotelian—imaginary. I have shown that in his rethinking of natural modes of being, he looks even further back than Aristotle to the pre-Socratics and archaic understandings of *physis*. Yet, as is beginning to become apparent, Castoriadis's reflections on nature also include an engagement with modern scientific forms of knowledge: His interpretation of being as self-animated and heterogeneous is informed by the limitations of the metaphysical presupposition of classical modern science of a fully rational (and rationalizable) world. His argument consistently revolves around his understanding that *what we can know tells us something about how the world is*. As mentioned, Castoriadis did not systematically pursue and elucidate the shift toward radical *physis*: His later trajectory requires reconstruction. The following chapters flesh out the different aspects in greater depth, beginning with his deepening critical engagement with the problematic of objective knowledge and its ontological implications.

6

Objective Knowledge in Review

Castoriadis's ongoing reflections on science were critical in paving the way for a new reflection on *physis*. Although he subsumed his epistemological critique to the discussion of the proto-institutions of *legein* and *teukhein* as a critique of elementary reason at the time of the *IIS*, it later developed its own momentum. During the 1980s Castoriadis's epistemological reflections go beyond the *IIS* to further relativize the claims of science while simultaneously liberating a space for philosophical reflection, in general, and, in particular, for deeper reflection on nature. He claims that science provides not only knowledge about nature, but also that underpinning this knowledge lies a philosophy of nature. These two strands of thought are foregrounded in his elucidation in "The Ontological Import of the History of Science" (1997), which provides the focus of discussion for the present chapter. In OIHS we see him moving back and forth between these two aspects, although finally they will converge in his overall thought. Castoriadis's questioning not only of the objectivist imaginary and the scientific enterprise, but also of mainstream philosophical reflection on their problems, takes two forms. First, Castoriadis critiques modern science for its dependence on the Cartesian and Baconian notion of, as he terms it, the "unlimited expansion of rational mastery over nature." This aspect of his critique emerges from his political thought and theory of modernity as the dual institution of autonomy and rational mastery.[1] Second, Castoriadis criticizes what he sees as the vicious circle of objectivist imaginary and subject-centered reflection but does so in philosophical terms through a sustained consideration of the ontological basis of the modern epistemological project, and, in so doing, a reactivation of the need to reassess the importance of *Naturphilosophie*.

The modern philosophical shift toward epistemology has generally downplayed the importance of ontological questions. Philosophical critiques of objective knowledge gathered particular momentum in the twentieth century, partly as a response to the discovery of the so-called "crises" in mathematics and physics, their epistemological foundations, and their underlying ontologies.[2] Castoriadis's particular concerns focus on the philosophical consequences of the radical separation of "subject" and "object" and their determinations as presumed in the traditional onto-epistemology; he shares this with the broader phenomenological field. His specific argument is that that every epistemology assumes an ontology, and this argument endures throughout his entire philosophical trajectory,[3] while, of course, leaning on Heideggerian insights as presented in the *Kantbuch*.[4] Although agreeing with Heidegger—contra Kant—that one cannot separate epistemology from ontology, Castoriadis goes further than Heidegger, not only in terms of radicalizing notions of the imagination and time, but also in contesting the Heideggerian ontological difference of Being/beings. Castoriadis links up with phenomenological critiques of the subject/object demarcation in that he does not approach objects as entities in themselves, but regards them as also existing for a subject/observer, in extension of Kant's "knowledge is always knowledge of something" and Husserl's "consciousness as consciousness of something," as well as Merleau-Ponty's enduring quest to rethink the dilemmas of the "subjective" and "objective" worlds.[5] However, Castoriadis goes beyond Husserlian phenomenology to post-transcendental (or even to post-phenomenological approaches), in that he pursues the ontological role of the *imagination* in Kant and Heidegger, and burrows down into its transcendental workings in the creation of the world.

During the early to mid-1980s, Castoriadis simultaneously explores various sides of an argument concerning the rethematization of the idea of *physis*. In the *IIS*, Castoriadis's discussion of natural phenomena—especially in the chapter on *legein* and *teukhein*, as well as in the final *IIS* chapter—foreshadowed the later shift toward a new reflection on *physis*, as did his continued questioning of objective knowledge. Should a philosophy of nature be revived, then a justification is required vis-à-vis the exclusive claims of modern science and its technological mastery of the natural realm. Even in his early work, Castoriadis demonstrated a curiosity for epistemological matters: His unfinished doctoral dissertation dealt with epistemology and logic.[6] The early MSPI addresses these themes further, albeit in that text "science" is conceived broadly and refers to both the "natural and social" sciences. In regard to the history of science, and its inability to be inserted within classical scientific frameworks, even pre-*IIS*, Castoriadis had begun to move in a clear direction.[7] His idea of truth as a social-historical "doing"—and concomitantly the debunking of absolute truth—is already evident at this early (pre-*IIS*) stage, as is the rejection of the demarcation between science (epistemology) and philosophy. Thus the centrality of the conundrum of science as a *history* of science is an articulated but as yet not systematically developed theme in the 1970s.[8] In elucidating key shifts in Castoriadis's later itinerary, the aim is not to reconstruct a linear trajectory, as his later writing does not lend itself to that. Post-*IIS*, Castoriadis elucidates the "world in fragments"; his work is less systematically developed, and it operates on a number of levels. From around the early to mid–1980s, Castoriadis's intellectual energies are directed at three *niveaux*: the seminars at the EHESS,[9] published essays, and the phantomesque *L'élément imaginaire*.[10]

OIHS provides a mature elaboration of Castoriadis's epistemological engagement in which the key aspects of his general ontology of reconfigured *physis* as *à-être* are increasingly delineated and made apparent.[11] Parts of OIHS were first presented in May 1982: Shortly after the publication of OIHS itself, a transcript of the original presentation was published as "Imaginaire social et changement scientifique" (1987), which makes clear the link between social imaginaries and scientific change (or social-historical change, more broadly). In this context, our primary text for the current chapter will be OIHS, as, of the two, it is the more systematically developed for publication.[12] Three themes are evident in Castoriadis's approach to the questioning of objective knowledge: First, the post-Kantian tradition in the history of science; second, the continuity of the modern project with the ancient Greeks; and third, the rehabilitation of a philosophy of nature as central to modern concerns. More particularly, Castoriadis proposes to link post-Kantian visions of science and its transformation to a pre-Kantian vision of philosophy and its tasks, whereby he begins to fuse key elements from Aristotelian and Kantian approaches.[13] This allows him to interpret the history of science and the ontology of the social-historical as interrelated.

The title of OIHS presents us with an indication of the ensuing anti-Kantian argument: That a "history of science" exists problematizes the project of science as being either only open to epistemological elucidation, or purely resting on transcendental grounds. Castoriadis's manner of proceeding in OIHS is by means of a critique of inherited thought and established presuppositions in modern classical ontology; from this it follows that he must take issue with what passes for knowledge in modernity and its basic assumptions. Second, Castoriadis provides a comprehensive concept of institution as the establishment of the precondition of knowledge in general, and of science in particular. The institution of knowledge is therefore integral to his rethinking of the social-historical (and the shifting interrelations of *physis* and *nomos*).[14] Third, Castoriadis has to articulate more thoroughly that knowledge is knowledge of an "external world"; that is, of beings and their modes of being. In making his main point—with which he begins OIHS and ISCS—Castoriadis insists that the subject and object are not, as classical conceptions would have it, radically distinct, but rather are perpetually interwoven (what he terms the "principle of the undecidability of origins"), and are in mutual implication. For him the social-historical context of the "subject" is as important as the "natural object" in the production of knowledge. Nor can the subject, contra Kant, be the privileged site of knowledge production. The subject, moreover, needs to be understood in its social-historical context: Knowledge is ultimately *transsubjective*, not egological, and as such ushers us toward post-phenomenological contexts and arguments. As social-historical, knowledge for Castoriadis can never be interpreted as absolute—but neither is it arbitrary. Rather, it must be understood as a history and process of social-historical *creation*.[15] On the other hand, the fact that we do have knowledge of the world tells us something of the being of the world; it is not the impenetrable in-itself of Kant's first *Critique*.

The history of science holds ontological implications for an elucidation of being. In his philosophical articulation, Castoriadis looks to ancient Greek imaginary schema to support his image of being as the entwining of chaos and kosmos. The world reemerges as a theme in OIHS, mainly as the physical universe, but also as the physical world as it is always already "made be" or "made real" (or given "meaningful existence") from the supports offered by social imaginary schemas. As Castoriadis moves into the *physis* register, the beginnings of a "realistic" schema of knowledge as a version of "transcendental realism" begins to emerge, in both stronger and weaker forms, as different layers of transcendental reality.[16] We find that primordial being exists before the social-historical encounters it; as such, it is not yet the "natural world." Raw being is not yet the natural world as social-historically "instituted": The world as *kosmos* is always already an *order of meaning*, in that it is social-historically imagined and articulated.[17] The natural world is primordial being as we encounter it—and as primordial being gives itself of itself to us—as we interpretatively create and institute it according to imaginary constellations of meaning, such as the two mentioned by Castoriadis in OIHS (leaning on

Koyré 1957): the "closed world" and the "infinite universe." Even the ensidic layering of the first natural stratum will be encountered in other ways by diverse social-historical milieu: As such, the "truth" of ensidic reality is more about correlation than correspondence. The world of nature is always already entwined with the cultural social-historical world of meaning as it is transcendentally instituted: transcendental in that it frames *how* we encounter the world and reality, not *what* we encounter there, yet historical, as the radical imaginary self-alters itself *as* history.[18] Natural being, with its links to an excess of creative *physis,* deploys itself as diverse and heterogeneous strata, which form themselves in sometimes more or sometimes less ensidically "dense" ways than others.[19] The social-historical (the psyche, the living being) encounters the most densely ensidic stratum as the first natural stratum, of which it must (in the emphatic sense of the German *müssen*) take account.[20] The ensidically dense first natural stratum most easily lends itself to stronger interpretations of "the real"—an ensidic reality—as it is the most stable and regular of natural being: Cows give birth to calves and not kittens. Of all the strata of primordial being, the first natural stratum is the most crystallized in form, but not so fully crystallized that it cannot (does not) undergo further ontological alterations through its encounter with the radical imaginary of the social-historical. Other strata of being are not always so ensidically dense and stable—the quantum level, for example—and are less amenable to strong interpretations of transcendental realism. However, there is still another layer of transcendental argumentation that needs to be taken into account.[21]

Castoriadis begins OIHS with some preliminary reflections (p. 342). Once a reflection regarding scientific knowledge is commenced, it is only valuable with a concomitant reflection on ontology; in this particular context, the ontological interrelations of subject and the object is the most relevant. Rethinking the problematic of science must incorporate *naturphilosophical* issues and themes: If science is knowledge of nature, it is also an ontology of nature and, more broadly, a philosophical reflection on the overall problematic of nature. OIHS opens with comments on the ways in which Castoriadis's version of transcendental realism links up with his three reasons for undertaking a critique of knowledge (pp. 342 ff). Castoriadis begins with the realist postulate: Knowledge is of natural beings. The realist postulate may seem elementary and a fundament shared by many, but Castoriadis interprets it in such a way as to incorporate the sense of institution and the social-historical. The real exists, but can only crystallize for us in overlap with the imaginary element (this goes beyond intersubjective realities of the lifeworld), which makes it become what it is for us. In essence, he starts from the argument that the transcendental approach presupposes things about knowledge and about reality. The gap, or tension, between external knowledge and internal knowledge (between subject and object) reappears in a different guise, reminiscent of Kant's move reenacted on a grander scale (although Castoriadis does not relapse into Kantianism).[22] In asserting that the two aspects of knowledge—the "subjective" and the "objective"—are ultimately indissociable (what he calls the "principle of the undecidability of origins" p. 345), Castoriadis is not suggesting that they should be collapsed into one; instead, knowledge is envisaged as a coproduction. There is a need to (at least analytically) separate the two aspects, but it must also be recognized that this can only be achieved incompletely and contingently. The *mise en forme du monde* of Merleau-Ponty—or "cultural articulations of the world," as Arnason renders it—can focus on the imaginary or ensidic element of the world. Forms of objective knowledge single out the ensidic element as it looks to the world as object. Objective knowledge takes us beyond the world of the social-historical, that is, of core significations, to the world of the object, that is, as one of the ways in which the social-historical formalizes its encounter with the natural world. This leads us to post-transcendental phenomenological contexts and, to draw on Merleau-Ponty again, the entwining of nature and culture as the "true transcendental" of world articulation in its twofold sense.

How then does Castoriadis reflect on these three aspects of knowledge? He begins by rejecting an epistemological approach in favor of a properly philosophical—that is ontological—interrogation, in so far as classical epistemology is based on the illusion that subject and object can be separated. In an extension of his earlier *IIS* argument that every logic is supported by an ontology, Castoriadis goes against modern epistemology that bases itself on the illusion that the subject is radically separate from the object. As such, Castoriadis rejects the modern attempt to replace first philosophy with epistemology (or its heirs). Castoriadis criticizes Kant's exclusive focus on what the subject (of scientific knowledge) imposes on the object, to the detriment of their mutual consideration and interrelation. He insists that more philosophical reflection is required—on both the subject and the object; before him, Aristotle and Heidegger had each suggested that epistemology reflects on the being of the subject and therefore is part of a more general ontological project. I have mentioned Castoriadis's elucidation of the subjective conditions of Heidegger's *Kantbuch* in the first section of the book, but here he approaches this elucidation from a different perspective and a broader context in that the natural world does not just appear at the social and natural interface but is the central context and object of his concern. Castoriadis's first point asserts that "a certain knowledge of [natural] being [*l'étant*] exists" (p. 342). This is the precondition for this discussion—and indeed, any discussion—on human forms of knowledge. To challenge this point would be to surrender all discussion: Discussion itself presupposes recognition *of* and *in* the other of a "natural and supranatural being" and this assumption is shared with the other. With respect to this first point, the remainder of his discussion can be read as a rejoinder to Habermas by making a point about the transcendental preconditions of communication. Castoriadis discusses what it means that "the other is there as natural being"; that is, as a finite being in space and time (not the Absolute or God). There is an incipient presencing of his epistemological realism, in that his examples are those taken from our mundane life: We make these assumptions every time we come into discussion with the other (in everyday life or as part of our lifeworld). It nonetheless makes a certain sense to speak of quasi-transcendental conditions of discussion, within which a twofold assumption about the other is discernable.

Second, Castoriadis briefly addresses the historicity of knowledge (pp. 342–43). He points out the indisputable fact that knowledge changes— and changes itself—over time, as do knowledge claims. Knowledge is a diachronic process, not a synchronic system; hence, it is never total or absolute. In this way, there is no Progress (toward total knowledge), nor even a case for the idea of "progress" as primary to the pursuit of knowledge. The history of science teaches us a general lesson about the historicity (*Geschichtlikeit*) of science/knowledge in that it displays structural changes over the course of time.

Third, Castoriadis asserts that there is not just an essential historicity to knowledge but that the process of knowledge itself is social-historical (p. 343). By incorporating the "social" as well as the "historical" element, this in turn critiques the assumptions of the egological (post)Kantian tradition, as knowledge is not just *historical* but *social-historical*, that is, not just as self-altering, but as self-altering within the context of particular imaginary constellations of meaning. In that there is no process of knowledge or thought without language, an essentially social aspect sustains the knowing subject. Furthermore, in a reiteration of *IIS* themes, in that language itself is a "total part" of the social-historical world (p. 343), language is not reducible to its ensidic aspects: It is always entwined with an imaginary dimension as well. Castoriadis challenges the dominant assumptions of the egological tradition from the Kantian up to and including the Husserlian. There is no process of knowledge without language (allowing us to glimpse a quasi-linguistic turn as part of his own framework); in turn, language is an essential part of the social-historical, and is, as such, a medium of knowledge.

Castoriadis continues to elaborate on the process of the "social" as a counterpart to conceptions of the individual as separate from the social (pp. 343–44). Again, he points to the properly historical dimension of knowledge and science. In this instance, Castoriadis argues that no one model of historicity can be taken for granted—be it "absolute progress" or "absolute discontinuity." Rather, *history* is the mode by which ruptures relate to tradition, and by which it creates itself as other. Castoriadis sees a fundamental requirement to historicize, that is, to reject conventionally transcendental, ahistorical approaches to being and science. His critique could be read not just as a critique of Kant, but also as a critique of Kuhn (toward whom he otherwise tends to be sympathetic) in that to impose an *apriori* model of revolution on science and its history can be seen as indeed "unhistorical." Castoriadis prefers rather to point to the level of ongoing historical self-alteration that alters that which it maintains at the very moment that it alters it.

A Critique of Kant

His opening gambit completed, Castoriadis embarks on a critique of Kant (p. 344). He does so, however, by incorporating an Aristotelian aspect in that he reformulates the distinction between form and matter. Leaning on Heidegger, Castoriadis observes a latent ontology in the Kantian theory of knowledge: "The mere existence of this process of knowing says something about what *is*—therefore about *what* is—as well as about *the one who knows*—therefore about another aspect of being" (p. 344). Despite its epistemological focus, Castoriadis suggests, as did Heidegger before him, that the first *Critique* involves assumptions of the being of the subject. However, it is also the case that assumptions of the being of the subject entail other assumptions of "externality"; if the subject can indeed know the world, then certain things are implied about the being of the world.[23] It also leads Castoriadis to the conclusion of that the "subject" and "object" are indissociable; Castoriadis takes the case of quantum physics as a case in point that both supports this postulation and moreover effectively negates the Kantian "in itself," as quantum particles have properties only "for us." He then offers a caveat that strengthens the case for the interpretation of his epistemological realism. Still discussing the case of quantum physics, Castoriadis notes the impossibility of "mak[ing] a lamb give birth to a cow, or even, at the level of quantum mechanics, mak[ing] particles appear . . . without their having some relation to the available levels of energy in use" (p. 345). The structuring of nature in all its heterogeneity is not arbitrarily malleable. Although the "real" for Castoriadis in general refers to the ensidic layer of the world, it is a transcendental realism of the first natural stratum as only "elaborable" not "interpretable." Yet for all that it is ensidic, increasingly the first natural stratum, although perhaps densely ensidic, is not seen as exhaustively so.[24] Rather, nature as elemental being is a magmatic flow that crystallizes into forms prior to its ontological alteration as imaginary element by the social-historical. Here Castoriadis's critique of Kant has moved to a variation of Aristotle's thought and to a consequent reformulation of the distinction between form (*eidos*) and matter (*hyle*): "reality resists."[25] He takes for granted that Aristotle's way of distinguishing form and matter is applicable to the question of knowledge. Thus he translates Kant for critical purposes to Aristotelian language—specifically, the inseparability of form/matter in the natural world—to lend weight to his argument that the subject and object are inseparable. From this it is evident that Castoriadis implies a double *Stellungnahme* in the title of "The Ontological Import of the History of Science." First he suggests that we need to think of science—the enterprise of securing objective knowledge—in terms of its history and its social-historical history in particular. Second, the fact of its history has ontological implications: Science must then be also thought of in terms of its ontology—which is where philosophy beyond mere epistemology reenters the dialogue.

In place of Kant's "pure reason," Castoriadis argues that the idea of elementary reason is better considered as an institution, as the mode of being of the social-historical (as discussed in Chapter 2). His main target in this respect is the radical separation between subject and object. Castoriadis positions himself against Descartes, Newton, Kant, and the classical idea of "objective" knowledge with its accompanying imaginary of mechanistic nature. Not only does Castoriadis ask how the subject must be in order for us to have (objective) knowledge—as per Kant in the *Critique of Pure Reason*—but also how the object—that is, the ensidic stratum of the world—must be. This, it should be noted, is different from the phenomenological problematic of the twentieth century, which sought to elucidate how objects presented themselves to us and takes us into postphenomenological currents (although suggested in the discussion of the magma in Chapter 4, he does not fully leave phenomenology behind).[26] The problem with Kant, as Castoriadis sees it, is that the Kantian framework cannot explain the apparent correspondence and correlation of the knowledge produced by the subject to the object. Kant, as Castoriadis explains it, is forced to acknowledge this conundrum and is reduced to explaining it as a "happy accident" in the introduction to the third *Critique*. Castoriadis dismantles Kant's reduction of knowledge as being only a particular kind of knowledge; that is, deterministic (scientific, Newtonian) knowledge. While acknowledging the efficacy of causally articulated knowledge, Castoriadis doubts that knowledge can be reduced to just that, for then there could be no knowledge of magmata (the living being, the psyche or the social-historical). In this vein, Kant's "*glücklicher Zufall*" (pp. 347–48), to which Castoriadis returns repeatedly in his various writings, is best interpreted metaphorically. Part of what it shows is that once the transcendental realist turn is taken, it inevitably incorporates philosophy, and ultimately a philosophy of nature, within the very foundations of science. To lean on Merleau-Ponty, the problematic of science also takes us to the "true transcendental" of nature and culture in world articulation. Here Castoriadis radicalizes Kant and Heidegger's *Kantbuch* in two ways: In terms of the subject of knowledge, the social-historical context of the institution needs to be incorporated. In terms of the object, Castoriadis paves the way for a transcendental realism and the early Romantic constellation of post-Kantian thought, in that the presuppositions of science inevitably incorporate a philosophy of nature and the problematic of the world.

On Castoriadis's account, the correlation between the subject and the object can be explained only because the world itself—in-itself—is organized to a minimum degree such that it is organizable. If the social-historical ultimately brings into being a-world-as-its-world, rather than merely organizing found objects/information, which it then orders into a comprehensive framework, then it is impossible to ultimately decide what comes from the subject and what comes from the object (for example, quantum phenomena): "There is no way of getting around the solidarity of the two dimensions "the 'subjective' and the 'objective'—their perpetual intertwining" (p. 345). "What is" cannot be reduced to "what is known," yet neither are they completely separable, for what is observed depends on the observer's theoretical framework and imaginary schema but, conversely, the objects are not completely determined by the particular theory applied. Thus, Castoriadis rejects the Kantian noumenal. Although it is true that there cannot be absolute knowledge of being, nevertheless, that anthropos exists—that the living being exists— demonstrates that we can and do have some knowledge of the world. For there to be knowledge at all, there must be something knowable in the world that we discover/create. In the end, Kant reduced all "objective" knowledge in the strong sense to "deterministic" knowledge (p. 346), which, as Castoriadis points out, excludes any thinking on the living being, the psychical and the social-historical spheres. To be sure, in *The Critique of Judgment*, Kant rediscovered a philosophy of the organism but does not—could not within the parameters of his critical philosophy—grant it the constitutive status of objective knowledge. However, Kant does posit a teleology of nature: The organism creates itself according to its own ends. In Castoriadis, this is extended and radicalized: The living being (and the world) forms itself. The world is not only formed, but formable; or better, it is partially formed and partially formable. In this sense, the world and being are not fully determined. Nonetheless, the ensidic exists as relatively stable and durable; the mistake of classical physics (and the inherited tradition of determinacy) is to assume that this stability and immanence of the ensidic exhausts the world. It does not. The "new objects" of the natural sciences (the living being, quantum physics) present a modified and postmechanistic understanding of nature, non-nomological in content and thus challenging the legacy of determinism. Being consists of—creates itself as—an irregular stratification, as a heterogeneity that underlies the possibility of the emergence of new forms and is implied by such new forms and their accordingly multiple strata of being. Each stratum that we discover/create is heterogeneous in its relationship to other strata. Different strata—to take Castoriadis's example, those pointed to by Newtonian and Einsteinian physics—although ostensibly "contradicting" each other, nonetheless have "local" validity; they are compatible, but irreducible to each other, and ultimately are not reducible to a single homogenized stratum of being. Rather they need to be seen as co-existent alterities."[27]

Genetic and Genealogical Reflections

Castoriadis then makes another decisive turn (p. 348) and proceeds to a genetic and genealogical reflection of knowledge. He follows an unconventional method, raising a general philosophical argument about the need for a general ontological level of analysis. He begins an analysis of nature (in particular the living being) that will in the end converge with his philosophical argument. Castoriadis's analysis of the living being in OIHS is directed at raising three philosophical issues. First, it introduces a prehistory of the subject: He asserts that there is knowledge, even at the level of the living being. Second, this presupposes something about "external" reality, that is, about our affinity with the natural stratum. Third, it highlights the discontinuity and heterogeneity of being: The living being itself is to be understood as a rupture and a break with other strata of being. Castoriadis repeats the three-point argument at higher levels of being, especially at the social-historical, which in turn emerges as a more radical version of the living being in its relation to the natural world especially—in this context—in its recreation of a more complex version of the ensidic. Social-historical creation is much more than attaining cognitive affinity with the "external" world. At the social-historical level, knowledge is pursued as a constant activity, whereas at the level of the living being, its proto-knowledge is instituted once and for all. The culminating point concerns the heterogeneity of being. The rupture of being is duplicated/redoubled at the level of the social-historical which undergoes its own internal ruptures. This links up with Castoriadis's argument regarding science and the discontinuities of the social-historical.

The genetic discussion is aimed at further dismantling the Kantian edifice by consistently following the principle Castoriadis spelled out at the beginning of the paper: to wit, the historicity of knowledge. If epistemology is to be embedded in ontology, then the historicity of knowledge needs to comprehend historicity through a genealogy of knowledge that precedes a history of sciences. In this context, Castoriadis returns to the living being *qua* living being to consider proto-knowledge—as the prefiguration of knowledge—that is palpable in the living being.[28] Important here is that this postulate prefigures the tension between *physis* as object of knowledge and *nomos* as the subjective side of knowledge. There are two steps in the analysis. First, the living being creates (forms) its own world, that is, a proto-subjective side is indicated. Second, at the same time, the living being cannot exist without performing a certain amount of ensidic encoding of the world. Castoriadis therewith focuses on the cognitive as opposed to the creative side: The living being cannot function without "classifying" and so forth. However, it is possible to proceed further and distinguish a tension between the creative and the cognitive aspects. The living being creates its own world but within constraints of functionality or instrumentality (purposiveness): It submits to something like a natural law. On the cognitive side, "classifying," for example, points to the living being registering the ensidic aspects of the first natural stratum, but it does so *in its own way*. However, the living being is also caught up in contexts of "meaning": It imposes new properties on the first natural stratum, brings the "world" into existence as meaningful. In this way, ontological creation is broader than creation of the *Eigenwelt* of the being for itself, as being for itself remains in a relation of purposiveness to the world, whereas the living being creates new levels of being (for example, colors) that go beyond that. It grafts thereby new levels of reality onto the first natural stratum.

Castoriadis points to the idea of creation that partially appears in Kant and is retheorized by Heidegger—the living being creates a world for itself vis-à-vis the chaotic "X" or "world fragment" (pp. 349–50). In noting that creation takes place "once and for all" in the living being (p. 352), Castoriadis observes its transcendental nature, that is, absence of historical variety. The general conclusion to be drawn concerns the essential onto-logical heterogeneity of the various strata of being. With that general les-son in mind, Castoriadis continues onto the social-historical where the genealogy of knowledge turns into a real history of knowledge. There are some fundamental points to be made in this respect, for example, the het-erogeneity and discontinuity (p. 353) that is synonymous with the emer-gence of humanity and society. Discontinuity occurs on both levels, that is, on the level of the ensidic and of the imaginary creation of the I/me. In discussing the rupture of the human psyche from the animal psyche, its defunctionalization and relation to the first natural stratum, Castoriadis points to the irrevocable way in which the ensidic is each time social-historically instituted and inextricably linked to the signitive and imagi-nary as a *sui generis* creation/organization of the first natural stratum. He points to von Neuman (p. 357) who first distinguished between the lan-guage of the mind and the language of mathematics, as well as to the inability of Artificial Intelligence to reconstruct a magmatic organization in the threefold interrelationship of the psyche—thymic, logical, and ore-ctic. This is because at every level mutual interference between the ensidic level and creative imaginary occurs. In this way, the ensidic acquires new meanings and contexts. The closest Castoriadis comes to acknowledging this is via mathematics. He begins to reflect upon the "unreasonable effec-tiveness" of mathematics as an area in which the nonseparability of the ensidic and creative aspects coexist. The ensidic organization belonging properly to the social-historical region is of a different kind from that of the living being: The social-historical needs to each time create anew "basic natural data" (pp. 356–57).

Castoriadis next moves from the genetic to the historical plane, where he identifies three ruptures of being (p. 357). The first rupture inaugu-rates history. It includes traditional (stateless) societies and archaic high cultures whose processes of knowledge and organization of the first natu-ral stratum, he argues in a direct critique of Lévi-Strauss, cannot be re-duced to bricolage: Their knowledge was tradition bound, not reflective, and was monopolized by the guardians of tradition. The second rupture occurred with the ancient Greeks, who transformed the idea of knowledge from being bound to tradition to being within the public arena as an ac-cumulation and discussion of observations (p. 358–59). They invented a form of "rational thought" that was characterized by two novel features: The first was the idea of unlimited questioning; the second was the necessity of demonstration—or a giving of reasons—in the form of *logon didonai*.[29]

The third rupture—to which Castoriadis devotes more detailed discussion—occurs in Western Europe with the moderns.[30] As in ISCS, Castoriadis imputes continuity to the whole of the Western scientific project from Aristotle onwards. This project is concerned with two imaginary significations, which, in Castoriadis's view, profoundly differentiate the moderns from the ancients: infinity and artificiality. Castoriadis initially discusses the idea of infinity in relation to mathematics, where it has been most effectively expressed, and in which the work of the creative imagination can be clearly seen. In reflecting on the subject of knowledge, not only do the social-historical aspects become apparent, but so, too, does the mixture of the social-historical and psychical aspects.[31] The active, knowing subject cannot do without the reactivation of the radical imagination, and from that point of view cannot do without a subversive or anarchic aspect to it, that sees a rejoining of the partially chaotic *physis* to *nomos*.

In his discussion on the mathematization of infinity, Castoriadis does not merely refute Kant but ventures beyond him. He takes on the standard argument against Kant that science has a history. In accord with Kuhn, Castoriadis does not view the history of science as cumulative knowledge, but rather as one that is punctuated by ruptures and revolutions.[32] Drawing on Kuhn, Castoriadis integrates the idea of the sciences as changing schemes and frameworks, the creation of which might seem to make science seem subjective. However, in radicalizing Kuhn, Castoriadis does not posit this as an *apriori* condition. He makes the ontological point, moreover, that the idea of a science that changes suggests the heterogeneity of being. Thus, even in science, the creative imagination (as related to generative ideas and schema, p. 370) becomes fundamental to grasping being. In regard to the idea of objective knowledge, the place of the infinite is best—and most beautifully—encapsulated by Koyré's (1957) notion of the shift *from the closed world to the infinite universe*.[33] Castoriadis suggests that it is not the case that the Greeks were incapable of thinking infinity. Despite Aristotle's understanding of infinity as virtual, Castoriadis discerns in the Greek imaginary, particularly in Democritus's "infinity of space and of worlds" (p. 361), the invention of infinity in mathematics and physics. Democritus accepted the infinity of space (p. 361), but Aristotle looks to Plato: The point for Castoriadis, however, is the idea that "infinity" matters to different understandings of knowledge.

Castoriadis concludes that for the ancient Greeks, especially with respect to the imaginary of "infinity," there were two worlds of signification, hence a radical choice between models of the real and therefore between models of knowledge was available. With the advent of modernity, the context changed: Infinity was positively valued, as well as being taken as a cornerstone of mathematics and physics. Yet Castoriadis's argument that the Judeo-Christian imaginary was irrelevant to this process (p. 362) seems weaker, as later medieval philosophy from the thirteenth century was instrumental in the transition to modernity.[34] Nonetheless, the general point about infinity remains important. It could be read as Castoriadis suggesting that it is less helpful to attempt to demonstrate that a particular historical culture was incapable of thinking a certain idea, rather, as in this example of the ancient Greeks, although the idea (of infinity) was present, a context that was conducive to positively value them was absent. Finally, in returning to Koyré's metaphor of the early modern transition from the *closed world* to *the infinite universe*, Castoriadis links infinity to capitalism. He therewith succinctly demonstrates the parallels between the underlying ontology of modern science and that of modern capitalism.[35]

Turning to address the idea of artificiality (p. 362), Castoriadis returns once more to the ancient Greeks, where we encounter the *physis/nomos* problematic. On Castoriadis's account, the Greeks were fundamentally uninterested in theoretical artifacts as such. Castoriadis traces this apparent lack of interest to the Greek philosophical imaginary of *physis* and *nomos*. For the mainstream of the ancient Greek world, knowledge *qua* science was interpreted in the context of *physis,* not *nomos*. In this way, science was understood as true knowledge of *physis* and did not concern *nomos*. In principle, the Greeks were not incapable of thinking of knowledge as an artifact, as Castoriadis likes to support by way of reference to Democritus and Protagoras and the idea of knowledge as an institution, and hence pertaining to *nomos*; Aristotle, however, represses the sophist insight. In his own account, Castoriadis wants to emphasize the idea of knowledge as *nomos* (institution and convention). In this way, he sees scientific knowledge as knowledge that interpenetrates *physis* and *nomos*. In turning to the moderns, Castoriadis notes that "artificiality" becomes unshackled from its previous imaginary constraints. He sees this historical disentanglement most plainly in the boundless inventiveness of creation of new mathematical models. The conventional aspects of knowledge were subsequently rediscovered—albeit for practical purposes—by moderns.

A general implication of the relation between ontology and the history of science seems plain. On one hand, the history of science, if taken seriously, illustrates, as nothing else does, the principle of ontological heterogeneity and rupture: Repeated ruptures instantiate new levels of being. With respect to ontology, there is a fundamental tension in the specifically strong notion of a history of knowledge that Castoriadis offers that is liable to be overlooked: the tension of *physis* and *nomos* as internal to knowledge. It is to be regarded as internal, as no knowledge is possible without an effort to grasp the domain of *physis*, but neither is knowledge possible without the imposition of a specific kind of *nomos*. As we have seen, these operate at transcendental, as well as mundane levels, and are interwoven through the creation and interpretation of history.

The radicalized idea of historicity that is Castoriadis's starting point for his version of the transcendental-realist argument does not mean that Castoriadis envisages a completely discontinuous version of history. As well as discontinuities, the history of science is characterized by important continuities, of which for him the most crucial concerns the link between the modern scientific project with that of the ancient Greeks (pp. 363ff).[36] Castoriadis argues for a unity to the ancient and modern projects as represented by the invention and renewal of the principle of *logon didonai* (mathematics providing a good example). In reference once more to the imaginary significations of "infinity" and "artificiality," he notes two important divergences between the modern and the ancient magma (p. 363). For Castoriadis, modern science is equated with the eternal elaboration of ensidic logic as it corresponds to—discovers—"real" strata of being/the world that lean on the imaginary schema of physical being as completely rational and graspable. The Greeks, on the other hand, did not assume the world to be a perfect continuum of rationality. Castoriadis's use of the philosophical idea of *hyle* can be interpreted as a continuation of the original idea of *chaos*, which emerged in archaic Greece. In this context, the reality of the world is never more than partly rational, which of course affects the way infinity can be thought, which is important in terms of the idea of the infinite progress of knowledge. Despite the differences, however, Castoriadis is confident that Aristotle's approach to knowledge could be aligned with the moderns, as it is a tenet of Aristotle that the operative assumptions of science consider being as *in* and *for itself*; this is indicative of what we might call a "methodological atheism" on the part of Castoriadis. To sum up, there are two lines of thought: Ruptures are inherent to the history of science and yet there is a basic continuity and common ground with Aristotle (p. 372) as part of the overall project of western science, itself, in its inauguration, part of the project of autonomy.

Castoriadis argues that the fundamental interplay between mathematics and physical reality expresses something ontological about the world (p. 369). In this vein, knowledge for Castoriadis cannot be reduced to an eternal—and interminable—elaboration of the ensidic (p. 370), but is rather always already imbued with an imaginary element of the society in question, thus incorporating a properly social-historical and ontological dimension. The imaginary dimension of knowledge points to the heterogeneous nature of being and the discontinuous, ruptural nature of science via the emergence of new imaginary schema: The differences between the ancient Greek and modern approaches to science are cases in point. Scientific knowledge does not merely accumulate, or follow visions of progress, but proceeds historically. That is, it changes: Gains in knowledge can only be understood as such on the basis of being "re-taken, re-conquered, re-interpreted" (p. 371). Although Castoriadis sees the continuity between the ancient Greek and the modern scientific project as the key illustration of this, he sees a certain discontinuity in their elaboration and direction as internal to the affinities that bind them together. Later he refers again to the continuity with the ancient Greek project and the invention of *logon didonai* (pp. 371–72), where he insists that *logon didonai* cannot be thought of as just an abstract idea, but signifies the ultimate internal criterion (overlapping with but not identical to the external referent).

The Heterogeneity of Being

Castoriadis concludes OIHS by reposing the three main philosophical questions informing his discussion (p. 372). First, how must the world be in order for a particular kind of objective knowledge to be possible? For Castoriadis, the world must be understood in its heterogeneity and stratification as locally ensidic with local validity, and the relationship between the strata as other, that is, not ensidizable. Second, how must the world be in order for a noncumulative history of science to exist? Fragments of the world may be indefinitely ensidizable but not the totality of the world. Finally, how must the "knowing subject" be to create/maintain/overthrow science and its history? For Castoriadis, the subject of knowledge cannot be ego(logical) or transcendental (as per Kant and Husserl, each in their own way); it can only be understood within a social-historical context and existence, in a creative interplay between the radical imaginary of the social-historical and the radical imagination of the singular psyche. Finally, and crucially, Castoriadis ends his discussion by suddenly reintroducing the idea of *à-être* in an ontological summation (p. 373): Being in its heterogeneity is to be understood as self-creation and radical temporality. Truth, which really does exist, is to be *imagined, created, made, done.*

Castoriadis's epistemological adventure in OIHS gathers momentum beyond that of the *IIS*. It relativizes the claims of science, while freeing a space for philosophical reflection. If the history of science is simultaneously a disclosure of its mode of being as it auto-forms itself, ontological issues resurface in the face of epistemological interrogation. As has been argued, Castoriadis's approach to the epistemological and ontological status of science and objective knowledge is distinctive in that he combines a critical reflection on science with a philosophical reflection on nature and natural being. Castoriadis positions himself against the tradition of the history and philosophy of science by reasserting his argument that an epistemology must ask not simply after the object but also the subject of knowledge. Contrary to Castoriadis's own usage, the natural kosmos and natural being were differentiated. The natural world is always already instituted as kosmos, and as such, is embedded in an instituted order of imaginary significations. It is diachronic, that is created by social-historical action, and disclosed and recreated via historical interpretation. The recognition of the interpenetration of *nomos* and *physis* at the level of objective knowledge is taken in his later works in an ontological *naturphilosophical* direction within post-phenomenological contexts. It opens a space for further reflection on the creative aspects of *physis* that has been revived within a critical reclamation of the Romantic *natura naturans/natura naturata*. His increasingly insistent summation of being as heterogeneous paves the way for a gradual enquiry into transregional *physis*. It simultaneously calls for the elucidation of further regional ontologies that are evoked by the magma metaphor. As we shall see in the next chapter, the living being becomes the region where the overlap of both strands is most apparent.

7

Rethinking the World of the Living Being

The living being emerges as a central theme for Castoriadis's rethinking of creative *physis*.[1] His reengagement with the mode of the living being sees the simultaneous reappearance of the *physis* and *nomos* problematic, although it is reconfigured at a new level. In line with the more general trend evidenced in Castoriadis's philosophical path during the 1980s, the living being is now less characterized as *self-organizing*—which implies an ensidic logic—and more properly theorized in terms of *self-creation*. Castoriadis's elucidation of the living being to some extent obscures the previously clear boundary between anthropic and non-anthropic regions of being. As will become clearer, this is particularly the case with respect to his emergent polyregional ontology of the being *for-itself* (*pour soi*). In revisiting the living being, Castoriadis not only deepens his long-term discussion with Francisco Varela, but also continues to radicalize and fuse key motifs in Aristotle and Kant in innovative ways. With the growing elaboration of the living being as ontologically creative, nonhuman nature came to be seen more in terms of continuity with anthropic modes of being in Castoriadis's thought. Indeed, in the 1980s, Castoriadis reassessed the lines of continuity and discontinuity between anthropic and non-anthropic being and, as a result, redefines them in variety of ways. Nonetheless, there remain crucial points of difference between them; that is, Castoriadis does not reduce the human world to the animal world. This becomes especially clear in Castoriadis's elucidation of autonomy as it pertains to the various regions and modes of the *for-itself*, as his discussions with Varela's notion of biological autonomy show. Not only was the living being autopoietic in the wider sense of being *qua* being, it also signified the emergence of an archetypal *self* as autopoietic and to that extent an imaginary element is present in its self-creation that ruptured with physical regions of being. This appearance of what Castoriadis was to call "the subjective instance" entailed the "self" and the emergence of "the world" as a horizon of (proto)meaning (PSS 119).

Previous chapters have provided a close reading of a single text to critically interpret and elucidate Castoriadis's philosophical trajectory (with amplification from selected additional primary sources). This chapter takes a slightly different approach, however, as Castoriadis's elaboration of the living being depends for much of its theoretical import on its contrast with other modes of being; in the first instance, with respect to the spectrum of the polyregionality of the various modes of being *for-itself* (for example, the living being, the psyche, or the social-historical); in the second instance, in comparison to nonliving nature. There is an abundance of material on the living being to be found in Castoriadis's various essays and seminars, but no single text that focuses exclusively on it. For this reason, the strategy of the present chapter is to take the most relevant passages—especially in "The State of the Subject Today," "Pour soi et subjectivité," and from the posthumously published seminars from SV (Seminar IV, 21 January 1987, and Seminar V, 28 January 1987), as well as important passages from DD, PA, and OIHS that engage directly with the problematic of the living being—that will be discussed in order to paint an overall picture of the shifts in Castoriadis's conception of these strata of being and heterogeneous regionality of the *for-itself.*

The puzzle of the living being had long interested Castoriadis. He elucidates it in three distinct phases over the course of his ontological trajectory. The first stage encompasses the period up to, and including, the publication of the *IIS* in 1975. As early as 1971 in MSPI, as well as in the *IIS,* the living being was a recurring if somewhat marginal theme. In these publications, Castoriadis's theorizing of the living being incorporates a preliminary interlacing of both ontological and epistemological aspects. In the 1970s, however, the regional ontology of the social-historical was his prime concern; the living being figured either as a limit case, or as an interesting point of contrast to anthropic modes of being. Prior to the mid-1980s, Castoriadis tended to describe the living being in terms of "self-organization" rather than "self-creation," and from as early as MSPI, Castoriadis situated his discussion of the living being as a critique of information and cybernetic theory. The most significant argument of this phase concerned the living being and its organization/"creation" of what for it will exist as "information," rather than the more conventional idea that "information" was already "existing" in nature waiting for the living being to happen upon it. The "new biology" emerges in the early 1970s (for our purposes, it is important to note that this occurred after the composition of MSPI) and announces itself with Maturana and Varela's landmark text *Autopoiesis and Cognition* (1973). It included theoretical novelties that stemmed from von Neumann, where the living being is still understood by way of the idea of the "auto" but more specifically as the *automaton*.

The middle phase coincides with Castoriadis's shift toward transregional *physis* during the 1980s, and is the most relevant for the purposes of the present chapter. This second phase begins to gather pace with Castoriadis's review (1980) of Varela's *Principles of Biological Autonomy* (1979), and his increasing engagement with Atlan (1979), Morin (1977), Prigogine and Stengers (1979), and various discussion groups and colloquia, as mentioned in Chapter 5. It starts to really flourish in the mid-1980s, however. During this time, Castoriadis wrote a handful of papers over an eighteen-month period (May 1985–January 1987), all of which directly discuss the living being. In May 1985, Castoriadis delivered "The State of the Subject Today" (1986) to an audience of the psychoanalytic Fourth Group. In December 1985 he completed "The Ontological Import of the History of Science" (1997); "Pour soi et subjectivité" (1990) transpired out of the Cerisy Colloque in honor of Edgar Morin (June 1986); and Castoriadis presented his paper "*Physis* and Autonomy" (1997) in Florence during October 1986. Finally, the years 1986–1987 saw him deliver a seminar series on human creation (posthumously published as *Sujet et vérité* [2002]), in which the living being was discussed on several occasions.

The third and final development in Castoriadis's philosophy of the living being begins, generally speaking, in the 1990s. It is visible, however, in the transitional essay "Done and to Be Done" that Castoriadis completed in December 1988, written as a response to his critics. In that essay, his elucidation of the living being takes a further philosophical turn in that it is now more directly linked to the meaning of the Aristotelian soul as imagination and marker of life, especially as is clear in "Psychoanalysis and Philosophy," written in 1996. Further development of his thought on the living being can be found, for instance, in his radio discussion with Varela from December 1995 (Castoriadis 1999).

The Self-Creation of the Living Being

Francisco Varela represents Castoriadis's most important interlocutor concerning the maturation of his later views on the living being. Castoriadis (1980) was the first to review Varela's (1979) *Principles of Biological Autonomy* and their mutual interest and engagement continued throughout the 1980s where Varela was a participant in the discussion group "Groupe Interdisciplinaire" at CNRS and was involved in many of the same Cerisy Colloques on auto-organization during the 1980s that Castoriadis was.[2] Their discussions continued into the 1990s and beyond: Varela presented a paper, entitled "Du bios au *Logos*," at the 1990 Cerisy Colloque in honor of Castoriadis; he participated in a radio discussion with Castoriadis in the mid-1990s (Castoriadis 1999) and even, after Castoriadis's death in 1997, Varela presented a conference paper in New York in 2000, entitled "Autonomy and Closure: The Resonances of Castoriadis's Thought in the Life Sciences," that remains, to the best of my knowledge, unpublished.

Castoriadis is receptive to much of what Varela argues, but is critical of his notion of "biological autonomy." In their 1995 radio discussion, he acknowledged his debt to Varela, observing not only the shared interest in autonomy that had first brought them to each other's attention, but also his embracing of Varela's understanding of the living being's organizational and cognitive closure (Castoriadis 1999). They share a perspective on science that is critical of (scientism's) reductionism, as do some of their contemporaries, for example, Atlan (1979), Morin (1977), and Prigogine and Stengers (1979). More particularly, Castoriadis and Varela criticize the idea of informational input/output in cybernetics, especially as it applies to the living being; their critique centers on the presumption that *information* is already formed in nature and "waiting" for the living being to discover and process. For Varela, the living being is an autonomous system in that it preserves its self-identity and organizational closure, which highlights the closure and autonomy of its cognitive domain. As autopoietic, the living being produces itself constantly, and as such, brings itself into being as *living being*, that is as *that which is for itself*. Although Castoriadis and Varela have a mutual interest in autonomy, their respective approaches vary quite considerably and lie at the basis of Castoriadis's critique of Varela.[3]

Castoriadis's elucidation of the regional ontology of the living being emerges as part of the articulation of a wider dimension of being *for-itself*. The dimension of the *for-itself* incorporates six overlapping levels or regions. Four of these Castoriadis designates as "real": the living being, the human psyche, the social individual, and the social-historical. The remaining two are not so much "real" but rather point toward an "emergent capacity" in anthropos: the human subject (the autonomous subject, properly speaking), and autonomous society (SST 11; PSS 119).[4] Castoriadis's discussions of the living being often take place in the context of the more encompassing elucidation of what I term his *polyregional* ontology of the *for-itself*, on the one hand, and the overlap and demarcation of their respective levels, especially significant in that this dimension of being incorporates anthropic and non-anthropic regions, on the other. From the 1980s, Castoriadis begins to elaborate all regions and modes of natural being as autopoietic, but the living being holds especial significance in that it represents a rupture of inorganic nature, and as such a rupture of and within being itself. With the emergence of the living being, the "subjective instance" as the (proto)self first appears with the simultaneous creation (invention) of the world properly speaking, as kosmos: as an order of (proto)meaning, and the emergence of the imaginary element.[5] The problematic of the world, which was half-exorcised in the social-historical domain, reappears in Castoriadis's thought in the guise of the *Eigenwelt* that is created by all modes and levels of the *for-itself*.[6] The articulation of the living being's ontological creation of its own world proper to its level of being not only highlights Castoriadis's ongoing shift toward an expanded ontology of creative *physis*, but also a further shift in emphasis from the more strictly phenomenological stance of *being-in-the-world* evident in his early paper on Merleau-Ponty (SU), to the ontological-phenomenological, in which particular modes of being do not merely *organize* and *act* in the world in which they find themselves, but, on Castoriadis's account, indeed create it. The living being, as the archetypal self—the first of diverse subjective instances—creates a world, creates its own world as an "absolute creation" (PSS 121), as opposed to merely organizing the world in which it dwells, or responding, however creatively, to its "environment." Here, the world *qua* world first comes to "visibility" as constitutive of the phenomenological field. As with the discussion of social-historical worlds in Chapter 4, it also suggests a limit in Castoriadis's treatment of the *for-itself*. The *for-itself* is also *for-the-world*. As suggested in the previous chapter, the world as kosmos needs to be understood as an order of meaning; this extends to the living being's self-creation as the autocreation of a meaningful world.[7] The creation of the world as kosmos is, moreover, *apriori* to the mode of being in the world (on Castoriadis's account): The world is instituted transcendentally not just at the anthropic level but at all levels of the *for-itself*.

The living being as the archetypal being for-itself is characterized by three interconnected attributes: first, self-finality; second, creation of its own world; and third, the *Eigenwelt* which consists of representations, affects, and intentions (*SV* 83). Drawing on Adolf Portmann (*SV*), Castoriadis explains auto-finality as the mode by which everything that appears on the living being's horizon is subordinated to the goal of its own conservation, both as a singular living being with respect to self-preservation, and as a species in terms of self-reproduction.[8] *Self-finality* presumes in turn the *Eigenwelt* in and through which everything must not only appear, but also appear as meaningful for the living being. Here Castoriadis expands his genealogy of knowledge from the human world to include the living being—as discussed in the previous chapter—to the extension of a genealogy of meaning as essential to the imaginary element (as encountered in the final two chapters of the *IIS*). A self-created world of meaning always exists *for a self* (as a version of subjectivity) and is in contrast to the physical regions, where the action of one entity on another has meaning for neither of the entities in question. The creation of an *Eigenwelt* and "information" assumes a "putting into meaning" or proto-meaning as characteristic of the living being. Central to the idea of the creation of an *Eigenwelt* is the view that nothing can exist for the living being that does not enter the *Eigenwelt* in question, and nothing enters into that world without being organized/endowed with meaning according to the organization and laws peculiar to that world of the *for-itself* in question. As suggested in the previous chapter, Castoriadis's approach partially echoes the approach of transcendental realism; this applies not only at the level of the social-historical institution of the world, but also extends to the level of the living being in that the organization of each *Eigenwelt* forms its *a priori* condition—we might say, its *apriori* condition of *being-in-the-world*. It also leads to post-phenomenological contexts and the *mise en forme du monde* as the entwining of nature and culture, here understood as primordial being, the natural world and the kosmos as instituted by the radical imaginary (DD 365). Castoriadis's interpretation of the living being's creation of the *Eigenwelt* is in contrast to what he calls "the new version of solipsism" on the part of Varela. Castoriadis interprets Varela's position as a restatement of the Kantian position at the level of the living being, where the subject (broadly understood) constructs the world, and exists in the interior of its categorical closure.[9]

Implicit in the creation of an *Eigenwelt* is the imaginative capacity, although not yet the "radical imagination" of the human psyche; the living being exhibits a corporeal imagination in the creation of an *Eigenwelt*. The elemental form of the imagination comes into play in creating "the image as image and as that image" (DD), by creating its own world such that anything that it encounters "externally" can only be processed or made "meaningful" by entering into its own world. The creaturely *Eigenwelt* consists of presentation, representation, and putting into relation various elements to form a world, relative to which the living unity reacts to, tends toward, and so forth.[10] Everything that presents itself in this *Eigenwelt* is also affect as a sign of value (positive, negative, or neutral). The living being can be characterized as possessing an intention that it is able to translate into action (toward self-conservation). In its self-constitution of an *Eigenwelt*, the *for-itself* exhibits three aspects: an aesthetic-noetic (representation and the image, or the "cognitive" in Varela's terms), affect, and intention/desire (SST 13).[11] The creation of information always involves a *mise en image* and *mise en relation*—that is, the dimensions of imaging and relating, or "sensorial" and "logical." Drawing on Aulagnier (1975), Castoriadis argues that "staging"—*mise en scène*—already contains some kind of meaning, and "putting into meaning"—*mise en sens*—cannot happen without a "presentification" of the sense, which requires a scene (SST 14). In *SV* Castoriadis approaches it from another angle: To put the world into meaning is not to be understood as a derivative operation, but rather as centrally connected to *putting into relation* or *staging*. This can be extended to Kant's separation of the Transcendental Aesthetic and Transcendental Logic (*SV* 68–70). As soon as an image is made, something is simultaneously made meaningful (*SV* 69). Critiquing Kant further, the receptive and spontaneous aspects of the "putting into image/concept" is not reducible to a receptivity of impressions (of the "X"), but involves a spontaneity on the part of all regions of the *for-itself*, including the living being. For Castoriadis, an *Eigenwelt* indicates that Kant's "X" of the external world is nothing in-itself, rather it is, to draw on Fichte, an *Anstoss*, or "shock" which becomes "something" only as the living being forms it—or rather transforms it—into something in its own manner: "Information" is a creation (SST 13; *SV* 66). From a different angle, the *Anstoss* can be thought of as an encounter with the world horizon. As such, the living being does not just "represent" the external world to itself, but rather, creates an interior, or an archetypal "subjective instance" (PSS). The living being must be "in contact" (*SV* 61) with the external world, choose elements in the world in an infinitely selective representation of the world. The living being leans on the ensidic elements of the first natural stratum to create what for it is information; it does not find information as such in nature. The X is transformed and put into form, but also into relation through recourse to proto-logical categories: Pieces of information do not exist in isolation.

At this level of being—that is, with the emergence of the living being—"existence" is given inaugural (subjective) meaning in its rupture from inorganic being by the *for-itself*. The living being creates the levels of meaning and the world, as well as their intimate connection. The *subjective instance*, as Castoriadis refers to it in PSS, is simultaneously the emergence of subjectivity as selfhood.[12] The living being—and the various regions of the *for-itself* more generally—not only create themselves as new strata of being, but create further strata of being that have *meaning for them*, and *exist for them*, but do not necessarily exist as such in other regions of being. Castoriadis often draws on the example of "color" in the natural world to make his point. Colors do not exist in the physical world as such, except as vibrations. The living being, however, creates colors as part of its *Eigenwelt*: That is, it brings colors into reality, and, as such, into ontological existence. This could be illustrated at the social-historical level by many examples that fit well with Castoriadis's project, but the situation can also be illuminated by one that does not: The creation of the *sacred* is seen in Castoriadis's second and final paper on religion (ISR) as a (inadequate) response to the abyss.[13] But, as with the creation of colors, it could also be interpreted as the creation of a new stratum of being which has neither reality nor meaning for those regions of being other than the social-historical (and anthropic being more generally).

Castoriadis's philosophical elaboration of the living being brings critical engagement with the scientific idea of autopoiesis to bear on a reactivation of the philosophical idea of modes of being *for-itself*.[14] I have characterized it as a partial fusion of Aristotelian and Kantian motifs, although at this juncture, it no longer resonates just with the Kant of the *Critique of Pure Reason*, but also of the *Critique of Judgment*. Kant's third *Critique* provides a useful analogy for Castoriadis's trajectory, ranging from the importance of the imagination (as taken up and altered by Kant in the first and second editions of the first *Critique*), to the increasing importance on the creative aspects of nature and aesthetic creation as an oblique form of autonomous questioning, or judgment, as trends in his later thought. In the third *Critique*, Kant embraces the creative and constitutive role of the imagination but without lending it ontological weight. As argued in Chapter 5, in turning to Aristotle's classic formulation of *physis*, Castoriadis rediscovers its creative aspect and subsequently radicalizes its philosophical implications to encompass all regions of being, but, most particularly in that essay (PA), Castoriadis emphasizes that living beings, "the beings (*étants*) of *physis* have in themselves principle of creation of form." Castoriadis situates himself against the "causalist" approaches within modern science, where the measurement of local movement with respect to inert bodies is prioritized over internal and self-animated movement. The *for-itself* is its own end. In PA, Castoriadis analyzes this in terms of teleonomy rather than teleology: Its finality is self-created. Castoriadis reinterprets and radicalizes Aristotle's classic formulation of *physis* from finalism as a variant of determinism, to self-creation of form. Thus, in terms of the shift in Castoriadis's conception of the living being from the time of the *IIS* to the growing importance of creative *physis*, the major discernable shift lies in the move from the living being's capacity to *organize* its world (at the time of the *IIS*), to *creating* its own world by the mid-1980s (with the attendant philosophical implications that this entails). Implicit in the creation of an *Eigenwelt* is the corporeal imagination, although not yet the "radical imagination" of the human psyche, that the living being exhibits in the creation of an *Eigenwelt*.

Biological Autonomy?

Is the living being autonomous? In posing this question, the *nomos/physis* problematic expands to the biological realm. Two further queries seem to underlie the first: Who can be autonomous? What is a self? Each of these questions is problematized within the context of Varela and Castoriadis's dialogue.[15] Varela's early approach to autopoietic systems did not theorize the "self" of the subjective instance as such; rather, the impersonal self of "auto-organization" was highlighted. Castoriadis utilizes both terms because, for him, they refer to different regions of being. Castoriadis's interpretative framework is at variance with the "self-organization of systems" approach in three ways: First, he radicalizes the idea of autopoiesis as self-*organization* to autopoiesis as self-*creation*, which, as we have seen, necessitates for him a radical reconsideration of ontology and epistemology that is not always evident in the broader debates on autopoiesis. Second, instead of the emphasis being on *systems* as self-organizing, Castoriadis would now argue that self-creation is characteristic of all regions of being. Third, Castoriadis maintains that at certain conjunction of being, a new level of being is created by the living being (or more generally, by the broader region of the *being-for-itself*) as the subjective instance or (proto)-self. It is at this level of the self as *for-itself* that Castoriadis primarily engages with autopoiesis and, in this way, the self—which manifests itself differently in a variety of subjective instances—acts as a bridge between *systems* and the *subject*.

Building on the above point, it is worth making more explicit that, as a second point of contrast to Varela and the exponents of autopoiesis more generally, Castoriadis does not rely on the vocabulary of systems theory.

He makes clear that, with respect to human modes of being, the concept of system has no relevance. Instead, Castoriadis introduced the magma metaphor, which he expounds upon in *IIS*. In the final chapter of the *IIS*, as we have seen, he extends the notion of magma into natural modes of being as well, with particular reference to the living being. With the emergence of the polyregional ontology of the *for-itself*, moreover, the living being is increasingly elaborated along the lines of a proto-self, not a system. One problem with the idea of "system" for Castoriadis is that it excludes a diachronic approach. However, is this problematic satisfactorily resolved with the idea of a proto-self that creates its *Eigenwelt* "once and for all," especially when the idea of a "once and for all" is interpreted as a marker of difference to the "incessant self-alteration" of the social-historical? In an earlier essay (MSPI), he seemed more at ease with the idea of the diachronic implications of a living system and argued that: "The same question arises in different fashion in biology, where the "system" only counts as a living system by virtue of its capacity to "evolve," whether at the ontogenetic level, the phylogenetic level, or the level of the global biosystem" (MSPI 203–4), but he did not systematically pursue this line of thought in his later reflections. In many respects, the earlier notion of the living system seemed to more satisfactorily address his problematic of the interplay of synchronic and diachronic approaches that he left unresolved in his philosophy of the living being in the 1980s.

The question remains: To what extent is there selfhood in the system? Concerning the idea of the "self" a possible confusion requires clarification. It is not always apparent in translations of the word "self" from French into English, whether it refers to the impersonal use of "*auto*" as in "auto-organization" or "autopoiesis," or if it refers to the "self" of a "subjective instance" as seen in Castoriadis elucidation of the various overlapping regions of the modes of *being for-itself*, or Morin's psychoanalytic self (*soi*), or the reflexive use, for example, *s'auto-créer*, that is not widely used in English, or the human "self" that in some contexts is interchangeable with the term human "subject," but is usually demarcated from nonhuman "selves." In this context, Ricoeur's (1992) introduction to *Oneself as Another* is helpful for its explication of the diversity of ways different languages (in what Descombes [1991] calls a "philosophical grammar") have to express the self. In the case of autopoiesis, the "self" of the subjective instance is not theorized as such; instead, the impersonal self of "auto-organization" is foregrounded. That notwithstanding, it is interesting that in an essay entitled "The Emergent Self" (1995), Varela argues that living beings have to be understood as a "mesh of virtual selves."[16] Certainly the living being does not just create a world of and by itself, but also for-itself; in this way, the instauration of the subjective level requires a kind of a *proto-self*. For Castoriadis, not only the living being but also being *qua* being creates itself. While I am not suggesting that for Castoriadis being is a *self* in the strong sense of the term, there is nevertheless a sense in which transregional being that *creates itself by itself* needs to be understood very generally in terms of an impersonal self or minimalist proto-self of creation.

How can we understand Varela's concept of biological autonomy? If the interest in autonomy first brought Castoriadis and Varela into conversation, it also reveals their differences in their respective approaches. For Varela, autonomy does hold significance at the level of biology and of the living being, as the ongoing maintenance of its identity in its organizational—that is, cognitive—closure. For Castoriadis, on the other hand, autonomy is not part (either *in actual fact* or *potentially*) of the *for-itself*'s mode of being in general, and he prefers the term *self-constitution* instead of "autonomy" to characterize the living being (see, for example, PA). However, this is not just semantics. On the contrary, the differences between *autonomy* and *self-constitution* are decisive for Castoriadis. Thus, although his ontology of creation is extended into nature, he continues to defend the idea of autonomy as limited to anthropos. The historical instauration of the autonomist imaginary can only be understood as a political and cultural project that entails (in varying aspects of explicitness and obliqueness) the recognition that collective law is self-instituted—that is, not extra socially instituted—*as well as* the explicit interrogation of the institution of the world on an ongoing basis, including self-limitation. The living being, on the other hand, creates the proto-meanings of its *Eigenwelt,* first, in (functional) closure; and second, once and for all. For Castoriadis, autonomy is centrally linked to the Greek philosophical invention of *nomos*. As indicated previously, Castoriadis tells us that "It is the term *nomos* that gives full meaning to the term and project of autonomy" (PA 332). For Castoriadis, *nomos* remains a mode of being specific to humankind; it enables a "self-reflexivity" that goes beyond the " 'blind' self-constitution" (PA) of the living being, and requires political activity (as *la politique*). For Varela, however, it is the ongoing achievement of self-creation, that is, the autonomous creation of an *Eigenwelt* (in Castoriadis's parlance) that signals the biological autonomy of the living being. Here Varela collapses *nomos* into *physis*, where *nomos* is understood as the culmination of self-creative *physis*, but without preserving the productive tension of the *nomos/physis* problematic. As discussed above, Castoriadis requires that self-creation of one's world is recognized per se, as well as being recognized in its ultimate openness, that is, able to be problematized in order for the project of autonomy to be more than an "emergent capacity" in the human realm.

Is there common ground between Varela and Castoriadis? The question of biological autonomy reintroduces the *physis/nomos* problematic, but this time it appears at an intradimensional level (of the polyregional ontology of the *for-itself*). If Varela articulates the autonomist imaginary within broad parameters so as to include the living being, Castoriadis conceives it more narrowly on the one hand, but also in a more complex sense, in that he includes dimensions that Varela does not really explore, on the other hand. Varela disputes the (then) conventional mechanistic notions of the living being, arguing instead that the living being is not *caused*, but autonomously creates its own world. Castoriadis argues against forms of determinism, too, but whereas he accepts that the living being creates its world in (functional) closure, his argument that the social-historical can rupture the overall tendency to closure by self-reflexive interrogation of the laws it gives itself—in a way that the living being simply cannot—is absolutely central. That being said, Castoriadis sometimes does seem to waver at the demarcation between *autonomy* and *self-creation* of a world in the human realm (especially evident in the final seminar of *CQFG*); and indeed, more generally, there is an overall tension between his ontology of creation and anthropology of the creative imagination, and the project of autonomy. In this sense, the autonomist imaginary is ambiguous in Castoriadis's thought. It incorporates overlapping aspects, not all of which are apparent in each region of the *for-itself*. *Nomos* can be thought of as a region—or dimension—that forms part of the wider horizon of the *eidos* of the *world* for the polyregionality of the *for-itself*. Creation of an *Eigenwelt* is the ontological creation of the most basic form for each mode of being for-itself. Self-creation of *eidos* is characteristic of the *for-itself*. The world, as an order that lends itself to meaning, can first "appear," is brought into "existence" (as a horizon conferred with meaning, broadly conceived) with the living being. Prior to the emergence of the living being, there is neither the existence of the "world" nor "meaning" in—or rather, for—strata of nonliving nature. The form of the world is created autonomously, in Varela's sense. However, it is only with the social-historical that it can be recognized as such, problematized and altered. Only in the human realm can the political promise of *nomos* be activated. Yet this, too, leaves a residue in Castoriadis's thought, as he conceives it, because *autonomy* is neither an anthropological category nor a widely shared historical characteristic: It is but an "emergent capacity" rarely actualized, let alone realized.[17]

The autocreation of a world is insufficient in and of itself to grant the living being participation in autonomy.[18] For Castoriadis, the recognition of the self-creating, self-constituting mode of the living being as being-for-itself is an important sign on the way to autonomy and reveals more durable lines of continuity between human and nature than at the time of the *IIS*. In line with Castoriadis's recourse to an archaic imaginary schema, it is possible that Hesiod could be reintroduced here and reinterpreted within a wider and more heterogeneous imaginary of *nomos* in which each kind of animal—or each level of the *for-itself*—is seen as self-creating its own world of *nomos*.[19] As Varela tends to dissolve *nomos* into *physis*—the self-creation of form is an autopoietic feature of creative *physis*—the advantages of keeping a strong version of biological autonomy is potentially more limited than it might first appear. With Castoriadis's shift from a regional ontology of *nomos* to a transregional ontology of *physis*, there is no concomitant collapse of *nomos* into *physis*. What we see instead might be called a relocation of Heidegger's ontological difference in that being is characterized by creative *physis* as *à-être,* that is variously and concretely manifested according to the level or region of being in question.

In conclusion, the living being has been elaborated as the archetypal form of the *for-itself;* its ontological qualities pervade each level and mode of the being *for-itself.* As self-creating, the living being is a concrete exemplar of radical *physis.* As being for-itself, the living being is its own end and creates its own proper world (*Eigenwelt*), through which no "information" can enter without being subjected to the laws and determinations of that world. The prime difference between the living being and other regions of the *for-itself* is that the living being lives within functional closure, whereas the defunctionalization of the human psyche ruptures the stratum of the living being at the anthropic level. The living being brings the "subjective instance" of a proto-self into existence; it constitutes itself as itself, and in contrast to inorganic nature, it creates a unity and an interior. As a "subjective instance" it creates the world as kosmos—a world of (proto)meaning. The kosmos is then concomitant to the subjective instance and imagination. Castoriadis's rethinking of the living being takes place within a more general shift in the 1980s, where the subterranean presence of creative *physis* as *à-être* take on transregional ontological importance. We can speak here of a sense of *creative emergence.* These developments emerged directly from his encounter with the problematic of autopoiesis. Although the autonomist imaginary remains an open field, Castoriadis does not dissolve *nomos* into *physis* with the emergence of his move to embrace the creativity of *physis* and its implications for his overall ontology. For him the living being cannot be considered autonomous; there is no biological autonomy. Castoriadis's introduction of the polyregional ontology of the *for-itself* in the 1980s is an innovation emerging directly from the shift to radical *physis*. It introduces the *for-itself* as overlapping modes/regions of being for the first time in Castoriadis's trajectory. It broadens the reach of meaning and the world, in that the creation of the world, even at the level of the living being, presume the activity of the (corporeal) imagination and the emergence of meaning. It thus broadens the problematic of world in terms of its mode of being and the reach of the phenomenal field in question. In addition, the creation of an *Eigenwelt* by the *for-itself* signals a shift from "organization" of the world *qua* living being, to *creation* of its own world. The emphasis on the creation of the world allows Castoriadis to extend the mode of being of the *for-itself* across anthropic and non-anthropic modes of being in such a way that they are configured more visibly in terms of continuity; the creativity of the living being is foregrounded and is understood as an important precursor to social-historical modes of being, in general, and to the project of autonomy, in particular.

8

Reimagining Cosmology

Castoriadis's cosmological considerations emerge from his reflections on the interconnectedness of time and creation. He seeks to offer a philosophical articulation of the physical universe—as one reducible neither to a purely scientific nor a religious imaginary—by an elucidation of the overarching meaning of time.[1] Castoriadis's dialogue with—and continual movement between—the ancients and the moderns continues to inform his elucidation, and he also draws on archaic mythopoietic motifs to anchor his image of the kosmos. Castoriadis's philosophical cosmology, in its radicalization of Aristotle via a rethinking of Kant, continues to resonate with pre-Socratic—more specifically Ionian—visions of nature (not least as composed of primordial elements), and the relationship between *physis* and being. Links to the "poetic ontologies" of Hesiod or Homer become discernable, particularly in his ancient Greek seminars (*CQFG*). His elucidations revise the interplay of scientific and philosophical articulation of the world, and in so doing, revive an older sense of philosophical cosmology (Gusdorf 1985). As Brague (1999) argues, *cosmology* implies an opening onto *anthropology*, as it presumes a reflexive relation to the world: As such the two are linked.[2]

For Castoriadis, proper time as such has not been thought by the inherited tradition. A primary part of his concern with philosophical cosmology is to question the inherited interpretation of time—as it is variously expressed—and its tendency to reduce time to a dimension of space, especially as it pertains to the physical world. As a consequence, he seeks to offer an interpretation of time at the cosmological level that would not be reduced to space, which he does through an articulation of time as qualitative, creative, and content-rich. From the time of the *IIS*, and in Heidegger's philosophical wake, Castoriadis has argued that the only way to think being was to think time; here he continues to expand and deepen this proposition. Castoriadis argues that traditional approaches to time—both in physics and philosophy—consistently theorize it as a dimension of, or as complementary to, space. In so doing they occlude the core aspects of temporality. He maintains that time as the emergence of alterity is not thematized; instead the conception of time remains caught within frameworks of identity, and, as such, cannot account for creation. He extends the notion of time as the concrete emergence of forms through which its content is constituted. His underlying proposition is that a new understanding of creation depends on a rethinking of the philosophical notion of time and vice versa. Castoriadis offers an interpretation which draws on the Greek imaginary as a distinctive grasping of the world, and highlights the radical temporality and heterogeneity of being as *à-être* as the incessant autocreation of other forms. His interpretation also foregrounds the image of being as creative *physis* and as *à-être*—a radically heterogeneous, *always-becoming* being.[3] In the same way that the regional ontology of the living being needed to be contextualized within a wider polyregional—or dimensional—ontology of the *for-itself*, so, too, does Castoriadis's philosophical cosmology exceed strictly regional limits, and provides a bridge to the transregional ontology of creative *physis*. Here time as the medium of creation links to Castoriadis's cosmology and simultaneously to the general ontology of transregional *physis*. Indeed, as Castoriadis notes elsewhere, "Ontology is also, necessarily, cosmology" (DD p. 362). As the creation of alterities and the time of alterity, overarching time is inseparable from transregional being.

Before proceeding further, it is worth returning to the early paper MSPI. In this essay, Castoriadis's discussion pursues a wide-ranging interrogation of the current state of the natural and the human sciences.[4] One conclusion to be drawn from his analysis is that each discipline has a particular grasp upon the world (upon a particular stratum of being), and has partial overlap with neighboring—and sometimes, too, with less related—disciplines: Each contributes to the elucidation of being *qua* being. As discussed earlier in Chapter 1, moreover, MSPI is best interpreted as the initial recognition and articulation of the social-historical as a separate region of being in need of its own philosophical elucidation, rather than as a setting out a programmatic research agenda that would lead to the development of creative *physis*. Simultaneously, however, MSPI is a defense of philosophical autonomy, although it requires the transformation and radicalization of the philosophical tradition in that the inherited tools and frameworks, not only of philosophy but also of the natural and anthropological sciences, are inadequate to the task of elucidating the mode of being of the social-historical. As such, there is a sense throughout in which Castoriadis sees philosophy—or at least a transubstantiated philosophy—as the queen of the sciences. It alone can provide a basis of unity to all the disciplines which are thus conceived as specific historical enquiries into—and, to use a less Castoriadian language, interpretative demarcations of—various levels of being. To achieve this, however, at the time of MSPI philosophy is mainly seen by Castoriadis as an elucidation of the *human* ontological condition (not of natural being) and more particularly, of the hitherto occluded mode of being of the *social-historical*. In MSPI neither the notion of the self-creation of the universe, nor the idea of creation in the natural regions, is indicated at this point.[5] Castoriadis's shift toward creative *physis* in the 1980s—and concomitant reconfiguration of the *nomos* and *physis* problematic—can be seen as broaching the other side of the ontological equation—nature—in a radicalization of the project of philosophical autonomy. Castoriadis is above all interested in "men in the city."[6] As with Plato's Socrates, to whom Castoriadis refers in this quotation (see the epigraph to Part II), Castoriadis is above all interested in "men in the city." However, Castoriadis, too, is eventually led to assign anthropos a "place in the world and to recognize their substantial kinship with stones and trees." In so doing, the "world" in which he assigns anthropos a place is reimagined. In MSPI, Castoriadis observed crises in mathematics, and more so in physics, where not only the nature of the physical object, but the activity of the physicist and the "physicist" himself is put into question. His critique is directed both against classic and contemporary forms of physics and, in particular, against their underlying metaphysics. The ideas that he was later to develop more fully were hovering on the horizon: the heterogeneous character of being; locally valid forms of knowledge; the overlap of discontinuity and continuity in the creation/discovery of new strata of being; and the philosophical import of the fact that science has a history. Castoriadis identifies the question that he takes to be at the end of the astrophysical endeavor: "In what sense can there be a theory of a unique object?" (MSPI 163). Castoriadis does not so much offer explicit answers or solutions but continues with his strategy of highlighting the aporias to which each suggested cosmological solution inevitable leads. Implicit throughout is the constant critique of (logico-mathematical) determinism. He notes the resurgence of philosophical questions among physicists that emerged during the crises that beset the endeavors of the natural sciences. They could not, however, provide an answer. All that was revealed was that each mathematical and cosmological theory presupposed a set of categories which were neither self-evident nor neutral, "which thus raises the issue of their interpretation, which from then onwards inevitably interferes with any theorisation of experience" (MSPI 164). At this point, Castoriadis identified the problem as the uncritical acceptance of these metaphysical postulates, and moved toward a preliminary response as an elaboration of the indeterminacy of being. As previously discussed, his first positive response to MSPI was to identify and elucidate the social-historical region of being. Later in the 1980s he returned to reinterrogate these fields of (natural) scientific endeavor, and began to elaborate an alternative account: the incessant auto-creativity of transregional being.

The period in which Castoriadis was chiefly occupied with cosmological considerations (the mid- to late 1980s) coincides with the latter part of his engagement with autopoietic thought more generally and is inseparable from this wider trend. As such, it is intimately linked to his gradual radicalization of *physis* as the self-creativity of all regions of being, which, as I discussed in Chapter 5, involved not only a rethinking of the philosophical idea of nature but also a deeper immersion in Greek sources. In this context, it is important to emphasize as part of Castoriadis's venture into cosmology a revitalization of ancient Greek visions of being/natural world as a *living being* (ISCS), that is, a self-animating being, in the broadest sense. As pointed out in the previous chapter on the living being, there are translation difficulties in distinguishing different connotations of the "self" (from French to English). Whereas the level of the living being created the dimension of being of the "self" as the *for-itself*, or "self" broadly understood as the subjective instance, this is not the case for physical regions of being. Nonetheless, they are still "self-creative" in the sense of "autocreative," and thus a very generalized and impersonal sense of a proto-living self can be imputed along the lines of the ancient Greek imaginary. These overlapping periods of Castoriadis's trajectory during the 1980s are reflected in the essay "Time and Creation," where the most sustained, albeit still fragmentary, engagement with philosophical cosmology is evident.[7] This essay is organized in five sections; each section corresponds to one of the seminars at the EHESS in 1987–88.[8]

The problematic that TC addresses constitutes a continuation and radicalization of Castoriadis's reflections of crucial sections of the social-historical chapter of the *IIS*, specifically "The philosophical institution of time," "Time and Creation," "The Social Institution of Time," and "Identitary and Imaginary Time," which were discussed in Chapter 1. The most pronounced difference is of course that that later TC includes or expands upon cosmological aspects that were not part of Castoriadis's main program at the time of the *IIS*. As discussed above, the scope of his project of philosophical autonomy in the 1980s reconnects with some themes of the early MSPI that he had left aside in the 1970s. Of particular interest was Castoriadis's introduction of the idea of *à-être* in the *IIS* during his discussion of the philosophical institution of time. Castoriadis's positioning of Plato's *Timaeus* in the *IIS* was understood as a counterpoint—even blockage—to the grasping of the temporality of being as *à-être*. Noteworthy, too, is Castoriadis's interpretation of cosmology—in his discussion of the *Timaeus*—as the *social-historical articulation of the world*. As I shall suggest, this phenomenological theme is deepened in the later TC seminars and writings. That being said, the TC sections that are devoted to an extension of social-historical and psychical modalities of time in a continuation of *IIS* themes are less relevant for our current purposes, and will not be dwelt with in the present context.[9]

The Philosophical Bifurcation of Time

Castoriadis opens TC with a restatement of Ricoeur's line of reasoning that there is an enduring bifurcation at the heart of the philosophical tradition of time: First, there is *subjective time* as time for us; and second, there is *objective time* as measurable time in the world (p. 374). Leaning on Ricoeur's *Time and Narrative*, Castoriadis notes (p. 377) that inherited philosophy has focused on *either* cosmological (as objective) *or* phenomenological (as subjective) time to the exclusion of the other, such that connecting them has been impossible. The occlusion of the social-historical means the occultation of the social-historical as transsubjective and transobjective mode of being and its elimination from the polarization of the subject/object opposition, which Castoriadis associates with the ego, animus, psyche, and transcendental consciousness on the subjective side; with the cosmos, creation, transcendence, nature, and world/Being on the objective side.[10]

Cosmological time has generally been viewed through the lens of ensidic time as the foundation of physicality. As such, time has needed to be measurable, or numbered; or regarded as the repetition of the identical in the production of difference. In other words, time becomes a dimension of space. Time as creation, in Castoriadis's understanding of it as the emergence of alterity as other forms, is not thinkable in these schemas.

Subjective time on Castoriadis's account has been rendered as an experienced, lived time on the part of the subject as anthropic being (although Castoriadis extends it to include all dimensions of the *for-itself*, hence, also the living being). The chief target of Castoriadis's criticism here is Heidegger and what Castoriadis terms his "utterly subjective" *je eigenes, je meines*, which makes a public and a cosmological time problematic, or, if such time were possible in Heidegger's schema, it would be at the cost of *Dasein*'s fall into inauthenticity. However, his critique of currents of subjective time also incorporates the phenomenological tradition more generally (including Merleau-Ponty).[11] In noting these two kinds of time, Castoriadis raises the question of time as such—overarching time—which makes this plurality of times possible. Although as yet unstated, this points to the idea of being in its transregional configuration of creative *physis*. In a reference to Aristotle, he draws attention to the plurality of times in the same way Aristotle conceived of the polysemy of "being." But Castoriadis goes further than Aristotle: Time is not just closely related to being, it is inseparable from it. Just as there are different regions of being, there are different "categories" (not just "meanings," in an oblique reference to Heidegger) of time. As discussed earlier, the failure of inherited philosophy to recognize the social-historical as a mode of being, or as radically temporal—that is, creative—has had consequences for all areas of philosophical questioning. So, too, in terms of philosophical cosmology as a philosophical elucidation of time, does this occlusion result in reductive tendencies, even and especially as it pertains to being *qua* being and its farthest regions. According to Castoriadis, it is only by due consideration of the social-historical that time in all its aspects and dimensions can truly begin to be grasped.

In discussing the philosophical idea of time with respect to the interrelations between subjective and objective times, the problematic of the world becomes more visible (pp. 376–77). Earlier in the *IIS*, Castoriadis saw the world as an "inexhaustible supply of otherness"; here in TC he writes "that the world (or being) considered by philosophy is thought irrespective of its social-historical construction (that is, creation) . . . with the results that inter alia *the true question of the world as the ground* for all the various social-historical creations of it is covered up" (p. 376, emphasis added). There is a further ambiguity in the being of the world in Castoriadis's thought between the social world, the natural world, being *qua* being, and the world as encompassing the combined social and natural worlds (as well as the various *Eigenwelten* of the regions of the *for-itself*). Castoriadis tends to entwine cosmological/objective meanings of the world with social-historical/subjective creations of the world and the latter needs to be distinguished from the phenomenological accounts of lived experience of our *being-in-the-world*.

Castoriadis does consider the phenomenological (or the subjective) mode of interpreting time *for us* to be a legitimate mode of elucidating time: He recognizes that it is, after all, our very mode of being. However, it does not exhaust all modes of being and thus the general ontological problematic reemerges.[12] For Castoriadis, the objective mode (beginning with Aristotle) as time in the world, has treated time as almost exclusively spatialized, quantified and measured. In contrast Castoriadis wants to elaborate a *qualitative* notion of time.[13] The meaning of the two varieties of time draws us to the conclusion that there must be a plurality of times, and thence an overarching sense of time that supports that plurality. But whereas Ricoeur in *Time and Narrative* approaches the problematic of time by a gradual deepening of the phenomenology of time and of the subjective perspective, Castoriadis turns to ontology to make sense of the distinction between cosmological and phenomenological approaches: For him, time as such is indivisible from being. Hence, the importance of Heidegger and his insight linking time to being. In this way Castoriadis can be thought of as forging a distinct post-Heideggerian path that is quite different from, for example, the better-known Derridean alternative. Castoriadis retraces his steps and asks why we are satisfied to remain with this distinction. His response? To be meaningful, time needs to be onto-logized; this in turn further affirms the diversity of times that need to be pluralized in new ways.

Castoriadis's tentative connection between the two currents—the cosmological and the ontological—stands in twofold contrast to Heidegger's explicit repudiation of the onto-theological error of the metaphysical tradition, which, in its articulation of the most excellent *Seiendes*, did not ask the question of Being *qua* Being, as well as of the cosmological error of equating being with the totality of beings. Although Castoriadis is clearly—if reluctantly—post-Heideggerian in that he reintroduces the *Seinsfrage* and the rethinking of being along temporal lines, he nonetheless just as clearly repudiates the *fundamental ontological* approach of Heidegger as the study of *Sein qua Sein* that is separate from concrete modes of being. Instead, as discussed earlier in Chapter 5, Castoriadis begins with a different premise: *Being* cannot be separated from *beings*. Taking that a step further, it is evident that Castoriadis does not so much pursue the meaning of Being, but, in more of an Aristotelian fashion, sees being as including a plurality of categories, and therefore encompassing various modes of being.[14] Another way of looking at this is to see Castoriadis as fusing together cosmological and phenomenological approaches within a broader ontological perspective. He interprets *Sein* as polysemic; that is, "to be" means different things in different regions. The most interesting ontological difference for him becomes then the difference between modes of being. In other words, Castoriadis relocates the ontological difference to the transregional ontology of *physis*, which is expressed in concrete modes specific to particular regions or clusters of regions/dimensions (as with the *for-itself*). *Nomos*, then, is the concrete mode of being specific to the social-historical. Instead, an interplay between cosmological and ontological renderings of the world become apparent; the cosmological aspects elucidate the existing order(s) of things (in and as the world), while the ontological aspects as creative *physis/à-être* indicate the modality of the existing order of things to forever become something other.

What then becomes of the arguments of the onto-theological and cosmological errors? If the initial premises are different, then they cannot mean the same thing as previously; nevertheless, it is clear that both are unacceptable to Castoriadis. For Castoriadis, the road to onto-theology, not least because of his theory of religion, leaves no space for the ultimate convergence of being and the Good. The cosmological path is closed, as, for Castoriadis, there needs to be more emphasis on discontinuity. In this way, a real—or true—totality is not possible from his perspective as there are too many gaps and jumps between different levels of reality. Thus, the relations between different strata of being are not fully ensidizable, as there is the element of *otherness*. Although he would have not welcomed the term, a detotalized, scaled down version of both arguments is palpable in his thought: There is clearly a sense that the social-historical is considered a special mode of being that is privileged over—or seen as more excellent than—other modes of being. So, on the one hand, while it is not onto-theological, it is ontological in a privileged fashion, in that the social-historical has its own logos. On the other hand, the strong link to *natura naturans/natura naturata* of the social-historical as instituting society and instituted society, as well as the social-historical as the creation of ontological form *ex nihilo*, leave the theological—or, at least, the religious—question still open.[15] As for the cosmological argument, there is no well-rounded totality existing, but there is a sense in which the social-historical remains in the natural order of things. At this juncture, a reflexive argument about cosmology can be brought in, namely, that constructing a cosmos, building a world order and situating the social (and anthropos more generally within it) is what most human societies have been doing most of the time.[16] Core imaginary significations are cosmological by definition: They articulate the world, in the double sense of *mise en forme du monde* as world *disclosing* and world *creating*. Both the cosmological and ontological aspects are linked to the social-historical; in this way, it is only by reconsidering the social-historical that the varieties of time can be thought. Conversely, however, the cosmological aspects form the background to the social-historical as a mode of being.

There is then a sense in which it is possible to suggest that Castoriadis pursues a negative cosmology: To the extent that he deconstructs positive cosmologies, it is loosely analogous to the procedures of negative theology. However, the possibility remains that Castoriadis can find promise in the old cosmologies and indeed he does find insights and points of support in the archaic Greek cosmologies for his own elucidation by drawing on a mythic-religious interpretative constellation of the world (see *CQFG* and SICS). The negative cosmology in the end becomes more than negative—a double negative—because Castoriadis discerns points of contact or insight from older cosmological constellations. Thus Castoriadis finds a mixture of insights and stimuli in the cosmological and onto-theological arguments that Heidegger rejects. Castoriadis's onto-cosmology can also be read phenomenologically as the interplay not only of culture and nature—in which the motif of the world as ultimate horizon is central—but also of the two modalities of philosophy that were encountered earlier in the "The Importance of *Nomos*": the philosophical (*le philosophique*) and philosophy (*la philosophie*). The former incorporates an articulation of the world, but the latter extends this to include an explicit problematization of the instituted world. Castoriadis presents us with a new imagining or articulation of being *qua* kosmos as it is now and thus puts into question the existing institution(s) of being *qua* kosmos. An image of philosophy as onto-cosmology moreover begins to emerge that would point to philosophy as being a bridge between—or the fusion of—two conventionally opposed traditions of reducing or homogenizing the world. The first refers to the objective/scientific approach, which reduces the world to its ensidic layer and thus empties the world of any meaning, and the second to the religious/mythic, which saturates, even overloads, the world with intrinsic meaning. Philosophy incorporates aspects from both currents that in turn relativize their polarization. Philosophy, then, mediates between science as a purely ensidic elaboration of the world and religion/myth (the distinction is not crucial to the argument here) as a purely imaginary elaboration of the world; it does so by drawing on imaginary schemas. Castoriadis, too, draws on a mythic constellation of the world—a specific version of the ancient Greek—as the interplay of chaos and order.[17]

At the onto-cosmological intersection the "world" as kosmos (as the "natural world" and as an "order of meaning") hovers on the horizon.

The parlance of "universe" (*uni*-verse) reveals a homogenizing, reductive tendency in modern thought, and the world reappears at the interface of the modern and archaic meanings of cosmology as well as in ontological terms: The double meaning of *mise en forme du monde* is important here.[18] In excavating the interconnections between the cosmological and ontological currents, we find that each can be further internally distinguished as including two interlacing aspects that more or less correspond to Castoriadis's own distinction between the ensidic and imaginary dimensions of being. The primary distinction revolves around the modern bifurcation of the world in its relation to meaning: In its natural aspects, it is regarded as intrinsically meaningless, and is only first invested with meaning by the social-historical. In this vein, first, Castoriadis offers a philosophical elucidation (and radicalization) of the objective, that is, scientific, ontological-epistemological articulation of the physical world that itself relies on the ensidic dimension of language as elaborative of the world *qua* physical world. That is, he assumes both that the (natural) world is meaningless and that it is capable—at least in some of its strata—of being grasped by scientific/objective frameworks that, in turn, *really* have a grasp on the physical world as it *really* is (in at least some of its strata). Philosophy in its articulation of the world in the double sense of *mise en forme du monde* cannot be seen as an elucidation of a "natural" world devoid of meaning. Neither is it satisfactory to imagine the world as meaningful in itself; rather, the world is *sinnfähig*. Second, Castoriadis's considerations—as with any cosmological reflection—must draw on interpretative patterns that incorporate mythic elements that narrate the beginnings of anthropos and the world. In this way, his cosmology also incorporates aspects of cosmogony. In so doing, the shape given to the world must support the philosophical elucidation of the objective elaboration of the natural, ensidic world and at the same time make the order of the world a meaningful order.[19] This second philosophical current—belonging to the imaginary dimension of the social-historical mode of being and the signitive dimension of language—creates the world as meaningful. In this context, philosophical cosmologies also rely on myth and mythic elements to articulate the world and vest the world with meaning: "There is no society without myth . . . Myth is essentially a way for society to vest with meaning both the world and its own life within the world—a world and a life that, otherwise, are obviously meaningless" (1997h: 11).[20]

First-order imaginary significations tend to invest the world with religious/mythic meaning; this goes for capitalism as much as it does for Christianity.[21] Although less explicit and more fragmentary in Castoriadis thought, it is clear that he draws on imaginary schema that have their roots in myth. He does this as a way of problematizing the presuppositions of the scientific worldview, and, subsequently, to reshape the kosmos in a new way. As indicated in "The Importance of *Nomos,*" "*Physis* and Romanticist Imaginary of Nature," and Chapter 5, Castoriadis reinterprets and combines ancient Greek religious motifs—most importantly here, Hesiod's chaos and the later notion of kosmos—to reinterpret the Greek notion of being as neither fully ordered nor fully chaotic. In a further usage of Hesiod (*CQFGI*) Castoriadis describes the origins of creation *ex nihilo* as self-creation from the abyss, from the groundlessness. We can here discern the increasing importance of archaic interpretative patterns to his thought, and his shift toward the transregional ontology of creative *physis,* along with his corresponding shifts in his articulation of the world, especially during the years spanning 1983–88. During this time he gave the seminars on archaic Greek imaginary significations of the world (*CQFG*), and further articulations are to be found both in the archival piece (AC, as discussed in Chapter 5) and in SCIS. Thus it can be seen that the overlapping currents in Castoriadis's philosophical cosmology and general ontology (each of the intracosmological currents pertain as well to the ontological) are multifarious and ambiguous; the respective interconnections pointed to above between cosmology and ontology and the links between the respective and various intracosmological and intraontological currents, which in turn all presuppose the centrality of the world as ultimate horizon and its articulation as *mise en forme du monde.*

Castoriadis discusses at length the most representative theorists of objective and subjective time: Aristotle and Augustine, respectively. When pushed to their limits, Castoriadis argues that each perspective only exists in interplay with its opposite. In line with our discussion of cosmological time, and our argument that Castoriadis—especially in his later philosophical trajectory—fuses key motifs of Aristotle and Kant, the focus of the present discussion is Aristotle. But first, a digression.

In choosing Aristotle as representative of objective time, it becomes significant to ask, what of Plato? The question is particularly pertinent given that the *Timaeus* (a text on cosmology) was the central point of discussion for Castoriadis's discussion of time and creation in the *IIS*.[22] At this juncture of the essay, Castoriadis—somewhat strangely in my view—offers only a brief allusion—or better, passing over—of Plato when opening his discussion of cosmological time in the TC essay:

> Leaving aside Plato—in the *Timaeus* (37d), time is clearly posited as an identitary, objective, measurable ordering of everything

worldly—we find in Aristotle the first systematic and thorough exposition of the objective, cosmological point of view (TC 379).

Why would Castoriadis pass over Plato at this crucial juncture in his mature elucidation of time? And does he, really? The response is negative: Plato (especially in reference to the *chora* as receptacle) remains Castoriadis's shadowy philosophical interlocutor in TC. But why, indeed, does the problem of Platonism remain ultimately unresolved in his thought (Along with—interrelatedly—the ontological status of mathematics)? How might this be interpreted? One interpretation might be attributable to the unsettling status of the *chora*: In his *IIS* discussion of Plato's *Timaeus*, Castoriadis argues that the philosophical tradition—which the *Timaeus* epitomizes in this context—is unable to think time as other than space, is unable to think time as alterity or as creation. Indeed, neither time nor space, strictly speaking, figures in the *Timaeus* (*IIS* 189). Later Castoriadis refers to time in the *Timaeus* as cyclical, in that it is that which allows *the return of the same* (*IIS* 190). He then moves to elucidate the notion of space more fully: Plato introduces the *chora* as a kind of separable/inseparable receptacle of that which is-becoming; it is in this context that time as *à-être* is introduced to indicate its irreducibility to "indetermination" alone. Instead, it needs to be interpreted as the surging forth of new, that is, other, forms and determinations (*IIS* 191).[23] Castoriadis discusses the ambiguities and *aporia* of the *chora*—not just as receptacle but also as a kind of "dream, *eidos,* participating in the sensible and the intelligible but neither one nor the other"—in terms of Plato's inability to locate it somewhere (all being must have its place). A little later, Castoriadis posits the *choral/topos* as inextricable from coexistence: The first possibility of the plural, excluded from imagining being as the one. Yet *topos* cannot accommodate the emergence of alterity, thus, coexistence/the plural signifies the repetition of the same. Clearly, at this juncture, Castoriadis was interpreting the *chora* along the spatial lines of the identical. Yet some years later—in "False and True Chaos"—he refers to the *chora*—along with Aristotle's *hyle*—as a pure chaos. He goes on to argue that it is starting from a strong form of chaos that being needs to be thought. Castoriadis does not discuss this at length, but interesting lines of thought begin to emerge, as discussed in Chapter 1, most intriguingly in terms of possibilities for a qualitative and dynamic notion of place/space. As emphasized throughout this study, Castoriadis reinterprets ancient Greek motifs—especially in this instance, chaos, but also chaos as linked to *kosmos*—in his image of being, especially in the sense of creative *physis/à-être* in all its onto-cosmological meanings. One such interpretation might, instead of linking *chora* to *topos* as coexistence of the identical, link it to Castoriadis's Aristotelian-influenced interpretation of the dyad as necessary to elucidate the idea of alterity, that is, creation of other forms, or, indeed, to pursue an elucidation of place/space as qualitative. However, is the relation between the ensidic dimension (of *topos/chora*) and the dimension of creation a relation of otherness? The relation between these two dimensions would be unensidizable, but they are not strictly other. In this context, it seems appropriate to reconsider the idea of an Adorno-esque relation of *nonidentity*. Thus, before there is a dyad of alterity, there is a primordial dyad of the nonidentical. Castoriadis's remarks on the dyad are part of a discussion on mathematics in an unpublished seminar on *Time and Creation* from 23/3/1988, entitled: "Introduction générale (suite et fin)," in which he refocuses the question of time as such (pp. 16ff). Castoriadis emphasizes the idea of time as the time of alterities (in the plural), in contrast to the (Platonic) idea of time as a pure receptacle, which was to be filled with elements. Time, for Castoriadis, is consubstantial and coemergent with that which is other. Thus, he continues in the archival seminar, it is necessary to posit a least two alterities when speaking of time: Alterity does not strictly speaking exist in the singular. Here the importance of the dyad for thinking alterity, and the reiteration of Aristotle's point that the number "two," rather than "one," must be considered as the first number. In Castoriadis's rethinking of Aristotle, he stresses the importance of this, for it is only with the emergence of "two"—of the dyad—that to think creation as alterity is possible.[24] Again, as with *nomos*, traces of primordial interlacing and mutual relativization of the spatial and the temporal becoming at the heart of being are apparent.

As mentioned, both the subjective and objective approaches to time engender aporias (pp. 378 ff), but when pushed to their respective limits, each version interlaces with its opposite. For Aristotle: "Time is the number (numbered number, measurement) of the before and after" (*Physics* 4.10–14: 217b29–224a17). However the "before and after" as a local movement is first a spatial ordering—Aristotle situates it in *topos,* with time only accompanying it. Time is that which can be measured; however, the "before and after" requires an observer and this implies also a subjective concept of time, or in Aristotelian terms, the subjective ordering of the soul. Kant interests Castoriadis as a thinker who bridges both subjective and objective approaches to time (p. 383). In Kant, time as *a priori* intuition forces whatever appears—be it in or externally—into one single dimension of succession. The application of this form to whatever appears/the phenomena requires the mediation of a transcendental schema, supplied by the transcendental imagination. This schema is the "line," which represents a shift away from the problem of "time" to the problem of "space." However, this, too, raises problems regarding the idea of the irreversibility of time, which clearly, a Kantian line cannot represent.

The Otherness of Time

Castoriadis begins to address time and the physical world from section four of TC (p. 389).[25] The imaginary dimension of time is a *Fähigkeit* of the social-historical: It is not manifest in the first natural stratum. The first natural stratum is an ambiguous region—or dimension—in Castoriadis's thought. It generally refers to physical nature as identitary, ensidic, but it also includes the living being, which, as we have seen, comes to be seen also a *creative* mode of being in Castoriadis's thought. While Castoriadis does not want to purge the first natural stratum of an identitary, ensidic dimension, he does want to highlight the poietic dimension of time that also occurs as part of the first natural stratum, while retaining a strict distinction between the meaningful time of the social-historical and the non-meaningful time of the world.[26] As Castoriadis states, "it is with this identitary dimension of the world that physics deals to begin with" (p. 389). Castoriadis's discussion of time seeks to identify its primary characteristics, especially in regard to its otherness from space. He pursues his characteristic strategy of dismantling conventional approaches toward the thematic in question (pp. 390ff). He considers conventional approaches in physics are deficient as they have neither explained satisfactorily the distinctiveness of time from space, nor the distinctive characteristic of time *qua* time. The "spectre of the spatialization of time that haunts physics" is the main subject matter of Castoriadis's critique: He argues that time has mostly been interpreted by analogy with space. In mathematical physics, too, if time is merely to be considered as part of a four-dimensional manifold, what then makes time distinct from other dimensions?

The irreversibility of time is generally called upon as the distinguishing characteristic of time from space: However, Castoriadis argues (or rather, asserts) that the reasons given are inadequate justification. First, it is not certain that all movements in space are irreversible (such as those close to black holes, for example); second, irreversibility is a cosmological "riddle" (in terms of the expansion and contraction of the universe); third, from Boltzmann onwards, irreversibility has not yet been successfully deduced from first principles; and fourth, physical irreversibility while locally indisputable, is still but a partial fact (p. 391). In this context, Castoriadis points out that irreversibility has been interpreted in terms of increasing entropy, yet this does not prevent the emergence of new forms at all strata of being, as forms are both created and destroyed. It is, in fact, the creation and destruction of forms that for Castoriadis will elucidate time and its "arrow." The spatialization of time is linked to the deeper problem of the mathematization of space within mathematical physics, resulting in the reduction of space to the ensidic layer as an ensidic dimension (p. 391). Castoriadis takes his assertion concerning the spatialization of physics a step further in criticizing the current conception of space as inadequate, in that spatialization of time in physics refers also to the mathematization of the ensidic layer, including space, as the quantifiable. Yet not all space is reducible to abstract, quantifiable space.[27]

Castoriadis starts to elucidate a positive notion of time in the cosmos. He maintains that any discussion that wants to go to the core of the idea of time must start from the idea of alterity and its emergence; that is, the creation and destruction of forms. The return of a radicalized *alloiosis* as a fundamental determination of being as such also emerges as a key element. Castoriadis moves on to differentiate between otherness and difference (as discussed in Chapter 1). However, now Castoriadis insists that his argument about creation *ex nihilo* does not stand in contradiction to determinism as such, but to universal determinism. He presents us with an implicit elucidation of *à-être* in its mature form: "Creation entails only that the determinations over what there is are never closed in a manner forbidding the emergence of other determinations" (p. 393). Following on from this, the contrast between time and abstract, mathematical space lies in the fact that abstract space is *extrinsic* to what is: It produces a receptacle which is filled with different objects. Time, on the other hand, is never empty. It is not abstractable from its content: "We cannot think of pure otherness as such." There is no pure time in which otherness could appear; there is not a "receptacle" of "otherness" that could be filled with different elements. Time coemerges as part of the new form, the time of alterity and the time of the new alterity. Otherness requires a dyad: Otherness always emerges as the otherness of something else:

> The dimension along which otherness is, is, in each case, consubstantial and co-emergent with that which emerges another in respect to something. It is inseparable from it—from the forms or events which make the otherness be, and which make be, in each case, another otherness. (p. 394)

The emergence of alterity—of a new form—is simultaneously the creation of a new time and the time of alterity as other times for other forms, and interlacing of times for overlapping forms.

In radicalizing Aristotle, Castoriadis concludes that time does not just accompany change but indeed *is* change, creation and being: "Time is being insofar as being is otherness, creation, and destruction. Abstract space is being insofar as being is determinacy, identity, and difference" (p. 395). There are two intertwining dimensions of being: alterity and determinacy. Castoriadis returns to the question of space (p. 395). He is clear that abstract space—the space of mathematical physics—is not to be reduced to space as such (that was Bergson's error). Abstract space correlates to the ensidic dimension of being. Space is qualitatively created by and for subjective modes of being; it contains not only an ensidic but also a poietic dimension such that being can deploy itself as a "heterogeneous multiplicity of coexistent alterities" (p. 396). And further, "There is poietic space, space unfolding with and through the emergence of forms. And there is identitary time, ensidic time embedded in poietic or imaginary time."[28] At this point, it would be interesting to return to Castoriadis's discussion of Plato's *chora* in the *IIS*, itself retaining a residue of *physis*, or to Merleau-Ponty's later idea of the flesh. Castoriadis argues that the emergence of forms is the unique characteristic of time, whereby the before and after of "the arrow of time"—its irreversibility—is "given by the scansion of creation and destruction" (p. 397). Time is the means by which the world can be meaningfully ordered. Time is not reversible, but not, on Castoriadis's account, as conventionally understood. Rather, the irreversibility of time is indicative of the emergence or self-creation of forms as the ultimate characteristic of being *qua* being. The self-creation of a new form (that is, as an *other* not merely *different* form) discloses *time* as creation (and destruction) of forms, and as such, cannot be linearly irreversible.

Time also entails space: The emergence of forms is an "organized multiplicity" and as such the emergence of a new coexistence (p. 398) is a necessary concomitant to time. However, when space is taken as prior, time *as* alterity, as auto-deployment of alterity is absent. The two aspects of time—difference and otherness—can moreover be aligned by introducing the idea of multiplicity as entailing a unity. However, the reverse is not the case. Castoriadis draws this paradox in terms of the statement that "being is—and is not one" (p. 399). Multiplicity as *difference* points to the existence of being as one in that the "plurality of particular beings is brought into one by the laws which produce and deduce beings from each other" (p. 399). However the unity of being is fragmented—it is not One—in that multiplicity also exists as alterity in being. In critiquing Heidegger, Castoriadis rejects the ontological difference, maintaining the solidarity of beings and their mode of being. New modes of being emerge or create themselves; being as such is each time altered. This points to the mode of being *qua* being as self-creation and self-alteration, whereby not only the new forms are a creation of otherness, but also alterity is exhibited in the modes of emergence themselves. For "we cannot think being as self-alteration and incessant to-be (*à-être*) without considering the modes of this self-alteration and the modes of being they bring about" (p. 400). Thus the ultimate characteristic of being for Castoriadis is a dyadic nexus of intertwining modes of being: Difference (as persistence and repetition of the same) and otherness (as the creation and destruction of forms). These characteristics are the very same ones for time: "the unfolding of otherness, the deployment of alterity, together with a dimension of identity/difference (repetition)" (p. 400). An identitary dimension alone is to be found in abstract (ensidic) space. Both dimensions occur in actual space, but unlike abstract space, actual space presupposes time. "The fullness of being is given—that is, simply is—only in and through the emergence of otherness which is solidary with time" (p. 401). Being is self-deployment and self-alteration through time as the emergence of otherness; as such this requires us to interpret being as essentially fragmented (as discussed in Chapters 6 and 7). It is exemplified with the emergence of the living being as rupture of inorganic being. Here, it suffices to note that each *Eigenwelt* of the various modes of the *for-itself* create their own time(s) and space, and thus "it fragments being, space and time." Unlike Heidegger, who sees only one temporality as authentic, Castoriadis sees a plurality of possible authentic times—be they cosmic or subjective. Yet the question of overarching time and being remains open.

To return to Castoriadis's opening distinction: Time has traditionally been divided into subjective time and time of the world "as receptacle and dimension of whatever may appear, and as order and measure of this appearance" (p. 374). Castoriadis offers an alternative account of cosmological time: No longer reduced to a dimension of space, there is also the time of otherness as emergence of alterity. Such time is not extrinsic to the emergence of new forms; it is rather consubstantial with this emergence. As such, time cannot be thought of as an empty receptacle (which clearly refers to the *chora*): Empty time abstracted from the concrete form is not thinkable. The world each time is created by the subjective mode of being for-itself (for example, living being or social-historical being) and consists of two kinds of multiplicities: an ensidic multiplicity of the simply different (receptacles, elements) and a poietic dimension of otherness.[29] Being is envisaged as *à-être*, as the creation and destruction of forms, as an essentially temporal mode of being, yet one with an irreducible ensidic dimension. The ensidic layer of being cannot be totally ensidized, and the poietic dimension cannot totally be without local determinations: Creation as the creation of form is also the creation of laws and determinations.

What is also increasingly apparent in this discussion in TC (and in this later period of his thought, more generally, in contrast to the *IIS*) is the shift from an emphasis on the creation of forms by the social-historical, to an emphasis on the *creation* and *destruction* of forms; a result of his thinking through the "arrow of time" via the dimension of otherness. Thus the two dimensions of being intertwine: the ensidic as persistence of the same, and the poietic as emergence of otherness. Within the context of Castoriadis's project of philosophical autonomy, the aspect left unexplained here is the relation of imaginary time to his philosophical cosmology, which Castoriadis practices as a philosophical interrogation of natural scientific frameworks. Imaginary time is strictly demarcated from identitary time: It at best "leans on" it. Identitary time is almost quasi-naturalized, in that it seems to appear in nature, whereas imaginary time of signification does not: It alone is the mode of being of the social-historical.

While there is an ensidic and poietic dimension to the world, which Castoriadis sometimes seems to equate with being itself (see, for example, TC 377), Castoriadis does seem to accept an Enlightenment—and in this sense also modern scientific—trend toward *Aufklärung* as *Ausklärung*. The world, on his account, is emptied of meaning, is strictly meaningless. Thus the elaboration or elucidation of its objective/cosmological aspects proceeds along quasi-objective lines.[30] It does and must of course draw upon imaginary schemes—in Castoriadis's case, that of the archaic Greek world—yet its elucidation would seem to proceed along "factual" rather than "imaginary" lines, "explanatory" rather than "interpretative." It is a *demagified* world that is to be elucidated cosmologically.[31] Yet the elucidation of objective time occurs within the subjectively instituted world of meaning and signification (in echo of Husserl's *Lebenswelt*). As has been discussed, the lines of continuity and discontinuity between natural and the anthropic, in particular social-historical modes of being, were reconfigured from the time of the *IIS*. Whereas at the time of the *IIS*, it was the social-historical that was considered to be the only region of being characterized by the creation of ontological form, now all modes of being for themselves, and even non-living modes of being, are understood to autocreate ontological forms. Ontological creation has become a transregional mode of being in Castoriadis's thought. On the other hand, Castoriadis has radicalized—or made more explicit—the imaginary dimension of time. The imaginary dimension of time is the social-historical regional manifestation of transregional poietic being, or, in this context, poietic time. Although a proto-meaning must be recognized at the level of the living being, as Castoriadis argues, the world *tout court* is meaningless (DD 364): The only mode of being that is in any sense meaning-creating and can hence confer meaning onto being and the world. Castoriadis's conception of the latter as instituting and instituted society may, with a further twist, be seen as a radicalization of the Romantic current of theorizing creative nature as *natura naturans/natura naturata*. Thus we find ourselves with the intertwining of both poietic and ensidic dimensions of being in a transregional context.

In his writings on time and creation, it is apparent that Castoriadis's main objective is to rethink the kosmos in all its aspects, including the physical, but especially in terms of the occlusion of the social-historical. To give the social-historical its fundamental due is to inevitably transform the philosophical landscape, and to reinforce the post-transcendental phenomenological trend to imagine the mutual entwining of the natural and cultural in the institution of the world. An interrogation of the existing institution of the world, and our knowledge of it, is the first and foremost part of Castoriadis's project of philosophical autonomy. The figure that remains in the shadow of his thought is the *world qua world,* as a phenomenological problematic. It is the ultimate horizon that links and separates natural and human modes of being, that is further always created/interrogated by subjective modes of being, and is the point at which cosmic and subjective times, regions and dimensions, overlap where cosmology merges into ontology. To turn Castoriadis upon himself, "The true question of the world as the ground for all the various social-historical creations of it" (p. 377) still awaits elucidation.

Conclusion

The Circle of Creation

The present study has taken the reader through the figurations—and re-configurations—of Castoriadis's philosophical path through ontology, and into the "crossroads in the labyrinth" emerging beyond. It offered a hermeneutic reconstruction of Castoriadis's ontological path, with a particular emphasis on his central concept of "creation." Its argument was twofold: First, it showed that over the course of his philosophical trajectory, Castoriadis extended his notion of ontological creation beyond the human realm to include regions of nature as well; that is, he shifted from a regional ontology of social-historical creation (as *nomos*) to a transregional ontology of creative emergence (as *physis*), but without diluting the productive tension between the two orders. Second, it argued that Castoriadis made an implicit hermeneutical turn at the end of the *IIS* that relativized his notion of *absolute* creation to *contextual* creation. In this regard, it detected an interpretative element integral to creation (and a creative element to interpretation), and opened onto a tension between the ontological and hermeneutical dimensions of Castoriadis thought, especially in light of the phenomenological problematic of "the world horizon."

By focusing on the *nomos* and *physis* problematic, we have been able to chart a path through Castoriadis's changing philosophical approach to being and creation. Over the course of the present study, the shifting configurations of *physis* and *nomos* in Castoriadis's thought, and the significance this held for his rethinking of being and creation in relation to nature, or, to be more precise, the significance this held for his rethinking of the place of anthropos within the natural world defined. The need to respond to a third question in addition to the *physis* and *nomos* problematic—that of the world horizon—emerged from the reflections (in Chapter 4) on the implications of the social-historical creation of "its world as the world." The need was reinforced on consideration of Castoriadis's polyregional ontology of the *for-itself* (Chapter 7). One implication that emerged from the later polyregional ontology was the need to elaborate an enlarged phenomenal field that went beyond the merely anthropic, and, concomitantly, a phenomenology that approaches the world of the living being with a view to elaborating more than "anthropological preconditions" (contra Heidegger). Although I would agree with Castoriadis's repudiation of biological autonomy, recognition of the world as a "meta-order" going beyond the orders of *physis* and *nomos*, yet simultaneously drawing into itself an overlapping of those orders, especially in the polyregional modes of the *for-itself* and its instauration of the "subjective instance," calls for a rethinking of the phenomenal field in question. The orders of *nomos*, *physis*, and the meta-order of the world, in turn, open onto three interweaving dimensions of creation—ontological, hermeneutical and phenomenological—and span physical, living, psychical, and social-historical regions of being.

Although important shifts in Castoriadis's ontological approach are evident, it is important to note that some of his other insights into being and creation were more enduring. These included, for example, the intimate nexus between time and creation; the notion that creation could only be understood as (auto)creation *ex nihilo*, that is, creation as immanent and absolute; and the qualitative and heterogeneous levels or regions of *being as creation*, and *creative being*, which illuminate being as irregularly stratified.

At the time of the *IIS*, Castoriadis's interrogation of "being and creation" was restricted to an elucidation of human modes of ontological creation. In particular, the being of creation was limited to excavating the region of *nomos* "for which no ontological place exists" (at least in conventional philosophical thought). As Castoriadis acknowledged, he could not explore the properly philosophical aspects of the "imaginary element" in the *IIS*, though its presence was increasingly felt, especially as the "being of doing" gradually became less important to his explicit elucidation, and the "being of signification" correspondingly more so. The creative imagination spanned the human psyche to the social-historical, but whereas the social-historical was emblematic of *nomos* and the project of autonomy, the psyche, although part of anthropic being, was of a different ilk: It was more than *physis,* yet not quite *nomos.* Although the autonomous subject (and the psychoanalytic perspective) became integral to his elucidation of autonomy, a few of his proposed solutions that emerged from the psychoanalytic domain, such as the relationships between the "first natural stratum," the psyche and the social-historical as one of *Anlehnung,* were not always systematically pursued. His elucidation of being and magma emerges from his psychoanalytic musings as well, but the relative weight given to psychoanalytic reflections tends to color some of his elucidation of the features of the social-historical. The most significant creation for Castoriadis was the social-historical creation of a world (of imaginary significations). Here, the ostensible problematic of human creation of ontological form, which is a creation of meaning in the proper sense, collides with the hermeneutic problem of culture and interpretation, and the phenomenological problematic of the world horizon—and an order of the world, more generally. Although Castoriadis repudiates the creative dimension to interpretation (and vice versa), the present study has demonstrated the converse to be the case.

The circle of *physis, nomos,* and world orders opens onto diverse contexts of meaning. It suggests a circle—or circles—of creation. In this sense, creative *physis* makes possible the specific mode of *nomos,* and *nomos* as the social-historical incessantly creates itself in a plurality of self-altering worlds. The world, too, is not limited to anthropic being, and the circle of creation emerges against the background of an enlarged and more heterogeneously constituted phenomenal field that crisscrosses the orders of *physis* and *nomos.* The circle of creation also suggests a hermeneutical circle—or circles. Here we see that Castoriadis has reinterpreted the ancient imaginary schema of *physis* and *nomos* within contemporary contexts, where their latent meanings are to be "created/discovered." Above all— and Castoriadis's protestations notwithstanding—the circle of *physis* and *nomos* suggests that these divergent moments (or circles) of creation and interpretation are inextricably linked, and linked, moreover, through the emergence of the polyregional order of the world. The meta-order of the world opens then onto ontological, phenomenological, and hermeneutical dimensions. While the issue of interpretation and meaning within the world of the living being is perhaps more thorny, certainly at the level of *nomos,* creation is better thought of as contextual, not absolute. In this way, creation is not only ontological but also always and already interpretative (and interpretation creative), and cannot occur without our ontological participation in the world. At some level, then, human creation revels an interplay of ontological and phenomenological-hermeneutical elements. There is agreement, then, with Merleau-Ponty's postulate that because we are in-the-world we are "condemned to meaning," and that these contexts of meaning are invariably creative and interpretative, explicit and latent. In agreement, with Castoriadis, however, elucidation of meaning without consideration of the centrality of the imaginary element is inconceivable: Meaning must be considered at the social-historical level and is irreducible to intersubjective domains or language.

The circle of *physis* and *nomos* ushers us toward terrain in which the questions of the order of the world and the enigma of the world horizon that encloses while opening the phenomenal field—and of our inescapable encounter with it and within it—first emerge. Within post-transcendental phenomenological approaches, the problematics of the cultural—or social-historical—institution of meaning, interpretation, and the world horizon are central foci. The post-phenomenological field draws on insights gained from phenomenology inspired by philosophical hermeneutics—and vice versa—and post-transcendental, transsubjective trends within phenomenology proper. The world problematic takes on increasing importance in allowing a deeper elucidation and questioning of the ever-entwining configurations of history, culture, and nature, and their ontological pre-conditions. As has been argued throughout this study, Castoriadis is central here. For him, meaning is the mode of being of the creative imagination in its divergent but overlapping aspects as the radical imagination and the radical imaginary; the social-historical as radical imaginary is beset by the inescapable horizon of the world, which it encounters and shapes, elaborates and recreates.

The world as a phenomenological problematic, as has been shown, tends to receive short shrift in Castoriadis's thought, but his contributions to its elucidation, albeit mixed, are nonetheless significant.[1] In his early reflections it hovers in the margins; in his later thought, it tends to be absorbed into radical *physis*. Overall, Castoriadis's approach to the world is ambiguous, although his elucidation of its ontological role is groundbreaking in fostering a greater understanding of the living being and subsequent enlargement and re-inscription of the phenomenal field. We can see that a general change in the status of the world is apparent in his thought, from the more or less phenomenological acceptance of action in the world—of experience as being-in-the-world as our mode of being in his early work—to the more radical notion of world creation and institution, in which our encounter with, and creative interpretation of, the always already instituted world in all its overlapping aspects, as well as our encounter with primordial being, tend to be downplayed and obscured. The creation of the world *ex nihilo* occludes the element of creative interpretation that is entwined therein. This is in contrast to Merleau-Ponty's notion of *être au monde*, which is more than *being-in-the-world*, but does not, in contrast to Castoriadis's ontological turn, do away with the experiential aspect of meaning altogether. Castoriadis's notion of *creatio ex nihilo* both obscures and aids clarification of the varying images of the world(s) and their ambiguous interrelations that are evident in his thought. In particular, various images of nature and world—in overlapping layers of natural being (where no world is yet existent), the appearance of world qua visible world (emerging with the for-itself), and nature as we encounter and institute it as kosmos (the social world, the world *qua* world and its ontological, that is, transcendental, pre-conditions) are discernable. The difficulty is that that the world—in its aspect as kosmos—is always an order of emergent meaning that is woven into diverse layers and regions of being, whether that be the chaos, the historical world of anthropos, or the natural world as social-historically encountered and instituted.

In a Greek text from 1944, Castoriadis observed that "Weber distinguished clearly the main characteristics of historical material from those of the natural. [In Weber's view] the historical phenomenon is always the bearer of meaning in contrast to the—meaningless—natural one" (1944, pp. 47–48).[2] Weber's view was shared by Castoriadis, although, as discussed earlier, this was relativized in his rethinking of the living being, and the wider *Eigenwelt* of the *for-itself*. Here we can begin to speak not just of the orders of *nomos* and *physis*, but a third dimension of the world that is characteristic of modes of being *for-itself*. However, the world *qua* world is not simply devoid of meaning; it is also external and amenable to it. Acceptance of the world as not-intrinsically-meaningful does not inevitably lead to Castoriadis's conclusion of the world as totally meaningless. We can refer here to his own critique of Kant's inability to acknowledge the mutual inherence of being *organized* with being *organizable*. For the world to be made meaningful there must be something in the world that lends itself to this; the world must be able to be made meaningful. To wit, the world needs to be considered *sinnfähig*.

The natural world, too, is also kosmos, and is imbued with imaginary and symbolic meaning that makes it "real" for us, yet points beyond this reality to imaginary dimensions of being. The natural world is no longer natural being, but is transformed through our encounter with it and elaboration of it as a field of meaning. The imaginary element, then, is intertwined with the emergence, encounter, and elaboration of the world. Perhaps the world does not indeed privilege any particular imaginary signification, as Castoriadis suggests in his critique of hermeneutical approaches to the world (DD 363), but this does not mean that the world is meaningless. The world always invites meaning; the world in this sense always comprises a horizon of meaning. The kosmos is a metaphor, in that it cannot be directly elaborated within the framework of a positive theory, although this is not to say that we cannot grasp its truth (or its always partial, always contextual truth). The world does not give itself to us directly, we do not encounter it directly, and we cannot elucidate it explicitly. But the world horizon as interpreted and transformed by the creative imagination into the kosmos is a historical order-bearing configuration of meaning: an order of meaning woven into the chaos (*IIS* 46). Meaning is an indefinite skein and it is open to creative interpretation. Indeed, constellations of meaning require ongoing interpretative creation and cultural elaboration. The world is configured through overlapping and ultimately open horizons of imaginary significations, which in yet another layer of opacity, present themselves to us through the symbolic—the "lost" layer in Castoriadis's later ontology. The kosmos emerges in and through the anonymous collective as history. Here again, the intrinsic overlap of interpretation and creation and the centrality of latent contexts of meaning are apparent. History is not just created, but interpreted (by definition). Historical worlds and their latent contexts of meaning are reactivated, encountered, creatively interpreted, and in constant need of reinterpretation.

There is a sense of heightened and accelerated temporality with the idea of the unmotivated "surging forth" of new forms: "the temporalization of the origin," as Ciaramelli refers to it.[3] Although the circle of creation assumes the self-presupposition of the origin, it does not, it is suggested, always burst forth in flames accompanied by claps of thunder from the abyss! What might appear as a "rupture" with the old may, on closer inspection, have its roots in a more distant past. New creations emerge as part of longer, historical processes. New epochs do not always mean the appearance of totally new questions and the eradication of the old. The same—or a similar problem—becomes visible within a historical context exemplified by the Greeks. Take the Athenian democratic *polis*, for example: Did it involve one creation or two? Was the autonomist imaginary unsaturated with its birth, or did it have its antecedents in Hesiod's interpretation of anthropos emergence from the chaos?[4] In a similar vein to his comments on the political side of autonomy in regard to Cleisthenes's reforms, Castoriadis effectively relativizes his strong position of the "bursting forth" of autonomy—in this case the more philosophical aspect—with the institution of the democratic *polis*, although, as Arnason notes in his discussion of Castoriadis and ancient Greece, Castoriadis's term of "long revolution" might be applicable here (Arnason 2001).[5] This leads to the relativization of Castoriadis's understanding of creation as absolute and *ex nihilo*; as has been argued throughout this study, it is more appropriate to elaborate creation as interpretative and therefore contextual. His later formulations of creation (as *ex nihilo* but not *in nihilo* or *cum nihilo*) acknowledge its circumscribing factors, but they tend to be minimized and its contextual and interpretative elements rejected. It also points us more generally to the metaphorical circle of *physis* and *nomos* as underscoring the ongoing dialogue between the ancients and the moderns and its importance for Castoriadis's overall reflections (as encapsulated, for example, in GMPI). The relevance of the ancients to the moderns is central to modernity's self-institution and search for "constitutive others" drawn not only from intercultural domains, but also intra-cultural classical contexts, distanced yet brought strangely near by history. It also points to modernity's hermeneutically privileged status as a self-revealing form of social reality.

To argue for an implicit interrogative moment in interpretation (and the imaginary) is neither to limit its scope to the Western tradition, nor to explicitly "critical" approaches (for example, the "hermeneutics of suspicion" found in Marx and Freud), which has been argued throughout this study, both in relation to the idea of *le philosophique* more generally. Within the scope of interpretative creation—within a given intercivilizational and intracivilizational context—an implicit *Auseinandersetzung* with older meanings and significations is inevitable, especially when it is considered, as Castoriadis did (*CQFG*), that underlying interpretative schema are always drawn upon. Castoriadis's own onto-cosmology (as a specific example of *world articulation*), for example, reinterprets archaic Greek religious or mythic motifs (the ongoing interplay of *chaos* and *kosmos* is also evident in radical *physis*) in a contemporary context that both problematizes the original Greek conception (the gods or *moira* do not figure in his conception, for example), as well as the current scientific, philosophical, and religious views of cosmology and ontology. If we take up Castoriadis's notion of the dyad, then the emergence of new forms needs to be interpreted as other *to another form*: Sometimes this aspect is obscured in thematizing the emergence of new forms. If this (preexisting) other form is not to be conceived in radical alterity from the new form, that is, as being separated by an ontological abyss such that to speak of it would be impossible, then they must stand in some kind of interpretative constellation to each other. This does not cancel out the novelty of the new; rather, it relativizes its absolute alterity.[6]

Over the course of this study we have tracked the changing configurations of *physis* and *nomos* in Castoriadis's ontology. The circle of *physis* and *nomos* points us to overlapping worlds of nature and culture, to the world *qua* world, and its overlap with primordial being, and the importance of the world brought into ontological visibility in Castoriadis's polyregional ontology of the *for-itself*. It points to worlds within worlds: The world *qua* world is simultaneously instituted and encountered as overlapping worlds, as *kosmoi* of meaning. Meaning—or at least some form of proto-meaning—is extended to the living being (along with the imaginary element) as characteristic of the for-itself. Historical worlds and their latent meaning-contexts are encountered, reactivated, creatively interpreted: The order of *physis*, for example, is emptied of intrinsic meaning in modernity (or at least in some Enlightenment versions of it), but vestiges of the world and meaning (but not a world-immanent meaning) reappear in the guise of the world as *à-être*, as that by which the world is *sinnfähig*. *Physis* is reconfigured in new contexts of meaning by Castoriadis in order to problematize the presuppositions of the scientific and capitalist kosmos of infinite rational mastery. As opposed to *physis*, history as *nomos* is the order that self-creates and self-institutes *kosmoi* of meaning.

In the first part of the book, we explored Castoriadis's elucidation of the region of *nomos* as the mode of being of the social historical and imaginary significations. At this point in his thought, the idea of *physis* was interpreted as an extra-social order in tension with *nomos*. As Castoriadis's reconsideration of *physis* took shape, he started—implicitly at least—to expand the notion of ontological creation of form to other regions of being. No longer confined to anthropic regions, the idea of self-creation began to metamorphose in his work. Both deeper and broader in scope, radical *physis* as *à-être*—an always becoming being—shapes itself as elementary to being, *qua* being. It is the flesh of the world and in-between worlds. The idea of *physis* evokes an element of the general creative process that pushes itself toward giving itself a form, and the regions of being with which Castoriadis begins to grapple are more in the manner of revealing the magma at work. *Physis* shifts from being interpreted primarily in opposition to *nomos* to being both the enabling ground of *nomos* and its point of culmination: They are mutually enveloping.

The idea of radical *physis* gives new meanings to being *qua* being, and the more circumscribed regions of nature. Elemental nature—*physis* as *à-être*—is also a reactivation of the archaic Greek thought. Castoriadis recontextualizes culture and nature—though a tension remains between nature as it appears for us (as per the discussion of the magma in Chapter 4) and its onto-cosmological aspects. Like Merleau-Ponty, Castoriadis's radicalization of *physis* takes place through a reinterrogation of the romantic conception of nature and the intermittent tradition of *natura naturans/*

natura naturata. As a contemporary version of *Naturphilosophie* it adds a Whiteheadian element to the philosophical project of autonomy in that it interrogates the imaginary presuppositions of scientific frameworks. This notwithstanding, Castoriadis's shift in register toward a context of radical *physis* does not always sit comfortably within the parameters of his earlier philosophical investigations, most easily discernible when his interpretation of the world comes into focus. The world remains a shadowy figure in Castoriadis's thought, yet it takes on a clearer hue as the post-phenomenological understanding of the world underlying his version of the cultural turn becomes more visible. Castoriadis's cultural turn is unusual in that he also rethinks the relation to the natural world; it resonates with the later Merleau-Ponty's thematizing of the world and its creative interpretation through the intertwining "true transcendental" of nature and culture. The world in Castoriadis's oeuvre is an abidingly ambiguous concept, mainly because he has not reconciled the two traditions of conceptualizing the world that he cultivates: the world as the sum of all natural beings (*Seiende*) and the more phenomenologically inspired *Ganzheit* of meaning. Finally, the reconfigured understanding of *physis* and its ontological creativity did not cancel out the uniqueness and importance of *nomos* as an anthropic order: The richness of the *physis* and *nomos* problematic was maintained, though its horizons were ever shifting.

And so the one circle is traversed and opens onto another. The interplay of elemental dyadic contexts—be they *nomos* and *physis*, culture and nature, kosmos and chaos—are preconditions of the chiasmic world and its ongoing elaboration. The anthropic encounter with the world horizon is inescapable and the variety of its cultural elaborations are concretized in social-historical constellations. The plurality of these historical worlds—in interplay with the unity of the overarching world horizon and the cultural clearing encompassed within it—weave an order of meaning into the chaos. Magmas of meaning are constantly reconfigured, and from these contexts of historical reconfiguration new ontological forms emerge. The ultimate *Sinnfähigkeit* of the world is neither a fully (self)determined something nor a formless nothing. The specific cultural configuration of the world emerges each time through historically shifting interconstellations of interpretation, creation, and problematization.

Notes

General Introduction: Castoriadis in Context

1. The question of the civilizational status of modernity is key to the current round of debates in historical sociology and civilizational analysis. See, for example, Eisenstadt (2001) and Arnason (2003). Some sections of this introduction have been published in earlier form in Adams (2009a, 2008a).

2. Although the imagination can be said to be central to Ricoeur's thought, he did not systematically pursue its elaboration. For discussions of Ricoeur on the imagination, see Arnason (1994), Taylor (2006), Kearney (2004), and Evans (1995).

3. See also Kearney (1998).

4. As such, both a "hermeneutic" of modernity, as well as a hermeneutic of Castoriadis's philosophical project as situated within modernity, are required. I return to this.

5. Hereafter referred to as the *IIS*.

6. The elaboration of the social-historical also incorporates an ongoing discussion of the imagination, or "the imaginary element." Although consideration of the "properly philosophical" aspects of the imaginary element was reserved for a forthcoming publication (p. 2), discussion of its various aspects is fundamental to the *IIS*. The coexistence of these two levels of discourse—"the social-historical"—or "anthropic being" more generally—and "the imaginary element" in the *IIS* was a point of productive tensions.

7. I return to this at length in Chapter 4.

8. This will be discussed in detail in Chapter 4.

9. Castoriadis explicitly denies, however, that Merleau-Ponty influenced his notion of creation, or, indeed that the idea of "creation" or "creativity" figured

in Merleau-Ponty's thought (2010: 8). For a different view on Merleau-Ponty's approach to the "experience of creation," see Delco (2005).

10. In particular, as Howard observes, Merleau-Ponty's thought was a significant, if little discussed, impetus for *Socialisme ou barbarie.*

11. See, for example, Castoriadis's 1948 text "Phénoménologie de la conscience prolétarienne." For contextualization of Castoriadis's political thought within the phenomenological field, see Howard (1988); within the French context of phenomenology more generally, see Waldenfels (1993). See also Piccone (1971), Arnason (1971), and Waldenfels, Broekman, and Pazinin (1984). Due to constraints of space, this book does not examine literature on Castoriadis in relation to *Socialisme ou barbarie,* his critique of Marx, or phenomenological Marxism. For discussion of these various aspects, see Howard (1988), Hirsch (1981), Hastings-King (1997), Poirier (2004), Arnason (1988a, 1991a, 2000, 2006), Tormey and Townshend (2006), and Caumières (2007).

12. See Howard (1974, 1975) for his introductions to Lefort and Castoriadis and the importance of thematizing bureaucracy with capitalism. See also Singer (1979). See Wolin (1985) for a discussion of Merleau-Ponty and Weberian Marxism. However, one of the earliest attempts at thinking Marx and Weber together—also emerging from a phenomenological background—appeared in the German context (Löwith 1932).

13. His critique of Marx was first published in *Socialisme ou Barbarie* in 1964–65 and then was included as the first part of the *IIS.* See also Lefort's paper "Marx: From One Vision of History to Another" (1978).

14. The above definition of the idea of a "trans-regional" ontology should be considered provisional. Further discussion and amplification is provided throughout this study, as is elaboration of Castoriadis's neologism of being as *à-être.* See especially Chapters 1, 4, and 5. Part II of the present work focuses in particular upon Castoriadis's shift toward this trans-regional ontology of creative *physis.*

15. It was composed in 1970 and was first published in the special issue on Merleau-Ponty in *L'ARC.*

16. For a discussion of Castoriadis's early homage to Merleau-Ponty, see Joas (2002) and Adams (2009a).

17. It was written in 1978. See Castoriadis (1993), "Merleau-Ponty and the Weight of the Ontological Tradition," *Thesis Eleven,* 36: 1–36. For discussions of the imaginary in Merleau-Ponty, see *Chiasmi International: Trilingual Studies Concerning Merleau-Ponty's Thought* (2003), No. 5, which devotes an entire issue to this thematic.

18. I elaborate this more fully in Chapter 1.

19. For a more extended elucidation of *à-être,* see especially Chapters 1 and 4 of this book.

20. Unlike these earlier phenomenological thinkers, however, Husserl was far more marginal to Castoriadis's thought.

21. Some recent Heidegger scholarship has emphasized the importance of "place/space" for Heidegger; see especially Malpas (1999, 2006). Others have

emphasized the shift to "Welt/*Lichtung*" in Heideggerian scholarship; see Sheehan (2001).

22. See Heidegger (2001 [1927]; 1929). Castoriadis is entirely dismissive of the later Heidegger. This is no doubt due, in part, to radically different political projects.

23. However, Castoriadis wants to replace the idea of pure intuition with pure representation by emphasizing the role of the transcendental, that is, radical imagination/imaginary, in creating the form of the image and its pre-conditions.

24. For an amplified discussion of post-transcendental phenomenology, see Chapter 4, especially the "*Excursus*: Johann P. Arnason's Phenomenology," albeit implicitly and unsystematically.

25. There is a tendency in some versions of "cultural analysis"—be it philosophical or sociological—to marginalize configurations of power. One way of doing justice to both dimensions is to elaborate various "cultural projects of power," such as, in Castoriadis's case, "the pursuit of rational mastery." See Arnason (2003).

26. Castoriadis was one of the earliest of Merleau-Ponty's interlocutors to point to the cultural underpinnings of subjectivity (SU). See also Adams (2009a).

27. Another contemporary strand of post-transcendental phenomenology emphasizes "life" as well as—or instead of—the "world." See in particular, Michel Henry (2003–4), Renaud Barbaras (2003, 2006, 2007), and Len Lawlor (2006).

28. See Putnam's essay of the same name (1975). Interestingly, Dummett (1981) has traced the origins of analytic philosophy to Frege as opposed to Russell. In tracing the origins of "analytic" philosophy to Frege, he can argue that a common *Schwerpunkt* for each of the main philosophical currents of the twentieth century—the so called, "analytic" and "continental"—is the enigmatic "meaning of meaning."

29. See Arnason (1988a). In social theoretical terms, the cultural turn was also a response to the deficiencies of the modernization paradigm. See Wagner (1994), Arnason (1982, 1988a, and Knöbl (2001, 2007). Emerging from the critique of modernization (and its concomitant cultural turn) are the relatively new and inter-related approaches of civilizational analysis and multiple modernities. See, for example, the *Daedelus* special issue on "Multiple Modernities" (Vol. 129, Winter 2000); Eisenstadt (2002), Arnason (1993, 1997, 2003), Delanty (1999), Arnason, Eisenstadt and Wittrock (2005), J. Smith (2006), Wagner (2008), and the special issue on civilizational analysis and modernities in the *European Journal of Social Theory* 13(1) (2010).

30. Castoriadis's understanding of the "imaginary" although very different from, must be situated within the same broad field as Sartre and Lacan, although he does not consider them as positive sources (see, for example, 2010, pp. 10–11). On the other hand, his elaboration of terms such as the 'social imaginary" and "radical imaginary" preceded Benedict Anderson's better known "imagined communities" (1982). Charles Taylor clearly drew on Castoriadis for interpretation of 'social imaginaries" as discussed in his *Modern Social Imaginaries* (2004)

and *A Secular Age* (2008), but he does not acknowledge Castoriadis as a source. The broad field of thought of "imaginaries" can be arguably understood as a variety of reconfigured and extended versions of Durkheim's notion of *collective representations*.

31. See Merleau-Ponty's well known essay "From Mauss to Claude Lévi-Strauss" (1964).

32. Durkheim and Weber are important for Castoriadis's theory of meaning, to which we return in Chapter 4.

33. Castoriadis was the first to translate Weber into Greek. See also Castoriadis's essay "Individual, Society, Rationality, History"

34. See Arnason (1982, 1988, 1989a, 1989b, 2003). For further discussion on Arnason, see the *Excursus* on Arnason's thought in Chapter 4 of this work. See also Adams (2009, 2011), Friese and Wagner (2000) and Knöbl (2000). Alfred Schütz (1932) also drew Weber in the direction of phenomenology, but with very different results.

35. From his book of the same title (1978); see also Ricoeur's review of this book (1991 [1980]).

36. For alternative approaches to the problematic of modernity, see also Wagner (2008), Eisenstadt (2002), Knöbl (2007) and Delanty (1999).

37. Thus cultural modernity is pluralistic (or from a different angle, a "unity as plurality"). But these "intra-cultural" constellations are pluralistic rather than monolithic, as well, as "the terrible twins" of empiricism and rationalism (Arnason) show. In this vein, interpretations of Romanticism and its significance vary widely. Two older collections of essays of especial interest are Prang (1968) and Klaus (1980). See also Ameriks (2000). For a recent interpretation of early Romanticism, see Beiser (2003); on the Enlightenment, see Cassirer (1985).

38. Korff's argument is specifically directed to the early Romantics, that is, the *Frühromantiker*—be they philosophers or poets—of the German Idealist period. Arnason discusses this aspect of Kant as part of a hermeneutic of modernity (1994). See also Freydberg (1994), Sallis (1987), Kearney (1988), and Engell (1981).

39. Castoriadis explicitly recognizes Kant as an important intellectual source for his theory of imagination (2010: 10), and, more broadly the "Great Four—Plato, Aristotle, Kant and Hegel" (2010: 10), indicative not only of his hermeneutic of modernity as a dialogue of Enlightenment and Romantic currents, but also of his enduring interest in the question of the significance of the ancients for the moderns (see GMPI).

40. In addition to the social-historical, Castoriadis also mentions the imaginary, representation and the imagination as modes or elements of being similarly not graspable by traditional thought. Although he touches upon these themes in the *IIS,* they are not given an exhaustive philosophical discussion. He acknowledges this limitation in the preface to the *IIS* (p. 2) where he expressed his intention to follow up these *topoi* in the forthcoming *L'elément imaginaire*, but this manuscript was unfortunately never completed. There are however extensive,

unpublished writings on various aspects of *L'Elément Imaginaire* held in the Castoriadis Archives, Paris. Following Castoriadis's own cue, these philosophical themes will not be extensively addressed in the current book.

41. Castoriadis's theory of meaning is the focus of Chapter 4.

42. This is an echo of Schleiermacher's stronger formulation of *Aufklärung ist Ausklärung*. See Arnason (1994).

43. The centrality of "autonomy" to Castoriadis's philosophical and political projects, as well as his rethinking of *logon didonai*, clearly draws on Enlightenment understandings of the importance of reason. So, too, does his interpretation of modern forms of heteronomy as the "pursuit of rational mastery," although his own writings neither makes this shared heritage clear, nor considers the tensions brought to bear on his own conceptualizations. Thus, for example, Foucault's arguments concerning the increasing disciplining of the body could be seen as more inclined to either autonomy or heteronomy, depending on the context. See, too, Norbert Elias (1994) *The Civilizing Process*. For a discussion of this aspect of Castoriadis's thought, see Arnason (1988a) and Wagner (1994).

44. See Howard and Pacom (1998).

45. I discuss the concepts of "politics" and "philosophy" more fully in the Introduction to Part I of this book, "The Importance of *Nomos*."

46. There is also a further link to the themes of Kant's third *Critique* evinced in Castoriadis's later trajectory, especially in the 1990s. An emergent trend in Castoriadis thought that highlights the autonomy of art becomes discernable. Enduring aesthetic creations were increasingly seen as an oblique form of autonomous activity (which he contrasted to the explicit form of autonomy as political autonomy [*la politique*]). Aesthetic autonomy was autonomous activity, in so far as "authentic art" interrogated the instituted meaning of the world. The autonomous aspects of aesthetic creation are oblique: An enduring cultural work (comprised of the author and concrete public) questions the signification of the world by rejecting transcendent sources of meaning and creating, in a Kantian moment, a new form in the giving form to the abyss (see Castoriadis 1994a).

47. I focus on the creativity of nature in the second part of this book.

48. I discuss these matters more fully in the "Introduction to Part II: *Physis* and the Romanticist Imaginary of Nature"

49. The same could be said of John McDowell's approach in *Mind and World* (1994).

50. The *Revue européenne des sciences sociales: Pour une philosophie militante de la démocratie* 25(86) contains a number of contributions that discuss aspects of Castoriadis's ontology. See also the special issue on Castoriadis in *Thesis Eleven* (1997), No. 49. Although specific aspects of his philosophy are discussed—especially the idea of creation—only few seem to have been systematically developed further, and even fewer that emphasize the ontological dimension. Apart from continued—and increasing—interest in Castoriadis in France and South America, there is a current upsurge of interest in Castoriadis in new settings. The Nordic Summer University formed a "Castoriadis Study Ring" for the years

2007–2010 (from which two anthologies are forthcoming), and the Swedish journal *Res Publica* published a special issue on Castoriadis (2003). Recently instituted annual gatherings in Belgium have produced fruitful discussion and the inauguration of a series of *Cahiers Castoriadis*. Another fairly recent issue of the journal *Thesis Eleven* (November 2005) reflects the sustained interest and engagement with Castoriadis's thought in the Australian context. See also the special issue *Castoriadis: Encounters and Extensions* in *The European Journal of Social Theory*, scheduled to appear in 2012.

51. Dick Howard's continuing engagement with the political philosophy of both Castoriadis and Lefort is important in this context. See, for example, Howard (2002, 2010).

52. The present study, while clarifying some crucial concepts in Castoriadis's work, is not intended as an introduction to Castoriadis's thought. There is not yet any thoroughgoing introduction to Castoriadis's work in English. Klooger's excellent book, though not an introduction in any conventional sense, focuses more directly on an elaboration and contextualization of key problematic in Castoriadis's overall oeuvre than the present book (Klooger 2009).

53. Ricoeur used this phrase in the 1963 debate with Levi-Strauss in *Esprit*.

54. DD is also in many ways a transitional paper and opens onto emergent trends in Castoriadis's thought, which continued to change into the 1990s. To adequately address these changes, however, would go well beyond the possible scope of this book. Hence DD seems an appropriate and convenient endpoint from this point of view as well. Emergent trends from the 1990s include a growing emphasis on the tripartite nature of the psyche (evident in his 1994 seminars from EHESS), as well as an increasing focus on the aesthetic aspects of autonomy, as previously mentioned.

Introduction to Part I: The Importance of *Nomos*

1. Generally, and for current purposes, "*physis*" is understood as "nature" and "*nomos*" as (human) custom and institution. These terms convey, moreover, a sense of different "orders" or "laws": the order of *physis* refers to a "natural order of things," while the order of *nomos* highlights human law, conventions, and institutions. Each term carries with it a plurality of meanings; this is especially pertinent for "*physis*" —and Castoriadis's philosophical engagement with it—as we shall discover throughout the course of the present work. The present introduction is limited to an interpretation of the importance of *nomos* for Castoriadis's intellectual trajectory rather than an assessment of the accuracy or idiosyncrasies of his account of the Greek world. Neither is it an attempt at a philosophical or historical contextualization of the *nomos/physis* antithesis more generally, although there is an extensive literature that does so; here I can only point the reader to a few references of particular interest. For a focus on the emergence of the *nomos/physis* distinction, the classic text remains Heinemann (1945); but see Pohlenz (1953) for a critique and Diller (1939) for an earlier view. For historical or historical-sociological perspectives on the emergence of the *polis* and

its importance for Greek thought, see Vernant (1962); Ostwald (1969); Finley (1985); Meier (1995, 2001); Raaflaub (2005); Vidal-Naquet (2000); and Ringvej (2004). For a very interesting comparative discussion of the *physis/nomos* antithesis in relation to both Greek and Chinese thought, see Sang-Rak Nam (1985). For a civilizational discussion of Eisenstadtian and Castoriadian approaches to the ancient Greeks that incorporates a critique—or better, relativization—of Castoriadis's interpretation of the invention of the Athenian democratic *polis* as the dual and instauration of politics and philosophy, see Arnason (2001). For a discussion of Castoriadis's interpretation of the Greeks and his relationship to them, see Vidal-Naquet (2004). See also the roundtable discussion between Lévêque, Vidal-Naquet, and Castoriadis (1996) in the essays devoted to Cleisthenes. For the most recent round of discussion, see Klimis, Caumières, and Van Eynde (2010). Earlier versions of some sections of this introduction have been included in Adams (2008a, 2001).

2. At this point, Castoriadis's interest in another ancient Greek problematic—*techne* and *physis*—was probably more evident in his thought (see, for example, his essay "Technique" from 1984). Castoriadis was originally more concerned to elucidated social-historical being as a mode of "creative doing" and "making" which he linked closely to *techne*. The being of doing slowly became more marginalized in his thought; I return to this in Chapters 1 and 2.

3. Yet Castoriadis occasionally displayed ambivalence about this, especially when reflecting on the problematic of environmental degradation (see, for example, Castoriadis 1984–85).

4. Static and dynamic forms of *physis*, however, seem to have been implicit or latent very early on (Mannsperger 1969).

5. The literature on "the beginning of philosophy" is vast. Classic texts include Cornford (1957), Nestle (1940), Kerferd (1981), Gigon (1959), Guthrie (1979), and Kirk (1970). These authors tend to argue for a clear demarcation between myth and philosophy as represented by the inauguration of pre-Socratic *physis*, as the book titles themselves already indicate: for example, Cornford's *From Religion to Philosophy* and Nestle's *Vom Mythos zum Logos*. Recent scholarship tends to argue more for the overlap of mythic and nonmythic elements in pre-Socratic *physis*. Arnason's designation, "Between Religion and Philosophy," sums up this trend (Arnason, 2001).

6. See Heidegger's essay on *physis* (1967).

7. The seminars were presented at the EHESS in the early 1980s and published as *CQFG* vols. I and II (with vol. III in the works at the time of writing).

8. The text of the published seminars shows that Castoriadis uses the untranslated terms of "*physis*" and "*nomos*," whereas he translates the others from the Greek. I have followed his convention here.

9. See Mannsperger (1969). However, see Plato's discussion of "disorderly motion" in the *Timaeus*.

10. However, as we traverse Castoriadis's philosophical trajectory, we shall see that, as he shifts toward an ontology of transregional *physis* in the 1980s, the

imaginary significations of pre-Socratic (in the broad, not narrow, sense) and archaic (as opposed to the ancient) worlds become more central to his philosophical elucidations, albeit unsystematically.

11. Interestingly, Castoriadis credits Democritus with recognizing the institutionalized character of *the world*. (VEJP 328). I discuss the problematic of the world in Chapter 4 and the conclusion. See also Castoriadis (2002) *On Plato's Statesman*.

12. Castoriadis's turn to the Greeks is evident also in the contemporaneous "Remarks on 'Rationality' and 'Development'" (1974 [1985]), but his most sustained engagement began in the early 1980s with his seminars at the EHESS, from which the important essay "The Greek *Polis* and the Creation of Democracy" was based. Posthumously, the first installment of the seminars was published in 2004 as *Ce qui fait la Grece I*; the second volume was published in 2008. As well, the seminars on Plato's *Statesman* have also been posthumously published, as well as several essays devoted to Greek tragedy, literature, and aesthetic creations more generally.

13. See VEJP, and "Remarks on 'Rationality' and 'Development'" (1984–85).

14. See also DD, especially pp. 372–73. These themes are pursued in greater detail in Chapter 6.

15. Autonomy has two aspects: Politics and philosophy. For discussion of Castoriadis's understanding of democracy and autonomy see, for example, Lambropoulos (1997) and Doridant (2005).

16. Contrast this with an earlier statement, in the 1964–65 section of the *IIS*, where he was more attuned to the phenomenological horizons and the problematic of the world: "Theory in itself is a doing, the always uncertain attempt to realize the project of clarifying the world. And this is also true for that supreme or extreme form of theory—philosophy—the attempt to conceive of the world without knowing, either before or after the fact, whether the world is actually conceivable, or even just what conceiving of something exactly means" (*IIS* p. 74), and then again to a later statement from 1989: "We then ask ourselves: How is the world *tout court*, since there effectively is this indefinite variety of worlds proper to each society? The response is: The world *lends itself* to (is compatible with) all these S.I.S. [social imaginary significations, *SA*]. This means: The world *tout court* is senseless, devoid of signification (save that of lending itself to . . . but that is not what we call a signification). The result is that, *at this level*, all 'hermeneutical' discussion, every attempt to see in the creation of S.I.S. 'interpretation' of the world, has no ground to stand on" (DD 363–64).

17. Drawing on Remi Brague's historical phenomenology, we might say that the emergence of *la philosophie* and *la politique* accompanied the shift from a cosmogony to cosmology (Brague 2004). Castoriadis's view of *nomos* and philosophy as *la philosophie* raises many questions to the status of pre-Socratic philosophical thought—that is, before *la philosophie* had been instituted—that go beyond the scope of the present work.

18. I will return to this in Chapter 4.

19. This marks a conceptual shift in his thought. In his earlier paper TE, he argued that the Greeks were unable to think "creation."

20. Although Castoriadis formally farewelled Marx in the first half of the 1960s, the autonomy/heteronomy divide can be seen as a reconfiguration of the earlier alienation/socialism problematic. However, in a 1983 interview with *Lutter*, he still explicitly equates heteronomy with alienation: "At a very deep level this something corresponds to the *alienation*, the *heteronomy* of people" (Castoriadis 1984g, p. 125).

1. Toward an Ontology of the Social-Historical

1. An earlier version of some sections of this chapter has been published in Adams (2008a).

2. Castoriadis prefers the term "elucidation" to "theorization" or "theory." For him, theory—at least in its traditional forms—refers to the construction of totalizing models of thought, whereas "elucidation" is creative activity (or *praxis*, strictly speaking) more appropriate to interpreting the social-historical world (See Arnason 1984).

3. In Castoriadis's view, Western philosophy has generally recoiled from ontological implications of the imagination. The *creative imagination* is Castoriadis's generic term for the radical imaginary and the radical imagination. I will return to this.

4. In Castoriadis's view Heidegger remains trapped in inherited frameworks.

5. Unless otherwise indicated, all page numbers in the first part of the present book refer to the 1987 English translation of the *IIS*, and all italics are in the original.

6. We will return to the theme of meaning in Chapter 3 and more fully in Chapter 4.

7. As discussed in the Introduction to Part I "The Importance of *Nomos*."

8. In the early 1980s, we find another reference to "interpretative creation" in the final seminar of *CQFG*.

9. This raises a number of important questions regarding the interpretative element of creation and the interrogative element of interpretation, which will be discussed more fully in Chapter 4 and again in the conclusion.

10. In this vein, Howard's (1988) allusion to "political ontology," as opposed to "political philosophy" or simply "ontology"—which he makes in reference to Castoriadis at the time of the *IIS* and the more or less contemporaneous essays published in the first *Carrefours du labyrinthe*—is suggestive.

11. See the interview with him entitled, "Does the Idea of Revolution Still Make Sense?" (1990).

12. For a discussion of Castoriadis's critique of determinism and formalist ontology, see Descombes (1989, 1991a).

13. This is apparent in the Preface to DH, written in 1983.

14. See the essay by Stoffel (2005). Within more phenomenological terms, it emerges from the centrality, and ultimate enigma, of the world horizon as the

ambiguous locus of various modes of being as they appear within, appear to, and appear as, the phenomenological anthropological field.

15. Other German critics—Habermas (1985) and Lövenich (1991)—have made similar criticisms. For a comparison of Habermasian and Castoriadian approaches, see Arnason (1988a). See Bernstein (1989) for a discussion of Habermas's criticisms of Castoriadis, and Kalyvas (2001) who critically contrasts Habermas to Castoriadis. See Castoriadis's response to Honneth in DD.

16. However, as I shall show, for Castoriadis, anthropology comes in at a second stage, via a reconsideration of psychoanalysis (see Chapter 3).

17. Written in 1970, MSPI was first published in 1973.

18. Castoriadis's early interpretation of the living being is discussed in the next chapter.

19. From various perspectives Vajda (1989), Mouzakitis (2007), and Arnason (2000) have discussed Castoriadis's connection to Heidegger.

20. I will return to this idea in Chapter 8 in the discussion of cosmology.

21. This is a recurring feature of late nineteenth century and twentieth century thought, from Nietzsche to Derrida. Merleau-Ponty, for example (1963) sees philosophy as an interrogation of the crisis of Western philosophy.

22. Nevertheless, it is not until the final chapter of the *IIS* that Castoriadis begins to mark out a new, positive program for philosophy. I will discuss this in Chapter 4.

23. Castoriadis's emphasis on "immanence" is particular clear in *The Institution of Society and Religion* (1993), which was written shortly after the *IIS*.

24. Castoriadis makes a sharp distinction between "creation" and "production." I return to this.

25. See Descombes's discussion of Castoriadis's approach to being as one of "categories" rather than "meaning" (1991a, especially pp. 52–53).

26. See Note 3, p. 394 of the *IIS*. Castoriadis makes this comment in relation to Heidegger and Husserl.

27. The literature on theories of history is vast. Current approaches—be they "analytic" or "continental"—generally share a common foe: Philosophies of History, writ large. A sample of twentieth-century thinkers of interest to Castoriadis at the time of the *IIS* might include: Ariès (1954), Braudel (1969), Löwith (1966), Toynbee (1934–61), R. G. Collingwood (1946), Jaspers (1949), Ricoeur (1967), and Gadamer (1960). Two texts seldom discussed but of especial interest are: first, the proceedings of a 1958 Cerisy Colloque on Toynbee (Aron 1961); second, a bilingual collection, edited by Gadamer, (1972) *Truth and Historicity/Vérité et Historicité*. Contemporaneous with the *IIS* and of particular interest to Castoriadis is Châtelet's two-volume publication on the birth of history as it emerged in ancient Greece (1974). The most interesting approaches to the idea of history in contemporary contexts are found in the revitalization of comparative civilizational analysis. In this vein, Arnason (2005a) has addressed the question of a philosophy of history for comparative civilizational contexts. But see also Carr (1974, 1991) for a contemporary phenomenological approach to history; see also the 2006 symposium on his thought in the journal *Human Studies* 29(4).

28. See Merleau-Ponty (1963, 1970), Lefort (1978), and the early book on phenomenology by Lyotard (1991), as well as his later teacher, Ricoeur (1980). In an unpublished radio discussion with Ricoeur from 1987, Castoriadis explicitly critiques Foucault's theory of history (and does so occasionally and implicitly in published works); but this could also be interpreted as part of his wider critique of structuralism as ahistorical, if not antihistorical.

29. See especially *CQFG*. See also the important essay that emerged from this immersion in Greek sources: "The Greek *Polis* and the Creation of Democracy" (1983).

30. Castoriadis's discussion occurs in the wake of the famous debate on these themes in *Esprit* between Ricoeur and Lévi-Strauss in 1963.

31. Interestingly, Merleau-Ponty (2003), in his seminars on *Nature*, points out that causalism and finalism became ultimately indistinguishable.

32. Castoriadis's critique of the Aristotelian "potentiality" and "act" is relativised as part of his shift to an ontology of trans-regional *physis* through his increasing recognition of the poietic aspects to *puissance*.

33. The proto-institutions of *legein* and *teukhein* are the focus of the next chapter.

34. Descombes (1989), for example, has remarked on this.

35. Castoriadis discusses Aristotle's imagination at length in "Radical Imaginary and Social Instituting Imaginary" (1994), and later in "Psychoanalysis and Philosophy" (1997 [1996]). He suggests in this context that Aristotle was not able to reconcile the imagination with *physis*. During the course of the present book, we shall see, however, that Castoriadis himself made great strides in doing so.

36. See p. 146, note 53; p. 391. See also Freydberg (1994).

37. For a discussion of the importance of the *Kantbuch* for Heidegger, especially as it relates to the thematic of time and including an important discussion of the imagination, see Sherover (1971). See also Weatherston (2002) where he traces the argument of the *Kantbuch* to Heidegger's lecture course on Kant in 1927–28 as a phenomenological interpretation of Kant's *Critique of Pure Reason*.

38. The philosophical enquiry into the imagination still remains quite marginal, although there are indications that it is emerging as a more important field (Cocking 1991). This is particularly the case in the French and English literatures. See Elliot (2005). In the North American context, Edward Casey's (1976) classic study on the imagination is important, as is the thought of John Sallis (1987, 2000) and adopted son, Richard Kearney (1988, 1989). The idea of the imaginary, especially as *social imaginary*, is gaining greater ground, from Anderson's *Imagined Communities* (1983) to Taylor's *Modern Social Imaginaries* (2004), although neither makes mention of Castoriadis as a precursor to their work.

39. For a related discussion, see Merleau-Ponty "Husserl at the Limits of Phenomenology" (2002). There is something in the idea of a particularly French obsession with mathematics. For another contemporary examples, that draws on set theory in a positive vein, see Alain Badiou (2005/1988).

40. He also reiterates this point in DD. I return to these themes in greater depth in Chapters 2 and 6.

41. We know from GI, which was written in 1973, that the individualist schema includes intersubjective frameworks as well.

42. As Castoriadis discusses in the first half of the *IIS*, as well as in "La Question de l'histoire du movement ouvrier" (1974).

43. Interestingly, Castoriadis was originally to entitle MSPI, in which he interrogates existing fields of knowledge in the natural and human sciences and their modes of grasping the world, "Le monde morcelé."

44. See Plato (1937, 1977) and Sallis (1999).

45. As Fink notes in the Heraclitus seminar with Heidegger, the pre-Socratics were also pre-metaphysical (1993).

46. Note 25, p. 395. The manuscript was unfortunately never published. It is held in the Castoriadis Archives, Paris. Castoriadis wrote it around 1970 and it can be best characterized as a running commentary of the *Timaeus*. It consists of some few hundred pages of handwritten manuscript in French and Greek; many sections are covered by mathematical equations. It seems to have been intended as an appendix, or series of appendices for *Les Carrefours*. Castoriadis indicated his intention to organize the appendices around three sections: I. The Mathematics of the *Timaeus*; II. The Date of the *Timaeus*; and III. The Composition of the *Timaeus*.

47. In the *Philebus* it is referred to as the *apeiron*.

48. *Timaeus* 48b–e.

49. Discussion of the *chôra* has become more significant to continental currents of thought. The most representative examples include: Derrida (1993), Sallis (1999), Caputo (1997), Kristeva (1984), but see also Richir (1993), Karfik (2004), El-Bizri (2004), Bigger (2005), and Vallier (2009). For an East Asian reconfiguration, see Nishida Kitaro's discussion of "Basho" (1987) and the surrounding literature, especially Stevens (1995) and Berque (2000). I return to the *chora* in Chapter 8.

50. Castoriadis's dialogue with Plato remains in the background, but it provides points of impetus to Castoriadis's reflections. The *chora*, for example, crops up Castoriadis's later thought, where its chaotic rather than its spatial aspects are emphasized (See Chapter 8).

51. Note 36, p. 396.

52. See especially the later essay "*Physis* and Autonomy" (PA). This important paper is rarely discussed in the secondary literature. I return to it in the second half of the book.

53. See VEJP and "Remarks on 'Rationality' and 'Development'" (1984–85).

54. Unpublished seminars from the late 1980s also discuss Aristotle's and Heidegger's notions of time. In TC, this is evident in summarized form.

55. See p. 396, note 31. Derrida's text was first published in 1972, and written in 1968. Although their respective trajectories take very different directions, both Derrida and Castoriadis can be situated within the heterogeneous field of post-phenomenology.

56. He does point to Heidegger's notion of presence in a footnote, judging it to be well founded but ultimately derivative.

57. Castoriadis elaborates this further in the 1980s. Pastor (2003) takes up this theme in Castoriadis's thought.

58. It is difficult to adequately translate *à-être* into English. In some translations it is noted as simply *to-be*, and in others it is not noted at all. Acknowledgement that the original term *à-être* is being translated, and that, further, this is a neologism of Castoriadis's is rare. I shall return to this *à-être* shortly, but for now let me note that it points to a notion of "always-becoming-being." It also carries with it the sense of being as always in the process of self-definition and self-constitution, or, from a slightly different angle, of being that awaits a more complete determination. I thank Vincent Descombes for pointing this out to me.

59. In the second half of the book, we will return to the dyadic context from the perspective of the creation of alterity.

60. The quotation is taken from Castoriadis's later paper entitled "*Physis* and Autonomy" (PA, p. 335). The "philosopher" in question is Aristotle and Castoriadis writes these words as he begins to reconstruct and rediscover the creative aspects to Aristotelian *physis*.

61. The exception to this was his positing of the psychic monad. See Chapter 3.

62. Renaud Barbaras's rethinking of henology in relation to Jan Patočka and phenomenology offers a contemporary reactivation of this problematic (Barbaras 2010), but not with especial reference to the chora.

63. We know this to be his understanding of creation as *ex nihilo*, although he does not use the term explicitly here.

64. See Ciaramelli (1997). His discussion combines these two aspects of *Ursprung* in his reflection on the self-presupposition of the origin.

65. For a critical discussion of *creatio ex nihilo* and "the beginning of the universe" from a theological perspective, see Ehrhardt (1951–52, 1968). See also Young for a discussion of the emergence of the idea *creatio ex nihilo* as Christian doctrine (1991).

66. See Blumenberg (2000) for a detailed discussion on *mimesis*, *poiesis*, and *techne* that considers the emergence of the (philosophical and ontological) idea of humans as creative beings as this overlaps, is reinterpreted, and transformed from classical, to medieval and modern contexts.

67. This is most clearly apparent in STCC (p. 43). Castoriadis speaks of this but does not develop its implications further: "*La création populaire, 'primitive' ou ultérieure, permet certes et même rend activement possibles une variété indéfinie de realisations, de meme qu'elle fait une place à l'excellence particulière de l'interprète qui n'est jamais simple interprète mais créateur dans la modulation: chanteur, barde, danseur, potier ou brodeuse. Mais ce qui la caractérise par-dessus tout, c'est le type de rapport qu'elle soutient avec le temps. Même lorsqu'elle n'est pas faite explicitement pour durer, elle dure en fait quand même.*"

68. See p. 46 and p. 162.

69. Castoriadis's later interpretation of Aristotle and the measure of time develops the line of argument differently. See Chapter 8 of this book.

70. See Chapter 6 of this book.

71. See Braudel (1984), 3 vols.

72. I will return to this discussion in Chapter 8.

73. Interestingly, Castoriadis also points to the exclusion of diachronic approaches within the canon of "science"; later he develops this further into a questioning of the foundations of objective knowledge. See Chapter 6.

74. These two regions will be developed later as part of his shift toward radical *physis*. See Chapters 7 and 8.

75. Many thanks to Angelos Mouzakitis for his summary of Castoriadis's arguments from the Greek.

2. Proto-Institutions and Epistemological Encounters

1. Some sections of this chapter have been published in earlier form (Adams 2008a).

2. Sherover (1971) discusses Heidegger's interpretation of Kant, especially as it pertains to the imagination and time, as does Kearney (1998).

3. Löwith (1966) has argued this in relation to Heidegger. I return to the idea of *Anlehnung* later.

4. See also Beiser (1987), Gadamer (1979), and Arnason (1996) for various analyses of and approaches to reason and its transformations.

5. The term "ensemblistic-identitarian" will be explained more fully throughout the present chapter.

6. The work of Charles Taylor and Maurice Merleau-Ponty is especially interesting in this context. While they both move beyond the strict transcendentalism of Kant and post-Kantian approaches, they nonetheless retain a qualified form of transcendentalism. See Taylor's "Transcendental Arguments" (1995). Merleau-Ponty came to understand the "true transcendental" in his later work as the entwining of nature and culture. See Merleau-Ponty (1968). See also Arnason (1993) and Rechter (2007). We will return to this at length in the second part of the book and link it more closely to Castoriadis's later thought.

7. As does Johann Arnason (1989, 1994, 2003). For a contrasting approach to the "other of reason" see the brothers Böhme (1983) and Arnason's critique (1987 and 1996a).

8. It becomes especially innovative when the link between social imaginaries and culture (that is, as transsubjective contexts of meaning) is emphasized. Castoriadis's link between the creative imagination and meaning is discussed more closely in Chapter 4.

9. For a discussion, see Arnason (1994), Kearney (1998), and Sallis (2005, 1987).

10. A concern with mathematics is especially noticeable in the French philosophical context. See especially Badiou (2005 [1988]), who makes set logic central to his ontology, in contrast to Castoriadis's critique of mathematical sets.

11. Another critic in this vein is Ludwig Klages, especially his main work of *Geist als Wiedersacher der Seele* (1929–32). Klages as a politically contentious and radical proponent of *Lebensphilosophie* has long been marginalized in twentieth-century thought. Unlike Heidegger, he has proved much more difficult to bring into the mainstream of contemporary philosophy. There are some signs however that this is changing, especially within the context of the phenomenological current in Germany. See, for example, Grossheim (1994). For Nietzsche's influence on Klages, see Löwith (1927) and Bishop (2002). See also Grätzel (2000). Some aspects of *Lebensphilosophie* more generally have been critically considered by some of the third generation of critical theory, see Honneth (1984) and Joas (1992), and have been revitalized in some recent currents of French phenomenology; see, for example, Michel Henry (2003, 2004) and Renaud Barbaras (2007), although from a different perspective.

12. Some thinkers have explicitly characterized Castoriadis as an antistructuralist. See Joas and Knöbl (2009).

13. As mentioned in the previous chapter, see contributions from Lévi-Strauss and Ricoeur in *Esprit* (1963).

14. For an extended discussion of the idea of *Anlehnung* in Castoriadis's thought, see Klooger (2009). Castoriadis's further critical engagement with the idea of objective knowledge is taken up in Chapter 6.

15. An early sketch of Castoriadis's understanding of the living being, which becomes particularly relevant in our later discussion of his developing ontology of radical *physis*, becomes discernable here. See the discussion in Chapter 7.

16. See Dreyfus (2004) on Taylor's phenomenological anti-epistemology for a different view.

17. We note that in the contemporaneous GI, Castoriadis speaks of the autonomization of particular spheres of social life as alienation. It seems particularly apt in this context.

18. For a discussion of the principle of determination, especially as it pertains to Castoriadis's philosophy, see Descombes (1991a).

19. See below in the discussion of "external" and "internal" aspects to *Anlehnung.*

20. As I discuss in Chapter 4, Castoriadis does make a hermeneutical turn, yet it remains implicit to his thought.

21. We will return to this. The actual term *Anlehnung* first appears on p. 289 of the *IIS*.

22. We will see in the second section of this book that *Anlehnung* is better thought of as an *encounter with the world*. Castoriadis moves some way to this, in fusing Aristotelian and Kantian motifs, but this, too, remains implicit in his thought. We note, however, that as Castoriadis began to shift toward an ontology of radical *physis*, especially in light of his multiregional ontology of the *for-itself* (*pour soi*), the idea of *Anlehnung* lapses in the discussion. For a contemporary approach to this problematic from within a very different philosophical current, see McDowell's *Mind and World* (1996).

23. Habermas's Kantian position, on the other hand, prevents human access to nature. For a critical discussion, see Whitebook (1979) and Dews (1995).

24. I will return to this theme in Chapter 6.

25. See OIHS. We discuss this more fully in Chapter 6.

26. At this point in the *IIS*, the human psyche has not been mentioned.

27. I discuss this in the chapter on the living being.

28. Arnason questions the adequacy of Castoriadis's transposition of *Anlehnung* from the psychological to the social-historical realm, as the leaning on of the social-historical ontologically alters the first natural stratum in a way that the psyche does not (1989b).

29. Lévi-Strauss found points of support in Mauss and Durkheim's *Primitive Classification*, considered a forerunner to Durkheim's later *Elementary Forms of the Religious Life*.

30. The chapter opens with: "Causation, finality, motivation, reflex, function, structure are simply pen names or *noms de guerre* assumed by necessary and sufficient reason. The latter, an offspring of reason as such, has become its exclusive representative, at the end of an evolution and following an interpretation whose roots lie deep within the social-historical" (p. 221).

31. Written in 1968, Castoriadis stays very close to the texts in a reading of Merleau-Ponty that is not just a "faithful rendition"—to use his own characterization of hermeneutics—but as a moment of interrogative interpretation. For discussions of this paper, see Joas (2002) and Adams (2009a).

32. At this stage of his trajectory, Castoriadis was still engaged in a dialogue with Merleau-Ponty, as SU (1971) shows us. By the time of his second paper on Merleau-Ponty, "Merleau-Ponty et les poids de l'heritage ontologique," he had withdrawn from the dialogue. The text was written in 1976–77; it was first published in English in 1993 in *Thesis Eleven* 36, and in French in 1997.

33. See, for example, the posthumously published *Zu den Sachen und Zurück* (Blumenberg 2002) for a critique of Husserl's phenomenological approach as a *plaidoyer* for the indirect and metaphorical approach to things.

34. Castoriadis begins to focus on operations that echo the radical operationalism of the Kantian problematic of the neo-Kantian, German philosopher, Friedrich Kambartel (1968) in that we see the analytic isolation of one basic operation or element: *Legein* as designation.

35. See Ricoeur (1984) for a discussion of "reference" and "world."

36. See the recent entry for "Institution" by Pechriggl (2004). Merleau-Ponty develops the notion of institution further in the posthumously published seminars devoted to that theme (2003). See also Vallier's (2005) interpretation of the importance of "institution" for Merleau-Ponty's thought.

37. In the *IIS*, Castoriadis tends to be critical of *logon didonai*. In the 1980s, he reevaluated its meaning and incorporated it into his account of the Greek instauration of philosophy as part of the project of autonomy (1997n).

38. But it is practical reason as Aristotelian *phronesis* for Castoriadis, rather than the Kantian version (although in DD he distances himself from "neo-Aristotelian approaches" such as MacIntyre's). In the paper on the creation of

democracy (1997n), Castoriadis discusses some philosophers—for example, Arendt—taking up of the third *Critique* for support for practical reason. He is, moreover, critical of ethics as a poor substitute for politics.

39. For an elaboration of the idea of technique, see Castoriadis (1984).

3. Anthropological Aspects of Subjectivity: The Radical Imagination

1. There is considerable literature concerning the psychoanalytic aspects of Castoriadis's thought. A selective list includes Whitebook (1996), Uribarri (1999, 2002), Elliott (2005), Klooger (2009), Pechriggl (2005), Gourgouris (2010), and Smith (2010). See also the special issues of *Free Associations* (1999, 7:3), *Constellations* (2002, 9:4), *Thesis Eleven* (2002, 71) and *Zona Erógena (1993,* 15), as well as articles in the French psychoanalytic journal *Topique* and *Cahiers Castoriadis* 3 (2007). Castoriadis's psychoanalytic theory has been significant in Argentina, and many papers may be found in the journal *Zona Eró- gena.* Although reception of Castoriadis's work in the German context has been mixed, that of his psychoanalytic work in Vienna has been more constructive. See, for example, the 1991 collection of essays edited by Pechriggl and Reitter. An earlier version of a section of this chapter was published in Adams (2008a).

2. At the time of the *IIS*, Castoriadis does not include in his philosophical anthropology explicit theorizing of the subject within the natural world; such a reconstruction is made possible by his later thought on radical *physis*.

3. See Freud (1989). See also Arnason (2002).

4. Castoriadis's interpretation of subjectivity revolves around an elucidation of the social individual and the (autonomous) subject. Although in the 1980s he develops a greater sense of the modes and interconnecting levels of the *for- itself*—ranging from the living being to the autonomous society—a fully fledged theory of the self is lacking. Smith (2010) broaches this absence by way of Charles Taylor's historical phenomenology of the self (see especially Chapter 3). See also Klooger (2008) for an account of the psychoanalytic self and Pechriggl for the gendered dimensions of the self (2005).

5. The social individual holds an ambiguous place in Castoriadis's thought, especially in regard to his notion of the subject. In later works—that is, from the 1980s as part of his development of a multiregional ontology of the *for-itself* as an aspect of his shift to creative *physis*—an otherness is postulated between the social individual and the autonomous subject as diverse modes of being for-itself. But at this point in the *IIS*, the social individual seems to evoke more of a generic notion of human subjectivity.

6. See Lacan (2002). His critique of Lacan appears as more of a focal point in the slightly later paper "Psychoanalysis: Project and Elucidation" (1977). As we shall see, this paper, along with the *IIS* chapter on the psyche, signals a shift in his thinking regarding Lacanian frameworks from his 1968 paper on psychoanalysis (ETSS).

7. For example, he had hitherto made this observation in the 1968 ETSS, 1970–73 MSPI and the 1971 SU, as well as in the previous two chapters of the

IIS. He continues to remark upon it also post-*IIS*, for example, in OIHS, DD, "The Institution of Society and Religion" (1993; this essay was written shortly after the *IIS* in 1978–80) and the 1983 paper "The Logic of Magmas and the Creation of Autonomy."

8. It is significant to note that Castoriadis's notion of the creation of an *Eigenwelt*, even at the level of the psyche, first appeared in the 1980s. At the time of the *IIS,* only the social-historical created a world of significations.

9. The idea of death is interesting in Castoriadis's thought. He discusses the idea of mortality as the lot of humankind (fated by *moira*) in his later seminars on ancient Greece (*CQFG*). To be mortal is in this sense anthropological. However, in a critique of Heidegger, as is evident by the psyche's unawareness of its own mortality, we are not born with an awareness of our impending death: It is an institution.

10. Husserl claimed that Kant constructed the content of the mind instead of describing it.

11. Merleau-Ponty, *The Phenomenology of Perception* (1962). See also Castoriadis's homage to Merleau-Ponty (SU).

12. In this context, the dyad as an emergent—or proto—motif makes its appearance in Castoriadis's work in the late 1980s in unpublished seminars. Castoriadis distinguishes between Platonic approaches—which uphold the primordial unity of the "one"—and Aristotle, who sees "two" as being the first number. In this vein, Castoriadis stresses the importance of the dyad as the first number, as it is only with the number "two" that we can start to think about alterity and creation. Consideration of the dyad leads us into the philosophy of mathematics, an area that the present author is not qualified to pursue further. But Castoriadis made regular forays into it. This takes on increasing importance when we remind ourselves of the curious and unresolved place of mathematics and its proto-ontological status in Castoriadis's thought. See Chapter 8 for further discussion.

13. These musings are to be found in archival fragments. We return to this in the second part of the book, in the chapter on cosmological considerations.

14. See, for example, SST and PSS.

15. Gauchet (2002). Gauchet argues for a rethinking of psychoanalytic theory, in particular in terms of the historicization of the unconscious as part of a historical anthropology of subjectivity. See also Smith (2005, 2010).

16. For discussions of Castoriadis and sublimation, see Whitebook (1996), Gourgouris (1997), Klooger (2008), and Smith (2010), respectively.

17. At this point, Castoriadis introduces his notion of a "corporeal imagination." He does not follow this much further. It would be interesting to do so—particularly in relation to the being of doing. Even though embodied subjectivity was a large part of Merleau-Ponty's focus, it was not an aspect that Castoriadis particularly addressed, perhaps partly because the body was a blurred context for him.

18. See Taylor (1995).

19. In later work, "language" fades into the background somewhat, whereas meaning as an imaginary mode of being is foregrounded.

20. The section of the *IIS* on "Individuals and Things" chapter is section x, the prejudice of perception and the privilege of "things" pp. 329–36.

21. As we shall see in the second part of the present book, in their later work both Merleau-Ponty and Castoriadis tend to view the entwining of culture and nature as the "true transcendental" in the institution of the world. See Arnason (1993).

22. However, *"être au monde"* is not reducible to *"in- der-Welt sein."* See Vallier (2005) for a discussion of Merleau-Ponty's usage. Dreyfus (2004) refers to *"être au monde"* as being *devoted to the world.*

23. There is an ambiguity in Castoriadis's own thought in this regard. For a discussion of this aspect, see Martuccelli (2002).

4. Hermeneutical Horizons of Meaning

1. I return to this point later in the chapter. Earlier versions of some sections of this chapter have been published in Adams (2005, 2007a, 2008a, 2010).

2. Although Merleau-Ponty hesitated when it came to the imaginary and its transsubjective and ontological implications, recent discussions have interpreted his later trajectory as evincing a cultural turn within post-phenomenological contexts. See in particular Arnason (1988a, 1993, 2003, and his essay "Merleau-Ponty and the Meaning of Civilizations," forthcoming in *Encounters and Interpretations: Essays in Civilizational Analysis*) and Rechter (2007). For discussions of the imaginary in Merleau-Ponty, see the special issue of *Chiasmi International* on the "The Real and the Imaginary." I will return to these themes in the second half of this study.

3. As Arnason argues, the enigmatic riddle of the world appears as the magma metaphor in Castoriadis. In this way, Castoriadis can be understood to have also ontologized the world through his focus on the being of magmas (Arnason 1989c), which among other things results in the virtual abandonment of the world as a *phenomenological* problematic.

4. My interpretation of Castoriadis's hermeneutical turn draws on insights from Johann P. Arnason's discussion of Castoriadis and social imaginary significations (see especially Arnason 1989b). Earlier versions of some parts of the following discussion have appeared in (Adams 2010, 2008).

5. Castoriadis writes, "Nearer to us, the trace of the difficulties and aporias to which the question of the imagination and the imaginary gives birth persist in Maurice Merleau-Ponty's *The Visible and the Invisible.* How else can we comprehend this hesitation which sometimes, in this work, makes of the imaginary a synonym for irreal fiction, for the nonexistent without further ado, and sometimes goes almost so far as to dissolve the distinction between the imaginary and real?" (1993, p. 4). These lines originally appeared in the "Avertissement" preceding "La découverte de l'imagination" in *Domaines de l'homme* (1986). They were added to the beginning of the English translation of "Merleau-Ponty and the Weight of the Ontological Tradition" first appearing in *Thesis Eleven* 36 (1993, translator's note, p. 36), but are absent from its subsequent English language publication in *World in Fragments* (1997).

6. The magma metaphor did not appear in the 1964–65 section of the *IIS*, but was clearly in gestation.

7. See K. Smith (2010, especially pp. 12–16) for a discussion of the image of the magma in Castoriadis's thought.

8. Castoriadis added an extra note to the English publication of MSPI in 1984, (n. 24a, p. 226) to include the most recent developments in theoretical biology; these were also important for his later shift toward radical *physis*: Atlan (1979), Prigogine and Stengers (1980), and Varela (1979).

9. He had earlier made a similar statement in MSPI.

10. Yet Castoriadis was to critique Husserlian and Merleau-Pontian phenomenology for this approach to philosophical elucidation, in his later paper on Merleau-Ponty, "The positing of this situation as primary and canonical carries with it an indeterminate number of prejudices and prior decisions henceforth imported irreflectively into *above* constitutions, descriptions of *what gives itself such as it gives itself,* and decisions to "let" the beings "be" and to let them 'come forth'" (1993, p. 5; emphasis added).

11. Levinas argues that "since Husserl the whole of phenomenology is the promotion of the idea of *horizon,* which for it plays a role equivalent to that of the *concept* in classical idealism" (Levinas 1969, pp. 44–45; emphasis in original).

12. Interestingly, Castoriadis does not mention Merleau-Ponty's distinctive approach to the creativity of language. See Waldenfels (1999, 2000) and Barbaras (2004, especially chapter 4).

13. The distinction is generally rendered as "sense" and "referent" in English. Tugendhat (1970) prefers to render *Bedeutung* as *significance,* but this would be potentially more problematic in the Castoriadian context, not least because the German translation of imaginary significations is rendered *imaginäre Bedeutungen* instead of, for example, *imaginäre Sinngehalte* (see also Arnason 1988a).

14. This becomes more interesting when we recall Dummett's argument that rethinks Frege as the founder of analytic philosophy—with then links to Husserlian thought—and the importance of meaning to twentieth-century thought (1981).

15. Although Castoriadis's reference on the previous page (p. 347) to the "illiterate fisherman," as opposed to the "linguist," not getting lost in the operations of language may be understood as a reference to this. This could then be read along Ricoeurian lines with its emphasis on action and discourse as two primary modes of human existence (Ricoeur 1991).

16. Habermas developed this current of thought as part of his theory of communicative action.

17. It is unusual to find Castoriadis referring in a negative fashion to things sophist. Perhaps the distinction lies for him between "sophistry" and the philosophical insights and reliance on *doxai* as opposed to *aletheia* that the fifth-century sophists offered.

18. Johann Arnason has developed an account of creation as "contextual" in a critique of Castoriadis's notion of creation as "absolute," his later qualification

of creation as "*ex nihilo* but not *in nihilo* or *cum nihilo*" notwithstanding (Arnason 1988a, 1989b. See also Castoriadis1997b).

19. The literature on meaning is too considerable to list here. The following selected texts have informed my own thinking: Arnason (1988a, 1989c), Luhmann (1984)—especially the chapter on "Sinn"; Merleau-Ponty (1968), Ricoeur (1981), and Descombes (1996).

20. For a discussion of the historical emergence and significance of the "world"—as "kosmos" and "cosmology"—as it first appeared in ancient Greek thought, see Brague (1999). For a more philological-philosophical approach to the emergence of *kosmos* in ancient Greek thought, see Kerschensteiner's classic text (1962).

21. Arnason (2003, pp. 226–34) notes this ambiguity in discussing Castoriadis's approach to imaginary significations and the world from the perspective of civilizational theory. His comments, however, limit themselves to addressing Castoriadis's consideration of the world from the earlier section of the *IIS*. For a further discussion of this point, see Adams (2011).

22. The English translation uses "develops," but since the original French word is "*élabore*," "elaborates" seems more appropriate, especially given the problematic connotations of developmental approaches for Castoriadis.

23. This gives rise to all manner of problematics to which we shall return in the concluding chapter.

24. "The Institution and the Imaginary: A First Approach" is the title of the third chapter of the *IIS*, and is the final chapter of the 1964–65 section.

25. Some of Arnason's main contributions include his distinctive approach to a hermeneutic of modernity, which includes an especially significant discussion of—and comparison between—Habermas and Castoriadis's respective approaches (1988a); an analysis of the Soviet case as an alternative modernity (1993b); a history of the Japanese path to modernity (1997); his major statement on civilizational analysis (2003); and its follow-up (2011); plus innumerable essays and edited collections focusing on a diversity of subjects, including ancient Greece, Islam and Islamic civilization, medieval civilizations, India, East Asia, the Nordic region, East-Central Europe, the Roman Empire, and the Axial Age.

26. While Heideggerian themes have been less prominent in his thought, Arnason's path through phenomenological Marxism, with particular reference to Marcuse, has meant Heideggerian problematics have been important to his overall trajectory, albeit in a more oblique fashion.

27. The notion of intersubjectivity still takes "the subject" as the primary ontological datum. Along with Castoriadis, Arnason maintains that meaning cannot be reduced to this level: It is, in Castoriadis's terms, the social-historical, or, in Arnason's terms, the cultural level of meaning that is the precondition both for the formation of sociopolitical institutions and intersubjective dialogue.

28. See, for example, Husserl (1941), and Fink (1958). Other thinkers of importance in this context include Patočka (1996, 1998) and Ricoeur (see, for example, 1981a, 1981b). See *Thesis Eleven* for a special issue on Post-Phenomenology (*Thesis Eleven* 90, August 2007). Discussion of Patočka's thought is

unfortunately beyond the scope of this study. Castoriadis refers to Patočka's work—in the "Institution of Society and Religion" (composed 1978–80)—but did not engage with his thought in any systematic way.

29. Arnason's emphasis on the world as a "unity in diversity" helps to mitigate against the potential difficulty that is presented when "culture" is taken as prime ontological datum: One suspects that a procession of cultural entities might end up replacing a procession of subjects but without resolving all the dilemmas. Not only does Arnason's enlargement of cultural "entities" to civilizational constellations (as broader than single cultures) help to circumvent this, so too does his relational approach to the world as a field of intercivilizational encounters, on the one hand, and as a shared cultural horizon and the hermeneutic field onto which this opens, on the other. At the time of writing, however, conceptualization of the shared cultural field onto which the world opens before/ as it diversifies itself has been more marginal to Arnason's concerns. It is the view of the present author that consideration of the current debates on Plato's *chora* within phenomenological circles, as a shared cultural clearing, could make a contribution here.

30. In some recent essays, such as "Merleau-Ponty and the Meaning of Civilizations" (2011), Arnason has begun to reinterpret Merleau-Ponty's phrase more closely to the original as "ways of worldforming," so as to make both the *world creative* and *world disclosing* aspects clearer.

31. However, Arnason does also sometimes discuss Castoriadis's approach to the "spirit of capitalism" in terms of a "global interpretive and practical relation to the world" in contrast to approaches that reduce them to "models of man" (1989b, p. 328).

32. The difference in their respective approaches to "world creation" and "world interpretation" is an enduring source of disagreement between Arnason and Castoriadis.

33. I notice, too, that Castoriadis is still haunted by Marx in that the nation state is here subordinated to the institution of capitalism (p.369). For a discussion of nation and modernity see Arnason (1996).

34. He used this term in DH. For a discussion of the circle of creation see Ciaramelli (1989).

35. See Arnason's discussion in *Praxis und Interpretation*, especially the chapter on Weber (1988a).

36. In light of Castoriadis's later shift to creative *physis*, the movement between Fichtean and Schellingian contexts becomes very interesting, especially considering Merleau-Ponty's later reception of Schelling's idea of nature (Merleau-Ponty 1995). In this vein, and especially in regard to our present discussion of the world, there is a very interesting paper entitled "Le double énigme du monde. Nature et langage chez Schelling et Merleau-Ponty" (Suzuki 2003).

37. Durkheim (1965). It is pertinent to note that Durkheim—and the anthropological turn evident in his later work, particularly *Elementary Forms of the Religious Life* (1965), and the essay *Primitive Classification* (1963) (in collaboration with Marcel Mauss)—inaugurated an important current of thought for

French social theory, anthropology, and philosophy the cultural implications of which were only fairly recently taken up in sociological thought.

38. Sometimes Castoriadis speaks of a "re-creation." I return to this in the conclusion of the book.

39. Religion—as experience or institution of the sacred—is a transcultural phenomenon. In this vein, see the phenomenological writings of Eliade (1978).

40. In Castoriadis's later thought on religion (ISR) we note two points: First, he comes to acknowledge "religious" experience as an experience of a bottomless abyss of which the sacred is its simulacra. Here the world returns (as a horizon in need of unending elaboration) as the indeterminate (abyss). Second, in ISR (written in 1977), his post-*IIS* theory of religion indicates that the idea of the sacred comes first, but for Castoriadis, nonetheless something still stands behind the "sacred," which, as we shall see, turns out to be *à-être*. For further discussion, see Adams (2011).

41. There is no exact English equivalent of the French *l'économique* in this context. "The economical" has a different meaning and "the economic" does not really make good sense in English. Hence I prefer to utilize the original.

42. See Arnason (1976, 1988a). In GMPI, first published in 1990, Castoriadis talks of the rarity of transhistorical constants.

43. It is worth noting that both Aristotle and Montchrestien were writing in times of social crisis. The problematic of a transcultural clearing could be fruitfully developed through recourse to discussions on Plato's *chora*.

44. The French term *conscience* evokes both "consciousness" and "conscience" in English.

45. See the discussion of Castoriadis and theories of history in Chapter 1 of this study.

46. See Descombes (1994) and Ricoeur (1980).

47. Arnason has long argued for the importance of hermeneutics to interpret Castoriadis (see especially 1988a, 1989a and 2003). See also Klooger (2005). Excavating the hermeneutical dimension in Castoriadis's thought would itself be a long journey. An important (and little discussed) text in this regard would be one written soon after the *IIS*: the 1977 Preface to CL where not just anti-Kantian themes—in terms of the fact that both science and philosophy have histories, themes that become important in the second half of the book—are raised, but several passages have a strong phenomenological-hermeneutical flavor.

48. The term employed in the English translation is "orientation," but as the French word is "origination," "orientation" seems misleading.

49. A transcript of a 1987 radio discussion between Ricoeur and Castoriadis is held in the archives. An important theme addressed therein is their respective and conflicting approaches to interpretation, production, and creation (*ex nihilo*). We shall return to this in the conclusion.

50. In Part II of the book, we shall see that the living being creates its own world, albeit in functional closure.

51. See Weber (1977). See also Arnason's discussion of the world (2003) in which he points to the Weberian interpretation of "world orders" and links their modern constellations to Romantic and Enlightenment currents.

52. Social imaginary significations—in that they create the mode of being of other societies for it—set the scene not only for encounters with other societies and civilizations, but they also represent a step toward a theory of culture, although, these two points are not explicitly elaborated upon and developed in the *IIS*. Finally, for Castoriadis, in that society is both instituting and instituted, society is history as self-alteration (p. 371). Creation then can only be understood as one moment in a more complex relationship or process which also involves (relatively stable) self-identification and self-relativization (p. 372).

53. This is in reference to the 1987 radio discussion between Ricoeur and Castoriadis.

54. A central difficulty it seems to me is the ambiguity and status of Castoriadis's idea of creation as "absolute creation." As will be seen in Chapter 7, Castoriadis regarded the creation of the living being's *Eigenwelt* as an "absolute creation." How much more so, then, the social-historical world, which does not even lean on the natural world for its imaginary creations? Some like Vajda (1989) and Waldenfels (1989) interpret Castoriadis's notion of creation as "absolute creation"; others, like Ciaramelli (1997), in a critique of Waldenfels, do not equate *"ex nihilo"* with "absolute." Once Castoriadis's qualification of "re-creation" is drawn upon, then, as I see it, we are already in the realm of interpretative creation, and hence, not "absolute creation".

55. Interestingly, a couple of years before this discussion took place, Ciaramelli (1985) observes that Ricoeur himself had acknowledged that the idea of creation is characteristic of his endeavour. Ciaramelli suggests that what interests Ricoeur most is a hermeneutic of poietic—that is creative—action within the framework of practical philosophy.

56. See, for example, the final seminar in *CQFG* and a text first presented in 1991, "Culture in a Democratic Society" (1997).

57. The emergence of the *polis*, for example, can be interpreted as a response to the crisis of sovereignty (Vernant 2002, Arnason 2006).

58. SIS is Castoriadis's shorthand for *social imaginary significations*.

59. See seminar 2 in *CQFG*.

60. See Ricoeur, "Word, Polysemy, Metaphor: Creativity in Language" (first presented as a lecture in 1972) and the 1984 interview (with Richard Kearney) "The Creativity of Language," both appearing in Valdes (1991). The latter piece contains a reference to Castoriadis and the *IIS* and the importance of his elucidation of the social imaginary (p. 470). Castoriadis tends to underemphasize the poetic dimension of the symbolic as language (especially in the 1965 section where he concentrates mainly on the symbolic of institutions) as to-be evoked. Poetry in general is underrepresented in his work (although it creeps in after 1990) as instances of the creative imagination. Bachelard's poetic imagination would be further interesting in this context. See Bachelard (1942, 1960), Gagey (1969), and Kearney (1998).

61. However see Castoriadis's early essay on Merleau-Ponty (SU, 1970), where the being of the world provided a rich context for his thought, which at that stage he elaborated more explicitly within the phenomenological universe. For a discussion of this paper, see Joas (2002) and Adams (2009).

Introduction to Part II: *Physis* and the Romanticist Imaginary of Nature

1. His later image of *physis* could thus be said to be *transnormative*. Some sections of this introduction have been published in earlier forms in Adams (2007b, 2008b).

2. As discussed in the General Introduction, the term *Frühromantiker* is used here in the Korffian sense. See also Beiser (2003) and Arnason (1994). For a discussion of *Naturphilosophie* in German Idealism, see Gloy and Burger (1996), as well as Kaulbach (1984a and 1984b). For the changes wrought with the Latinized transformation of the Greek imaginary of *physis*, see Bremer (1989).

3. See the classic texts on Goethe and the *Goethezeit* by Korff (1923–57).

4. Some of Klages's insights have been interpreted in light of a phenomenology of nature. See Hauskeller (1997); see Böhme (1997) for discussion of its Goethian variants.

5. This is especially the case in reflections on Merleau-Ponty's reactivation of Schelling's "barbaric principle "as "brute" or "savage" being. See especially Haase (2003), Suzuki (2003), and Vallier (2005).

6. See the well-known essay by Prigogine and Stengers (1978), *La Nouvelle alliance* (published in English under the title *Order Out of the Chaos*, 1984).

7. See Schelling (1988), Sandkuehler (1984), and Cattin (2002, esp. pp. 171–73).

8. This is in no small part due to the efforts of the trilingual journal devoted to Merleau-Ponty studies: *Chiasmi International: New Series*. See in particular issue 2 (2000), with the thematic Ontology and Nature (Barbaras's paper in this issue is particularly significant); issue 5 (2003) on the Real and the Imaginary; and issue 7 (2005) on Life and Individuation. See also Barbaras's monograph on Merleau-Ponty's ontology (2004).

9. The context of the *Abgrund* and the *naturans* also would require a discussion of the religious thematic, but due to confines of space I am unable to pursue this further here.

10. See Barbaras (2000), Van der Veken (2005), Cassou-Noguès (2001), and Robert (2005) develop this thematic further. Castoriadis, too, considers Whitehead to be one of the most important philosophers of the twentieth century ("The Ethicist's New Clothes," p. 108).

11. See, for example, Whitehead (1961).

12. Although this, too, is a fruitful way to interpret Castoriadis's mature thought, it is not meant to obscure the points of tension between Castoriadis and Merleau-Ponty—for example, their differing conceptions of the imaginary, the institution and, as previously mentioned, the world. Interpretations of the Merleau-Pontian approach are beginning to gather momentum in considering,

for example, the place of the imaginary, and the institution (see Robert 2000, Suzuki 2003, and Vallier 2005), which are conducive to further dialogue with Castoriadis's thought.

13. In this vein, the suggested overlap of Romantic and Enlightenment themes in Castoriadis's thought is evident also at the level of his theory of modernity. However, Castoriadis's radical opposition at this level between the project of autonomy and the infinite pursuit of rational mastery is questionable in that both draw on the autonomist imaginary for support, although they are interpreted in divergent directions (Wagner 2005). This overlap highlights the cultural basis of each trend as a different meaning-orientation in the world; each imaginary signification shapes and is shaped by cultural projects. For a discussion of how this relates to reason and imagination, see Arnason (1989a, 1994).

14. I have mentioned this previously. See EA and the 1993 text "The Revolutionary Force of Ecology." See also Moscovici (1972).

5. The Rediscovery of *Physis*

1. Although Castoriadis was pursuing discussions on the political aspects of environmental degradation even earlier. See, for example, "Remarks on 'Rationality' and 'Development'" (1984–85), which was first given as a presentation in 1974. Some sections of this chapter have appeared in earlier versions (Adams 2007b, 2008b).

2. The review appears not to have been published.

3. Cornelius Castoriadis, "Merleau-Ponty and the Weight of the Ontological Tradition," *Thesis Eleven* 36, pp. 1–36. For discussions of *the imaginary* in Merleau-Ponty, see *Chiasmi International* 5. Castoriadis's earlier meditation on Merleau-Ponty's thought, "The Sayable and the Unsayable: Homage to Maurice Merleau-Ponty," was first published in 1971.

4. Castoriadis generally preferred to avoid the term "emergence," seeing it as ultimately too close to "production" and "causality." We notice it creeping into his writing more often in his later trajectory, however. For a discussion of the problematic of *creative emergence*, see Arnason (1996).

5. Post-*IIS*, Castoriadis increasingly came to emphasize being *qua* being not just as creation of forms but also as creation/destruction of forms. See ISR and *CQFG*.

6. See, for example, Ciaramelli (1989, 1997). I suggest that the circle of creation is simultaneously the hermeneutical circle. I discuss this problematic more fully in the conclusion.

7. See Castoriadis's earlier discussion of Merleau-Ponty's critique of Heidegger's ontological difference in SU. See also Arnason (2000).

8. Although there is scope to interpret a philosophy of the body or of embodied subjectivity as part of Castoriadis's later *naturphilosophical* concerns—he makes *ad hoc* reference to the psyche-soma connection, for example—it was not part of his later agenda and will not be covered here.

9. In Part II of this study, I follow Castoriadis's own shift in terminology from *ensemblistic-identitarian* logic at the time of the *IIS*, to the shortened form, *ensidic* logic or, simply, the *ensidic*, as evidenced in later texts.

10. As also signalled in Chapter 4, the world increasingly is developed and expanded as the *Eigenwelt* as a key element in the multiregional ontology of the *pour soi*. We return to this in Chapter 7. We return to the problematic of being/world/*à-être* from various perspectives in Chapters 8 and 9.

11. I discuss this in Chapter 7.

12. See *La Nature* (1995), and *The Visible and the Invisible* (1968 [1964]).

13. The literatures on ancient Greek philosophy in general, and the various strands on the pre-Socratics, Aristotle, and the idea of *physis* in particular, are extensive. I have found the following of interest in the context of this study. On historical and philosophical accounts of the idea of *physis*, see Spaemann (1973), Bremer (1989), the two Collingwoods—Francis J. (1972) and R. G. (1945); Godin (2000), and Diller (1939). On the pre-Socratics, see the collection of essays edited by Gadamer (1968), Bröcker (1965), and Sandywell (1996). On Aristotle, see Cherniss (1964), Seeck (1975), Thayer (1979) and Broadie (1982).

14. See, for example, the posthumous publication of Castoriadis's 1983 seminars on ancient Greece (*CQFG*), as well as the paper on the social imaginary and scientific change (ISCS) and his contrast of ancient and modern approaches to the political (GMPM). For a discussion of Aristotle, radical *physis,* and Varela, see PA.

15. This was the first published usage (Maturana and Varela 1973). In a later paper (1995), Varela speaks of inventing the idea/term in 1970.

16. Autopoiesis is an important natural scientific and theoretical development; indeed, in a later paper (1999d), Castoriadis singles out the new biology as the only "creative" cultural innovation in the post–World War II era of general conformism. Castoriadis qualifies this compliment by pointing out that it leaned on von Neumann's work in the first half of the century. This proviso, however, points rather to the limitations of Castoriadis's strong notion of creation *ex nihilo* as excluding an interpretative element, rather than to a lack of originality or inventiveness within the new biology itself.

17. Some of the Cerisy Colloquia included the one on self-organization in 1981 (Dumouchel and Dupuy 1983, Castoriadis 1997a); 1983 in honor of Prigogine (Brans et al 1988, Castoriadis 1997b); 1986 in honor of Morin 1986 (Bougnoux 1990, Castoriadis 1989 and 1990); and 1991 in honor of Barel (Amiot et al. 1993, Castoriadis 1993).

18. See Varela (1986). Although the autopoietic field historically emerged from cybernetics, biology, and mathematics, its influence is now also felt in the social sciences and humanities; Luhmann's autopoietic systems theory is the classic example.

19. ISCS was first presented at a conference in 1985. From it two publications emerged: SICS, which comprises a transcript of the presentation, as well as OIHS, to which we turn in the next chapter.

20. The meeting was chaired by Yolande Benarrosh.

21. The document comprises 9 A4 sized pages: The first page is a record of attendance, the remainder a report of the discussion. The minutes are not written by Castoriadis himself, but comprise a detailed summary of his intervention and the ensuing discussion. Its status could be considered similar to Merleau-Ponty's (1995) posthumously published seminars on nature.

22. The title is given in English in the minutes. It was published in August of the same year in the *Journal for Theoretical Biology* 102(4), pp. 523–47.

23. To avoid confusion with the multiple meanings of "self" in English, I leave *auto* for the most part untranslated. I return to a discussion of "self" and "*auto*" in Chapter 7.

24. In ISCS, Castoriadis explicitly links myth and religion to Greek imaginary schema. We return to the overlap of the ontological and the cosmological, as well as to the inescapability of mythic elements in Chapter 8.

25. Castoriadis did start to develop a theory of (human) power as *pouvoir* in PPA (see also GMPI). In later works, particularly noticeable in the unpublished Time and Creation seminars, he tends more often to utilize *puissance* in terms of nature (and the psyche). This is a shift away from his earlier rejection of the Aristotelian *acte/puissance* couplet at the time of the *IIS* as being one of the most insidious forms of determinacy. It is noteworthy, however, that in his later usage of *puissance*, he does not use it in reference to *acte*.

26. The issue of Plato's *chora* ultimately remains unresolved for Castoriadis. I return to this in Chapter 8.

27. I return to this theme later.

28. As mentioned in the first part of the book, the dyadic context is a motif that emerges in the later 1980s in Castoriadis's thought. Discussions of the dyad are found in the unpublished Time and Creation seminars. I return to the idea of the dyad in Chapter 8.

29. The acceptance of a kind of "chance" seems partially reminiscent of Kant's "happy accident," which Castoriadis elsewhere criticizes.

30. In ISCS, Castoriadis goes so far as to note the similarity between contemporary physicists' view of the world to that of the pre-Socratics. On a different but related note, it is also curious to note the ways in which current "string theories" draw on Pythagorean themes.

31. I return to this at length in Chapters 7 and 9.

32. Sometimes Castoriadis refers to the self-constitution of the living being, other times to its creation. The latter version appears more often in later texts. I return to this in Chapter 7.

33. Although in ISR, for example, Castoriadis emphasizes the chaotic element of being at the expense of its entwinement with an ordering element.

34. Castoriadis further links *chaos* with the *apeiron* of Anaximander, not as infinity but as the indeterminate.

35. In the French version (1997), PA is entitled, "*Phusis*, Création et Autonomie," which highlights the connection between the idea of radical *physis* and

its radically creative implications. PA was first delivered as an oral presentation as part of a Florentine colloquium in 1986.

36. In ISCS, Castoriadis makes mention of the limitations within which Aristotle's imaginary schema formed itself; his cosmological theory, as part of his theology, is a particular example.

37. So, too, does Patočka in rethinking the importance of movement for the human condition (2006). More recently, Barbaras has taken up Patočka's elaboration of movement as part of his own phenomenology of life (2007). Each of them remains more clearly within the phenomenological universe than Castoriadis's reflections.

6. Objective Knowledge in Review

1. For the sociopolitical aspects of objective knowledge and the pursuit of rational mastery, see Castoriadis (1987c). For a recent discussion of Castoriadis's philosophical approach to science, see Crozon-Cazin and Dolaur-Liberté (2005) and Klooger (2009). For a systematic and sustained engagement with the objectivist imaginary and the sociopolitical as well as philosophical contexts of science, see Komesaroff (1986). For a discussion of Castoriadis's theory of modernity, see Arnason (1989a); see also Wagner (2008). An earlier version of a section of this chapter was published in Adams (2007b).

2. Philosophical critiques of science are many. They include, in the analytic tradition, Rorty (1991) and Davidson (2001). In the context of this book, those in the phenomenological and hermeneutic traditions are of particular interest. For a relatively recent debate on the possibility of hermeneutics in the natural sciences, see Markus (1987), Heelen (1989), Kockelmans (1991), and Kisiel (1997). For discussions between different views from hermeneutics and the natural sciences, see Connolly and Keutner (1988). See Gadamer (1991), Heelan (1991), and Feher, Kiss, and Ropolyi (1999).

3. See, for example, MSPI. It was also part of his broader Ph.D. topic, which he did not complete.

4. For an earlier paper on Castoriadis's approach to science, see, for example, MSPI. For a discussion of Heidegger's interpretation of Kant and time, see Sherover (1971, 1994).

5. Husserl draws on Brentano for this insight, whose idea of intentionality draws on Aristotle.

6. From archival sources in the period 1964–79, the thesis project addressed axiomatic logic and philosophical foundations of epistemology.

7. In the closing paragraph of MSPI, Castoriadis writes: "How, furthermore, can one hope to abolish this institution in its present form without profoundly disrupting the internal organization of knowledge and of the scientific work which is congruent with it? And what could this disruption be, if not an entire reconsideration of the question of knowledge, of those engaged in its pursuit, of the object of their pursuit, and thus, once again, and more than ever, philosophy that philosophy whose death some simpletons believe they can cause simply by pronouncing it?" (p. 224).

8. However, MSPI is as much about distinguishing the psyche, the social and history as separate regions not graspable by natural scientific frameworks as it is about internal crises within the natural scientific frameworks themselves. Thus, in its wide ranging enquiry into the state (or crises) of the natural and human "sciences," MSPI is best read as a preparatory step to the ontological turn of the *IIS*.

9. Some of which have been posthumously published, with more planned (for example, *CQFG*, *SV*).

10. As mentioned at the beginning, the promised manuscript for *L'élément imaginaire* (mentioned as early as the *IIS*) seems not to have been systematically pursued to completion.

11. Consequently, except where otherwise stated, all page numbers refer to this paper.

12. The 1989 paper "Philosophy, Politics, Anthropology" provides a mature exposition of his views. As we saw in Chapter 3, Castoriadis tended to emphasize the psychological elements in his philosophical anthropology, but this is not so evident here. The enigma of knowledge is not made explicit in the title, but is a pervasive theme. However, a lengthy discussion would take us beyond the parameters of the current work ("Done and to Be Done," the 1989 transitional paper and reply to his critics, represents the chronological limit for this study).

13. Arnason (2006) has argued that McDowell's *Mind and World* can also be interpreted along these lines.

14. As well as building on the later Durkheim's understanding of institution, Castoriadis also leans on and radicalizes the idea of institution as *Fundierung* in the later Merleau-Ponty, who in turn draws on Husserl,

15. While Castoriadis does not pursue a "correspondence" theory of knowledge and truth, neither does he pursue a kind of Heideggerian *aletheia*. For Castoriadis, the world is created not unveiled: Knowledge or the truth of being is a social-historical process, not a disclosure (as this would mean there is a "determinate thing" to be disclosed).

16. In this vein, the early Bhaskar (1975, 1979) is relevant, especially also in his attempt to link a philosophy of science to a socialist politics. Interestingly, Bhaskar in his early work preferred the term transcendental realism to critical realism.

17. Castoriadis does not use the term "primordial being." As I interpret it, there is some overlap between Merleau-Ponty's notion of brute or savage being and the idea of primordial being, although they are not reducible to another. Among other things, this has to do with the differing approaches to nature that Merleau-Ponty and Castoriadis take. For Castoriadis, nature is not just the "non-instituted" as it is for Merleau-Ponty (2003) (see also Barbaras 2000), it is always instituted by anthropic being as part of the "real," of the "natural world" and with diverse imaginary and symbolic contexts. The living being, moreover, takes on an ambiguous status in Castoriadis's thought (as I show in the next chapter), for as the "archetype" of the subjective instance, it, too, creates a world of (proto)meaning.

18. This takes us into phenomenological and post-phenomenological regions. See Merleau-Ponty (1961) for the fragment on the "true transcendental" of nature and culture and their interlacing. See also Arnason (1993). We return to post-phenomenological themes in the conclusion.

19. See Klooger's discussion (2009).

20. Castoriadis does not in the first instance make a primary distinction between living and nonliving nature, rather it is the first natural stratum (which includes diverse modes and regions of being) as that which the social-historical encounters as ensidizable nature, and its ontological relation as "different" or "other" to heterogeneous layers of being that interests him. See Klooger (2009).

21. See Taylor (1995) on the validity of transcendental arguments. Drawing on Heidegger and Merleau-Ponty in particular, he develops a phenomenological critique of the subject-object distinction via an articulation of our embodied subjectivity always already directly engaged in the world. See also Dreyfus's discussion (2004); and the pre-postmodern Lyotard (1991) on history and phenomenology.

22. In this vein, Klooger (2009) argues that Castoriadis smuggles in an established harmony between that which can be organized and our organization of it.

23. See Taylor (2005) for an interpretation of Merleau-Ponty's "anti-epistemology"—to use a term from Dreyfus—and its implications for the world.

24. See Klooger's discussion (2009).

25. This is a distinction that Castoriadis did not himself resolve satisfactorily in his later writings.

26. This has been further pursued in a somewhat different but related direction by the British critical realist school. See the special issue "Sociality/Materiality: The Status of the Object in Social Science," *Theory Culture and Society* (October–December 2002).

27. "If we are to think about what exists, it must be in terms of an organization of layers that in part adhere together, in terms of an endless succession in depth of layers of being that were always organized, but never completely, always articulated together, but never fully" (MSPI 172).

28. The next chapter focuses more extensively on the philosophical problematic of the living being.

29. See Gadamer (1981).

30. See Butterfield on the historical origins of modern science (1968), and Grant, Basalla, and Hannaway (1997) on the medieval antecedents to modern science. See Huff for a comparative historical account of the rise of science in Islam, China, and the West (2003). See also Patočka's discussion of the emergence of the worldview of modern science and its preconditions (2006).

31. Castoriadis devotes later papers and discussions to mathematics. See his discussion with Alain Connes in *Dialogue*, as well as "Remarques sur l'espace et le nombre," in *Figures du pensable*.

32. As mentioned in the first part of the book, but especially relevant in the present context, an absence in Castoriadis's account is Bachelard's epistemological elucidation. Bachelard, too, privileges discontinuity in science (Bachelard

1934). Although Bhaskar (1975) sees similarities between Bachelard and Popper, I think that links might also be made between Bachelard's approach to discontinuity and Kuhn's. There is also a connection between Bachelard's notion of an "epistemological break" and Althusser and Foucault. See Lecourt (1969). See also Van Eynde's very interesting discussion on Castoriadis, Bachelard, and the imaginary (2008).

33. See Koyré (1957). See also Blumenberg (1987) and Gusdorf (1969).

34. See the collection of papers edited by Arnason and Wittrock (2004) that considers the importance of the tenth through the thirteenth centuries in the breakthrough to modernity. See also Huff's comparative approach to the rise of science (2003).

35. For a discussion by Castoriadis that takes up the political implications of the marriage between capitalism and science, see *Dead End?* (1991).

36. See also GMPI for a discussion of contrasts and similarities between ancient and modern political imaginaries.

7. Rethinking the World of the Living Being

1. Some sections of this chapter have been published in an earlier form (Adams 2007b, 2008b).

2. As discussed in Chapter 5. See Barel's discussion on Atlan, Varela, and Hofstadter (1983), and Stengers (1985).

3. As previously indicated, recent debates in phenomenology, particularly in French currents of phenomenology, have reengaged with the importance of "life", which can be broadly understood as the renewal of the question of 'existence' rather than a return to *Lebensphilosophie*. As Barbaras, too, has devoted an essay to Varela's thought (Barbaras 2002), a comparison between his and Castoriadis's respective approaches could be fruitful. Provisionally, two differences stand out: Castoriadis highlights the idea of life as autopoiesis from an ontological rather than phenomenological level, and he also is interested in the question of political autonomy and hence pursues a discussion with Varela concerning the question of biological autonomy.

4. In *SV*, on the other hand, he prefers the terminology "*devenir être.*"

5. "Life" for Castoriadis is signified by the presence of the imagination, in the case of the living being, the corporeal imagination, and its construction of a world. This becomes increasingly clearer in his post-1990 thought.

6. Castoriadis variously uses the German term *Eigenwelt* or the French version of *monde propre*.

7. Obviously, "meaning" for the living being is of a different order than for the social-historical. In that sense it can be thought of as proto-meaning. However, the crucial difference between the living being and other regions of the *for-itself* is that the living being operates within functional closure—the defunctionalization of the human psyche ruptures the stratum of the living being at the anthropic moment.

8. See, for example Portmann (1961, 1990). See also Merleau-Ponty's discussion of Portmann in *La Nature* (1995).

9. See the debate between Varela, Castoriadis et al from 1981 (Dumouchel and Dupuy 1983, pp. 171–73). In the same context, Castoriadis criticizes the Varelan autonomous system (in its Kantian closure) by comparison to the closed world of the schizophrenic.

10. For a discussion of anthropic "creatureliness," especially in regard to autonomy, see Ambrose (2004).

11. Being able *to put into image, to make an image be*, is of ontological importance for Castoriadis.

12. Later developments in Castoriadis's thought highlight the role of the corporeal imagination in the living being and the rethinking of life vis-à-vis the Aristotelian soul. See especially the 1995 paper "Psychoanalysis and Philosophy."

13. Castoriadis's theory of religion changed quite dramatically from his discussion in the final *IIS* chapter (as we discussed in Chapter 4), to ISR written three years later. Castoriadis did not develop his theory of religion further into the 1980s. For further discussion of the sacred in relation to Castoriadis, see Adams (2011); for a discussion of religion and autonomy, see K. Smith (2007).

14. Castoriadis's resurrection of the category of "*being for-itself*" tends to minimize its essential openness toward the world.

15. A theory of the "self" and its difference from "the (autonomous) subject" is at best fragmentary in Castoriadis's thought. See Klooger (2009) for his discussion of the living being. See K. Smith (2010) for a comparative approach to the modern self and subjectivity in Castoriadis and Taylor. The current discussion is limited to the clues that the dimension of the *for-itself*, and the living being in particular, reveal in relation to the problematic of the autonomist imaginary broadly conceived. C. Ambrose (2004) first coined the term "autonomist imaginary," although I use it in a slightly different sense here.

16. Varela's later work in neurophenomenology and on "first person science" sees the interplay between "body" as object and lived experience (Husserl's distinction between *Körper* and *Leib*) in interesting ways.

17. Johann P. Arnason relativises and reconfigures Castoriadis's polarization of "autonomy" and "heteronomy" from a number of angles (see Arnason 1988, 2001).

18. See Dumouchel (1983) for different approaches to the problematic of autonomy.

19. See *Works and Days*. For Hesiod, *dike* separated animal from human *nomos*.

8. Reimagining Cosmology

1. For a different approach to Castoriadis's engagement with the physical world, see Klooger (2009). Whereas Klooger's critical discussion focussed on the implications of determinacy/indeterminacy for science, as well as a relativization of its applicability in terms of Castoriadis's own thought, the focus of the present chapter centers on the philosophical implications of Castoriadis's thought. An earlier version of some parts of this chapter was published in Adams (2007b).

2. The notion of "the world" is not a transhistorical concept. It was "discovered/created" in the Axial Age, where it first emerged in ancient Greek thought. According to Brague (1999), it appeared first in Pythagorean writings, as well as in Heraclitus and then in a form recognizable as such by us today by Plato. It was preceded, by ideas referring to "The All" or "All things" (see Brague 1999). Kerschensteiner (1962) reminds us in this context that the idea of kosmos is metaphorical. See also Gadamer (1998), and Dirks's (2004) entry on "Welt" in the *Historisches Wörterbuch der Philosophie*.

3. A later formulation again is the idea of *vis formandi*. It starts to appear in his writings from the late 1980s and into the 1990s.

4. By "the current state," Castoriadis is referring to the 1960s and the beginning of the 1970s.

5. With the benefit of hindsight, however, openings toward creative *physis* are discernable.

6. This is taken from the epigraph to Part II of this book, and which is, in turn, from the opening paragraph of MSPI.

7. TC was first prepared as a presentation for the 1983 Cerisy Colloque in honor of Ilya Prigogine. A reworked version was used as the basis for the lecture at the colloquium on "The Construction of Time," Stanford University in February 1988. Then in 1987–88, Castoriadis wrote a short series of seminars on Time and Creation that are held in the archives. The Time and Creation seminars contain in amplified form the arguments present in the final version of the published "Time and Creation" (TC) essay.

8. There are other typewritten fragments and short papers written at that time that we also draw upon in the following discussion that he may have written as part of his planned book. These as yet unpublished seminars and other writings of this period provide a rich source of Castoriadis's philosophical engagement with the cosmological aspects of being.

9. It is of course impossible to discuss cosmology without some reference to the social-historical, but the elaboration of social-historical modes of time per se will not be our primary focus here.

10. Although Castoriadis and Bergson form part of a broader philosophical lineage to foreground approaches to "time" and "becoming," Castoriadis does not explicitly engage with Bergson, and his ontological elaboration of time is far removed from Bergson's *élan vital*.

11. As his later paper on Merleau-Ponty shows—"Merleau-Ponty and the Weight of the Ontological Tradition"—Castoriadis did not regard him as having surmounted the supposed privileged viewpoint of perception and (inter)subjectivity.

12. See Dostall (1993) for a discussion of time in Husserl and Heidegger. I mentioned in the introduction to Part II of this book Castoriadis's interest in the connection between Whitehead and Merleau-Ponty. Similarly, although more strictly within phenomenological parameters (as opposed to the "post-phenomenology" of the later Merleau-Ponty), earlier attempts to build bridges between

Whitehead and Husserl and Whitehead and Heidegger are evident. See Laszlo (1966) and Schrag (1959).

13. That Castoriadis sees Aristotle's understanding of time as measurable and quantitative, but his notion of "change"/"motion" as qualitative, points to the unfinished and unsystematic approach to creative *physis* in Castoriadis's thought.

14. For a discussion of this thematic, see Descombes (1991).

15. Unfortunately, due to constraints of space, the question of religion, its relation to myth and its place in Castoriadis's thought, especially as it pertains to autonomy, will have to remain open.

16. See Brague (1999).

17. See Atlan's very interesting discussion on the relation between science and myth (1993). See also Bottici's distinctive account of the work of political myth (2008).

18. As Jula Kerschensteiner reminds us in her opening sentence of her now classic 1962 text *Kosmos*: "*Kosmos—'die Welt': Wir sind uns kaum mehr bewusst, dass dahinter eine grossartige Metapher steckt*" (Kerschensteiner 1962, p. 1).

19. See Brague (1999).

20. For my purposes here, myth is to be understood broadly as encompassing religion.

21. See especially Deutschmann (2001) and Arnason (2003).

22. See Brague's studies on Aristotle and Plato (1982).

23. Here also the *puissance-acte* distinction is explained as the most subtle way to suppress time. This is very interesting in terms of radical *physis* and his (general) interpretation of *physis* as *poussée,* not the more common *puissance* as per the secondary literature on *physis*/nature (see, for example, Goddard 2000). Yet, occasionally he refers to the psyche as *puissance* (see *IIS* 263). Moreover, in TC, he equates the psyche with *physis*.

24. The strange status of mathematics seems an omnipresent phantom in Castoriadis's thought. Later writings on mathematical themes include "Faux et vrai chaos" (1993), "Remarques sur l'espace et le nombre" (written in 1993, published 1999), and his discussion with Alain Connes in *Dialogue* (1999).

25. Some physicists incorporate a philosophical discussion to the physical world. See, for example, Mehra (1973), but also Brans, Stengers, and Vincke (1988), Honner (1987), and Prigogine (1997). Jantsch's text on the self-organization of the universe has been influential (1979). For philosophical discussions, see Whitehead (1978), Leclerc (1972, 1986), and van der Veken (1990).

26. The living being and the psyche represent the intermediate levels and the question of the meaningfulness of their respective worlds remains open.

27. See, for example, Casey (1993, 1997) for his interpretation of place within the phenomenological tradition of meaningful place.

28. Unfortunately, Castoriadis does not pursue a sustained elucidation of space; and he generally speaks of "space" and rarely of "place." Space generally figures as an oppositional figure to time.

29. I prefer here the term poietic rather than imaginary, as imaginary is limited to the social-historical mode of being, whereas "poietic" can more readily be envisaged to embrace all modes of being.

30. See p. 376: "The meaning of the term 'objective' is, here: the possibility offered to subjects as beings for-themselves by what there is, to exist in a world and to organize, each time in another way, what there is (this possibility being largely independent of these subjects)."

31. Instead of the term "disenchanted," I prefer this more literal translation of Weber's *Entzauberung der Welt*.

Conclusion: The Circle of Creation

1. Apart from Merleau-Ponty's *The Visible and the Invisible*, key texts that have informed my approach to the idea of the *world* include Arnason's essay "Weltauslegung und Verständigung" (1989c); Richir's essay "Nous sommes au monde" (1989); Dirk's long entry "Welt" in the *Historisches Wörterbuch der Philosophie* (2004); Weber's early essay on "Religious Rejections of the World" (1977); and a review of Nelson Goodman's *Ways of Worldmaking* by Ricoeur (1991d).

2. Many thanks to Angelos Mouzakitis for his translation.

3. See Ciaramellis's thoughtful discussion of the self-presupposition of the origin, where he provides a philosophical elucidation Castoriadis's notion of creation—the paradox of the immanent *Ur-Sprung*—as a mode of being in reflecting on the groundlessness of the "elsewhere" of creation (1997).

4. As mentioned earlier, in the final seminar of *CQFG*, Castoriadis traces the idea of anthropos as self-creation to Hesiod's chaos in the *Theogony*.

5. See Castoriadis (1996 [1993]) "Athenian Democracy: False and True Questions."

6. See Meier (1989) and Waldenfels (1997–99). Openings onto intercultural interworlds and the corresponding reconfiguration of "*Selbst*" and "*Anderes*" to "*Eigenes*" and "*Fremdes*" would be a central thematic to pursue further.

References

Primary Sources

Archival

(Per the archival inventory established by Myrto Gondicas, Paris)

Le Timée (1970). Manuscript in A2: materials philo.grecque (*Timée*, *Rép*, *Sophiste*, etc: *De Anima*).

B1 a B8: Materials on *L'Elément imaginaire* (Aristotle, Kant, Heidegger, etc.), 1957/87.

B13, B14; Magmas/amas: Colloque. Cerisy (1981; l'auto-organisation), materials 1970/87 (from p. 47 of catalogue).

B17: documents—Dupuy, Varela, Thom, etc.; notes (from p. 47 of catalogue).

(Mar) C3bis (chemise): Sur le temps, notes, 1986/88.

"Séminaire du 23/3/88. Introduction générale (suite et fin)." In Mar C15: sem. 87/88 "Temps et création." transcriptions d. de séance, annotées, materials ms.et d. ad TC classes en rubriques de livre.

D1: T&C: science, documents

Materials manuscrit et documents. 1985/86 (from p. 50).

(Mar) D2: Temps & création; seminar 1987/88.

Materials ad. Seminar: St. Augustin, Aristotle, Ricoeur, Kant.

"Discussion avec Ricoeur." In (Mar) D8: CH, seminar 86/87.

Entretien radio CC–Ricoeur (February 1985?), typed transcription, some missing.

Compte-rendu de la réunion du "Groupe de réflexion interdisciplinaire" du 17 mars 1983, "Autonomie et complexité." Rédigé par Yolande Benarrosh in (Bbis A) 1bis: Presse: Annonces de parutions et comptes redus (1979/1989).

"Compte rendu du *La Nature de la Nature*." In (Bquater) 10: Germinal (années 70).

Compte rendu critique par Cornelius Castoriadis du livre *La Nature de la nature* (vol. 1 de *La Méthode*); 2 lettres d'E. M. à C.C. en prévision du débat.

Published

Atlan, Henri, Cornelius Castoriadis, J. M. Domenach, Jean-Pierre Dupuy, P. Feyerabend, R. Girard, Edgar Morin, Ilya Prigonine, Isabelle Stengers, J. C. Tabarly, and P. Watzlawock (1987). *"Création et désordre." Recherches et pensées contemporaines.* Paris: L'Originel/Radio France.

Atlan, Henri, Cornelius Castoriadis, Michel Gutsatz, Pierre Livet, Benny Shanon, and Francisco Varela (1983). "Séminaire: Sur le problème du nouveau." In Paul Dumouchel and Jean-Pierre Dupuy, eds., *L'auto organisation: De la physique au politique.* Paris: Seuil.

Castoriadis, Cornelius (1944). "Εισαγωγή στον Max Weber." (Μετάφραση της Εισαγωγής απο το βιβλίο του Max Weber Οικονομία και Κοινωνία), Αρχείον Κοινωνιολογίας και Ηθικής, No 2, 'ανοιξη (επαναδημοσίευση στην Εποπτεία, τ. 11–12, Μάιος-Ιούνιος 1977). Τώρα στο Πρώτες δοκιμές.

———. (1973a). *La société bureaucratique*, vol. 1, *Les rapports de production en Russie*. Paris: Union Générale d'Éditions.

———. (1973b). "Introduction." In Castoriadis, *La société bureaucratique*, vol. 1, *Les rapports de production en Russie*, 11–61.

———. (1973c). "Phénoménologie de la conscience prolétarienne." In Castoriadis, *La société bureaucratique*, vol. 1, *Les rapports de production en Russie*, 115–29.

———. (1979a). *Capitalisme moderne et révolution, vol. 1, L'impérialisme et la guerre.* Paris: Union Générale d'Éditions.

———. (1979b). *Capitalisme moderne et révolution, vol. 2, Le mouvement révolutionnaire sous le capitalisme moderne.* Paris: Union Générale d'Éditions.

———. (1979c). *Le contenu du socialisme.* Paris: Union Générale d'Éditions.

———. (1979d). *La société française.* Paris: Union Générale d'Éditions.

———. (1980). "Francisco Varela, *Principles of Biological Autonomy*." *Le Débat* 1, 126–27.

————. (1984a [1968]). "Epilegomena to a Theory of the Soul Which Has Been Presented as a Science." In Castoriadis, *Crossroads in the Labyrinth*, 3–45.

————. (1984b [1973]). "Modern Science and Philosophical Interrogation." In Castoriadis, *Crossroads in the Labyrinth*, 145–226.

————. (1984c). "The Sayable and the Unsayable: Homage to Maurice Merleau-Ponty." In Castoriadis, *Crossroads in the Labyrinth*, 119–44.

————. (1984d). "Technique." In Castoriadis, *Crossroads in the Labyrinth*, 229–59.

————. (1984e). "Value, Equality, Justice, Politics: From Marx to Aristotle and from Aristotle to Ourselves." In Castoriadis, *Crossroads in the Labyrinth*, 260–339.

————. (1984f). *Crossroads in the Labyrinth*. Translated by Kate Soper and Martin H. Ryle. Brighton, UK: The Harvester Press.

————. (1984g). "Marx Today: An Interview." *Thesis Eleven* 8, 124–32.

————. (1985). "Reflections of 'Rationality' and 'Development.'" *Thesis Eleven* 9, 18–36.

————. (1986a). *Domaines de l'homme. Les carrefours du labyrinthe II*. Paris: Éditions du Seuil.

————. (1986b). "Preface" to *Domaines de l'homme. Les carrefours du labyrinthe II*. Paris: Éditions du Seuil, 7–15.

————. (1987a [1975]). *The Imaginary Institution of Society*. Translated by Kathleen Blamey. Cambridge: Polity Press.

————. (1987b). "Imaginaire social et changement scientifique." In L'Action Locale Bellevue, ed., *Sens et place des connaissance dans le société*, 161–83. Paris: CNRS.

————. (1987c). "Voie sans issue . . . ?" In Albert Jacquard, ed., *Les scientifiques parlent*, 261–98. Paris: Hachette.

————. (1987d). "L'auto-organisation, du physique au politique" (entretien à Radio France avec Gérard Ponthieu). In Création et désordre. Recherches et pensées contemporaines. Paris: L'Origine/Radio France, 39–46.

————. (1988). "L'utilité de la connaissance dans les sciences de l'homme et dans les savoirs: Table ronde." *Revue européenne des sciences sociales* 79, 87–91.

————. (1989). "The State of the Subject Today." *Thesis Eleven* 24, 5–43.

————. (1990a). *Le monde morcelé: Les carrefours du labyrinthe III*. Paris: Éditions du Seuil.

————. (1990b). "Individual, Society, Rationality, History." *Thesis Eleven* 25, 59–90.

———. (1990c). "Pour-soi et subjectivité." In Daniel Bougnoux, Jean-Louis le Moigne, and Serge Proulx, eds., *Arguments pour une méthode (Autour d'Edgar Morin)*, 118–27. Paris: Seuil.

———. (1991a). "The Crisis of Culture and the State." In Castoriadis 1991b, 219–41.

———. (1991b). *Philosophy, Politics, Autonomy: Essays in Political Philosophy*. Edited and translated by David Ames Curtis. New York: Oxford University Press.

———. (1991c). "Time and Creation." In John Bender and David Wellbery, eds., *Chronotypes and the Construction of Time*, 38–64. Stanford: Stanford University Press.

———. (1993a). "Complexité, magmas, histoire: L'exemple de la ville médiévale" (octobre 1991–février 1992). In Michel Amiot, Isabelle Billiard, and Lucien Brams, eds., *Système et paradoxe: Auteur de la pensée d'Yves Barel*, 55–73. Paris: Seuil.

———. (1993b). "Institution of Society and Religion." *Thesis Eleven* 35, 1–17.

———. (1993c). "La force révolutionnaire de l'écologie." *Les cahiers de Saint-Martin*, 7, 80–86.

———. (1993d). "Merleau-Ponty and the Weight of the Ontological Tradition." *Thesis Eleven* 36, 1–36.

———. (1993e). "Social Transformation and Cultural Creation." In *Political and Social Writings*. Translated and edited by David Ames Curtis. Minneapolis: University of Minnesota Press, 3:300–313.

———. (1993f). "Does the Idea of Revolution Still Makes Sense? Interview." *Thesis Eleven* 26.

———. (1994a). "En mal de culture." *Esprit* (December), 40–50.

———. (1994b). "Radical Imagination and the Social Instituting Imaginary." In Gillian Robinson and John Rundell, eds., *Rethinking Imagination: Culture and Creativity*, 136–53. New York: Routledge.

———. (1996a). "Athenian Democracy: False and True Questions." In Lévêque and Vidal-Naquet 1996.

———. (1996). La montée de l'insignifiance. Les carrefours du labyrinthe IV. Paris: Éditions du Seuil.

———. (1997a). "Anthropology, Philosophy, Politics." *Thesis Eleven* 49, 99–116.

———. (1997b). "Done and to Be Done." In Castoriadis 1971l, 361–417.

———. (1997c). *Fait et à faire. Les carrefours du labyrinthe V*. Paris: Éditions du Seuil.

———. (1997d). "Logic, Imagination, Reflection." In Castoriadis 1997m, 246–72.

———. (1997e). "*Phusis* and Autonomy." In Castoriadis 1997m, 331–41.

———. (1997f). "Psychoanalysis and Philosophy." In Castoriadis 1997l, 348–60.

———. (1997g). "The Discovery of the Imagination." In Castoriadis 1997m, 213–45.

———. (1997h). "The Imaginary: Creation in the Social-Historical Domain." In Castoriadis 1997m, 3–18.

———. (1997i [1983]). "The Logic of Magmas and the Question of Autonomy." In Castoriadis 1997l, 290–318.

———. (1997j). "The Ontological Import of the History of Science." In Castoriadis 1997m, 342–73.

———. (1997k). "Time and Creation." In Castoriadis 1997m, 374–401.

———. (1997l). *The Castoriadis Reader.* Edited and translated by David Ames Curtis. Oxford: Blackwell.

———. (1997m). *World in Fragments: Writings on Politics, Society, Psychoanalysis and the Imagination.* Edited and translated by David Ames Curtis. Stanford: Stanford University Press.

———. (1997n). "The Greek *Polis* and the Creation of Democracy." In Castoriadis 1997l, 266–89.

———. (1997o). "The Crisis of the Identification Process." *Thesis Eleven* 49, 85–98.

———. (1999a). "Mode d'être et problèmes de connaissance du social-historique." In Cornelius Castoriadis, *Figures du pensable. Les carrefours du labyrinthe* VI. Paris: Seuil, 261–75.

———. (1999b). *Dialogue.* Paris: L'Aube.

———. (1999c). "Anthropogonie chez Eschyle et autocréation de l'homme chez Sophocle." In Castoriadis, *Figures du pensable,* 13–34.

———. (1999d). "Imaginaire et imagination au carrefour." In Castoriadis, *Figures du pensable,* 93–114.

———. (1999e). "Notes sur quelques moyens de la poésie." In Castoriadis, *Figures du pensable,* 35–61.

———. (2002a). *On Plato's Statesman.* Translated by David Ames Curtis. Stanford: Stanford University Press.

———. (2002b). *Sujet et vérité dans le monde social-historique: Seminaires 1986–1987.* Edited by Enrique Escobar. Paris: Seuil.

———. (2004). *Ce qui fait la Grèce,* vol. 1, *D'Homère à Héraclite.* Paris: Seuil.

———. (2008). *Ce qui fait la Grèce,* vol. 2, *La cité et les lois.* Paris: Seuil.

Castoriadis, Cornelius, and Daniel Cohn-Bendit (1981). *De l'écologie à l'autonomie.* Paris: Seuil.

Castoriadis, Cornelius, and René Girard (1983). "La contingence dans les affaires humaines." In Paul Dumouchel and Jean-Pierre Dupuy, eds., *L'auto-organisation: De la physique au politique.* Paris: Seuil.

Castoriadis, Cornelius, Pierre Lévêque, and Pierre Vidal-Naquet (1996). "On the Invention of Democracy." In Lévêque and Vidal-Naquet 1996.

Secondary Sources

Adams, Suzi (2001). "The Enduring Enigma: *Nomos* and *Physis* in Castoriadis." *Thesis Eleven* 65, 93–107.

———. (2003). "Castoriadis' Shift Towards *Physis.*" *Thesis Eleven* 74, 105–112.

———. (2005). "Interpreting Creation: Castoriadis and the Project of Autonomy." *Thesis Eleven* 83, 25–41.

———. (2007a). "Castoriadis and the Permanent Riddle of the World: Changing Configurations Between Alienness and Worldliness." *Thesis Eleven* 90, 44–62.

———. (2007b). "Castoriadis and Auto-Poiesis." *Thesis Eleven* 88, 76–91.

———. (2008a). " 'Castoriadis' Long Journey Through *Nomos*: Institution, Creation, Interpretation." *Tijdschrift voor Filosofie* (Leiden) 70, 269–95.

———. (2008b). "Castoriadis and the Phenomenology of Life." *Cosmos and History,* 2:387–400.

———. (2009a). " 'Dimensions of the World: Castoriadis' Homage to Merleau-Ponty." *Chiasmi International: Trilingual Studies Concerning the Thought of Merleau-Ponty* 11.

———. (2009b). "The Intercultural Horizons of Johann Arnason's Phenomenology of the World." *Journal of Intercultural Studies* 30(3), 249–266.

———. (2011). "Arnason and Castoriadis' Unfinished Dialogue: Articulations of the World." *European Journal of Social Theory* 14:1.

Ameriks, Karl, ed. (2000). *The Cambridge Companion to German Idealism.* Cambridge: Cambridge University Press.

Amiot, Michel, Isabelle Billiard, and Lucien Brams, eds. (1993). *Système et Paradoxe: Auteur de la pensée d'Yves Barel.* Paris: Seuil.

Anderson, Benedict (1983). *Imagined Communities: Reflections on the Origin and Spread of Nationalism.* New York: Verso.

Ariès, Philippe (1954). *Le temps de l'histoire.* Monaco: Éditions du Rocher.

Aristotle (1982). *The Complete Works of Aristotle: The Revised Oxford Translation*. Edited by Jonathan Barnes. Oxford: Oxford University Press.

Arnason, Johann P. (1971). *Von Marcuse zu Marx: Prolegomena zu einer dialektischen Anthropologie*. Neuwied: Luchterhand.

———. (1984). "Progress and Pluralism: Reflections on Agnes Heller's Theory of History." *Praxis International* 3(4), 423–37.

———. (1986a). "Die Moderne als Projekt und Spannungsfeld." In Axel Honneth and Hans Joas, eds., 278–326. *Kommunikatives Handeln*. Frankfurt am Main: Suhrkamp Verlag.

———. (1987). "Das Andere der Aufklärung." In W. Weit et al., eds., *Antipodische Aufklärunge—Antipodean Enlightenments. Festschrift for Leslie Bodi*, 25–35. Frankfurt am Main: Peter Lang.

———. (1988a). *Praxis und Interpretation: Sozialphilosophische Studien*. Frankfurt am Main: Suhrkamp.

———. (1989a). "The Imaginary Constitution of Modernity." *Revue européenne des sciences sociales: Pour une philosophie militante de la démocratie* 25(86).

———. (1989b). "Culture and Imaginary Significations." *Thesis Eleven* 22, 25–45.

———. (1989c). "Weltauslegung und Verständigung." In Axel Honneth, Thomas McCarthy, Claus Offe, and Albrecht Wellmer, eds., *Zwischenbetrachtungen: im Prozess der Aufklärung. Jürgen Habermas zum 60. Geburtstag*, 66–89. Frankfurt am Main: Suhrkamp Verlag.

———. (1993a). "Merleau-Ponty and Max Weber: An Unfinished Project." *Thesis Eleven* 36, 82–98.

———. (1993b). *The Future that Failed: Origins and Destinies of the Soviet Model*. London: Routledge.

———. (1994). "Reason, Imagination, Interpretation." In Gillian Robinson and John Rundell, eds., *Rethinking Imagination: Culture and Creativity*. London: Routledge, 155–17.

———. (1996a). "L'autre de la raison et la raison de l'autre." In C. Bouchindhomme and R. Rochlitz, eds., *Habermas, la raison, la critique*, 9–37. Paris: Editions du Cerf.

———. (1996b). "Theorizing History and Questioning Reason." *Theoria* 87, 1–200.

———. (1996c). "Invention and Emergence: Reflections on Hans Joas' Theory of Creative Action." *Thesis Eleven* 47, 101–13.

———. (1996d). *Nation and Modernity: Reykjavik Lectures*. Stockholm: NSU Press.

———. (1997). *Social Theory and the Japanese Experience: The Dual Civilization*. London: Kegan Paul.

———. (2001). "Autonomy and Axiality: Comparative Perspectives on the Greek Breakthrough." In Arnason and Murphy 2001.

———. (2002). "Psychoanalysis and Civilization Analysis: Preliminaries to a Debate." *Thesis Eleven* 71, 71–92.

———. (2003). *Civilizations in Dispute: Historical Questions and Theoretical Traditions*. Leiden: Brill.

———. (2005). "The Axial Conundrum: Between Historical Sociology and the Philosophy of History." In Eliezer Ben-Rafael and Yitzhak Sternberg, eds., *Comparing Modernities: Pluralism versus Homogeneity: Essays in Homage to Shmuel N. Eisenstadt*, 57–82. Leiden: Brill.

———. (2007). "Roads Beyond Marx: Rethinking Projects and Traditions." In Jan Balon and Milan Tuček, eds., *Chaos a řád v sociologii a ve společnosti*, 150–64. Prague: Matfyzpress.

Arnason, Johann P., and Peter Murphy, eds. (2001). *Agon, Logos, Polis: The Greek Achievement and Its Aftermath*. Stuttgart: Franz Steiner Verlag.

Arnason, Johann P., and Bjorn Wittrock, eds. (2004). *Eurasian Transformations, Tenth to Thirteenth Centuries: Crystallizations, Divergences*. Leiden: Brill.

Aron, Raymond, ed. (1961). "Histoire de la philosophie et historicité." In *L'histoire et ses interpretations. Entretiens autour de Arnold Toynbee*. Colloques de Cerisy. Paris: Mouton.

Assmann, Jan (1992). *Das kulturelle Gedächtnis. Schrift, Erinnerung und politische Identität in frühen Hochkulturen*. Munich: Beck.

Atlan, Henri (1979). *Entre le crystal et la fumée*. Paris: Seuil.

———. (1993). *Enlightenment to Enlightenment: Intercritique of Science and Myth*. Translated by Lenn J. Schramm. Albany: State University of New York Press.

Aulagnier, P. (1975). *La violence de l'interprétation*. Paris: PUF.

Bachelard, Gaston (1934). *Le nouvel esprit scientifique*. Paris, PUF.

———. (1942). *L'eau et les rêves: Essai sur l'imagination de la matière*. Paris: J. Corti.

———. (1960). *La poétique de la rêverie*. Paris: Presses Universitaires de France.

Badiou, Alain (2005 [1988]). *Being and Event*. Translated by Oliver Feltham. New York: Continuum.

Barbaras, Renaud (2000). "Merleau-Ponty et la nature." *Chiasmi International* 2, 47–62.

―――. (2004). *The Being of the Phenomenon: Merleau-Ponty's Ontology.* Translated by Ted Toadvine and Leonard Lawlor. Bloomington: Indiana University Press.

―――. (2005). "A Phenomenology of Life." In Taylor Carman and Mark B. N. Hansen, eds., *The Cambridge Companion to Merleau-Ponty.* Cambridge: Cambridge University Press.

―――. (2010). "Phenomenology and Henology." In E. Abrams and I. Chvatík, eds., *Jan Patočka and the European Heritage: Centenary Papers.* Dordrecht: Springer.

Barel, Yves (1983). "Le 'Paradoxe de l'Auto.'" *Cahiers du CREA* 2, 187–229.

Beiser, Frederick (1987). *The Fate of Reason: German Philosophy from Kant to Fichte.* Cambridge, Mass.: Harvard University Press.

Berque, Augustin, ed. (2000). *Logique de lieu et dépassement de la modernité,* vols. 1–2. Brussels: Ousia.

Bhaskar, Roy (1975). "Feyerabend and Bachelard: Two Philosophies of Science." *New Left Review* 94.

―――. (1989). *Reclaiming Reality.* London: Verso.

Bishop, Paul (2002). "Ludwig Klages' Early Reception of Friedrich Nietzsche." *Oxford German Studies* 31, 129–61.

Blumenberg, Hans (2000 [1957]). " 'Imitation of Nature': Toward a Prehistory of the Idea of Creative Being." Translated by Anna Wertz. *Qui Parle* 12(1), 17–54.

―――. (2002). *Zu Den Sachen und zurück.* Frankfurt am Main: Suhrkamp.

Böhme, Gernot, ed. (1997). *Phänomenologie der Natur.* Frankfurt am Main: Suhrkamp.

Böhme, Hartmut, and Gernot Böhme (1983). *Das Andere der Vernunft: Zur Entwicklung von Rationalitätsstrukturen am Beispiel Kants.* Frankfurt am Main: Suhrkamp.

Bottici, Chiara (2007). *A Philosophy of Political Myth.* Cambridge: Cambridge University Press.

Bougnoux, Daniel, Jean-Louis le Moigne, and Serge Proulx, eds. (1990). *Arguments pour une méthode.* Paris: Seuil.

Brague, Rémi (1982). *Du temps chez Platon et Aristote: Quatre études.* Paris: Presses Universitaires de France.

―――. (1999). *La sagesse du monde: Histoire de l'expérience humaine de l'univers.* Paris: Fayard.

Brans, J-P., I. Stengers, and P. Vincke. (1988). *Temps et devenir: A partir de l'oeuvre d'Ilya Prigogine. Actes du colloque de Cerisy de 1983.* Geneva: Editions Patino.

Braudel, Ferdinand (1969). *Ecrits sur l'histoire*. Paris: Gallimard.

Bremer, Dieter (1989). "Von der *Physis* zur Natur: Eine griechische Konzeption und ihr Schicksal." *Zeitschrift für philosophische Forschung* 43, 241–64.

Broadie, Sarah (1982). *Nature, Change and Agency in Aristotle's Physics: A Philosophical Study*. Oxford: Clarendon Press.

Bröcker, Walter (1965). *Die Geschichte der Philosophie vor Sokrates*. Frankfurt am Main: Vittorio Klostermann.

Bruzina, Ronald (2002). "Eugen Fink and Maurice Merleau-Ponty: The Philosophical Lineage in Phenomenology." In Ted Toadvine and Lester Embree, eds., *Merleau-Ponty's Reading of Husserl*, 173–200. Dordrecht: Kluwer Academic.

Busino, Giovanni, ed. (1989). *Revue européenne des sciences sociales: Pour une philosophie militante de la démocratie* 25(86). Geneva: Librairie Droz.

Butterfield, Herbert (1968). *The Origins of Modern Science: 1300–1800*. Revised edition. Toronto: Irwin Clarke and Co.

Capelle, Wilhelm, ed. (1968). *Die Vorsokratiker*. Stuttgart: Kroener.

Caputo, John (1997). *The Prayers and Tears of Jacques Derrida*. Bloomington: Indiana University Press.

Carr, David (1991). *Time, Narrative and History*. Bloomington: Indiana University Press.

———. (1974). *Phenomenology and the Problem of History: A Study of Husserl's Transcendental Philosophy*. Evanston, Ill.: Northwestern University Press.

———. (1993). "Phenomenological Reflections on the Philosophy of History." In Phillip Blosser, Eilichi Shimomissé, Lester Embree, and Hiroshi Kojima, eds., *Japanese and Western Phenomenology: Essays from the Japanese-American Joint Seminar on Phenomenology Held in the Suburbs of Sanda-City (Japan) October 24–26 1989*, 393–408. Dordrecht: Kluwer Academic.

Casey, Edward S. (1976). *Imagining: A Phenomenological Study*. Bloomington: Indiana University Press.

———. (1993). *Getting Back Into Place: Toward a Renewed Understanding of the Place-World*. Bloomington: Indiana University Press.

———. (1997). *The Fate of Place: A Philosophical History*. Berkeley: University of California Press.

Cassou-Noguès, Pierre (2001). "Merleau-Ponty et les sciences de la nature: lecture de la physique moderne: confrontation à Bergson et Whitehead." *Chiasmi International* 2.

Caston, Victor (1997). "Pourquoi Aristote a besoin de l'imagination." *Revue Etudes Philosophiques* 1, 3–39.

Caumières, Philippe (2007). *Castoriadis: Le projet d'autonomie*. Paris: Michalon.

Châtelet, François (1974). *La naissance de l'histoire: La formation de la pensée historienne en Grèce*, vol. 2. Paris: 1018.

Cherniss, Harold F. (1964). *Aristotle's Criticism of Presocratic Philosophy*. New York: Octagon Books.

Cho, Kah Kyung, and Young-Ho Lee, eds. (1999). *Phänomenologie der Natur*. Freiburg/Munich: Verlag Karl Alber.

Christofides, C. G. (1961). "Gaston Bachelard's Phenomenology of the Imagination." *Romanic Review* 52(1), 36–48.

Ciaramelli, Fabio (1985). "Herméneutique et créativité. A propos de Paul Ricoeur." *Revue Philosophique de Louvain* 83(59), 410–12.

———. (1989). "Le cercle de la création." *Revue européenne des sciences sociales: Pour une philosophie militante de la démocratie* 25(86).

———. (1997). "The Self-Presupposition of the Origin: Homage to Cornelius Castoriadis." *Thesis Eleven* 49, 45–68.

———. (1998a). "Castoriadis." In Simon Critchley and William R. Schroeder, eds., *A Companion to Continental Philosophy*, 492–503. Oxford: Blackwell.

———. (1998b). "An Introduction to Cornelius Castoriadis' Work." *Psychomedia–Journal of European Psychoanalysis* 6, 87–91.

———. (1999). "Human Creation and the Paradox of the Originary." Translated by David Ames Curtis. *Free Associations* 7(3), 357–66.

Cocking, J. M (1991). *Imagination: A Study in the History of Ideas*. London: Routledge.

Collingwood, Francis J. (1972). *Philosophy of Nature*. Englewood Cliffs, N.J.: Prentice-Hall.

Collingwood, R. G. (1945). *The Idea of Nature*. Oxford: Clarendon Press.

———. (1946). *The Idea of History*. Oxford: Oxford University Press.

Cooper, Ron L. (1993). *Heidegger and Whitehead: A Phenomenological Examination into the Intelligibility of Experience*. Athens: Ohio University Press.

Cornford, Francis M. (1957). *From Religion to Philosophy: A Study in the Origins of Western Speculation*. New York: Harper & Row.

Delanty, S. (1999). *Social Theory in a Changing World: Conceptions of Modernity*. Cambridge: Polity.

Delco, Alessandro (2005). *Merleau-Ponty et l'expérience de la creation: Du paradigm au scheme*. Paris: PUF.

Derrida, Jacques (1982). "*Ousia* and *Grammé:* Note on a Note from *Being and Time.*" In *Margins of Philosophy.* Translated by Alan Bass. Brighton, UK: The Harvester Press.

————. (1993). *Khôra.* Paris: Galilée.

Descombes, Vincent (1989). "Un renouveau philosophique." *Revue européenne des sciences sociales: Pour une philosophie militante de la démocratie* 25(86).

————. (1991). "The Principle of Determination." *Thesis Eleven* 29, 47–62.

————. (1994). "Is There an Objective Spirit?" In James Tully, ed., *Philosophy in an Age of Pluralism: The Philosophy of Charles Taylor in Question*, 96–188. Cambridge: Cambridge University Press.

————. (1996). *Les institutions du sens.* Paris: Minuit.

Deutschmann, Christoph (2001). "The Promise of Absolute Wealth: Capitalism as a Religion?" *Thesis Eleven* 66, 32–56.

Dews, Peter (1995). *The Limits of Disenchantment: Essays on Contemporary European Philosophy.* London: Verso.

Diller, Hans (1939). "Der griechische Naturbegriff." *Neue Jahrbücher fuer Antike und deutsche Bildung* 114, 241–57.

Doridant, Raphaël (2005). "Democratie et Projet d'Autonomie." *Sciences de L'Homme et Sociétés*, 80, 32–36.

Dostall, Robert J. (1993). "Time and Phenomenology in Husserl and Heidegger." In Charles B. Guignon, ed., *The Cambridge Companion to Heidegger.* Cambridge: Cambridge University Press.

Dreyfus, Hubert L. (2004). "Taylor's (Anti-)Epistemology." In Ruth Abbey, ed., *Charles Taylor*, 52–76. Cambridge: Cambridge University Press.

Dummett, Michael (1981). *The Interpretation of Frege's Philosophy.* London: Duckworth.

Dumouchel, Paul (1983). "Mimétisme et autonomie." In Paul Dumouchel and Jean-Pierre Dupuy, eds., *L'auto-organisation: De la physique au politique.* Paris: Seuil.

Durand, Gilbert (1964). *L'imagination symbolique.* Paris: Presses Universitaires de France.

Durkheim, Emile (1965 [1912]). *The Elementary Forms of the Religious Life.* Translated by Joseph Ward Swain. New York: Free Press.

Durkheim, Emile, and Marcel Mauss (1963). *Primitive Classification.* Translated and edited by Rodney Needham. Chicago: University of Chicago Press.

Ehrhardt, Arnold (1951–52). "*Creatio Ex Nihilo.*" *Studia Theologica*, 4 (IV), 27–33.

———. (1968). *The Beginning: A Study in the Greek Philosophical Approach to the Concept of Creation from Anaximander to St. John.* Manchester: Manchester University Press.

Eisenstadt, S. N. (1995). *Power, Trust and Meaning: Essays in Sociological Theory and Analysis.* Chicago: University of Chicago Press.

———. (2001). "The Civilizational Dimension of Modernity: Modernity as Civilization." *International Sociology* 16(3), 320–40.

El-Bizri, Nader (2004). "ON KAI KHORA: Situating Heidegger between the *Sophist* and the *Timaeus.*" *Studia Phaenomenologica* 4(1–2), 73–98.

Eliade, Mircea (1975) *Myths, Rites and Symbols: A Mircea Eliade Reader.* Edited by Wendell C. Beane and William G. Doty. New York: Harper & Row.

Elliott, Brian (2005). *Phenomenology and Imagination in Husserl and Heidegger.* London: Routledge.

Engell, James (1981). *The Creative Imagination: Enlightenment to Romanticism.* Cambridge, Mass.: Harvard University Press.

Fichte, J. G (1982). *Science of Knowledge.* Cambridge: Cambridge University Press.

Fink, Eugen (1958). *Sein, Wahrheit, Welt: Vor-Fragen zum Problem des Phänomen-Begriffs.* The Hague: Martinus Nijhoff.

Frege, Gottlob (1892). "Über Sinn und Bedeutung." *Zeitschrift für Philosophie und philosophische Kritik* 100, 25–50.

Freud, Sigmund (1989). *Civilization and Its Discontents.* New York: Norton.

Freydberg, Bernard (1994). *Imagination and Depth in Kant's Critique of Pure Reason.* New York: P. Lang.

Friese, H., and P. Wagner (2000). "When 'the Light of the Great Cultural Problems Moves On': On the Possibility of a Cultural Theory of Modernity." *Thesis Eleven* 61, 25–40.

Furlong, E. J. (1961). *Imagination.* London: Allen and Unwin.

Gadamer, Hans-Georg (1960). *Wahrheit und Methode: Grundzüge einer philosophischen Hermeneutik.* Tübingen: JCB Mohr.

———. (1986). "Naturwissenschaft und Hermeneutik: Die hermeneutische Dimension in Naturerkenntnis und Naturwissenschaft." In A. Werner, ed., *Filosofi och Kultur,* 3:39–70.

———. (1991). "Natur und Welt: Die hermeneutische Dimension in Naturerkenntnis und Naturwissenschaft." *Gesammelte Werke,* 7:418–42.

———. (1998). *The Beginning of Philosophy.* Translated by Rod Coltman. New York: Continuum.

Gadamer, Hans-Georg, ed. (1968). *Um die Begriffswelt der Vorsokratiker.* Darmstadt: Wissenschaftliche Buchgesellschaft.

———. (1972). *Truth and Historicity/Vérité et Historicité.* The Hague: Martinus Nijhoff.

Gagey, Jacques (1969). *Gaston Bachelard: Ou, la conversion à l'imaginaire.* Paris: M. Rivière.

Gane, Mike, ed. (1992). *The Radical Sociology of Durkheim and Mauss.* New York: Routledge.

Gauchet, Marcel (2002). "Redefining the Unconscious." *Thesis Eleven* 71, 4–23.

Gloy, Karen, and Paul Burger, eds. (1996). *Die Naturphilosophie im Deutschen Idealismus.* Stuttgart: Frommann-Holzboog.

Goodman, Nelson (1978). *Ways of Worldmaking.* Indianapolis: Hackett.

Gourgouris, S., ed. (2010). *Freud and Fundamentalism: The Psychical Politics of Knowledge.* New York: Fordham University Press.

Gourgouris, Stathis (1997). "Philosophy and Sublimation." *Thesis Eleven* 49, 31–44.

Grätzel, Stephan (2000). "*Mythos* und *Logos* bei Klages." *Hestia: Jahrbuch der Klages Gesellschaft* 20.

Grossheim, Michael (1994). *Ludwig Klages und die Phänomenologie.* Berlin: Akadamie-Verlag.

Guibal, Francis (1989). "Imagination et création: Sur la pensée de Cornelius Castoriadis." *Revue européenne des sciences sociales: Pour une philosophie militante de la démocratie* 25(86).

Gusdorf, Georges (1985). *Le savoir romantique de la nature.* Paris: Payot.

Guyer, Paul (2000). "Absolute Idealism and the Rejection of Kantian Dualism." In Karl Ameriks, ed., *The Cambridge Companion to German Idealism.* Cambridge: Cambridge University Press.

Haase, Ullrich (2003). "Der Natur auf die Sprünge helfen? Bermerkungen zur Entwicklung des Naturbegriffes von Schelling bis Merleau-Ponty." In Margarete Maurer and Otmar Hoell, eds., *Natur als Politikum.* Vienna: RLI-Verlag.

Habermas, Jürgen (1985). "Exkurs zu Castoriadis: *Die Imaginäre Institution.*" *Der philosophische Diskurs der Moderne.* Frankfurt am Main: Suhrkamp.

Hastings-King, Stephen (1999). "L'internationale situationniste, Socialisme ou Barbarie, and the Crisis of the Marxist Imaginary." SubStance: A Review of Theory and Literary Criticism 90, 26–54.

Hauskeller, Michael (1997). "Natur als Bild: Naturphänomenologie bei Ludwig Klages." In Gernot Böhme and Gregor Schiemann, eds., *Phänomenologie der Natur.* Frankfurt am Main: Suhrkamp.

Hedwig, K. (1984). "*Natura naturans/naturata*." In Joachim Ritter and Karlfried Gründer, eds., *Historisches Wörterbuch der Philosophie*, 6:504–9. Stuttgart: Schwabe.

Heelan, Patrick (1989). "Yes! There is a Hermeneutics of Natural Science: A Rejoinder to Markus." *Science in Context* 3(2), 477–88.

———. (1991). "Hermeneutical Phenomenology and the Philosophy of Science." In Hugh J. Silverman, ed., *Gadamer and Hermeneutics: Science, Culture, Literature*, 213–28. New York: Routledge.

Heidegger, Martin (1929). *Kant und das Problem der Metaphysik*. Bonn: Verlag von Friedrich Cohen.

———. (1992). *The Concept of Time*. Translated by William McNeill. Oxford: Blackwell.

———. (2001 [1927]). *Sein und Zeit*. Tübingen: Max Niemeyer Verlag.

Heidegger, Martin, and Eugen Fink (1993). *Heraclitus Seminar*. Evanston, Ill.: Northwestern University Press.

Heinimann, Felix (1965). *Nomos und Physis: Herkunft und Bedeutung einer Antithese im griechischen Denken des 5. Jahrhunderts*. Darmstadt: Wissenschaftliche Buchgesellschaft.

Held, Klaus (1991). "Heimwelt, Fremdwelt, die eine Welt." *Phänomenologische Forschungen*, 24/25—Perspektiven und Probleme der Husserlschen Phänomenologie. Freiburg: Karl Alber, 305–37.

———. (1999). "Lebenswelt und Natur: Grundlagen einer Phänomenologie der Interkulturalität." *Phänomenologische Forschungen* 4(4), 31–44.

Hesiod (1978). *Works and Days*. Translated by M. L. West. Oxford: Clarendon.

Honner, John (1987). *The Description of Nature: Niels Bohr and the Philosophy of Quantum Physics*. New York: Oxford University Press.

Howard, Dick (1974–75). "Introduction to Lefort." *Telos* 22, 2–30.

———. (1975). "Introduction to Castoriadis." *Telos* 23, 117–55.

———. (1988). *The Marxian Legacy*. Minneapolis: University of Minnesota Press.

———. (2002). *The Specter of Democracy*. New York: Columbia University Press.

———. (2010). *The Primacy of the Political, From the Greeks to the American and French Revolutions*. New York: Columbia University Press.

Howard, Dick, and Diane Pacom (1998). "Autonomy—The Legacy of the Enlightenment: A Dialogue with Castoriadis." *Thesis Eleven* 52, 83–102.

Huff, Toby (2003). *The Rise of Early Modern Science: Islam, China and the West*. Cambridge: Cambridge University Press.

Husserl, Edmund (1941 [1931]). "Phenomenology and Anthropology." *Philosophy and Phenomenological Research* Vol. 2, No. 1, pp. 1–14.

Jantsch, Erich (1979). *Die Selbstorganisation des Universums: Vom Urknall zum menschlichen Geist.* Munich: Deutscher Taschenbuch Verlag.

Jaspers, Karl (1949). *Vom Ursprung und Ziel der Geschichte.* Munich: Piper Verlag.

Joas, Hans (2002). "On Articulation." *Constellations* 9, 506–15.

Joas, Hans, and Axel Honneth (1980). *Soziales Handeln und menschliche Natur. Anthropologische Grundlagen der Sozialwissenschaften.* Frankfurt am Main: Suhrkamp.

Joas, Hans, and Wolfgang Knöbl (2009). *Social Theory: Twenty Introductory Lectures.* Cambridge: Cambridge University Press.

Joy, Mavourneen M. (1990). *Towards a Philosophy of Imagination: A Study of Gilbert Durand and Paul Ricoeur.* Ottawa: National Library of Canada.

Kambartel, Friedrich (1968). *Erfahrung und Struktur. Bausteine zu einer Kritik Empirismus und Formalismus.* Frankfurt am Main: Suhrkamp.

Kant, Immanuel (1924). *Kritik der Urteilskraft.* Hamburg: F. Meiner.

———. (1964). *Die drei Kritiken in ihrem Zusammenhang mit dem Gesamtwerk.* Edited by Raymund Schmidt. Stuttgart: Alfred Kroner Verlag.

———. (1998). *Kritik der reinen Vernunft.* Hamburg: Meiner Verlag.

Kaplan, David M. (2003). *Ricoeur's Critical Theory.* Albany: State University of New York Press.

Karfik, Filip (2004). *Die Beseelung des Kosmos: Untersuchungen zur Kosmologie, Seelenlehre und Theologie in Platons Phaidon und Timaios.* Munich: Saur.

Kaulbach, F. (1984a). "Natur." In Joachim Ritter and Karlfried Gründer, eds. *Historisches Wörterbuch der Philosophie*, 6:422–78. Basel/Stuttgart: Schwabe.

———. (1984b). "Naturphilosophie." In Joachim Ritter and Karlfried Gründer, eds., *Historisches Wörterbuch der Philosophie*, 6:536–60.

Kearney, Richard (1989). *The Wake of Imagination: Toward a Postmodern Culture.* Minneapolis: University of Minnesota Press.

———. (1998). *Poetics of Imagining: Modern to Postmodern.* Edinburgh: Edinburgh University Press.

Kerferd, G. B. (1981). *The Sophistic Movement.* Cambridge: Cambridge University Press.

Kerschensteiner, Jula (1962). *Kosmos: Quellenkritische Untersuchungen zu den Vorsokratikern.* Munich: Beck.

Kerszberg, Pierre (1993). "La crise des sciences exactes comme amplification du monde." *Revue philosophique de Louvain* 91(92), 576–602.

Kisiel, Thomas (1997). "A Hermeneutics of the Natural Sciences? The Debate Updated." *Continental Philosophy Review* 30(3), 329–41.

Kitaro, Nishida (1987). *The Logic of the Place of Nothingness and the Religious Worldview.* Honolulu: University Press of Hawaii.

Klages, Ludwig (1960 [1929–32]). *Der Geist als Widersacher der Seele,* vols. 1–3. Munich: J. A. Barth.

Klimis, S., P. Caumières, and L. Van Eynde, eds. (2010). "Castoriadis et les grecs." *Cahiers Castoriadis* 5.

Klooger, Jeff (2005). "Interpretation and Being." *Thesis Eleven* 83, 15–24.

———. (2009). *Castoriadis: Psyche, Society, Autonomy.* Leiden: Brill.

Knöbl, Wolfgang (2001). *Spielräume der Modernisierung. Das Ende der Eindeutigkeit.* Weilerswist: Velbrück.

———. (2007). *Die Kontingenz der Moderne. Wege in Europa, Asien und Amerika.* Frankfurt: Campus.

Komesaroff, Paul (1986). *Objectivity, Science and Society: Interpreting Nature and Society in the Age of the Crisis of Science.* London: Routledge and Kegan Paul.

Korff, Hermann August (1929). "Das Wesen der Romantik." In *Zeitschrift für Deutschkunde* 43.

Koyré, Alexandre (1957). *From the Closed World to the Infinite Universe.* Baltimore: Johns Hopkins University Press.

———. (1971). *Études d'histoire de la pensée philosophique.* Paris: Éditions Gallimard.

Kristeva, Julia (1984[1974]). *Revolution in Poetic Language.* New York: Columbia University Press.

Kuhn, Thomas (1962). *The Structure of Scientific Revolutions.* Chicago: University of Chicago Press.

Lacan, Jacques (2002). *Écrits: A Selection.* Revised version. Translated by Bruce Fink. New York: Norton.

Laszlo, Ervin (1966). *Beyond Scepticism and Realism: A Constructive Exploration of Husserlian and Whiteheadian Methods of Inquiry.* The Hague: Martinus Nijhoff.

Lawlor, Leonard (1993). *Imagination and Chance: The Difference Between the Thought of Ricoeur and Derrida.* Albany: SUNY Press.

———. (1993). *The Implications of Immanence: Towards a New Concept of Life.* New York: Fordham University Press.

Leclerc, Ivor (1972). *The Nature of Physical Existence.* London: Allen and Unwin.

———. (1986). *The Philosophy of Nature.* Washington, D.C.: Catholic University of America Press.

Lefort, Claude (1978). "Marx: From One Vision of History to Another." Translated by Terry Karten. *Social Research* 45(4), 615–66.

Lenoble, Robert (1953). "L'Évolution de l'idée de 'nature' du XVIe au XVIIIe siècle." *Revue de Métaphysique* 1–2, 108–29.

Lévêque, Pierre, and Pierre Vidal-Naquet, eds. 1996. *Cleisthenes the Athenian: An Essay on the Representation of Space and the Time in Greek Political Thought from the End of the Sixth Century to the Death of Plato.* Translated and edited by David Ames Curtis. Atlantic Highlands, N.J.: Humanities Press.

Levinas, E. (1969 [1961]). *Totality and Infinity: An Essay on Exteriority.* Translated by Alphonso Lingis. Pittsburgh: Duquesne University Press.

Lévi-Strauss, Claude (1962). *La pensée sauvage.* Paris: Payot.

Lévi-Strauss, Claude, and Paul Ricoeur (1963). "Réponses à quelques questions." *Esprit* 31(322), 629–53.

Löwith, Karl (1927) "Nietzsche im Lichte der Philosophie." In Erich Rothacker, ed., *Probleme der Weltanschauungslehre.* Darmstadt: Otto Reichl Verlag.

———. (1966). *Nature, History and Existentialism: and Other Essays in the Philosophy of History.* Edited by Arnold Levison. Evanston, Ill.: Northwestern University Press.

———. (1988 [1932]). "Max Weber und Karl Marx." In *Hegel und die Aufhebung der Philosophie im 19. Jahrhundert—Max Weber. Sämtliche Schriften,* 5:324–407 Stuttgart: Kluwer.

Luhmann, Niklas (1984). *Soziale Systeme: Grundriss einer allgemeinen Theorie.* Frankfurt am Main: Suhrkamp.

Lyotard, Jean-François (1991). *Phenomenology.* Translated by Brian Beakley. Albany: State University of New York Press.

Malinowski, Bronislaw (1944). *A Scientific Theory of Culture.* Chapel Hill: University of North Carolina Press.

Malpas, Jeff. (1999). *Place and Experience.* Cambridge: Cambridge University Press.

———. (2006). *Heidegger's Topology: Being, Place, World.* Cambridge, Mass.: MIT Press.

Mannsperger, Dietrich (1969). *Physis bei Platon.* Berlin: de Gruyter.

Markus, György (1987). "Why Is There No Hermeneutics of Natural Sciences? Some Preliminary Theses." *Science in Context* 1(1), 5–51.

Martuccelli, Danilo (2002). "Cornelius Castoriadis: Promesses et problèmes de la création." *Cahiers Inernationaux de Sociologie* 113, 285–305.

Maturana, Humberto, and Francisco Varela (1973). *Autopoiesis and Cognition: The Realization of the Living.* Dordrecht: D. Reidel.

McDowell, John (1996). *Mind and World.* Cambridge, Mass.: Harvard University Press.

Mehra, Jagdish, ed. (1973). *The Physicist's Conception of Nature.* Dordrecht: Reidel.

Meier, Christian (1995). "Enstehung und Besonderheit der griechischen Demokratie." In Konrad H. Kinzl, ed., *Demokratia: Der Weg zur Demokratie bei den Griechen.* Darmstadt: Wissenschaftliche Buchgesellschaft.

———. (2000). "The Greeks: The Political Revolution in World History." In Arnason and Murphy 2001.

———. (2001). "The Greeks: The Political Revolution in World History." In Arnason and Murphy 2001

Merleau-Ponty, Maurice (1962). *Phenomenology of Perception.* Translated by Colin Smith. London: Routledge.

———. (1964). *Signs.* Translated by Richard C. McCleary. Evanston, Ill.: Northwestern University Press.

———. (1968). *The Visible and the Invisible.* Edited by Claude Lefort. Translated by Alphonso Lingis. Evanston, Ill.: Northwestern University Press.

———. (1974a). *The Prose of the World.* Edited by Claude Leforte. Translated by John O'Neill. London: Heinemann.

———. (1974b). *Phenomenology, Language and Sociology: Selected Essays of Maurice Merleau-Ponty.* Edited by John O'Neill. London: Heinemann.

———. (1995). *Nature: Notes de cours au College de France.* Edited by Dominique Seglard. Translated by Robert Vallier. Evanston, Ill.: Northwestern University Press.

———. (2002). *Husserl at the Limits of Phenomenology, Including Texts by Edmund Husserl.* Edited by Leonard Lawlor with Bettina Bergo. Evanston, Ill.: Northwestern University Press.

———. (2003). *L'institution dans l'histoire personelle et publique—Le problème de la passivité: Le sommeil, l'inconscient, la mémoire—Notes de Cours au Collège de France (1954–55).* Paris: Belin.

Milgram, M., and H. Atlan. (1983). "Probabilistic Automata as a Model for Epigenesist of Cellular Networks." *Journal of Theoretical Biology* 103(4), 523–47.

Morin, Edgar (1977a). *La méthode: La nature de la nature,* vol. 1. Paris: Éditions du Seuil.

———. (1977b). *La nature de la nature.* Paris: Seuil.

Moscovici, Serge (1972). *La societé contre nature.* Paris: Seuil.

Nestle, Wilhelm (1940, 1941). *Vom Mythos zum Logos. Die Selbstentfaltung des griechischen Denkens von Homer bis auf die Sophistik und Sokrates*. Stuttgart: Kröner.

Pastor, J-P. (2003). *Devenir et temporalité. La création des possibles chez Castoriadis*. Paris: Moonstone.

Patočka, Jan (1938). *Edmund Husserl zum Gedächtnis. Zwei Reden gehalten von Ludwig Landgrebe und Jan Patočka*. Prague: Academia.

———. (1996). *Heretical Essays in the Philosophy of History*. Edited by James Dodd. Translated by Erazim Kohák. Chicago: Open Court Press.

———. (1998). *Body, Community, Language, World*. Edited by James Dodd. Translated by Erazim Kohák. Chicago: Open Court Press.

———. (2006). *Andere wege in die Moderne: Studien zur europaischen ideen geschichte von der Renaissance bis zur Romantik*. Würzburg: Königshausen und Neumann.

Pechriggl, Alice (2004). "Institution." In Helmuth Vetter, ed., *Wörterbuch der phaneomenologischen Begriffe*, 290–91. Hamburg: Meiner.

Piccone, Paul (1971). "Phenomenological Marxism." *Telos* 9, 3–31.

Plato (1937). *Plato's Cosmology: The Timaeus of Plato*. Translated by Francis MacDonald Cornford. London: Routledge and Kegan Paul.

Pohlenz, Max (1953). "*Nomos* und *Physis*." *Hermes* 81, 418–38.

Poirier, Nicholas (2004). *Castoriadis—L'imaginaire radical*. Paris: PUF.

Portmann, Adolf (1961). *Animals as Social Beings*. Translated by Oliver Coburn. New York: Viking Press.

———. (1990). *Essays in Philosophical Zoology by Adolf Portmann: The Living Form and the Seeing Eye*. Translated by Richard B. Carter. Lewiston, Maine: Mellen.

Prang, Helmut, ed. (1968). *Begriffsbestimmung der Romantik*. Darmstadt: Wissenschaftliche Buchgesellschaft.

Prat, Jean-Louis (2007). *Introduction à Castoriadis*. Paris: La Decouverte.

Prigogine, Ilya (1997). *The End of Certainty: Time, Chaos and the New Laws of Nature*. New York: Free Press.

Prigogine, Ilya, and Isabelle Stengers (1979). *La nouvelle alliance*. Paris: Gallimard.

Putnam, Hilary (1975). "The Meaning of 'Meaning,'." In *Mind, Language and Reality: Philosophical Papers*, 2:215–71. Cambridge: Cambridge University Press.

Raaflaub, Kurt (2004). *The Discovery of Freedom in Ancient Greece*. Chicago: University of Chicago Press.

Ramsay, A., I. S. Straume, and F. Theodoridis, eds. (2011). *Creation, Rationality and Autonomy*. Malmö: NSU Press.

Rechter, Susan (2007). "The Originating Breaks Up: Merleau-Ponty, Ontology and Culture." *Thesis Eleven* 90, 27–43.

Richir, Marc (1989). "Nous sommes au monde." In J-B. Pontalis, ed., *Le temps de la réflexion*, 237–58. Paris: Gallimard.

Ricoeur, Paul (1967). *Histoire et vérité*. Paris: Seuil.

———. (1970). *Freud and Philosophy: An Essay on Interpretation*. Translated by Denis Savage. New Haven: Yale University Press.

———. (1975). "Ideology and Utopia as Cultural Imagination." *Philosophic Exchange* 2(2), 17–28.

———. (1978). *The Rule of Metaphor: Multidisciplinary Studies in the Creation of Meaning in Language*. London: Routledge.

———. (1981). *Hermeneutics and the Human Sciences: Essays on Language, Action and Interpretation*. Translated by John B. Thompson. Cambridge: Cambridge University Press.

———. (1984–88). *Time and Narrative*, vols. 1–3. Translated by Kathleen Blamey and David Pellauer. Chicago: University of Chicago Press.

———. (1991a). *A Ricoeur Reader: Reflection and Imagination*. Edited by Mario J. Valdés. Toronto: University of Toronto Press.

———. (1991b). *From Text to Action*. Translated by Kathleen Blamey and John Thompson. Evanston, Ill.: Northwestern University Press.

Ringvej, Mona Renate (2004). *Interpretation of a Political Idea—The Radical Democracy of 508–462 BC*. Oslo: Unipub.

Robert, Franck (2000). "Fondement et Fondation." *Chiasmi International* 2, 351–69.

———. (2005). "Whitehead et la phénoménologie. Une lecture croisée du dernier Merleau-Ponty et du Whitehead de Process and Reality." *Chiasmi International* 7.

Rosengren, Mats (2006). "Radical Imagination and Symbolic Pregnancy: A Castoriadis-Cassirer Connection." In *Embodied Thought*. London: Routledge.

Sallis, John (1987). *Spacings: Of Reason and Imagination*. Chicago: University of Chicago Press.

———. (1999). *Chorology: On Beginning in Plato's Timaeus*. Bloomington: Indiana University Press.

———. (2000). *Force of the Imagination: The Sense of the Elemental*. Bloomington: Indiana University Press.

———. (2005). *The Gathering of Reason*. 2nd edition. Albany: SUNY Press.

Sandkuehler, Hans Joerg (1984). *Natur und geschichtlicher Prozess: Studien zur Naturphilosophie F.W.J. Schellings*. Frankfurt am Main: Suhrkamp.

Sang-Rak, Nam (1985). *Das Problem "Physis"-"Nomos" im griechischen Denken im Verhältnis zur chinesischen Philosophie*. Ph.D. dissertation, University of Heidelberg.

Sartre, Jean-Paul (1936). *L'imagination*. Paris: Alcan.

Schrag, Calvin O. (1959) "Whitehead and Heidegger: Process Philosophy and Existential Philosophy." *Dialectica* 49, 42–56.

Seeck, Gustav Adolf, ed. (1975). *Die Naturphilosophie des Aristoteles*. Darmstadt: Wissenschaftliche Buchgesellschaft.

Sheehan, Thomas (2001). "A Paradigm Shift in Heidegger Research." *Continental Philosophy Review* 32(2), 1–20.

Sherover, Charles M. (1971). *Heidegger, Kant and Time*. Bloomington: Indiana University Press.

Siebeck, H. (1890). "Über die Enstehung der Termini *natura naturans* und *natura naturata*." *Archiv für Geschichte der Philosophie* 3, 370–78.

Singer, Brian (1979). "The Early Castoriadis: Socialism, Barbarism and the Bureaucratic Thread." *Canadian Journal of Political and Social Theory* 3, 35–56.

Smith, Jeremy (2006). *Europe and the Americas: State Formation, Capitalism and Civilizations in Atlantic Modernity*. Leiden: Brill.

Smith, Karl E. (2005). "Re-Imagining Castoriadis's Psychic Monad." *Thesis Eleven* 83, 5–14.

———. (2007). "Religion and the Project of Autonomy." *Thesis Eleven* 91: 27–47.

———. (2010). *Meaning, Subjectivity, Society: Making Sense of Modernity*. Leiden: Brill.

Spaemann, Robert (1973). "Natur." In Hermann Krings, Hans Michael Baumgartner, and Christoph Wild, eds., *Handbuch Philosophischer Grundbegriffe*, 4:956–69. Munich: Kösel.

Stengers, Isabelle (1985). "Les généalogies de l'auto-organisation." *Cahiers du Centre de Recherche en Épistémologie Appliquée (CREA)*, 8.

Stevens, Bernard (1995). "Basho et khōra. Nishida en son lieu." *Etudes Phénoménologiques* 21, 81–109.

Suzuki, Marcio (2003). "La *double énigme du monde. Nature et langage chez Schelling et Merleau-Ponty.*" *Chiasmi International* 5, 235–58.

Taylor, Charles (1995). *Philosophical Arguments*. Cambridge, Mass.: Harvard University Press.

———. (2004). *Modern Social Imaginaries*. Durham, N.C.: Duke University Press.

———. (2008). *A Secular Age. Cambridge*, Mass.: Harvard University Press.

Tormey, S., and J. Townshend (2006). *Key Thinkers from Critical Theory to Post-Marxism*. London: Sage.

Toru, Tani (1999). "Phänomenonologie und Metaphysik der Natur." In Kah Kyung Cho and Young-Ho Lee, eds., *Phänomenologie der Natur*. Munich: Verlag Karl Alber.

Toynbee, Arnold J. (1934–61). *A Study of History*. London: Oxford University Press.

Tugendhat, Ernst (1970). "The Meaning of 'Bedeutung' in Frege." *Analysis* 30, 177–89.

Urribarri, Fernando (1999). "The Psyche: Imagination and History: A General View of Cornelius Castoriadis's Psychoanalytic Ideas." Translated by Nora Stelzer and Veronica Chehtman. *Free Associations* 7(3), 374–96.

———. (2002). "Castoriadis: The Radical Imagination and the Post-Lacanian Unconscious." *Thesis Eleven* 71, 40–51.

Vajda, M (1989). "La philosophie de la création absolue." *Revue européenne des sciences sociales: Pour une philosophie militante de la démocratie* 27(86).

Vallier, Robert (2005). "Institution: The Significance of Merleau-Ponty's 1954 Course at the Collège de France." *Chiasmi International* 7.

van der Veken, Jan (1990). "Process Thought from a European Perspective." *Process Studies* 19(4), 240–47.

———. (2005). "Merleau-Ponty and Whitehead on the Concept of Nature." *Interchange* 31(2–3), 319–34.

Van Eynde, Laurent (2008). "Castoriadis et Bachelard. Un imaginaire en partage." *Cahiers Critiques de Philosophie* 6, 159–75.

Varela, Francisco (1979). *Principles of Biological Autonomy*. Amsterdam: North Holland.

———. (1986). "Interview (by Isabelle Stengers)." *Cahier CREA* 9, 271–93.

Vernant, Jean-Pierre (1981). *Mythe et pensée chez les grecs*. Paris: Librairie François Maspero.

———. (2000). "The Birth of the Political." *Thesis Eleven* 60, 87–91.

Vidal-Naquet, Pierre (1996). "Democracy: A Greek Invention." In Lévêque and Vidal-Naquet 1996.

———. (2000). "The Tradition of Greek Democracy." *Thesis Eleven* 60, 61–86.

Wagner, Peter (1994). *A Sociology of Modernity: Liberty and Discipline*. New York: Routledge.

———. (2005). "The Problématique of Economic Modernity: Critical Theory, Political Philosophy and the Analysis of Capitalism." In

Christian Joerges, Bo Stråth, and Peter Wagner, eds., *The Economy as a Polity: The Political Constitution of Contemporary Capitalism*. London: UCL Press.

———. (2008). *Modernity as Experience and Interpretation*. Oxford: Polity.

Waldenfels, Bernhard (1989). "Der Primat der Einbildungskraft." *Revue européenne des sciences sociales: Pour une philosophie militante de la démocratie* 25(86).

———. (1993). *Phänomenologie in Frankreich*. Frankfurt am Main: Suhrkamp.

———. (1997–99). *Topographie des Fremden: Studien zur Phanomenologie des Fremden*, vols. 1–4. Frankfurt am Main: Suhrkamp.

———. (1999). "Fair voir par les mots. Merleau-Ponty et le tournant linguistique." *Chiasmi International: Trilingual Studies Concerning Merleau-Ponty's Thought*. Paris: Memphis, 57–64.

———. (2000). "The Paradox of Expression." In L. Lawlor, ed., *Chiasms: Merleau-Ponty's Notion of the Flesh*, 89–102. Albany: SUNY Press.

Waldenfels, Bernhard, Jan M. Broekman, and Ante Pazinin, eds. (1984). *Phenomenology and Marxism*. Translated by J. Claude Evans Jr. Boston: Routledge.

Weatherston, Martin (2002). *Heidegger's Interpretation of Kant: Categories, Imagination and Temporality*. London: Palgrave Macmillan.

Weber, Max (1977 [1948]). "Religious Rejections of the World and Their Directions." In H. H. Gerth and C. Wright Mills, eds., *From Max Weber: Essays in Sociology*, 323–59. London: Routledge and Kegan Paul.

Whitebook, Joel (1979). "The Problem of Nature in Habermas." *Telos* 40, 41–69.

———. (1989). "Intersubjectivity and the Monadic Core of the Psyche." *Revue européenne des sciences sociales: Pour une philosophie militante de la démocratie* 25(86).

———. (1996). *Perversion and Utopia: Studies in Psychoanalysis and Critical Theory*. Cambridge, Mass.: MIT Press.

Whitehead, Alfred North (1961). *The Interpretation of Science: Selected Essays*. Edited by A. H. Johnson. Indianapolis: Bobbs-Merrill.

———. (1978). *Process and Reality: An Essay in Cosmology*. New York: Free Press.

Wittgenstein, Ludwig (1953). *Philosophical Investigations*. Cambridge: Cambridge University Press.

Wolin, Richard (1985). "Merleau-Ponty and the Birth of Weberian Marxism." *Praxis International* 5(2), 115–30.

Woodbridge, Frederick (1965). *Aristotle's Vision of Nature.* New York: Columbia University Press.

Young, Frances (1991). " *'Creatio Ex Nihilo'*: A Context for the Emergence of the Christian Doctrine of Creation." *Scottish Journal of Theology* 44, 141–68.

Index

195, 206, 208, 211–12, 240, 250–51, 256; intra-, 205

cosmology, 41, 47, 58, 103, 143, 151, 154, 195–96, 198–99, 202, 204, 213, 220, 230, 232, 243, 255–56; philosophical, 14, 147–48, 162, 195–96, 198, 200, 205, 212; negative, 203

cosmos, 199, 202, 209. See also *kosmos*

creatio ex nihilo, 2, 119, 125, 149, 218, 235. *See also* creation, *ex nihilo*

creation(s): absolute, 2, 49, 185, 214, 246; aesthetic, 119, 188, 227; auto-, 28, 48–49, 155, 185, 193, 196; autonomous, 191; being and, 214–15; being of, 2, 4, 13–14, 50, 215; contextual, 130, 214; *cum nihilo*, 129, 220, 243; and destruction, 209–12; Divine, 2, 28; *ex nihilo*, 2, 14, 51, 59, 98, 118, 121, 127, 129, 156, 205, 209, 215, 249; human, 1–2, 5, 7, 13, 19, 24, 51, 61, 116, 183, 216; *in nihilo*, 119–20, 243; interpretative, 9, 24, 52, 59, 127–30, 219–20, 231, 246; of the living being, 160, 184; radical, 4, 129, 145, 149; re-, 130, 174, 245–46; self-, 3, 12, 14, 23–25, 31, 70, 129, 155, 160–61, 180–82, 184–85, 189, 191–93, 197, 205, 210–11, 221, 258; social, 70; social-historical, 4, 25, 38, 59, 109, 129, 166, 174, 214–16; theological, 42; of a world, 24, 70, 109, 216; of the world, 112–13, 132, 164, 185, 194, 217

creative: emergence, 4, 10, 147, 193, 214, 248; imagination, 2, 6–7, 9, 13, 25, 27, 32, 36–37, 48, 61, 75, 83–84, 93, 98, 100–1, 119, 128, 140, 176, 192, 215, 217, 219, 231, 246; imagination and meaning, 116, 236

physis, 3, 10, 13–14, 30, 46, 60, 68, 102, 127, 132–33, 139, 142, 144, 146–48, 150, 161–62, 167, 181, 185, 189, 191, 193, 196–97, 200, 202, 205–6, 216, 224, 239, 244, 256–57

Critique of Judgment, 10, 159, 173, 188. *See also* Third Critique

Critique of Pure Reason, 5, 60–61, 76, 104, 171, 188, 233. *See also* First Critique

culture, 5–7, 61, 93, 104, 114, 116, 125, 143, 168, 172, 177, 186, 203, 216–17, 221–22, 236, 241, 244, 246, 253; problematic of, 6, 116

cultural: articulation(s) of the world, 24, 114–16, 168; configurations, 6; constellations, 6, 226; currents, 8–9, 133, 138; horizons, 138; imagination, 6, 279; interpretation, 6; memory, 6; modernity, 81, 138, 226. See also *mise en forme du monde*

culturalist, 115, 123

culturological, 10, 113, 115–16, 123

cybernetics, 35, 67, 149–50, 184, 249

Dasein, 29–30

defunctionalization of psyche, 84, 126

de-historicize, 123

Demiurge, 42, 52, 152, 154. *See also* Artisan

democracy, 23, 50, 70, 230, 239; ancient Greek, 230, 233; Athenian, 9, 22, 258; direct, 22

democratic ideals, 21

Democritus, 21, 153, 176–77, 230

denotation, 106

Descartes, René, 1, 152, 171; Cartesian, 142, 163

Descombes, Vincent, 10, 31, 190, 231, 233, 235, 237, 243, 245, 257, 270

desire, 91, 94, 187; desiring, 90

destruction, 64, 108, 209–12, 248

Destruktion, 41, 107

determinable, 39, 56

determinacy, 50, 55, 62–65, 67, 69, 78, 90, 102, 104–5, 108, 110, 129, 138, 146, 150, 159, 173, 210, 250, 255; of being, 27, 37, 38, 52; frameworks of, 13, 30, 41

determination, 32, 36–38, 43–44, 46, 52–53, 106, 206, 209, 235, 237

determine, 21, 55

determinist, 156, 160; imaginary of, 27, 36, 39, 71, 73, 95

diachrony, 47, 58; diachronic, 57–58, 105, 169, 180, 190, 236

difference, 30, 36, 39, 40, 48–50, 112, 117, 147, 164, 190, 193, 202, 209–11, 248; production of, 31, 36, 45, 199

field: phenomenal, 114, 164, 185, 194, 215–17, 224, 232; of tensions, 8, 133, 138

First *Critique*, 8–10, 37, 45, 60, 69, 71, 75, 119, 141, 166, 170, 188

first natural stratum, 30, 37–38, 54, 56, 62–36, 65, 67–71, 90, 104, 109–11, 121, 125, 128–29, 148, 167, 171, 174–75, 187, 208, 216, 238, 253

flesh, 210, 221

flux, 13, 76, 84, 87, 89, 94–95, 98, 142

forgetting of Being, 5, 31

for-itself, 55, 91, 98, 110, 148, 181–82, 184–94, 196, 198, 200, 202, 211, 215, 218, 221, 237, 239, 255; being for-itself, mode(s) of, 66, 147, 155–56, 161, 181–82, 186, 188–90, 192–93, 211, 218, 239, 255

form(s), 3, 44–45, 51, 74, 81, 104, 111–12, 125, 129, 135, 153–55, 159–61, 170–71, 187–89, 192–93, 210–12, 220–21, 227; civilizational, 8; ontological, 53, 69, 147, 202, 212, 216, 221–22; social-political, 24. See also *eidos/eide*

Forms, the, 93, 146, 209; immutable, 21; platonic, 48

Foucault, Michel, 58, 227, 233, 254

fragment/-ed/-ation/-s, 39–40, 47, 57, 94, 130, 165, 175, 179, 210–11, 240–41, 253

framework(s): interpretative, 8, 28, 35, 130, 189; scientific, 10, 165, 204, 212, 222, 252

freedom, 6, 22, 54

Frege, Gottlob, 106–7, 225, 242

Freud, Sigmund, 37, 39, 83–85, 87–89, 91, 93, 130, 220, 238

Frühromantiker, 11, 139, 226, 247. *See also* Early Romantics

functional, 35, 80, 117, 191–93, 245, 254; -ity, 174; non-, 34, 117; trans-, 34, 117. *See also* defunctionalized

functionalism, 34, 106–7

functionalist, 33–35, 117

Gadamer, Hans-Georg, 11–12, 20, 123, 128, 232, 236, 249, 251, 253, 256

Galileo Galilei, 152

Gauchet, Marcel, 92, 240

generation, 19, 44, 160

genesis, 42–43; ontological, 50, 53, 146

The German Ideology, 34

God, 28, 51, 118–21, 129, 140, 152, 154, 160, 169

gods, 20, 70, 112, 120, 220

Goethe, Johann Wolfgang von, 139, 247

Goodman, Nelson, 8

Greece, 20, 28, 34, 55, 128, 178, 219, 232, 240, 243, 249

Greek, 2, 11, 14, 19–23, 28, 34, 40, 52, 63, 103, 107 117, 131, 148–49, 151–54, 156, 159, 162, 176–77, 179, 195, 198, 203, 205–6, 212, 218, 220–21, 226, 228–30, 233–34, 236, 238, 243, 249, 256; breakthrough, 20; imaginary, 24, 147, 149, 152–54, 156, 159, 161–62, 166, 176–77, 196, 198, 205, 247, 250; philosophical creation, 20, 191

Gusdorf, Georges, 139–40, 195, 254

Habermas, Jürgen, 29, 114, 138, 169, 232, 242–43

happy accident, 72, 81, 85–86, 172, 250

Hegel, G. W. F., 34, 36, 45, 110, 115, 123, 226

Hegelian-Marxism, 34–35

Heidegger, Martin, 4–5, 11, 20, 30–31, 37, 45, 48, 53, 60, 75, 107, 111, 115, 160, 164, 168, 170, 175, 200–1, 203, 210–11, 215, 224–25, 231–34, 236–37, 240, 253, 256–57

hermeneutic/al/s, 2, 6, 11, 15, 20, 27, 31, 38, 65, 100–1, 112–13, 115–16, 118, 123–24, 127, 131, 133, 138, 142, 214–16, 218, 220, 223, 226, 230, 237–38, 241, 243–46, 248; aspect, 2, 123; cultural, 7, 116, 138; dimension, 2, 6–7, 114, 123, 214, 216, 245; implicit, 2, 101, 214; method of critique, 11; philosophical, 10, 13, 132–33, 217; reconstruct/-ed, 12; reconstruction, 14, 24, 133, 153, 157, 214

Herodotus, 21

Hesiod, 20, 149, 156, 193, 195, 205, 219, 255, 258; Hesiodian, 28, 43, 137

heterogeneity, 3, 5, 12, 52, 56, 102, 108, 149, 161–62, 167, 173, 179–80, 182, 193

heterogeneous, 3, 5, 12, 52, 56, 102, 108, 149, 161–62, 167, 173, 179–80, 182, 193, 196–97, 210, 215, 234, 253; logics of being, 3

heteronomy, 15, 23, 57, 154, 227, 231, 255

heteronomous, 23, 98, 131, 152

historical: a-, 139, 170, 233; preconditions, 1; world, 26, 71, 86, 92, 112, 118, 123, 129–30, 133, 156, 167, 169, 218, 231, 246; trans-, 35, 120–21, 245, 256

historicity, 11, 80, 123, 169–70, 174, 178, 232

history, 19–59, 163–80; creativity of, 3; Greek, 21; and meaning, 7; philosophy of, 33, 232; of science, 163, 165–66, 169, 171, 176, 178–79, 183. See also social-historical

Honneth, Axel, 29, 232, 237

horizon(s): cultural, 24, 113–14, 126, 244; of horizons, 97, 117; of meaning, 93, 100–11, 113, 182, 192, 219; meta-, 111, 143; phenomenological, 114; ultimate, 7, 205, 213. See also world

Howard, Dick, 2, 224, 227–28

human: being(s), 17, 155. See also anthropos

human condition, the, 2, 12, 20, 26, 70, 100–1, 114, 116, 121, 130, 133, 251; self-interpreting, 7, 116; world-interpreting, 116

human creation, 1–2, 5, 7, 13, 19, 24, 51, 61, 116, 183, 216

humanism/ist, 1, 7

humanity, 112, 139, 175

humankind, 155, 160, 191, 240

Husserl, Edmund, 55, 62, 76, 87, 107, 115, 117, 142, 179, 224, 242–43, 251–52, 256–57

hyle, 104, 157, 171, 178, 206

hyper physis, 4

ideal types, 123. *See also* typology/typologies

ideal typical, 123

identitarian. *See* ensemblistic-identitarian

identity, 25, 33, 35–37, 42, 45, 48, 53, 55, 57, 64, 74–75, 89, 102, 117, 184, 191, 196, 210–11

image, 56, 75, 89; of being, 3, 40, 52, 149, 153–54, 166, 196, 206; counter, 30; Hesiodian, 28; of *physis*, 247; rival, 8

imaginary/ies: ancient Greek, 149, 152, 156, 161, 166, 198; autonomist, 129, 191–93, 219, 248, 255; determinist, 27, 36, 39, 71, 73, 95; Enlightenment, 143; Greek, 24, 153, 159, 176, 196, 205, 247, 250; institution, 2, 11–13, 17, 19, 25, 50, 80, 110, 137, 143; of nature, 13–14, 134, 137–41, 148, 205, 227, 247; radical, 11, 13, 36, 48, 51, 54–56, 60, 83–84, 93, 96, 98–99, 101, 117, 19, 124–25, 128, 132–33, 167, 179, 186, 217, 225, 231, 233; religious, 195; Romantic, 140, 148; schema, 149, 151–54, 156, 159, 161, 166, 172, 178–79, 193, 203–4, 216, 250–51; scientific, 152; social, 6, 36–37, 56, 74–76, 80, 112, 147, 152, 165–66, 225, 233, 236, 246, 249. *See also* social imaginary; social imaginary significations

imaginary signification(s). *See* social imaginary significations

imagination: creative, 2, 6–7, 9, 13, 25, 27, 32, 36–37, 48, 61, 75, 83–84, 93, 98, 100–1, 116, 119, 128, 140, 176, 192, 215, 217, 219, 231, 236, 246; as ground of reason, 9; modern, 152; productive, 2; radical, 13, 38, 75, 82, 83–85, 87–91, 93–95, 97–99, 101–3, 128, 176, 179, 186, 189, 217, 225, 231, 239; transcendental, 5, 43, 141, 207

Imagined Communities, 7, 225, 233

immanence, 101, 142, 173, 232

immanent, 41, 53, 58, 63–64, 95, 215, 221, 258

indeterminacy, 22, 53, 66, 69, 71, 102, 105, 108, 110, 154, 157, 198, 255

physicalism, 34–35, 38–39

physics, 14, 44–45, 85, 149, 151, 154, 158, 164, 170, 173, 176–77, 196–97, 207–10

physis/phusis/physei: creative, 3, 10, 13–14, 30, 46, 60, 68, 102, 127, 132–33, 139, 142, 144, 146–48, 150, 161–62, 167, 181, 185, 189, 191, 193, 196–97, 200, 202, 205–6, 216, 224, 239, 244, 256–57; general ontology of, 145–46; hyper-, 4; non-anthropic dimensions of, 22; ontology of, 21, 66, 103, 193, 202; radical, 14, 22, 28, 30, 40–41, 47, 59, 67, 69, 85, 133, 147–48, 153, 157, 159, 161–62, 193–94, 217, 220–22, 236–37, 239, 242, 249–50, 257; transregional, 12, 14, 147, 155, 180, 183, 196, 229, 233

physis and *nomos*. See also *nomos* and *physis*), 14–15,19, 22, 147, 151, 155, 157–58, 161, 166, 177–78, 181, 214–17, 220, 222

place, 37, 44, 48–49, 53, 76, 78–79, 96, 111, 133, 135, 176, 197, 206–7, 224, 257; ontological, 17, 19, 21, 24, 27, 143, 215

Plato, 20–21, 31, 41–43, 45, 49–51, 53, 62–63, 103, 134, 176, 205–6, 226, 234, 256–57

platonic, 21, 51, 86, 89, 153–54, 157, 207, 240

pleasure, 91; organ, 94; principle, 91; representational, 94

poiesis, 51, 149, 235. See also *auto-poiesis*

poietic, 98, 208, 210–13, 223, 246, 258

Poirier, Nicholas, 224

polis/poleis, 19, 21, 57, 128–29, 153, 219, 228–30, 233, 246

political, 4, 6, 10, 24, 34, 98, 137, 145, 158, 161, 163, 191–92, 219, 224–25, 227–28, 231, 248–49, 254, 257; animal(s), 21; dimension, 143; freedom, 22; revolution, 22; the, 22

politics, 6, 9, 21–23, 157, 227, 229–30, 239, 252; institution of, 22

la politique, 9, 22–23, 57, 191, 227, 230

le politique, 22–23

polity, 22

Pontalis, Jean-Bertrand, 90

Post-Durkheimian, 7

potentiality, 36, 46, 92, 128, 233. *See also* actuality

power, 1, 22, 46, 79–80, 104, 153, 255, 250; impersonal, 20. *See also* potentiality; *puissance*

praxis, 97, 231, 244; philosophical, 26

pre-modern, 1

pre-*nomos*, 20

presence, 31, 46, 70, 118, 125, 127, 161, 193, 235

presentification, 90, 187; presentifying, 80, 91, 125

pre-Socratic, 20, 43, 45, 128, 143, 149, 153, 195, 229–30

presocratics, the, 42, 137, 154, 162, 234, 249–50

project, 164–65, 176, 178–79, 188, 191, 223, 230, 239, 251; of autonomy, 179, 191–2, 194, 197, 199, 212–13, 215, 222, 238, 248; ontological, 168. *See also* autonomy

Protagoras, 21, 177

protocreativity of nature, 10

proto-institution(s), 13, 37, 56, 59, 60–61, 72, 81, 98, 118, 125, 163, 233, 236. See also *legein*; *teukhein*

psyche, 83–99; -soma, 248

psychic, 88, 90, 155; flux, 13, 76, 87, 93; monad, 98, 235

psychical meaning, 13

psychoanalysis, 3, 83–84, 86–87, 98, 183, 232–33, 239, 255

psychoanalytic, 10, 62, 66, 84, 98, 183, 190, 216, 239–40

psychogenetic, 94

psychological, 76, 95–96, 238, 252

psychosis (psychotic), 93–94, 126

puissance, 153, 233, 250, 257

question, 26–27, 30–36, 39, 41–42, 44, 49, 64–65, 70, 91, 97, 102, 108, 117, 120, 132, 171, 189–90, 192, 195, 197, 200–3, 207, 210–11, 213, 215, 226, 232, 234, 241, 251, 254, 257; of being, 30–31, 39, 201; to put into, 23–24, 197

sensible, 21, 42–44, 206
set(s), 38–39, 64, 68, 95, 198; ensemblist-identitarian, 105; mathematical, 64, 233, 236; natural, 35; social, 35
shock, 66, 156, 187. See also *Anstoss*
signification(s), web of, 118, 122. *See also* social imaginary significations
signitive relation, 74–79, 81
Sinn, 106–7, 123, 243. *See also* meaning
Sinnfähigkeit (*sinnfähig*), 85, 204, 218, 221–22
SIS. *See* social imaginary significations
Smith, Karl E., 11, 239, 242, 255
social: extra-, 221; individual, 84, 88, 92–94, 96–99, 185, 239; institution, 54–56, 61, 76, 92, 95, 98, 101, 199; life, 9, 36, 64, 121, 237; representation, 56, 58, 122
social facts, 110
social-historical, 1–15, 25–59, 60–82, 83–93, 101–12, 117–34, 144–62, 163–80, 185–86, 192, 194, 196–204, 208, 212–13, 214–22; temporality of, 5
social imaginary/ies. *See* imaginary/ies
social imaginary signification(s), 2, 7, 67, 99, 101, 103–4, 108–9, 111–12, 114, 116–17, 120–23, 133, 230, 241, 246; central, 121, 123, 125; primary, 122
social sciences, 7, 165, 249
social theory/social theoretical, 6, 11, 33, 113, 225, 228, 245
socialism, 12, 231
Socialisme ou Barbarie, 3, 12, 34, 46, 224
sociality, 100, 109, 253
socialization, 83, 88, 92–93
society, 4, 6, 10, 27, 32–59, 60–82; ancient Greek, 117; anthropological aspects, 7; capitalist, 94; image of, 35
sociocentric, 7, 114, 116, 119
sociology, 6–7, 113–14, 223
Solon, 128
soma, 89, 248
Sophist(s)/sophistry, 20–21, 75, 107, 177, 242
Sophocles, 21
Sozialität, 109
source(s): ancient Greek, 11, 14, 28, 138,

148–49, 151, 162, 198, 233; extra-social, 131; intellectual, 2, 26; phenomenological, 113; philosophical, 86, 152
space. See *chora*; receptacle; time, spatialization of; time and space
space-time, 44
Sparta, 56, 117, 129
spatial, 14, 41–44, 48, 50, 142, 206–7, 234
spatialization, 95, 151, 208–9
species-being, 34
Spinoza, Baruch, 10, 141
Sprachspiele, 107
Stengers, Isabella, 150, 152, 183–84, 242, 247, 254, 257
stratification, irregular, 3, 173
structuralism, 35, 57, 62, 114, 233
structuralist(s), 33–35, 58, 61, 73, 84, 106, 237
subject(s): autonomous, 98, 185, 216, 239, 255; -oriented, 5; proto-, 86, 91, 174; transcendental-, 61–62, 85, 96, 104
subject-centred, 163; metaphysics, 1
subjectivity, 11, 13, 23, 83–85, 98, 186, 188, 225, 239–40, 248, 253, 255–56
sublimation, 54, 83–85, 92–94, 99, 240
surplus: of meaning, 35, 93, 132
symbolic, 6, 41, 87, 102, 105, 107, 119, 124, 132, 218, 252; order, 6 (*see also* order); the, 124, 132–33, 219, 246
symbolism, 132
symbols, 65, 132
synchronic, 57–58, 105, 169, 190

Taylor, Charles, 7, 115, 223, 225, 236, 240, 253, 255
techne, 1, 51, 153, 229, 235
teleology, 10, 21, 159, 173, 189
teleonomy, 159, 189
telos, 159
temporal, 5, 13, 27–28, 31–33, 39–41, 43, 48, 50, 53, 57–58, 60, 129, 142, 200–1, 207, 211
temporality, 5, 30, 48, 55–56, 58, 142, 196, 199, 211, 219; radical, 25, 40, 180, 196
temporalization, 37, 40, 95, 98, 219

Perspectives in
Continental Philosophy
John D. Caputo, series editor

Karl Jaspers, *The Question of German Guilt.* Introduction by Joseph W. Koterski, S.J.

Jean-Luc Marion, *The Idol and Distance: Five Studies.* Translated with an introduction by Thomas A. Carlson.

Jeffrey Dudiak, *The Intrigue of Ethics: A Reading of the Idea of Discourse in the Thought of Emmanuel Levinas.*

Robyn Horner, *Rethinking God as Gift: Marion, Derrida, and the Limits of Phenomenology.*

Mark Dooley, *The Politics of Exodus: Søren Kierkegaard's Ethics of Responsibility.*

Merold Westphal, *Overcoming Onto-Theology: Toward a Postmodern Christian Faith.*

Edith Wyschogrod, Jean-Joseph Goux, and Eric Boynton, eds., *The Enigma of Gift and Sacrifice.*

Stanislas Breton, *The Word and the Cross.* Translated with an introduction by Jacquelyn Porter.

Jean-Luc Marion, *Prolegomena to Charity.* Translated by Stephen E. Lewis.

Peter H. Spader, *Scheler's Ethical Personalism: Its Logic, Development, and Promise.*

Jean-Louis Chrétien, *The Unforgettable and the Unhoped For.* Translated by Jeffrey Bloechl.

Don Cupitt, *Is Nothing Sacred? The Non-Realist Philosophy of Religion: Selected Essays.*

Jean-Luc Marion, *In Excess: Studies of Saturated Phenomena.* Translated by Robyn Horner and Vincent Berraud.

Phillip Goodchild, *Rethinking Philosophy of Religion: Approaches from Continental Philosophy.*

William J. Richardson, S.J., *Heidegger: Through Phenomenology to Thought.*

Jeffrey Andrew Barash, *Martin Heidegger and the Problem of Historical Meaning.*

Jean-Louis Chrétien, *Hand to Hand: Listening to the Work of Art.* Translated by Stephen E. Lewis.

Jean-Louis Chrétien, *The Call and the Response.* Translated with an introduction by Anne Davenport.

D. C. Schindler, *Han Urs von Balthasar and the Dramatic Structure of Truth: A Philosophical Investigation.*

Julian Wolfreys, ed., *Thinking Difference: Critics in Conversation.*

Allen Scult, *Being Jewish/Reading Heidegger: An Ontological Encounter.*

Richard Kearney, *Debates in Continental Philosophy: Conversations with Contemporary Thinkers.*

Jennifer Anna Gosetti-Ferencei, *Heidegger, Hölderlin, and the Subject of Poetic Language: Towards a New Poetics of Dasein.*

Jolita Pons, *Stealing a Gift: Kirkegaard's Pseudonyms and the Bible.*

Jean-Yves Lacoste, *Experience and the Absolute: Disputed Questions on the Humanity of Man.* Translated by Mark Raftery-Skehan.

Charles P. Bigger, *Between* Chora *and the Good: Metaphor's Metaphysical Neighborhood.*

Dominique Janicaud, *Phenomenology "Wide Open": After the French Debate.* Translated by Charles N. Cabral.

Ian Leask and Eoin Cassidy, eds., *Givenness and God: Questions of Jean-Luc Marion.*

Jacques Derrida, *Sovereignties in Question: The Poetics of Paul Celan.* Edited by Thomas Dutoit and Outi Pasanen.

William Desmond, *Is There a Sabbath for Thought? Between Religion and Philosophy.*

Bruce Ellis Benson and Norman Wirzba, eds., *The Phenomoenology of Prayer.*

S. Clark Buckner and Matthew Statler, eds., *Styles of Piety: Practicing Philosophy after the Death of God.*

Kevin Hart and Barbara Wall, eds., *The Experience of God: A Postmodern Response.*

John Panteleimon Manoussakis, *After God: Richard Kearney and the Religious Turn in Continental Philosophy.*

John Martis, *Philippe Lacoue-Labarthe: Representation and the Loss of the Subject.*

Jean-Luc Nancy, *The Ground of the Image.*

Edith Wyschogrod, *Crossover Queries: Dwelling with Negatives, Embodying Philosophy's Others.*

Gerald Bruns, *On the Anarchy of Poetry and Philosophy: A Guide for the Unruly.*

Brian Treanor, *Aspects of Alterity: Levinas, Marcel, and the Contemporary Debate.*

Simon Morgan Wortham, *Counter-Institutions: Jacques Derrida and the Question of the University.*

Leonard Lawlor, *The Implications of Immanence: Toward a New Concept of Life.*

Clayton Crockett, *Interstices of the Sublime: Theology and Psychoanalytic Theory.*

Bettina Bergo, Joseph Cohen, and Raphael Zagury-Orly, eds., *Judeities: Questions for Jacques Derrida.* Translated by Bettina Bergo and Michael B. Smith.

Jean-Luc Marion, *On the Ego and on God: Further Cartesian Questions.* Translated by Christina M. Gschwandtner.

Jean-Luc Nancy, *Philosophical Chronicles.* Translated by Franson Manjali.

Jean-Luc Nancy, *Dis-Enclosure: The Deconstruction of Christianity.* Translated by Bettina Bergo, Gabriel Malenfant, and Michael B. Smith.

Andrea Hurst, *Derrida Vis-à-vis Lacan: Interweaving Deconstruction and Psychoanalysis.*

Jean-Luc Nancy, *Noli me tangere: On the Raising of the Body.* Translated by Sarah Clift, Pascale-Anne Brault, and Michael Naas.

Jacques Derrida, *The Animal That Therefore I Am.* Edited by Marie-Louise Mallet, translated by David Wills.

Jean-Luc Marion, *The Visible and the Revealed.* Translated by Christina M. Gschwandtner and others.

Michel Henry, *Material Phenomenology.* Translated by Scott Davidson.

Jean-Luc Nancy, *Corpus.* Translated by Richard A. Rand.

Joshua Kates, *Fielding Derrida.*

Michael Naas, *Derrida From Now On.*

Shannon Sullivan and Dennis J. Schmidt, eds., *Difficulties of Ethical Life.*